THE
UNHOLY GHOST

Anti-Catholicism in the American Experience

Mark J. Hurley

Our Sunday Visitor Publishing Division
Our Sunday Visitor, Inc.
Huntington, Indiana 46750

International Standard Book Number: 0-87973-529-5
Library of Congress Catalog Card Number: 92-60315

PRINTED IN THE UNITED STATES OF AMERICA

Cover design by Rebecca J. Heaston

529

Acknowledgments

The author and publisher are grateful to the copyright holders of materials cited in this work. The author would like to thank all those who have made this work possible, especially Monsignor Thomas W. Keys of the diocese of Santa Rosa as well as Veronica Beard. Special thanks go to those who have provided the editorial cartoons (please refer to the cartoon section for the names of those individuals and publishers who have graciously granted permission to use their materials). If any copyrighted materials have been inadvertently used in this book without proper credit being given, please notify Our Sunday Visitor in writing so that future printings of this work may be corrected accordingly.

*Not only for every idle word
must a man render an account,
but for every silence.*
— St. Ambrose, c. 340-97

To P.H.P. and J.D.H.

Table of Contents

Introduction

"As a nation we began by declaring that 'all men are created equal.' We now practically read it 'all men are created equal, except Negroes.' When the Know-Nothings get control, it will read 'all men are created equal, except Negroes and foreigners and Catholics,' " wrote Abraham Lincoln.

As the twenty-first century approaches on the horizon, the people of the United States can justly look down the arches of the years of their history, some two centuries, with a great deal of satisfaction but without any smugness. As the Founding Fathers had hoped, God did bless this nation and this people abundantly, a noble experiment in republican structures with democratic aspirations. The wonder of it all was that a country so large and so varied, of people so diverse in history, culture, race, and religion, could form a union that would endure over two centuries.

Some have called it the American experiment, others the American proposition, while the patriotic orators down the years refer to it as simply a singular opportunity in the history of nations granted by Divine Providence, and a model for other people and nations. Nevertheless, no one would deny that the United States has much unfinished business to redress any past grievances and to grow and develop yet further into the twenty-first century.

The American proposition was founded upon certain fundamental truths, its basic patrimony, said to be self-evident, anterior to government because it was based upon the essential dignity of each individual who was endowed by his Creator with certain inalienable rights, some of which were not enumerated in law. This human dignity, equal justice, and true freedom were the concepts forming the substratum of the nation. To put these fundamentals into practice demanded a true consensus among the citizens, not one simply of majority, but one free from unjust passion and prejudice.

Americans, by and large, have agreed to accept pluralism in their society, to agree that each group be entitled to maintain its identity and that according to its own definition. The two most important questions at issue have been race and religion: the first because immigrants have come to America from all corners of the globe; the second because of their heritage at once Protestant, Catholic, Orthodox, Jewish, Muslim, Hindu, Buddhist, Taoist, Sikh, and others, plus secular humanist, agnostic, and atheist. The translation of this ongoing heritage into a consensus has been the exigent pursuit of over two centuries.

The end of the twentieth century has witnessed great progress in the elimination of racial and religious prejudice. Of particular note is the *de jure* exorcising of racial discrimination from the lawbooks. "Separate but equal" schools, poll taxes, redlining in real estate, separate facilities in public accommodations, methods of hiring and promotion in employment — all have come under the scrutiny of the law. *De facto* discrimination based on race is a more difficult matter. There are some sunny spots, with the vast majority of the largest American cities electing Afro-Americans and Hispanics as governors, mayors, and other public officials. Progress has been made; much more needs to be done. The *de facto* virus of racial discrimination has been dealt a serious blow, but it has not been killed. Similarly, slowly and painfully the unjust gender discrimination against women in society is being met in the courts and in society.

The virus of religious discrimination is yet another matter. The specific virus of anti-Catholicism and more specifically Nativism have not been evicted from the bloodstream of American society, neither *de jure* nor *de facto*.

Lincoln's words just quoted may well describe the Nativism of the nineteenth century; Father John Courtney Murray, S.J., may equally well describe the same virus of the twentieth century: "Nativism in all its manifold forms: ugly and refined, popular and academic, fanatic and liberal ... the Neo-Nativist as well as the Paleo-Nativist addresses to the Catholic community substantially the same charge: 'You are among us but not of us.' "

While the progress of Catholics in the United States is unmatched in history, yet there remains the underlying suspicion that a Catholic cannot be a true believer in the American scheme of things. Contrariwise, many Europeans, including Vatican curial prelates, were skeptical that a true believer in the American proposition could be a true believer in Catholicism. "Catholic" and "American" were judged an internal contradiction in the seventeenth-century Colonies before independence; during the early days of the Republic, the assumption took hard political form in the nineteenth century and has been kept alive in the twentieth.

Perhaps the *Baltimore Sun* during the Al Smith presidential campaign in 1928 editorialized best: "The people who believe that Catholicism is the enemy of Americanism will continue to believe it no matter how cogent proof to the contrary." Or was it better said by a current historian? "Anti-Catholicism is the most luxuriant tenacious tradition of paranoiac agitation in American history." Is it the ghost that will not die?

Did not the election in 1960 of John F. Kennedy as President put to rest any question of a Catholic's patriotism to trust him to fulfill conscientiously the office to which he is elected? And faithful to the Constitution? Moreover, did he speak for all Catholics or even truly reflect Catholic teaching when he, like Al Smith before him, opted for a complete and all but absolute separation of Church and State? And even to the denial of parental rights in education?

Governor Mario Cuomo of New York and U.S. Supreme Court Clarence Thomas have had to face a special litmus test with two facets: the perennial school-aid question and the abortion predicament. Is there a religious test in the last decade of the twentieth century for public office or public trust in government positions? Or was the British politician on the right track when he said that a politician must be a hypocrite in practice but a saint before the law?

Must a Catholic governor park his religion at his office door, or a Catholic professor at the entrance to his lecture hall, or a newspaper reporter at the lintel of the pressroom? How is it that the Internal Revenue Service can suffer myopia when Jesse Jackson openly violates its regulations by using the tax-exempt churches for patent political purposes and at the same time warn the American Catholic Church that it faces loss of tax exemption for opposing abortion and its political supporters? Or the IRS threatening the one issue of pro-life campaigners while turning a blind eye on the single issue of pro-abortion Planned Parenthood, the National Organization for Women, the National Abortion Rights Action League, and similar groups?

The Catholic Church in America has not accepted the secularist interpretation of the First Amendment, the theory that it meant absolute separation not merely of the state from the establishment of religion but of religion itself from public life. Back to the sacristy for all religions! Nor have Catholics been reconciled to the tilting of the balance between the no-establishment clause and the free-exercise clauses of the First Amendment against them and other religious people. That balance is still being cast in new forms; the present tension between the two counterbalancing clauses has not been resolved, and its present state, in the words of Justice Antonin Scalia, is chaotic.

As they read the account of this American problem, no doubt Jews, Afro-Americans, Hispanics, Chinese, and Native Americans will see compelling parallels with their own struggles against injustice and discriminatory practices. So too may the other and especially the more recent immigrants recognize a certain affinity with the trials and crises they have endured that are so contrary to the expressed sentiments of the American experiment and proposition. Still, Catholics labored under an incubus not shared by other religious people, for they were members at once of a worldwide church with headquarters in Rome and citizens of the great country grown into a super-power.

This volume, however, does not present itself as a comprehensive history of anti-Catholicism, much less of Nativism. The thoroughgoing treatment must await the professional historians to bring to light not only the facts but also an interpretation of the events and their causal relationships. This work dips into history to provide adequate documented samples that illustrate the reality of anti-Catholicism and Nativism, sufficient to maintain the thesis that these ghosts of the past two hundred years have not been laid to rest.

The treatment, like Gaul, is divided into three parts.

The first "book" traces the subject from 1776 up to Vatican Council II, illustrating at once the nineteenth-century's "no popery" passions, and also its more subtle transition into the twentieth century. The primary question was: Were Americans safe with Catholics? or were Catholics safe in America? Could Catholics be trusted to be at once fully American and fully Catholic? The record shows that American Catholics were held suspect both in the halls of government and in the Roman Curia in the Vatican.

The second "book" presents an analysis of the Second Vatican Council's "Declaration of Religious Liberty" as an excellent answer both to the Nativism and no popery of the past and to the Vatican's condemnation of Americanism. The document itself is seen as a triumph of the development of doctrine to meet modern needs and of the American Church's stamp and seal upon it.

The third "book" traces the reactions of Americans with the narrowing down of the two-century conflict to two major topics: public support for all bona fide schools, and the volatile question of abortion. These two controversies have engendered litmus tests for public office and a proliferation of one-issue political campaigns, both dangerous to the common good.

Some, especially Catholics, will no doubt object that by emphasizing the negative, by underlining injustices and grievances, this presentation will beget a "victimology" for Catholics. The objection does have some merit. Yet what worthwhile campaign against injustice did not find its source and motivation in its beginnings with perceived injustice? The Civil Rights Movement? The campaign against AIDS? Against smoking? Similarly the Anti-Defamation League scarcely apologizes for its very title. Injustice — whether against immigrants, Asians, Afro-Americans, Native Indians, women, or gays — cries out first for recognition and then redress according to the circumstances.

In plain words, Catholics have been and are victims of injustice, and education and verification of their history may well awaken citizens of good will to the elimination of second-class citizenry.

For two centuries Catholics have striven to alleviate the apprehension and doubt of their fellow citizens, declaring full acceptance of the First Amendment with its disestablishment and free-exercise clauses. While these efforts have in the main been successful, yet a surprisingly significant part of mainstream American society continues to entertain doubts.

The Vatican Council afforded Catholics a disinterested and splendid opportunity to set the record straight. The Church was able to distance itself from the harsh inquisitions of its history, to accept modern democracy, constitutional government, and to refuse to bless one single form of government, and on the positive side to show how the Church too can move with the times. Moreover, the worldwide Church could and did follow in large measure the American model on religious liberty.

The Vatican Council's "Declaration on Religious Liberty" must be regarded as a seminal document in the same genre as the "Universal Declaration of Human Rights," the Helsinki Accords, *Pacem in Terris*, and other similar testimonials to individual and corporate freedom.

American Catholics have a reasoned and compelling position on the relationships of Church and State. They hope that the unholy ghost of both anti-Catholicism and Nativism may be given an exit visa to the history books. Americans, all of them, deserve to be treated as endowed by their Creator with certain inalienable rights and must enjoy equality *de jure* and *de facto*. God bless us all!

Bishop Mark J. Hurley
SAN FRANCISCO

BOOK 1

Chapter 1

The Ghost That Will Not Die

From the very first days of the Republic, the American Catholic has been forced to live under a cloud, a cloud of suspicion. Because of his perceived allegiance to a foreign power, namely the Pope in Rome, a Catholic citizen, it has been alleged, cannot at the same time and under the same circumstances be faithful to the doctrines of his Church and the United States Declaration of Independence and the Constitution. George Washington warned against "foreign entanglements" and surely nothing was more foreign and more alien to "the American way" than an "infallible" pontiff representing a culture and history inimical to a free society — so the argument ran in 1776 and so it runs in mitigated form in the 1990s.

George Washington felt compelled to denounce those politicians and military leaders who questioned the patriotism of his Irish troops; he roundly condemned the observance of the virulently anti-Catholic Guy Fawkes Day, a celebration inherited from Great Britain, the motherland. The Protestant historian Ray Allen Billington in his classic study opened his book with these words: "Hatred of Catholics and foreigners had been steadily growing in the United States for more than two centuries before it took political form (in the 19th century). . . . (It was) steeped in anti-papal prejudice."[1]

The evidence cited against Catholics often began with an account of the Spanish Inquisition of 1478 and its grand inquisitor, the Dominican priest Tomás de Torquemada. While there was no denying that the Inquisition was indeed inimical to democratic theory and practice, the imputation to Catholics came from sources that could not escape the same strictures.

Historians, especially English ones, have dwelt at length on Torquemada, who led the Inquisition in Spain, all the time generally neglecting a similar inquisition in England. If Spain had its persecution, aimed largely but not exclusively at converted Jews, the Marranos, with few Protestants as victims, England had not only its "Bloody Mary" executing Protestants but its "Bloody" Elizabeth I who executed many more, a fact submerged by the historians. If the Church and Spain had its Torquemada, the Protestant Church and England had its Topcliffe, described by a Jesuit prisoner in the Tower of London in 1597 as a prosecutor of "bloody and butchery mind . . . the man is not opened to reason."

The punishment called *piene forte et dure* in England was not abolished until 1827. A Catholic Englishwoman, Jane Wiseman, was convicted on June 30, 1598, for hiding priests in her home: "The sentence is that Jane Wiseman shall be led to the prison of the Marshalsea of the Queen's Bench and there naked except for a linen cloth about the lower part of her body be laid upon the ground, lying directly on her back: a hollow shall be made under her head and her head placed in same; and upon her body in every part let there be placed as much stones and iron as she can bear and more; and as long as she shall live, she shall have of the worst bread and water of the prison next her; and on the day she eats, she shall not drink, and on the day she drinks she shall not eat, so living until she die."[2]

Was this torture any worse than the *murus strictus* in Spain with its solitary confinement on "bread and water of affliction"? Or its *de heretico comburendo*, the burning of heretics? Queen Mary proceeded against Archbishop Thomas Cranmer; Isabella and Ferdinand through Torquemada prosecuted the Catholic Bishop Aranda of Calaborra. Queen Mary was named "Bloody Mary" by historians, while Elizabeth was dubbed "Good Queen Bess."

The *British Encyclopedia* passes judgment: in England in 1401 (before the Reformation) the inquisitions were "a violent assertion of secular absolutism," and in Spain "a combination of secular jealousy, national pride, and religious bigotry," a rather apt description for most of Europe's nations after Martin Luther. Muslims and Jews suffered in most countries of Europe under the threat "Convert or go into exile."

Thus neither the American Protestants nor the American Catholics could appeal to their ancestral heritage in Europe, to their ancestors as progenitors of religious liberty. Both carried with them certain historical impediments, really baggage, that were inimical to the new spirit of freedom in the U.S.A. Protestants, however, enjoyed majority numbers.

New England inherited the Statute of Elizabeth of 1562, which made witchcraft a crime and its penalty death. Belief in witchcraft and the overmastering dread of it pervaded the Massachusetts Colony. No less a person than the Reverend Cotton Mather, a literary maven, persecuted alleged witches with absolute fanaticism and merciless cruelty. His anti-Catholicism as well was legendary: in his *Magnalia* he labeled Ann Glover "a scandalous old Irishwoman, very poor, a Roman Catholic and obstinate in idolatry." She was hanged as a witch at Salem, Massachusetts. This Puritan historical dowry lasted down through the years of American history.

Sam Adams, cousin of John Adams, signer of the Declaration of Independence from Boston, member of Congress, and governor of Massachusetts, perpetuated this particular bit of Puritan heritage. "Much more is to be dreaded," he wrote, "from the growth of Popery in America than from the Stamp Act or any other acts destructive of men's civil liberties." He applauded John Locke's exclusion of Catholics from laws of toleration because they "teach doctrines subversive of civil government . . . in the states under whose protection they enjoy life, liberty, and property . . . leading directly to the worst anarchy and confusion, civil discord, war and bloodshed."[3] Yet this same public servant hoped for the restoration of a Christian commonwealth continuous with the Puritan ideal of the founders of Massachusetts.

To their credit more than half the signers of the Declaration of Independence were Anglican laymen, many with very close ties to England. Of the one hundred twenty-nine clergy residents in Virginia in 1775, at least seventy-four supported the American cause. During the war years the Congress and provincial assemblies ordered the churches to be opened on stipulated days for prayer and fasting for the American cause. After July 4, 1776, prayers for the King were considered "treasonous"; yet the clergy had by oath upon appointment sworn allegiance — a dilemma peculiar to the Anglicans alone. The clergy asked for a ruling from the bishops of London who replied that the Anglican clergy (in 1779) should do the best they could, omitting the prayers for the King but not prayers for the Congress. American legislatures quickly disestablished the Anglican Church, terminating salaries for its clergy. Britain did not formally surrender until 1783. The Anglican Church took a new name: Episcopal.[4]

Nor is it surprising that this historical inheritance found its way into the constitution of the state of Massachusetts in 1780 whose chief architect was no less a personage than John Adams.

Every Christian denomination enjoyed the protection of law with but one exception: the Catholics who were excluded from office precisely because "some of them (sic) in some countries will not disclaim the principles of the spiritual jurisdiction of the pope . . . which are subversive of a free government established by the People."[5]

Nine of the thirteen original states had official churches, established by law, all of them Protestant; it took many more years before the First Amendment of the federal Constitution with its clear prohibition against state establishment of religion was seen to apply to the several states.

In spite of the Constitution, it took at least a century for the disestablishment of Protestantism in the public schools. Professor Howard K. Beale of the University of North Carolina points out: "While sectarianism was increasingly discouraged, practically all schools still included religion in their curricula. School opened with a prayer. The Bible was read and portions of it memorized. Hymns were sung. The principles of Protestant Christianity, so far as they were accepted by all Trinitarian sects, were instilled into children."

As for Catholics, "they contributed taxes to the support of schools in which their teachers were not allowed to teach. . . ."[6]

Leading citizens, however, continued to play the "Americanism card." John Jay, chief justice of the U.S. Supreme Court (1789-95) and governor of New York, demanded that Roman Catholics be deprived of their civil rights unless they swore to the Supreme Court that no pope or priest had "the authority to absolve them from their allegiance to the State."[7] As outrageous as the demand was, it was the result of the baggage that Catholics had to carry from Europe: in 1570 Pope Pius V excommunicated Queen Elizabeth I and "absolved" Catholics from allegiance to her. It was still another shadow, like the Inquisition, that plagued American Catholics down the years into the twentieth century.

As late as 1870, New Hampshire prohibited Catholics from election to governor or legislator; the Congregational Church enjoyed a special hegemony there. New Jersey barred Catholics from state office in 1776, as did Georgia and North Carolina, all under the perceived double allegiance of Catholics, which was seen as a direct threat, indeed a positive menace to the fledgling Republic. New York legislated an oath that had the effect of excluding Catholics from public office. There was universal anti-Catholic bias in all Thirteen Colonies from Massachusetts to Georgia, even though Catholics, a small minority, gave full assent to religious liberty.

Actually Pope Paul III, as early as 1537, in his encyclical *Sublimis Deus*, had given some direction for Catholics in the New World: "The said Indians and all other people who may be discovered by Christians are by no means to be deprived of their liberty or possession of their property, even though they may be outside the faith of Jesus Christ."

The Catholic leaders in Baltimore — the Calverts in 1649 and Governor Thomas Dongan of New York in 1683 — had declared religious liberty for all Christians. These acts of toleration were soon overturned by the establishment of the Church of England. Yet while the American majority was persecuting other Americans in the Colonies, it was simultaneously wooing the Catholic Canadians in 1774, who had won religious toleration from Great Britain, to join the Revolution, promising religious liberty to them.

The Quebec Act of 1774 not only recognized French Canadian sovereignty throughout the Northwest Territory and down to the Ohio River but allowed the French Catholics to eliminate the traditional oath of loyalty to the King. Americans on the contrary considered the act one of the five intolerable acts perpetrated by the English Parliament that is alluded to in the Declaration of Independence. The King has, it declared, given "his assent to their Acts of pretended Legislation . . . for abolishing the free system of English Laws in a neighboring Province," a threat to the Thirteen Colonies. But while the Americans were denouncing the Quebec Act in these terms, they were at the same time quite willing to woo the Canadians to join the Revolution against the Crown. With one hand it was dogmatically rejecting Catholicism as inimical to liberty and with the other hand stretching out an invitation to Canadian Catholics to join them. An American wit put the point to poetry:

> If Gallic Papists have a right
> To worship their own way
> Then farewell to the Liberties
> Of poor America.[8]

Notwithstanding, leaders of the American Revolution assigned Father John Carroll, cousin of Charles the signer of the Declaration of Independence, to a delegation to visit Canada in February 1776 to persuade the Canadians. Later the first American bishop, Carroll wrote of his hesitation, precisely on Church-State grounds: "I have observed that when ministers of religion leave the duties of their profession, they generally fall into contempt and sometimes even bring discredit to the cause in whose service they are engaged."[9] The delegation to Canada in fact failed in its mission.

Now archbishop of Baltimore, John Carroll told his priests to hold themselves aloof from politics. Nor did he favor a Catholic political party. His was a prescient vision and stance as his successor bishops (numbering three hundred seventy-five) two hundred years later would vote to keep priests out of "partisan" politics and be opposed to a "Catholic" political party as in Europe or to "Catholic" labor unions.

The most celebrated observer of the American scene, Alexis de Tocqueville, the French lawyer and judge, described as "an observer to the degree of genius with a Gallic capacity to generalize," in his *Democracy in America*, appraised the Catholics that he met in his famous tour of the Thirteen Colonies in 1835: "The Catholics are faithful to the observances of their religion; they are fervent and zealous in support and belief of their doctrines. Nevertheless, they constitute the most republican and the most democratic class of citizens which exists in the United States; although this fact may surprise the observer at first, the causes by which it is occasioned may easily be discovered upon reflection.

"The Americans combine the notion of Christianity and of liberty so intimately in their own minds, that it is impossible to make them conceive of one without the other. . . . Despotism may govern without faith but liberty cannot."

Theory met practice in American schools; education became the battleground par excellence. The first schools in America were Church-sponsored: the Lutherans had over four hundred schools in the colonial period and about two hundred forty schools by 1820 in Pennsylvania alone, with a stronger system soon to grow in the Midwest. The Episcopalians began in 1838 in earnest to build schools and by 1862 had parochial schools in eleven states. Presbyterians were even more dedicated and in the 1845 Synod of New Jersey adopted a resolution affirming the principle of public support for denominational schools.[10] By 1840 there were over two hundred Catholic schools, most of them west of the Allegheny Mountains; by 1900, over four thousand.

Sparked by the impassioned rhetoric of the Reverend Lyman Beecher, a rioting mob torched the convent school at Charleston outside Philadelphia in 1834. Ten years later thirteen Catholics died in the arson destruction of two churches. Young Abraham Lincoln was prompted on June 12, 1844, to propose the following resolution to his political party: "Resolved that the guarantee of the rights of conscience as found in our Constitution is most sacred and inviolable and one that belongs no less to Catholics than to Protestants."[11]

In 1837, the American bishops at the Third Baltimore Council counseled patience to the Catholic people. Archbishop Carroll earlier had directly advised his priests to hold themselves aloof from partisan politics; the assembled bishops agreed.

New York Governor William Seward in 1840 proposed state aid to religious schools: "I do not hesitate . . . to recommend the establishment of schools in which [the children of immigrants] may be instructed by teachers speaking the same language and professing the same faith." His secretary of state, John Spencer, issued his report on the question: "It can scarcely be necessary to say that the founders of these [religious] schools, and those who wish to establish others, have absolute rights to the benefits of the common burthen; and any system which deprives them of their just share must be justified, if at all, by a necessity which demands the sacrifice of individual rights, for the accomplishment of a social benefit of paramount importance. It is presumed no such necessity can be urged in the present situation."[12] His stand cost him his office.

The pattern was similar in San Francisco in 1850 where all elementary schools — public, Protestant, and Catholic — shared tax funds until 1855. The public schools were seen as an "almost total failure" directed by Protestant ministers, with the people "not anxious to avail themselves of the advantages of a free public school," choosing rather the religious schools.[13] There were cries of "godless" and secularism and antireligion. Nevertheless, California public schools had twenty-three thousand pupils, once a virtual monopoly was secured for the public schools. Supporting that monopoly in the state of California the Supreme Court in 1868 declared tax exemption unconstitutional and California became the only state in the country to impose property taxes on nonpublic schools, a condition not reversed until 1958. The result was the virtual collapse of Protestant schools at all levels. Tax exemption was granted colleges and universities in 1914.[14]

Since the public schools were anything but "nonsectarian," rather under the control of Protestants and particularly of Protestant ministers, Catholics found themselves, in the nineteenth century, fighting Protestantism in the public schools and in effect contributing to their secularization.

When Horace Mann began his work for the common free public school, the Nativist movement had already reached alarming proportions. Not only was the Protestant Bible read, but offensive commentaries and even textbooks that alluded to Catholics as "deceitful" and the Pope as "the man of sin, mystery, iniquity, son of perdition" were part of the curriculum. Monasteries were described as "seats of voluptuousness . . . (of) luxurious pleasures."[15]

22

The Philadelphia controversy over Bible reading in the schools erupted into violence with twenty people dead, scores wounded, and entire blocks of homes of Irish immigrants put to the torch as well as three Churches and the seminary of the diocese. Grand juries and special investigation placed the blame on the Irish because of "the efforts of a portion of the community to exclude the Bible from our Public schools."[16]

The irony of it all was that Catholics were working to excise one bit of religion and contributing directly toward the secularization of the common schools in which in the years to come their own children would be educated. This sustained effort boomeranged and became a source of deep regret in the twentieth century.

On May 10, 1855, for example, the *San Francisco Chronicle* accused the public school superintendent, the Reverend Thomas J. Nevins, of forcing Catholic children to read the Protestant Bible and having them whipped for refusal. It further noted that the ninety Protestant youngsters in the Catholic schools of San Francisco were not taught sectarian doctrines.

Just a year before, when priests and nuns arrived in San Francisco, the *Christian Advocate* greeted them in these words: "The large company of European priests and sisters [they were Irish] who arrived yesterday morning by the *Cortez* should obtain heavy damages from the Nicaragua Steamship Company for bringing them past their port. . . . We trust these ladies and gentlemen may be able to return without delay . . . particularly as the institutions of our Protestant and Republican country are known to be obnoxious to their sentiments and taste. . . .

"In case they do not commence suit against the Nicaragua Company for damages in bringing them here" the U.S. attorney general will.[17]

American Catholics, however, were still carrying an albatross around their necks: the checkered history of their Church in various countries. Protestants, led by an overzealous clergy afflicted for the most part with a convenient amnesia about the Protestant countries of Europe, aimed their barbed spears at papal teachings in illustration of antidemocratic theory, Spain being its exemplar in practice. Anti-Catholic societies proliferated and moved easily into the political action committees for other groups that preferred to remain in the shadows, such as the Freemasons and anti-Irish as well as anti-immigrant sects.

The battle cry of "Rum, Romanism, and Rebellion" through the nineteenth century boded no good for the original pioneers of French, German, Irish, and Spanish ancestry. These "super-Americans" contributed to an atmosphere of xenophobia and virulent odium against immigrants from the so-called "Catholic" countries, against the Jews, against dark-skinned newcomers, and finally against Afro-Americans.

To reiterate what was pointed out in the introduction to this book, Abraham Lincoln in a letter to Joshua Speed in 1855 was quite explicit: "As a nation we began by declaring that 'all men are created equal.' We now practically read it 'all men are created equal, except Negroes.' When the Know-Nothings get control, it will read 'all men are created equal, except Negroes and foreigners and Catholics.' "[18]

Actually the religious prejudice was mostly against Catholics and Irish when identified as Catholic. The Celtic cross at Gettysburg commemorating the service of the famous Irish Brigade of five hundred soldiers — forty percent of whom were casualties on July 2, 1863, in the Union cause — made no palpable impression on the general public. Yet it was here on this battlefield some three months later that President Lincoln made his famous address. Ironically their sacrifice was indeed forgotten. Scotch-Irish Presbyterians, however, as well as Scots, Welsh, and English Protestant immigrants, were welcomed to the United States and soon gave birth to future presidents, senators, governors, and leaders of all types. Birth in Ireland as such was no handicap.

Sadly it should be noted that Catholic ethnics were so preoccupied with their own problems of freedom and security in a hostile atmosphere that they largely neglected the plight of the blacks after the Civil War. The Healys (eight brothers and sisters), who were half black, made their mark when one became the bishop of Portland, Maine (1875-1900), and another the president of Georgetown University in Washington, D.C. A few other black priests were also ordained along the years until the founding of the Society of the Divine Word in 1875 with its specific purpose of training blacks for the priesthood and leadership in the Church. But it was not until the 1930s that the Church took radical steps in seeking true freedom for blacks in education, in employment, as well as in cultural and social life in America, "a most powerful . . . church stance on behalf of racial justice."[19]

The constitution of the American Society to Promote the Principles of the Protestant Reformation began with the words: "Whereas, the principles of the court of Rome are totally irreconcilable with the gospel of Christ; liberty of conscience; the rights of man; and with the constitution and laws of the United States of America . . . endangering the peace and freedom of our country. . . ." The constitution of the American Protestant Association opened with its preamble: "Whereas, we believe the system of Popery to be, in its principles and tendency, subversive of civil and religious liberty. . . ." So too the constitution of the American Protestant Society and the other groups dedicated to preserving true liberty against Romanism.

The contradiction in the Protestant position, given the heritage of Great Britain's history of a state church, was not lost on Cardinal John Henry Newman who spoke from the pulpit in the 1830s in England precisely on "State Churches": "I do not know any more palpable absurdity than the theory of national Churches. . . . It is sacrificing Christianity to nationality; it is putting Caesar before Christ. It is a denial of the Church's catholicity. It is a returning to the old pagan ideal of state supremacy."

24

He pointed to what he considered an egregious current example of the vice of the Middle Ages, namely the lay investiture of bishops: "Just imagine . . . Christian bishops pleading before a half-infidel Parliament for liberty to teach; imagine that half-infidel Parliament rejecting that proposal contemptuously and the bishops submitting lamely. . . . The Crown claims . . . supreme jurisdiction not only in temporalities but in spiritualities. In other words the Church is a mere creation of the State."

U.S. historian Henry Steele Commager concluded that "from 1880 on, the Catholic Church was one of the most effective agencies for democracy and Americanization." But contradictions were no barrier to the xenophobes: they took political action.

Along with these types — the demagogues, the bigots, the "rednecks" — there were people of good will, men and women who were genuinely concerned about "the Catholic Menace," precisely because of the papal pronouncements of the times.

In the U.S. Senate in 1875, Senator George F. Edmunds, in support of the Blaine Amendment, quoted at length from the encyclical letter of Pope Pius IX, the famous *Quanta Cura* of 1864, which in turn quoted Pope Gregory XVI (Pius IX's immediate predecessor) that it was "insane" to say that liberty of conscience and worship was the right of every man and that all should be unrestrained in the exercise of every liberty. The senator also entered into the *Congressional Record* Pope Pius IX's *Syllabus of the Principal Errors of Our Time* (or, more popularly, the *Syllabus of Errors*), a list of propositions on liberty and the commonweal condemned by the Holy Father.

Senator Edmunds, a Republican, concluded his plea for support by expressing astonishment that any Democrats could in light of these revelations oppose the Blaine Amendment, which in effect would outlaw religious schools. The Democrats responded that the Blaine Amendment would harm religious activities in all government hospitals, orphanages, prisons, and veterans' homes. Many saw the amendment as an invasion of states' rights, since education was not even mentioned in the federal Constitution.

The proposed amendment to the Constitution was defeated, but the melody lingered on. When Blaine was the Republican candidate for the presidency of the United States in 1884, the Reverend Samuel D. Burchard, a prominent Presbyterian clergyman, attacked Blaine who although a professed Protestant, yet was of a Catholic mother, and who had sent his daughter to a "Romish convent" school. "We are Republicans and don't propose to leave our party and identify ourselves with the party whose antecedents have been rum, Romanism and rebellion" quoted the cleric.

Blaine tried to counter on two grounds: there should be no religious test for public office; he would not "for a thousand presidencies speak a disrespectful word of my mother's religion."

Catholics became something of a political football because of their call for state aid for their schools, for their opposition to Bible reading in the public schools, and for their requests for equal treatment in the fields of social work and charities, equal, that is, to what Protestants enjoyed.

Rutherford B. Hayes in 1875 tarred the Democrats as subservient to Catholics, followed by Ulysses S. Grant who campaigned on the plank that unless parochial schools were stopped, another civil war might be started. It was the doomsday scenario. President Grant called for a constitutional amendment forbidding public funds or property for sectarian schools, clearly inferring that the Constitution did allow aid, for example, to Catholic schools.[20] The contrary opinion took new life from the Supreme Court only in 1947.[21]

After the Civil War the Pope became once again a prime target, now that Jefferson Davis was out of the way. But the target was always the bishops and priests, not the people.[22]

The American Protective Association, the APA, was founded by Henry F. Bowers in 1887 at Clinton, Iowa, dedicated to opposing Catholicism, to curbing immigration, and to preserving the public schools from Catholic subversion.[23] Keeping its membership secret, it plunged headlong into partisan politics between 1891 and 1897.

By 1894 there were seventy APA daily papers publishing spurious documents: one contained instructions by bishops to Catholics to massacre Protestants; a second, a papal bull exhorting such a massacre, in a word, a bogus encyclical. Bowers himself reported that the appointment of Archbishop Francis Satolli as papal delegate to the U.S.A. was the greatest stimulus to the growth of the APA. Historian John Higham calls the incident "minor."

A year later another bogus encyclical attributed to Pope Leo XIII was published absolving Catholics from all loyalty to the U.S.A., calling for the extermination of all heretics, and stating that there were seven hundred thousand papal soldiers in the cities ready to rise up in insurrection.

It would be a misreading of history and an injustice to so many men and women of good will to attribute their questioning and even opposition to Church teaching on religious liberty solely to prejudice and religious bigotry. After all, there was a Spanish Inquisition, an Italian, and a Portuguese Inquisition as well. Nor is it sufficient in refutation to point out the countries with Protestant (not to mention Buddhist and Islamic and other nations') ascendancies, where quite similar atrocities and religious persecutions had been and are still taking place.

The years healed many things but not all: during the early twentieth century, antiradicalism and anti-Catholicism surfaced almost everywhere in the country.

Protestants could more easily throw off direct connections with their European counterparts and fellow churchmen in a way not possible to

Catholics: one had a pope, the other no similar authority, no easy center of attribution. And there were voices of Protestants that defended Catholics against these attacks, such as Theodore Roosevelt, Senator George Hoar of Massachusetts, and the Reverend Washington Gladen. This last's contrary voice, for example, came from him as a Congregationalist minister who defended Pope Leo XIII as perhaps "the most enlightened and most progressive pontiff who ever occupied the throne," who affirmed the right of people to govern themselves under republican institutions.[24]

Cardinal James Gibbons of Baltimore in 1887 spoke for all Catholics: "For myself, as a citizen of the United States, without closing my eyes to the defects as a nation I proclaim with a deep sense of pride and gratitude and in this great capital of Christendom (Rome) that I belong to a country where the civil government holds over us the aegis of its protection without interfering in the legitimate exercise of our sublime mission as ministers of the Gospel of Jesus Christ. But thank God we live in a country where liberty of conscience is respected. . . . I say, America with all your faults I love thee still. Perhaps there is no nation on the face of the earth where the church is less trammelled and where she has more liberty to carry out her sublime destiny than in these United States."[25] Nor was the cardinal alone.

The laymen of his own Baltimore Catholic Congress of 1889 stated forthrightly: "We repudiate with equal earnestness the assertion that we need to lay aside any of our devotedness to our Church to be true Americans, the insinuation that we need to abate any of our country's principles and institutions to be faithful Catholics."[26]

As might be expected, Catholics fought back against the charge of un-Americanism, organizing into various associations and groups, often with an ethnic basis. Perhaps the most successful was the Knights of Columbus, founded in 1882. Its purpose was basically in the field of charity: social welfare, war relief, public relief, and very explicitly "patriotism." It conducted war relief services during the Mexican border wars of 1916 and World War I, and provided scholarships for families who lost a son or daughter in World War II.

The Knights, however — sensitive to the exigencies of the times in which they live — became champions of the Catholic schools and, with the advent of the abortion deluge in the U.S.A., actively and fervently pro-life. The Knights campaigned vigorously to include the words "under God" in the Pledge of Allegiance and opposed legal efforts to have them deleted. Thus they placed themselves squarely in the midst of the two most fundamental problems in American society involving religious liberty and Church-State relationships as well as the specter of secularism.[27]

Archbishop John Ireland of St. Paul, Minnesota, added his support, citing America as a country that lived by the scriptural injunction to render to Caesar and to render to God. He boasted that "rulers govern by the will of the people and derive their just powers (from) their consent." In 1897, Irish-born Father Denis O'Connell (future bishop of Richmond, Virginia) spoke in Fribourg, Switzerland, in defense of true Americanism as not in conflict with the Catholic faith. Cardinal Gibbons ruefully remarked: "Little that American (Catholic) writers have said to the contrary has been successful in disabusing many European Catholics of this opinion," that is, on the nature of the American scheme of things.

Particularly sensitive to the accusations of being un-American were the Irish immigrants. On May 14, 1890, the Ancient Order of Hibernians held its national convention in Hartford, Connecticut. It opened with a parade of five thousand men, a parade reviewed by the governor of the state and mayor of the city and featuring American and Irish flags and green streamers. At St. Joseph's Cathedral a solemn Mass opened the day with the Reverend J. J. Quinn, chaplain of the Hibernia Rifles as preacher.

His theme was that the Catholic Church was "a faithful protector of the Christian commonwealth." More specifically he added that "it is the fashion nowadays in certain quarters to question the loyalty of Catholics to our government, to assert the incompatibility of the Catholic Church with American citizenship."

He continued, "But the history of our country is a sufficient proof." Catholics had been among the best citizens, loyal and devoted and their Church "the mother of civil and religious liberty in America."

Moreover, he pointed out, "Our actions are closely watched by those not of our faith. Foreigners (as some of us are unjustly called) are looked upon with an unfriendly eye, and there are public men, who by attacking our religion and race, seek to sow the seeds of civil discord. Men of this stamp are the real enemies of the republic, and not the Catholics. We are at home in this land of the free."

Father Quinn noted the role of Catholics in the Civil War, pointing to the heroic work of priests, chaplains, and nuns as nurses —these spoken, he said, "not in any spirit of self-glorification, but in self-defense."[28]

The noted convert to Catholicism and controversial activist Orestes Brownson, a contemporary of Gibbons, tried to put a more philosophical base to the "American dream." In his book *The American Republic*, he reiterated a theme as dear to Protestants as to Catholics: "The American Republic has been instituted by Providence to realize the freedom of each with advantage to the other. . . . Its mission is not so much the realization of liberty as the realization of the true idea of the state which secures at once the authority of the public and the freedom of the individual — the sovereignty of the people without social despotism, and individual freedom without anarchy . . . the dialectical union of authority and liberty of the natural rights of man and those of society."

Brownson further stressed that the ancient Greeks and Romans placed the state above individual freedom, and modern states tended either to do exactly the same or in other instances assert individual freedom to the detriment of the state. Shades of Father John Courtney Murray at the Vatican Council to come three quarters of a century later, seeking such balance in regard to religious liberty!

But the suspicion would not die down, the apprehension that Catholics had a secret agenda and were obligated to make some mental reservations when taking an oath to uphold and defend the Constitution. They could not be trusted to hold to both their faith and their constitution in spite of protestations to the contrary, in spite of willing service in wars and especially World War I.

Mark Twain could write that "I have been educated to enmity towards everything that is Catholic and sometimes in consequence of this I find it much easier to discover Catholic faults than Catholic merits." Similarly in high places, America's premier historian George Bancroft could write that the Pope controlled politics and the conduct of Catholics throughout the world. He went further: "I adhere to the Protestant principle, the great teachings of Martin Luther, that every man is his own priest."

Wars usually bring citizens together in common defense. Such was not the case during World War I: a resuscitated Ku Klux Klan sprang into action in 1915, attacking Catholics, Jews, and Negroes, even carrying out dozens of lynchings of this last group. But its special target was the Catholic school.

So powerful had the Klan become that it greased the political machinery in the state of Oregon to push through the legislature and the electorate a bill to outlaw Catholic and other nonpublic elementary and secondary schools entirely, creating a monopoly for the public school establishment in pursuit of true Americanism. The year 1925 witnessed a big KKK parade in Oakland, California, against not the Klan but the Klan's targets — the same year the U.S. Supreme Court invalidated the Oregon School Law as unconstitutional; the same year that the Klan claimed 8,900,000 members.

During these times the Catholic bishops were enunciating through the National Catholic Welfare Conference and its famous "labor priest," John A. Ryan, the directions that both American society and the American government should take in the social and economic order. On February 12, 1919, Lincoln's birthday, Ryan issued what might rightly be called the "bishops' manifesto," signed officially by the U.S. bishops.

It urged Congress to pass minimum-wage laws, unemployment protection, old-age insurance, child-labor laws, legal enforcement of the right of workers to organize, measures for public housing, a national employment service. Ten years later the American bishops made twelve similar proposals, all of which became law by 1945 except the one asking for a share in management for the workers.

The proposals of 1919 were bitterly denounced by the National Association of Manufacturers as socialist propaganda and pro-labor union, seconded by the New York Committee on Seditious Activities.

On the matter of racial equality, The Catholic University of America under the control of the U.S. bishops was the first all-white school in the District of Columbia to integrate and did so in 1936, long before the courts had sorted the matter out in 1954. Cardinal Patrick O'Boyle, then an archbishop, desegregated Catholic churches, schools, and hospitals in the District in 1948.

The chief rabbi of Israel, Isaac Herzog, paid tribute to the American Catholic: "Catholics have been in America for four centuries with a maximum of loyalty and service to every fundamental ideal and principle upon which the Republic was founded and has endured." While such a judgment was justified, yet as Archbishop O'Boyle looked over the ruins of Washington, D.C., and saw on television the similar devastation wreaked in the race riots in Los Angeles (Watts), Detroit, and other cities, he could only cry out: "We should have done more."

Nevertheless, Catholics were still the object of unjust religious discrimination. Between 1789 and 1955 only fourteen Catholics had been in a presidential cabinet, ten after Roosevelt in 1933; only six in the Supreme Court. Historians Arthur Schlesinger, Sr., and Henry Commager attest to the fact that Catholics have never threatened American institutions "except in the imagination of men." Politically, however, Catholics have never carried their weight. As early as 1908 Archbishop Ireland of St. Paul had complained that the seventeen million Catholics were "not represented as they should be." Could there ever be a Catholic president? "When the right man is presented, the United States will choose him and not discriminate because of his religion." But were Catholics carrying their weight? The answer was again in the negative.

A prime target of the Nativists was Alfred E. Smith, the Democratic nominee for President in 1928. Senator Thomas J. Heflin of Alabama became the most notorious, as his anti-Catholic speeches were franked and 556,000 copies distributed at government expense.[29] Leaflet reprints were produced by a magazine called *The Menace*, its title targeting the Catholic Church; it was joined by another bitter periodical named simply *The Protestant*.

Charles C. Marshall, writing in the *Atlantic Monthly* (1927), had his own inquisition on Governor Smith, aimed at impugning Smith's Americanism. The school issue was paramount in Marshall's view: explicit and exclusive support for the public common schools to the exclusion of parochial (and by implication other religious) schools became the litmus test. Catholic politicians were suspect.

"Smith will get the united wet and papal vote . . . in large measure the Jew and Negro vote . . . the gamblers, the red-light and dope vote . . . of the Jew-

Jesuit movie gang," trumpeted *The Rail-Splitter*. Along with Senator Heflin, the Reverend Bob Jones, evangelist and founder of Bob Jones University, stumped the South with inflammatory statements such as "I would rather see a saloon on every corner than a Catholic in the White House" and "I'd rather see a nigger as President."[30] It was vintage Nativism.

A review of these loyalty tests aimed at the Catholic religion illustrated clearly that the very first question concerned the parochial school and possible federal assistance, whether direct or indirect. The answers demanded of Catholics would go beyond what the First Amendment says but be consonant with an *absolute* separation of Church and State. Anything less was considered un-American. Both candidates Smith and later John F. Kennedy felt compelled to bend over backward on the school question to satisfy the critics who included men and women of good will as well as ill will, and organizations anti-Catholic in theory and practice.

A doctrinaire secularism was demanded largely on the assumption that the common public school was inherently more American than the "parochial" (meaning Catholic almost exclusively) school. The conclusion was all the more curious and downright unjust, since the same criterion was not applied to colleges and universities: private, like Harvard and Stanford; religious, like Georgetown, Notre Dame, Brigham Young, Yeshiva, and Brandeis. The "principle" halted at grade 13. Nor did the historical fact that almost none of the presidents of the U.S.A. ever attended a common school bring into question their Americanism.

During the 1928 presidential campaign a Republican, Dr. Nicholas M. Butler (in *The Shadow of the Pope*), reported his sorrow at finding how widespread anti-Catholicism was in America, "in circles quite remote from the KKK." There are "widespread exhibitions of ignorance, intolerance and religious bigotry manifested on every side." He called the bigots "Judases" betraying Christ, Thomas Jefferson, and Roger Williams, and added that it was a duty to stamp out, without regard to party affiliation, "this invading snake with iron heel."

He continued: "The foundations of America are under attack. . . . This is no time for cowardice, timeservers, legalistic wordsplitters or well now's." Butler was responding to widespread attacks such as the following in the *Wesleyan Christian Advocate* of July 13, 1928: "Governor Smith has a constitutional right to run for President even though a Catholic. This we confess and we have a constitutional right to vote against him because he is a Catholic. This we assert" because, it went on, Catholicism is "a degenerate form of Christianity."[31]

Lutheran pastor Dr. Charles L. Fry added his piece of insight: "Shall we have a man in the White House who acknowledges allegiance to the autocrat on the Tiber, who hates democracy, public schools, Protestant parsonages, individual rights? . . . We must fight a second war for independence."[32]

31

Nor was it surprising that the professionally anti-Catholic periodical *The Rail-Splitter* would attack in similar fashion, on the matter of crime, a time-tested chestnut in almost all national elections: "We do not claim that all Al Smith men are crooks, but we know that all crooks are Smith men."

So much for Archbishop Ireland's counsel in 1908 — Governor Smith was not the man!

But the Catholic school remained the litmus test, overshadowing other questions: Do you believe in the separation of Church and State? Do you want the United States to spend taxpayers' money establishing diplomatic relations with the Vatican? Prayer in the schools? All these problems were exacerbated by the question of abortion that began in the 1970s.

What about the obverse of these positions? While vehemently denying that they are anti-Catholic, some people are unabashedly anti-Catholic school; others are so vehemently pro-abortion that their bias has been projected on the Catholic Church far beyond the premises of the question. The bashing of U.S. bishops, the vituperation against the Church, the none-too-subtle charge of un-Americanism, and even the imputation of disloyalty reached a new crescendo in the 1990s.

Catholics were once again perceived as "a problem" in the United States, not quite to be trusted on the matter of religious freedom, especially in view of the history of the Catholic Church in Europe. It is worth expanding on what was touched on earlier regarding the fact that during the Hoover-Smith campaign in 1928 *The Baltimore Sun* editorialized: "Persons who think that a single expression of denial will affect this ingrained prejudice have little knowledge of human nature. A man convinced against his will is of the same opinion still. The people who believe that Catholicism is the enemy of Americanism will continue to believe it no matter how cogent proof to the contrary."[33]

Was European Catholicism a perpetual albatross around the neck of American Catholics? Would Catholics running for public office always face a special litmus test? Is Nativism the ghost that will not die?

Chapter 2

The American Catholic's Stumbling Block

Since Catholics and other religious people for over two centuries fought a losing battle on the matter of equal justice for their schoolchildren and parental rights, they were tagged with the label that they did not believe in the separation of Church and State. Further, they were pictured as being opposed to the public schools, even though a majority of their children attended them. The metaphor of the "wall of separation" was sufficient, however, to deny even the most paltry aid to nonpublic schoolchildren, causing some dissenting U.S. Supreme Court justices along the way to question its relevance: "The wall which the Court was professing to erect between Church and State has become even more warped and twisted than I expected," wrote Justice Robert H. Jackson in the Zorach case of 1952.

The point, however, was made over and over again that the public school was really *the* American school. While the Supreme Court found little or no problem in supporting a pluralistic solution to the question of support of schools above grade 12 — tax money could be appropriated for private universities like Harvard and Stanford and religious like Georgetown, Southern Methodist, and Brandeis — it choked on the question when the same "principle" was applied to secondary and elementary schools. There would be no pluralistic solution to a problem of pluralism at the lower levels; the Court reasoning rested on the premise that "the public school is at once the symbol of our democracy and the most pervasive means for promoting our common destiny."[34]

It was most disconcerting to find out that even the Supreme Court justices were reading and citing the most virulent anti-Catholic sources. About Hugo Black, a Ku Klux Klan member in 1925 and a Supreme Court justice from 1937 to 1971, his son has written: "The Ku Klux Klan and Daddy so far as I could tell, had only one thing in common. He suspected the Catholic Church. He used to read all of Paul Blanshard's books exposing power abuse in the Catholic Church. He thought the popes had too much power and property."

When Mr. Black was nominated for the Supreme Court by President Franklin D. Roosevelt on August 12, 1937, he ducked the question on membership in the Ku Klux Klan with a "no comment." The next day a subcommittee of the Senate Judiciary Committee voted 5 to 1 to forward the nomination to the committee, which, only three days later, approved 13 to 4 and the full Senate on August 17 by a vote of 63 to 16 confirmed the President's choice. One senator raised the question, but it was ignored. On

September 13 a Pittsburgh *Post-Gazette* reporter broke the story with documentation that Black had been a Klansman for about three years in the 1920s.

Roosevelt maintained that he did not know the fact. After Black's death, however, a memorandum written by the justice gave another version: "When I went up to lunch with (FDR), he told me that there was no reason for my worrying about having been a member of the Ku Klux Klan. He said that some of the best friends and supporters he had in the State of Georgia (FDR's second home) were strong members of the organization."[35]

The Supreme Court's decision most damaging to the cause of private and religious schools was written by Justice Black in a 5 to 4 decision in the Everson case in 1947. He denied aid to all religions using Jefferson's analogy of a "wall of separation." It was a distinction that could not endure.[36]

Blanshard was a professional anti-Catholic whose book *American Freedom and Catholic Power* sold 165,000 copies in just two years. The Catholic Church was portrayed as a present dire threat to American democracy. He told of the Catholic ideal state that would repress all heresy: "The Catholic hierarchy could never make the United States into a clerical state unless it captured the public school system or regimented a majority of American children into its own parochial school system."[37]

Its most common premise was that Catholics deep-down could not be full-fledged Americans as long as they held to Catholic teaching, and most especially on the question of religious liberty. America's most famous educator, John Dewey, added his voice to the chorus that parochial schools were "inimical to democracy."

Dewey was a strong believer in secular humanism, devoted to science and democracy with an atheistic base or presumption. As the most famous educator in the U.S.A. in the twentieth century, he was the ideological father of "progressive education" and an avowed secularist that opposed religion in schools and religious schools. He stood in opposition to Horace Mann, the reputed founder of the common schools, who, a century before, favored excluding all religious instruction from schools but permitting the common schools to teach one official religion, allowing each denomination in the majority to choose. The opposition to religious schools was not only springing from a theoretical foundation but in the practical order as well.

Another idol of the public school establishment of the second quarter of the twentieth century was Ellwood P. Cubberley of Stanford University who paid so little attention, as a renowned historian of education, to the nonpublic schools that they were perceived as nonentities, negligible on the American scene, "treating them as false starts or regrettable aberrations along the way to the glorious rise and triumphant procession of the public school system."[38] Lawrence Clemin in *The Wonderful World of Ellwood Patterson Cubberley* states that there was a "terrible bias and evangelistic spirit which imbued the writing of public school historians between 1910 and 1950."[39] In a word, religious schools at best got short shrift.

The theory and practice of exclusion took on a new, virulent, and powerful form after World War II, now that there was once again open season on the Catholic Church and its schools.

In the Methodist Temple in Chicago, on November 20, 1947, there was born an organization devoted almost exclusively to prevent the Catholic Church, that is, "the Menace," from leading America into a clerical state.

Its founders were prominent Americans, none from the lunatic fringes of American society. Its name revealed much and revealed little: Protestants and Other Americans United for the Separation of Church and State. Its origin was to be found not only in Protestant circles but in Scottish Rite Freemasonry as well; the National Education Association (NEA), the establishment of the public schools; the various humanist societies; and the American Jewish Congress.[40]

The "big three" of the founding fathers were Glenn L. Archer of the NEA; Paul Blanshard, a Congregationalist minister and former employee of the U.S. State Department; and the last, C. Stanley Lowell, a Methodist minister. Archer called the Catholic Church a tyranny behind the purple curtain of Roman clericalism; Blanshard described Catholicism as "a dictatorial society within America's democratic society"; and Lowell averred that a Catholic education might qualify a person for citizenship in a totalitarian society but not in a free country, adding that "I do not want my child in a school directed by officials who are under the control of a foreign potentate." Testifying before the U.S. Senate against aid to nonpublic schools he named himself as speaking for "militant Protestantism."

One Presbyterian, Frederick Sullens, editor of the *Daily News* of Jackson, Mississippi, took issue and described the POAU in these words: "Their activities would indicate that their sole concern is to see that people in parochial schools receive no aid and that the supporters of these schools be held to several taxations . . . and that anti-Catholic prejudices be kept alive and inflamed."

When in 1955 the U.S. Catholic bishops issued a statement that said that "both systems (public and private) made a profound and indispensable contribution to the American scene . . . both a noble partnership in education," Archer accused them of trying to take control of all education.[41]

Adding his organization's weight against Catholic schools, Rabbi Richard S. Hirsch for the Committee on Social Action of Reform Judaism opposed all and every form of assistance. Ignoring the hundreds of Protestant and Jewish schools and thousands of children, he testified in Congress that "America is facing a hundred years war over tax appropriations to Catholic schools."[42]

Blanshard, who may justly be characterized as a professional anti-

Catholic, warned about "the Menace" in 1949, writing that Catholics would repeal the First Amendment and effect a union of Church and State; would exempt Catholics from facing U.S. courts; would forbid public worship and operations to all non-Catholics; would supervise all schools, whether public or private, wherein Catholic pupils were enrolled; would outlaw coeducation; and would teach that "direct abortion is murder of the innocent."[43]

What was the solution? "Resist the appointment or the election of Catholic judges in all states where sterilization laws applied to the unfit are on the statute books unless the Catholic judges publicly repudiate the Roman directives to defy such laws." Shades of the 1980s and '90s!

Blanshard's advice to the two major political parties was predictable: "The platform should stand for the public school from kindergarten through college as the foundation of democracy." He neglected to stop at grade 12 in his charge of un-Americanism. But this school of un-Americanism was "for the benefit of the social policies of the hierarchy."

What was — and indeed continues to be — most disconcerting to Catholics is to find a Supreme Court justice citing Blanshard in his opinion, and many university professors doing the same, illustrating all too well that underneath a veneer of tolerance or evenhandedness there lay the virus of Nativism.

Surveying the history of the Republic, historian John Tracy Ellis concluded that "few matters of public policy have separated Catholics from their fellow citizens more markedly than that of their differences over private schools."[44] In 1966, Milton Himmelfarb passed similar judgment: "Catholics therefore have a real grievance. To remove this grievance would be just. It would also be statesmanlike and would help improve education."[45]

At a seminar of thought leaders in the field of education in the 1940s, even the most liberal and respected voices expressed similar reservations. Maurice B. Fagan of the Philadelphia Fellowship Commission, for example, weighed in with his opinion that "on aid to religious schools there is a real fear of where are we going? and where will it stop? . . . And there are many people who will tell you that they are opposed to federal aid to private schools, not because they have any fear of the Catholic Church but because they think it impossible to have a democracy unless there is one school system."

James Hastings Nichols of the Federated Theological Faculty of the University of Chicago added that "the Roman Catholic Church is the only church large enough to constitute a national threat to this public school system. . . . (It) is censored education. It is irresponsible in the technical sense in that it is not subject to the criticism and the review of the community. . . . To most Protestants the expansion of the Roman Catholic education is a threat to a free society. . . . The Church's power 'approximates structures and methods characteristic of Spain, France and Italy.' "

36

President John A. Mackay of Princeton Theological Seminary continued in a similar vein: "If I understand the classical Roman Catholic position of religious freedom and freedom of thought, it is that error, which is defined by the Roman Catholic hierarchy, can never have the same rights as truth and if the church had the power then the voice of error will not be freely heard. ... Would the Roman Catholic Church repudiate (the classical doctrine) so that there would be an absolute guarantee of religious freedom. . . ?"

There were dissenting voices such as Professor Will Herberg of Drew University: "The public school must understand that its position is different from what it was in immigrant days. The surest way to ruin the public school is to assure the American people that it is a school of non-religiousness."

Curiously, this symposium featured as a principal speaker Father John Courtney Murray, S.J.; among other speakers were Robert M. Hutchins, president of the Friends for the Republic, Leo Pfeffer of the American Jewish Congress, Stringfellow Barr of Rutgers University, Rabbi Abraham Joshua Heschel of the Jewish Theological Seminary of America, Dr. Paul Tillich of Harvard Divinity School, and one hundred ten others, including Paul Blanshard, Martin Marty, Paul Ramsey, Mark Tannenbaum, George Higgins, Alan F. Westin, and Benjamin Epstein.[46]

Whether it was the Blaine Amendment of 1870, the state of Oregon amendment of 1922, the Supreme Court decision of 1947 in the Everson case, the direct property taxation of nonpublic schools up until 1952 in California, or the presidential campaigns of Alfred E. Smith of 1928 or John F. Kennedy of 1960, the conclusion had to be drawn that anti-Catholicism was alive and well in the U.S.A.

It was not simply a question of the lunatic fringe, or small esoteric groups, or clandestine Catholic haters and baiters, but of extraordinary statements and actions found in the highest strata of American society: in universities, law firms, the judiciary, the legislatures, city halls, labor unions, as well as fraternal, religious, and ethnic societies and associations.

The opposition so historically against Catholic schools would later include the explosive question of abortion — and it would be argued out on the perception of the Church's teaching on religious freedom.

The American bishops en route to Vatican Council II carried with them that extra baggage of history, a mixed history at best, on the question of religious liberty and a tradition that would be at once defended and simultaneously rejected. The papal declarations of the nineteenth century so dear to the campaigns of anti-Catholicism in the twentieth century, special fodder for "no popery" drives, could not be and indeed were not discarded as irrelevant; nor were they passed over as ancient history. History was alive and well at the Council; especially reviewed were the papal writings and encyclicals.

The most common target, whether pro or con, was Pope Pius IX who published his famous letters the *Syllabus of Errors* and *Quanta Cura* in 1864. The publication of them was forbidden in France and in parts of Italy, and they were largely ignored in the U.S.A., which was then engaged in civil war.

Pius IX reacted to the false freedoms he saw among nations, freedoms of a dogmatic and doctrinaire character that were the heritage and legacy of the French revolution of eighty years previous. In the *Syllabus*, he flatly condemned the proposition, Number 80, that "the Roman pontiff can and ought to reconcile himself and come to terms with progress, liberalism, and modern civilization." The Holy Father was looking down the years of persecution of the Church as well as the birth of Communism, with the publication especially of *Das Kapital* and the *Communist Manifesto* of Karl Marx and Friedrich Engels, the antics of the Napoleons and Bismarck — in a word, the rise of totalitarianism and the threat of the absolute state.

He clearly targeted naturalism by which states and statesmen claimed that "the best interests of the state and the progress of civilization absolutely demand that human society should be constituted and governed without any consideration for religion, just as if it did not exist or at least that no distinction should be made between true and false religions. . . ." *Quanta Cura* called this and like opinions "absurd" and as "advocating a liberty of perdition."

Seen in the context of the nineteenth century, Pius IX condemned rationalism, which affirmed that man was in religion subject to no law; freedom of worship as indifferentism, meaning that it really didn't matter what a person believed, that one religion was as good as another; the absolute separation of Church and State, which would drive the Church into the sacristy, with religion a private matter only, and in the long run would reduce the Church to subjection to the state. All was summed up in the philosophical tenets of laicism, the nineteenth-century heresy that claimed that the Church and indeed all religion had no relevance in public life.

At the same time the Holy Father defended the position of the Catholic Church in Spain, which was established by law to the exclusion of other churches and the synagogue. The Pope's objection to a right "to all kinds of liberty, to be restrained by no law in the propagation of any ideas whatsoever" evoked a response and support from John Henry Newman: "Perhaps (a man) will say, why should the Pope take the trouble to condemn what is so wild? But he does; and to say he condemns something which he does not condemn, and then to inveigh against him on the ground of that something else, is neither just nor logical."[47]

In effect, Newman was demanding that critics of the Church get on target and quit fighting straw men: "All that the Pope has done is to deny a universal and what a universal! . . . It is a liberty of self-will. What if a man's conscience embraces the duty of regicide or infanticide? or free love? You may say that in England the good sense of the nation would stifle and extinguish such atrocities. . . . (What is condemned) of all the conceivable absurdities it is the wildest and most stupid."[48]

During these same years in the nineteenth century some thought leaders contributed to the development of a new approach to religious liberty. The Irish emancipator Daniel O'Connell based his claim to religious liberty for Catholics on what he called "the new score of justice — of that justice which would emancipate the Protestant in Spain and Portugal, the Christian in Constantinople. . . . There can be no freedom without perfect liberty of conscience." O'Connell spoke up for Jews: "No man can admit that sacred principle (of freedom of conscience) without extending it equally to the Jew as to the Christian."

In a particularly perceptive and even prophetic insight, O'Connell added: "I think not lightly of the awful responsibility of rejecting true belief but that responsibility is entirely between man and his creator. . . ." It would appear that he had difficulty in rejecting "error has no rights" but did want to do so.

Quite understandably his expressed thoughts on religious liberty were not readily accepted in the Roman Curia, and his rejection of the doctrine of infallibility of the Pope on matters of faith and morals scarcely endeared him to the same Roman authorities. It should be pointed out that O'Connell died before the doctrine of infallibility was defined at Vatican Council I. But he opposed the French liberals because of their hostility to religion; he argued that freedom was inseparable from religion and religion as its basis. Finally he applauded the revolution in Italy against the Papal States, for he considered the union of Church and State "an adulterous connection."[49]

Liberal Catholics in the Papal States, in Italy, and in France saw him as a prototype and "A Man of the Age" and a significant influence on the nineteenth-century Church.

One of the most liberal clerics of the century who remained a true son of the Church, Gioacchino Ventura di Raulica, preached a funeral oration in St. Peter's in Rome on the occasion of the death of O'Connell in 1847. He glorified O'Connell as one who held to the union of religion and liberty. Father Ventura supported the Sicilian revolution, advocated the separation of ecclesiastical and temporal powers.

Another contemporary, Father Jean Baptiste Lacordaire (1801-61), a Dominican friar, warned: "Catholics, remember that if you desire freedom for yourselves, you must desire it for mankind. If you desire it only for yourselves it will never be granted to you: give it where you are masters so that you will be given it where you are slaves."[50] These priests and others like them were often held under suspicion as not being quite orthodox and not pro-papal.

Neither was Archbishop John Baptist Purcell of Cincinnati so persuaded by the Roman Curia's model state. Describing what he submitted in writing to the First Vatican Council in 1869, the archbishop explained his intervention given to the Pope and the Church's bishops from over all the world:

> In it I took occasion to show that ours is, I believe, the best form of human government. That source of government is placed by God in the people. . . .
> Our civil Constitution grants perfect liberty to every denomination of Christians. . . . All that we want is a free field and no favor.
> In Spain the Catholic religion is persecuted; in Portugal . . . persecuted, the very Sisters of Charity driven from the country; in Italy monks, priests and people are driven away from their homes . . . the desolation that Victor Emmanuel has made, and all this contrasts with the best form of government, which I thanked God, we had adopted.[51]

Purcell's views reflected the ideas shared by a majority of the American bishops who had established for themselves a reputation "for fairness and clarity in the matter . . . and (were) especially opposed to groups like the Italians who wanted to universalize their own sad experience of government and make it the basis for general laws."[52]

Nor were these contrasting positions and divergent opinions lost to some leaders in Europe. England's Prime Minister William E. Gladstone saw the American Church's chance to exert its influence: "Of all the prelates at Rome, none had a finer opportunity, to none is a more crucial test applied, than to those of the United States. For if these, where there is nothing of covenant, of restraint, of equivalent between Church and State, the propositions of the Syllabus are still to have the countenance of the episcopate, it really becomes a little difficult to maintain in argument the civil rights of such persons to toleration, however conclusive be the argument in favor of granting it."[53]

But who was listening to the American bishops either in Rome or in America?

Through the years into the twentieth century many bishops, priests, religious, and Catholic laity followed these same lines of argument influenced by the American Constitution, the history of Church-State problems, and the effect on the Catholic community in the U.S.A. But all came into sharper focus with the work of the Jesuit theologian Father John Courtney Murray, who did not escape the curial cloud of suspicion.

As early as 1948 Father Murray faced the question of the right of civil government to repress heresy: "This statement and others similar to it have been widely understood to mean that the principle of civil intolerance is inherent in the Catholic doctrine of the Church and of the State, that it is inhibited from operation only by lack of political power on the part of Catholics to enforce it; and that the limiting measure of its operation is simply the necessity of avoiding the evil of serious social disturbance. In a word, with us civil intolerance in greater or lesser measure is 'the principle.' ... (These) statements of Catholic doctrine that lead to the understanding stated above cannot but generate suspicion, prejudice and hostility ... a serious obstacle to the work of the Church."

He then appealed to history and not abstract teachings such as "error has no rights" for a proper resolution and perhaps unwittingly took on the mantle of a true prophet: "The doctrine of the two powers (the spiritual and the temporary) has had a long history and has seen much development; and there is no reason to suppose that the development is entirely ended."[54]

The American theologian, at Rome in 1963, stated very plainly that had he been living at the time of Pope Pius IX he would have supported the Holy Father in his opposition to the nineteenth-century laicism and totalitarian regimes and philosophies of government then sweeping Europe. On the other hand, another Jesuit, Petrus Huizing of Louvain, looking at the *Syllabus of Errors* years later, asserted that it cannot be rescued from a philosophical, untenable contradiction in that its closed concept of Catholicism is so absolutist that "truth is degraded into a system which is closed to life and freedom.

"The Syllabus of Errors rightly exposes the errors of a political order divorced from moral and spiritual order and a conscience detached from all norms, values or truths.

"Its solution seems in accepting the Catholic Church as a State religion. .... The Syllabus does not rescue (the Church) from a closed concept of Catholicism ... closed to life and freedom."[55]

The next step forward in the history of religious liberty was taken by the succeeding pope.

In the eyes of many, Pope Leo XIII by distinguishing between the two powers — the two fully constituted ("perfect") societies, namely the state generally in matters temporal and the Church generally in matters religious — was opening up new vistas for a true development of doctrine within the Church. In his encyclical letter *Immortale Dei*, the Holy Father affirmed a legitimate autonomy for the temporal power of the state as well as spiritual power for the Church.

Adding further to the burdens of the American bishops and the American Church were the papal condemnations of Americanism by Leo XIII in *Testem Benevolentiae* in 1899 and of modernism, *Pascendi Dominici Gregis*, in 1907, by Pope Pius X.

This sally of papal authority directed in large measure toward the U.S.A. — and certainly perceived as such by American bishops and seized upon by those who doubted the Church's devotion to true religious liberty — caused great confusion and debate within and without the Church in America, a debate that continued right into the Second Vatican Council in 1962.

France's Abbé Paul Naudet, editor of *Justice Sociale*,[56] asked whether

Americanism was a doctrine or a state of mind. The whole gamut of American values was at stake: democracy, pluralism, cooperation between religions, state neutrality toward churches. Bishops in the U.S.A. were aligned on both sides with Cardinal James Gibbons and Archbishop John Ireland as "liberals" and Bishop Bernard McQuaid of Rochester and Archbishop Michael Corrigan of New York as "conservatives."

Pope Leo's encyclical letter did not outright condemn Americanism, noting that accusations had come from foreign sources; but he warned that if the doctrines he enumerated were being taught, these were erroneous. He said these errors were called by some "Americanism." Cardinal Gibbons spoke for all Catholics in the United States, saying that "this Americanism as it is called has nothing in common with the views, aspirations, doctrine and conduct of Americans." The American bishops tried to explain that while they did not consider the Spanish model ideal, much less suited to a pluralistic America, yet they were not presenting the U.S.A. arrangement as ideal either but quite suitable for Americans.

Some American theologians in a somewhat tongue-in-cheek posture expressed, in something of a Machiavellian stance, their agreement with Pope Leo's strictures precisely because they believed that Americanism did not exist in the U.S.A. but only in the imagination of some French theologians who were the "foreign accusers" mentioned by the Pope.

It was quite understandable that the lines between what was Catholic dogma, doctrine, theological opinion, political judgments, practical politics — and even personal opinion, whether of pope, priest, politician, or peasant — were not always crystal clear. Anything said or printed by pope or priest, especially if he were in the Roman Curia, became fair game in the polemics and debates that swirled around the American Catholic Church. The dialogues, often acrimonious, engaged protagonists both outside and inside the Church.

Modernism presented Pope Pius X with his greatest challenge and concern to protect the philosophical, biblical, and theological traditions of the Church. Books were put on the official index; some theologians were censured; and official condemnations were published in quick succession in just eighteen months beginning in July 1906. Sixty-five errors imputed to modernism were condemned, and what was termed a "résumé" of all the heresies was strongly condemned in the papal encyclical *Pascendi* of September 8, 1907.

At the same time the Vatican's Holy Office issued a momentous directive entitled *Lamentabili*, which sharply restricted the seminaries training future priests and prescribed an oath against modernism to be taken by all professors and clerical students. Moreover, a new and vigorous censorship was instituted on ecclesiastical writings.

As a theoretical analysis of modernism, called "the synthesis of all heresies," the action of the Holy See was quite in order. Philosophical agnosticism wherein the existence of God was compromised; the reduction of religion to the subconscious and to immanence wherein history was nullified; the recasting of religion into an entirely subjective and private role — all these were actually propositions that orthodox Protestants would agree with. Revelation both immanent and transcendent in character was a gift of God in both traditions. It was the attendant disciplinary measure that cast the chill on Catholic scholars and became grist for the mill for those doubting the Church's commitment to religious liberty.

The repressive measures gave rise to excesses fomented by a new society called the League of St. Pius V, whose members were the Integralists, self-appointed watchdogs and enforcers of papal decrees. The society was secret, with codes and pseudonyms: it engaged in anonymous attacks on specific persons, taking pieces of writings out of context being one of its common tactics; the accusations of unorthodoxy and of outright heresy were circulated through a network of newspapers and periodicals to attract the attention of ecclesiastical authorities. The net result was a cloud of suspicion over literally hundreds of leading theologians, religious superiors, and bishops. While the league eventually disappeared, the Integralist mentality remained still very much alive.[57]

Pope Pius X's *Pascendi* was judged to be a major setback for an emerging intellectual life in the U.S.A.[58] Scholars lost heart. One splendid journal, the *New York Review*, produced by three priest-professors at St. Joseph's Seminary, Dunwoodie, New York, sensing the Roman climate, simply ceased publication in 1907. The Roman authorities seemed to see a threat from "scientific theology"; their strictures on American Catholic intellectuals cast their spell over the Church in the U.S.A., in France, in Germany, and elsewhere. The Catholic leaders, religious and lay, were put on the defensive, and nowhere more so than in the United States.

Chapter 3

The American Church and the Roman Curia

A lowering cloud of something wavering between outright suspicion and positive distrust on the one hand and dubious indecision and ambivalent benevolence on the other has hung insecurely over the Catholic Church in the United States. This climate of skeptical uncertainty about the Church had its origin both in the U.S. and in Europe, especially in the Roman Curia, the Vatican's bureaucracy and the Pope's cabinet. That cloud of suspicion has survived on both sides of the Atlantic throughout the twentieth century.

The most intractable indictment against Catholics was not only that noisily and malevolently posited by Nativists and those who share an unholy affinity with them, but more importantly and significantly by well-balanced, intelligent, tolerant, and reasonable Americans, most of whom were not themselves far removed from Europe. The allegation made was that a foreign potentate, some called him a dictator, was in fact in control of the millions upon millions of American citizens and would not scruple to intervene even in an American election. The suspicion was that Catholics could not really be fully American, devoted to the Bill of Rights precisely because of the record of the Church in Europe.

At the same time the Roman Curia was perceived as exceedingly narrow, as thinking almost exclusively in terms of Europe, of the confiscated Papal States, and when dealing with the United States concentrating almost exclusively on the Italian immigrants, this Roman sense of priorities "not necessarily malevolent but certainly out of tune with the aspirations of those American churchmen who believed that the United States was 'the choicest field in which Providence offers (Catholicism) in the world today.' "[59]

The American bishops were American. Meeting for the first time in a formal fashion in the First Plenary Council of Baltimore in 1852, the bishops — thirty-three in number, with an American archbishop, Francis P. Kenrick of Baltimore, as the papal legate — promulgated twenty-five decrees, the first being a formal acknowledgment of the Pope as successor of St. Peter, Vicar of Christ, head of the whole church, with universal authority to govern the Church. The Council urged the erection of Catholic schools. It paid tribute to the U.S. government for the wise noninterference of the U.S. civil authorities in religious matters.

Rome was not entirely pleased. The Roman Curia authorities sent a private letter to Archbishop Kenrick expressing concern lest the U.S. Church take on the appearance of a national church.

Close upon the end of the Civil War the bishops, numbering forty-five, met in the Second Plenary Council of Baltimore in 1866. Archbishop Martin J. Spalding of Baltimore was the papal legate to the Council. The Roman Curia sent its proposed agenda, which included proposals for care of the recently freed Negro slaves. President Andrew Johnson attended the final session.

Archbishop Peter Kenrick (brother of Francis) opposed the move by the Roman Curia to send a Roman theologian to "assist" the plenary council. Afterward he protested to Cardinal Alessandro Barnabò in Rome that the decrees adopted at the Council did not represent the real wishes of the bishops. Emphasis on the role of the episcopate brought Kenrick and others into conflict with the process of centralization at Rome.

The Third Plenary Council of Baltimore in 1884 provided further evidence. The Roman authorities intended to send an Italian archbishop as papal legate. The Americans persuaded the Curia that Cardinal Gibbons should preside over the seventy-two bishops instead. The Council became most remembered for its promotion of Catholic schools and the publication of the Baltimore Catechism.

Manifestly the Church in America had to ride a sinuous rail between these competing exigencies, a complex conundrum that left the reigning Pope often in a difficult dilemma. George Washington had set the mood with his advice: "no foreign entanglements." Repeating that same sentiment more than anyone else was John Ireland, the distinguished archbishop of St. Paul, Minnesota. "Americans have no longing for a Church with a foreign accent," he thundered from the pulpit. "Americans are fair to the Catholic Church. . . . Prejudices exist where Catholics give cause for them and seldom else-where."[60] It was not so clear that he felt the same benevolence toward many members of the Roman Curia; moreover, he met with strong resistance within the Church in the U.S.A., not so much because of his view of America, but because of his view of the Vatican Curia.

Archbishop Ireland found it simple to correlate his faith in the Church and in the United States; he was prescient on some of the social problems, especially race and poverty.

> The equality of men is an American principle; it is also a religious teaching. . . . We are all brothers in Christ and brothers do not look at color or race.
>
> There is but one solution of the problem and it is to obliterate all color line. [He went into detail: the color line on marriage, political rights, industrial and professional employment must be obliterated and corrected on the basis of ability.]
>
> I rejoiced in my soul when slavery ceased. I will rejoice in my soul when this social prejudice shall cease and I will work in the name of humanity, of religion and of patriotism to kill it.[61]

His advice to his fellow Americans was as direct: "Glance mercifully into factories of etiolated youths and infancy. Pour fresh air into the crowded tenement quarters of the poor. Follow upon the streets the crowds of vagrant children."[62]

The archbishop's profession of faith in the Church and in America and its traditions, that profession joined in by millions of American Catholics, including more churchmen, did not convince a few Catholics and left a majority of non-Catholics still skeptical. Over in Rome the American Church was being accused of "modernism" and "Americanism," charges that bedeviled American Catholics all through the twentieth century. Nowhere was the controversy more keen than in the field of scholarship. The Catholic University of America — because it was owned and controlled by the bishops' conference (until the 1970s) — was an easy target for the Roman inquisitors.

The Catholic Church had its own internal arguments about education and the schools on the American scene. In 1891, a CUA professor, Thomas Bouquillon, wrote a pamphlet entitled "Education: To whom does it belong?" His answer was that it "belongs to the individual, physical and moral, to the family, to the state, to the Church and to none of these solely and exclusively but to all four combined in harmonious working. . . ." The state could rightly found schools, pass compulsory-education laws, determine minimums of instruction, appoint capable teachers, and inspect hygiene and public morality.[63]

Bouquillon was breaking new ground not just for Catholics but for all education and Church-State theorists. While his theories needed some refinement, especially wherein he skirts the question of the state as a teacher per se, he seems to have been quite supported a half century later by Vatican II in its "Declaration on Education" and "Declaration on Religious Liberty."

American Catholics and their scholars were working out the implications of the American experience and history, but they were not trusted by the Roman Curia members who often assumed superior knowledge.

Archbishop Francis Satolli in 1892 arrived as papal legate (actually as a temporary representative) to the Chicago World's Fair. His advent elicited overt opposition both without and within the Catholic community. Protestant Episcopal Bishop A. Cleveland Coxe of New York called Satolli a "vice pope"; he was supported by the famous inventor of the telegraph, Samuel F. B. Morse, a bitter anti-Catholic. There was one major charge: "The Roman Catholic Church is the enemy of our public school system"; the conclusion was the advice to voters: "no ballot for the man who takes his politics from the Vatican."

While, according to historian John Higham, Satolli's arrival might have been "minor" in the public arena, it caused a great deal of consternation in the Catholic hierarchy.

The Third Plenary Council of Baltimore in 1884 had called for Catholic schools — which already numbered 2,246 with an enrollment of 400,000 children — in each parish, with parents enjoined to send their children to them. The ideal was impossible of fulfillment, although the subsequent growth of the schools was one of the wonders of the world, perhaps the largest private enterprise of its kind in history. By his delineation of the legitimate role of the state in education, Bouquillon sparked a bitter controversy. Archbishop John Ireland of St. Paul had sought to work out a cooperative arrangement with the local Fairbault and Stillwater public schools; further he praised the work of the public schools at the National Education Association (NEA) convention in St. Paul in 1890.[64]

"I beg to make at once my profession of faith. I declare unbounded loyalty to the constitution of my country. I deserve no favors; I claim no rights that are not consonant with its letter and spirit. . . . I am a friend and advocate of the state schools. In the circumstances of the present time I uphold the parish school. I sincerely wish that the need for it did not exist. I would have all schools for the children of the people to be state schools." In a peroration, he cried out: "The free school of America! Withered be the hand raised in sign of its destruction!"

Why then the parish school? Ireland said he spoke for Protestants as well as Catholics because of the irreligion infecting the public schools, the materialism, and the practical denial of God or the agnosticism that reduces Him to an unknown. In something of a prophetic posture, he concluded: "Secularists and unbelievers will demand their rights. I concede their rights. I will not impose upon them my religion, which is Christianity. But let them not impose upon me and my fellow Christians their religion which is secularism.

"Secularism is a religion of its own kind, and usually a very loud-spoken and intolerant religion."[65]

To solve the various dilemmas, the archbishop suggested the English model with religion in the public schools and a second model of denominational schools that would be subject to inspection and full review, with tax money paying the tuition.

Jesse B. Thayer of the Wisconsin NEA bitterly attacked Ireland's speech immediately, "bitingly and sarcastically": "The ultramontane jesuitical element of the Roman Catholics in America was ready to defy the state." He threatened conflict "between the jesuitical hierarchy of the vatican (sic) armed with the syllabus of errors and the American people."[66]

For his pains some of his fellow bishops in the U.S.A. dubbed him "anti-Catholic school." Roman curial authorities received many protests from America; Monsignor Denis J. O'Connell defended Archbishop Ireland at the Curia when he learned that a censure was being considered. Further, Roman authorities thought it not fitting that nuns should teach pubescent boys, as was commonly thought in much of Europe.

The papal secretary of state, Cardinal Mariano Rampolla, got into the act, requesting a new commentary on Ireland's speech at the NEA, which the archbishop obligingly composed in an elaborate exegesis. But he warned: "A public condemnation from Rome of the address would set America in fury, as it would be an attack on principles which America will not give up. . . . The reproof would be taken as a censure of my Americanism and as a proof of the hopeless foreignism of the Church. This too is what my German friends are hoping for. They hate America, and they hate me for being an American."[67]

Cardinal James Gibbons of Baltimore in a letter to the Pope supported Ireland. Ireland had earlier pleaded with the cardinal: "Have we no duty toward our fellow-citizens on the way of assuring them officially and formally we are Americans? Are we satisfied to let base calumnies go out to Rome against us, our priests and our people without refuting them? Ought we not take this opportunity to assert ourselves before Rome and compel her to have in the future some regard for us? . . . At home we are surrounded by spies and traitors. . . ."[68]

Meanwhile Ireland denied having been influenced by Bouquillon, although he undoubtedly agreed with him on most points and in fact heartily supported him. The Bouquillon pamphlet stirred up a storm of controversy; priests and editors vied in denouncing it as advocating an intrinsic right of the state to educate and thus denying the primary right of parents.

In 1892, Ireland visited Rome where he found as his adversaries the Jesuits and a German faction among the cardinals, "abetted by certain influential American Catholic laymen who took exception to his 'liberalism,' and one Miss Edes who did a clipping service of items unfavorable to the Archbishop which she duly sends to the Roman Office of the Propagation of the Faith." One of the most vociferous opponents was the semiofficial periodical, *La Civiltà Cattolica*, a Jesuit magazine that equated "liberals" with "revolutionary men." "Archbishop Ireland is well known in Rome as a liberal revolutionary bishop," its editor, Father Salvatore Brandi, wrote.

Archbishop Satolli came equipped with fourteen propositions to "settle the school question," which was being sharply debated. Satolli ordered the bishops to agree with the civil authorities or members of school boards, to conduct schools with due consideration for respective rights. When Satolli had finished, both sides claimed victory: where the Church could, it should build parochial schools; where not, the Catholic children could attend the public schools.

Bishop Bernard McQuaid of Rochester, New York, wrote to Archbishop Michael Corrigan of New York, both opponents of Archbishop Ireland, saying: "We are all in a pickle, thanks to Leo XIII and his delegate. . . . If an enemy had done this! It is only a question of time when present Roman legislation, having wrought incalculable mischief, that we, schoolchildren of the hierarchy, will again receive a lesson in our Catechism from another Italian sent out to enlighten us."[69] Non-Catholics were not the only ones who would prefer that the Pope and the Roman Curia leave such matters in America to the bishops, religious, and laity of the U.S.A.

But the school question was not the only one in Satolli's mandate. On the Pope's authority he asked that a permanent apostolic delegation be established "with the kind concurrence of the Most Reverend Metropolitans (Archbishops)." The bishops, with Ireland alone dissenting, were quite critical of the proposal. When Satolli was asked to answer some pointed questions, "he stormed out of the room and refused to return." He judged quite accurately that the archbishops would not resist once the delegation was established in Washington, D.C.

In reporting to his superior, Cardinal Rampolla, Satolli described Archbishop Ireland as "a prelate exceptional in the goodness of his heart and the nobility of his actions: with high regard among American civil authorities, but in ecclesiastical circles outside St. Paul, he inspired neither trust nor sincere affection. . . ." He cautioned against giving Ireland a cardinal's hat, which would "cause too many difficulties."[70]

Curiously Archbishop Ireland supported Satolli and the establishment of the delegation. Not so Bishop John Lancaster Spalding of Peoria who said: "There is and has been for years (among American Catholics) a deep feeling of opposition to the appointment of a permanent delegate for this country. This opposition arises in part from the fixed and strongly-rooted desire . . . to manage as far as possible one's own affairs. . . . (American Catholics) are devoted to the Church; they recognize in the Pope Christ's Vicar, and gladly receive from him the doctrines of faith and morals; but for the rest, they ask him to interfere as little as may be."[71] The delegate will be seen as a foreign intruder.[72] As to Satolli's 14 propositions, out of 84 American bishops only 11 supported them, with 53 opposed in one form or another.

Over the intervening years the same tensions have perdured between the Roman Curia — which, like civil-service employees everywhere often outlive the incumbent — and the American Church. The anti-American bias in much of the Curia, its interference in truly internal affairs of the Church in America, its acceptance of unsupported and secret charges against bishops, its predilection for alleged "orthodox" bishops over alleged "liberal" bishops, its harboring of the ultramontane (read ultraconservative) functionaries constituted a facile framework for anti-Americanism that has perpetuated itself down the entire twentieth century.

The list of such conflicts is long and painful. Some of the more salient ones caused much confusion and sorrow in all spheres of American life. Roman authorities became obsessed with "Americanism" as a heresy, and not a little nettled that the Americans were holding to a thesis that Anglo-American common law was superior to Roman law and thus to canon law and that the American Church-State arrangement was superior to that of the French and indeed to that of the other nations of Europe. These sentiments were expounded and expanded in the *Life of Isaac Hecker*, whose subject was the founder of the American community of priests known as the Paulists. It was, on curial orders, withdrawn from circulation.

This challenge was taken up by Abbé Charles Maignen who pronounced Hecker a fraud; Monsignors Ireland, John J. Keane, and O'Connell virtual schismatics; and Americanism a dark conspiracy. The Spanish-American War gave him more fodder: America was a money-mad place full of Protestants, Masons, and Jews, all of whom conspired to snatch Cuba and the Philippines out of Catholic hands. His anti-American book even had a Vatican imprimatur stamped upon it: Satolli wrote a laudatory introduction. Ireland is credited with writing that Americanism was cradled as well as entombed in Europe; in America it was unknown until it was condemned.

Monsignor Denis O'Connell, rector of the North American College in Rome, was forced to resign; Edward J. Hanna, later archbishop of San Francisco, as well as Professors Edward Pace and Bouquillon remained suspect.

In September 1896, Cardinal Gibbons, who was chancellor of The Catholic University, summoned Bishop John J. Keane to Baltimore to inform him of his removal as rector of CUA, presumably because he was not controlling the tendencies toward Americanism. Yet the *Catholic Encyclopedia* concluded that "little that American writers have said to the contrary has been successful in disabusing many European Catholics of this opinion."

In 1924, the CUA chairman, Cardinal William O'Connell of Boston, opposed Father John A. Ryan's support of a child-labor law and asked Archbishop Michael J. Curley of Baltimore to censure him. Curley replied, "Let Ryan disagree." In 1935, Bishop James Hugh Ryan was removed as rector, allegedly for secularizing the university, again not possible without curial intervention. Archbishop Fillippo Bernardini of the Vatican Secretariat of State later called it "a big mistake. I fought with Cicognani (Archbishop Apostolic Delegate to the U.S.A.) about it."[73]

The banning of books directly from Rome, the censuring of university professors, the suspension of priests, the clouds floating over the lives and actions of priests and bishops in the twentieth century presented American bishops with dilemmas very similar to those of the nineteenth century. The problem was not that some books ought not to be banned, or priests and religious not censured, or bishops not called to account; the problem was (and is) that the Roman curial intervention is seen as a sign of distrust of the American bishops and of the Catholic Church in the U.S.A., and is just as often perceived as clumsy and heavy-handed.

The assumption that what the Roman Curia does concerns only the Church, even where the question at issue is truly internal, is simply naïve.

When the Jesuit magazine *La Civiltà Cattolica* — explicitly approved article by article in the Vatican Secretariat of State — defended the Spanish model of religious liberty, the Presbyterian minister Robert McAfee Brown, later to be an official observer at Vatican II, wrote: "I have since seen it reproduced in at least a half dozen Protestant books and twice as many Protestant articles, all of which subjoin appropriately Protestant comments."

What had he seen multiplied over and over again? *La Civiltà Cattolica*'s assertion that "the Church cannot blush for her want of tolerance, as she asserts it in principle and applies it in practice."[74] As applied not only to the United States but to most nations, this kind of pronouncement was disastrous. Modern communications cover the world swiftly, and each motion of the Church is carefully promulgated and recorded. The Roman Curia enjoys no immunity even in non-Catholic circles.

The encyclical letter of 1987, *Sollicitudo Rei Socialis*, of Pope John Paul II, affords an example: well-intentioned and written with a spirit of objectivity and evenhandedness. Without naming countries as such, it weighs in the balance the Western and Eastern blocs in the world, one inspired by liberal capitalism and the other Marxist collectivism, each with its "own forms of propaganda and indoctrination," "both concepts being imperfect and in need of radical correction," the Church "being critical of both: both guilty of neo-colonialism," harboring "in its own way a tendency towards imperialism," the West with "selfish isolation" and the East with lack of cooperation. The point here is definitely not to question the criticisms of the United States by the Vatican; there are undoubtedly sufficient reasons for such questioning and criticizing. But the evident equating of the United States with the U.S.S.R., the assumed equipoise between the two, the equation of the ills of one with the other caused great confusion in the U.S.A. Some bishops quietly protested to the Vatican that this seeming evenhandedness was not only an insult to Americans but tragically wrong and patently unfair. Moreover, the passages cited illustrated either an abysmal ignorance of the American social order and political aspiration or what was suspected by responsible observers as just another instance of curial prejudice against the U.S.A.

At any rate, the events in Eastern Europe since 1987 have more than vindicated the judgment that trying to balance the two blocs was an exercise in folly. The latest encyclical of 1991, *Centesimus Annus*, with the option of hindsight, restores a balanced and fair, if sometimes critical, appreciation of American democracy and its economic system.

Furthermore, quite like the shenanigans of the previous century, unsupported and secret accusations without any opportunity for redress, the deleterious slurs by unknown libelers, the acceptance of favors from rich and important citizens and from politicians (as in the nineteenth century) — all these have been entertained by the highest echelons of the Curia. Without judging the cases, it seems fair to say that the Roman establishment would not trust the American conference of bishops to handle the celebrated cases of Father Charles Curran at The Catholic University, of the Jesuit Father Robert F. Drinan, and of Archbishop Raymond Hunthausen of Seattle, to cite some examples. The Roman intervention in these cases was resented by many Americans, Catholic and non-Catholic, conservative and liberal, religious and lay, bishops and priests, mostly because the Vatican could not bring itself to trust the local church.

These and other incidents rightly caused legitimate concern in both Catholic and non-Catholic circles. The Roman Curia, notoriously uninstructed and untutored in things American, and hiding behind the anonymity of a Byzantine bureaucracy, continued to make mischief right into the 1990s to the despair of many bishops as well as others. Archbishop Rembert Weakland of Milwaukee was denied an honorary degree by the veto of Archbishop Pio Laghi of the Congregation for Catholic Education on the specious grounds that Laghi did not have sufficient time to review the proposal.

The repressions, quiet censorship, removal from office, and other actions gave non-Catholics, in particular, grounds for concern as to where the Church stood on basic liberties, the American bishops to the contrary notwithstanding.

Thanks in large measure to the Roman curial actions over the years, two centuries to be exact, those who viewed the American Catholics with distrust were not fighting straw men. There were legitimate doubts and both legitimate and illegitimate reactions. Thoughtful men and women asked fair questions; demagogues ran wild.

Through the 1920s, into the Al Smith campaign for President in 1927, American Catholics were subject to fierce criticism as citizens not quite fully American. World War II tended, as did the Civil War between the States, to quiet all dissension in the interest of the war effort; but, soon after, the same controversies arose, with Catholics again on the defensive.

One of the more famous public debates was carried on by Father John Courtney Murray and Dean Walter Russell Bowie of New York's Union Theological Seminary in 1949.[75]

Bowie, while expressing admiration for the Church's opposition to the creeping secularism in the U.S.A., yet warned that the Catholic Church's stated purpose to make all Americans Catholic would jeopardize both the religious and civil liberties that had been the glory of Protestantism in countries of Protestant majorities and culture. Catholics, he said, did not include Protestants in the Church of Christ but rather viewed them as schismatics wallowing in error. To support his thesis he cited Italy, Argentina, and Spain as well as the papal statements of Pius IX and Leo XIII. In addition, he pointed to the contemporary writings of a Jesuit in Rome, Father F.

Cavalli of *La Civiltà Cattolica*, and the American Redemptorist moral theologian Francis J. Connell.

Murray, himself a Jesuit, sharply attacked Bowie, making national headlines in *Time* magazine and elsewhere. Asserting that Bowie had taken his objections completely out of context and was thus fighting straw men, he dismissed Bowie as speaking historical, theological, epistemological, and ethical nonsense. He added, "It is always a bit difficult to convince anyone that a bogeyman does not exist. ... Dr. Bowie does have a few scattered bones ... but I have more sense to regard past Catholic documents on Church and State as so many crystal balls in which to discern the exact shape of things to come."[76]

Murray rejected both the Spanish and the Cavalli model and predicted the end of the concept of the religion of the state. Moreover, "the peril of a Catholic America is a chimera; the real problem is secularism as represented by Blanshard. Men more learned than Blanshard have given (the new Nativism) a philosophical armature which they call evolutionary scientific humanism.

"In the presence of this enemy I consider Catholic-Protestant polemic to be an irrelevance."[77]

Murray perceived the growth of secularism in the American government, which meant that religion had no role in the public sphere and that the pluralism in religion in American society demanded an exclusion of religious belief from all activities of government. The rising role of the central federal government tended to blur the distinction between society, that is, "we the people," and the state with its government.[78] Thus the notion of people logically was antecedent to the notion of the state. Murray expressed it in these words:

> The State is not the body politic but that particularly subsidiary functional organization of the body politic whose special function regards the good of the whole. The State is not the person of the ruler; in fact it is not personal at all. ... It is a rational force employed by the body politic in the service of itself as a body.
>
> It is the power ordained of God, the author of nature but deriving from the people. ... Its functions are not coextensive with the functions of society. ...
>
> In accordance with the primary principle of the subsidiary function the axiom obtains: As much State as is necessary; as much freedom as possible.[79]

At the same time the eminent historian-philosopher Arnold Toynbee was delivering a quite similar message: a secular liberalism is grievously afflicting the human race with its sins of cruelty, militarism, tyranny, intolerance, violations of conscience, suppression of truth, and propagation of falsehood

— and all done by men and women of Western civilization and culture. Only Christianity, he wrote, can give the answer; democracy as such cannot because freedom comes from God and not the state,[80] and, it might be added in light of the twentieth century, the bloodiest and most tyrannical in history, the promises of the French Revolution to the contrary notwithstanding.

As Murray had warned, the real question was the secular state assuming more and more power over individuals, families, groups, associations, and alliances, excluding the role and contribution of these to a just and happy society. The private sector stood in danger of losing more of its rights in the name of a secular god, the state.

The polemics, however, were not confined to a Catholic-Protestant debate or even dialogue: it arose simultaneously within the Church itself and also in the Church in America. A less-than-gentle controversy broke out in Rome as well; Murray was swept into the middle of the tide.

With his basic thought resting on a clear distinction between society and the organized government within a given society, he could not accept Spain as an acceptable model for the U.S.A., much less a model ideal for any country. Further he could brook no sympathy whatsoever with totalitarian regimes, whether to the right or to the left — pace Beijing, Lisbon, or Moscow — for invariably they tended to identify society and the state. It was a French monarch who cried: *"L'etat, c'est moi"* ("The state, I am the state"); but he had dozens of successors in the twentieth century.

Murray further enunciated the principle of subsidiarity which holds that smaller entities and units in the state should be given as much leeway and freedom that are consonant with the common good.

The government is the servant, not the master, of society, of "we the people."

The totalitarian state then opted for an official religion of official atheism — official science, official art and music, official culture, official history, and even official athletics. The state became a teacher, not simply a facilitator of education. Contrariwise, freedom of religion, assembly, and the media were severely compromised if not banned outright in the all-mighty state.

Father Cavalli, writing from Rome in the Jesuit periodical *La Civiltà Cattolica* in April 1948 on the condition of Protestants in Spain, ran shivers through not only Dean Bowie who quoted him but many others as well.

"The Roman Catholic Church, convinced of its divine prerogatives of being the only true church, must demand the right for freedom for herself alone because such a right can only be possessed by truth, never by error," he wrote.

"As to other religions, the Church will certainly never draw the sword but she will require that by legitimate means they shall not be allowed to propagate false doctrines."

He then pointed out that Catholics in majority numbers in a state would deny legal existence to error but would allow minorities to exist *de facto* but without the opportunity to propagate their beliefs. In a minority, Catholics will seek "all possible concessions."

He concluded, "The Church cannot blush for her own want of toler-ance. . . ."

Murray, in response, paid tribute to the First Amendment as "recognition of the primacy of the spiritual, a recognition that is again unique in that it is a recognition of the primacy of the spiritual life of the human person as a value supreme over any values incorporated in the state. . . .

"In other words, the First Amendment rescues the American State from the monism which has characterized the modern laicized state. Its premise is the Christian dialect concept of man."[81]

Ten years later Murray called the Cavalli article "dreadful" and wondered if *Civiltà* still held the same view. "If not, I further wonder if perhaps they do not owe a debt to the world to say so, in some fashion."[82]

But Murray's troubles were only beginning. Even though chosen by the National Conference of Catholic Bishops to be the primary adviser for Church-State problems and openly supported by the hierarchy, he was cas-tigated by some who believed he had contradicted the classic and time-honored teachings of the popes. The American bishops as a body were not deterred and issued (presumably with Murray as a principal adviser) in November 1948 a statement on secularism and religious liberty.

As president, Archbishop John T. McNicholas of Cincinnati published the document that dubbed secularism "the most deadly menace to our Christian and American way of living," and asked for a reversal of the Supreme Court decisions that seemed to favor a secular humanism, in essence an atheism, as the mandate of the First Amendment. The bishops further disclaimed any in-tention of changing the original American tradition of free cooperation be-tween government and religious bodies "with no special privilege to any group and no restriction of the religious liberty of any citizens."[83] This proclamation seemed the type of Americanism condemned by Pope Pius IX to some theologians, notably Monsignor Joseph Fenton and Father Francis Connell, both at The Catholic University of America in Washington, D.C.

Murray as editor of *Theological Studies* and Fenton as editor of the *American Ecclesiastical Review* carried on a mutual vendetta both "angry and tense" for two years, 1952-53, with a mutual reconciliation in June 1953, as Murray was hospitalized with "extreme fatigue, rooted in cardiac insufficiency."

But while the debate went on in America, the eyes and the tongues in Rome were on Murray and Fenton, each of whom had friends and advocates in the Eternal City.

Behind the scenes but not at all in secret fashion, Murray received rebukes from the Holy Office in Rome under the leadership of Cardinal Alfredo Ottaviani, from the U.S. Apostolic Delegation under Archbishop Amleto Cicognani, and from The Catholic University itself; in addition, the Jesuit headquarters in Rome felt pressure from each of the above to curb Murray's public expressions, whether vocal or in script.

These nagging contretemps between the Roman Curia and the American Church continued right into the final decade of the twentieth century. There were always natural tensions to be expected to arise between a central authority and its diaspora; between a legitimate concern for faith, morals, and discipline and the responsible use of conscience in a Church of almost one billion people; between an Old World culture and the New. The history of the question, however, illustrated that in the twentieth as well as the nineteenth century, the American bishops and the Church in the U.S.A. were not supinely subservient to the tergiversations and arbitrary vagaries of the Roman bureaucracy. They were quite capable of distinguishing between the essentials and the nonessentials in faith, morals, and discipline in their own country.

At times the American bishops did not meet the challenges to faith, morals, or discipline in the American Church, thus forcing the Curia to step in and do the vexatious, difficult work for them. The very interventions, however, tended to discourage the bishops to take matters in their own hands. At no time was there any question of loyalty to the Holy Father as the successor of St. Peter. When the Pope intervened personally, there was all but universal acquiescence, even if there were some doubts as to the wisdom of it all, as, for example, the *Syllabus of Errors*, or the problem of Americanism, not to mention trivia such as allowing girls to serve Mass, or Communion given in the hand, issues that sent some curial officials into paroxysms of emotion.

A study of U.S. Church history reveals quite convincingly that the American bishops, except on the matter of faith and morals, were not always in agreement with each other; they did not walk in lockstep, especially on matters of deep concern to America. However, on religious liberty the American bishops were all but unanimous, the Roman Curia to the contrary notwithstanding, as the discussions and debates of the Vatican Council proved beyond any doubt. They were truly bishops, truly Catholic, and they were truly American.

While American Catholics seemingly had to prove to their fellow citizens that they were fully American, they had at the same time to prove to the European Church and especially the Roman Curia that they were fully Catholic. A consummation devoutly to be wished for, the American Catholic never did fully and unequivocally succeed in either endeavor.

While non-Catholics in America were for the most part quite unaware of the reciprocal actions of the Church in America to the Vatican and its Curia, they were unfortunately made aware of curial interventions of the Roman authorities, which they saw as a decree from a foreign source. No matter how valid the intervention might be, it was seen as unwarranted interference in American affairs.

When two priests, U.S. congressmen, for example, were ordered by the Roman authorities to leave office, this order was commonly perceived as negating the will of the American electorate, an overseas veto. It would not have been regarded as such if the action had been taken by the American bishops' conference, but that body did not have the courage to face the question, leaving the matter to devolve upon the Roman Curia by default.

The acrimonious debate on religious liberty and Church-State relations that was going on in both Rome and the United States was fomented and aggravated, not by Murray or Fenton, but by the assessor of the Holy Office of the Roman Curia, the redoubtable Cardinal Ottaviani on March 2, 1953.[84]

Chapter 4

The Contest Joined

The traditions of the Middle Ages sanctioned a sort of sacred dualism: two organized societies that had within themselves all the things necessary for the securing of their ends and purposes. Thus the Church had within its powers those things essential to its spiritual purpose and the state to its temporal object. Each was considered "sacral," whether in Catholic, Protestant, Islamic, or other sections of the world. Each was considered as *societas perfecta*, dreadfully translated as "perfect," and equally misunderstood. Both were independent with all powers needed for their purposes, hence worked or made whole without dependence on other societies.[85]

The Catholic nation, so-called, was enclosed by the Church itself, and the divine right of kings, in Protestant as well as Catholic countries, included in its purposes the care of religious unity as well as political. It was axiomatic that *cujus regio, ejus religio*, that is, the religion of the prince was the religion of his subjects. No less a sage than the poet Dante as early as 1307 in his *Purgatorio*, Canto XVI, warned about the union of Church and State:

> The Church of Rome
> Mixing two governments that ill-assort
> Hath missed her footing, fallen into the mire.
> And there herself and burden much defiled.

Was Dante not suggesting a separation?

Americans of the final decade of the twentieth century can confidently judge that neither Protestants nor Catholics, neither Jews nor Muslims, neither atheists nor secularists, can invoke images of their past histories as primary and exclusive prototypical patterns of the American solution to Church-State problems. Contributions came from all sides; the First Amendment and its applications to religious liberty were worked out, ever painfully, sometimes violently, seldom patiently, always distressingly over the two centuries since 1776.

In the sixteenth century, Protestant reformers like Calvin in Switzerland and Knox in Scotland set the Church above the state in the fashion of Popes Sixtus V and Boniface VIII.[86] The French Huguenots taught that the state should use force to suppress heresy and idolatry. Cardinal Robert Bellarmine was persuaded that the Pope had no secular authority as such, that secular authority is independent of the Church and must not impose religion on a people. However, he left a big loophole, so dear to the leaders of the various inquisitions, the "indirect power" of the Church over the state "for the common good," for the greater good of eternal salvation. Jesuit Juan Mariana modified Bellarmine by agreeing that all kings are subordinate to the Pope in things spiritual but denying that kings held their authority directly from God but only through the people who can reserve certain things to themselves, for example, legislation, power to tax, what forms religion takes, and laws of succession. He was seen to justify tyrannicide.

The theory that kings and queens rule by divine right and that rebellion against them is tantamount to a rebellion against God was commonly held down the years of history, whether in France, England, Spain, Sweden, Russia, Turkey, or elsewhere. The theocratic states of Islam, Buddhism, and Hinduism, of ancient Israel — not to mention the failed and collapsed atheistic countries of Marxist persuasions with their ideologies and traditions — were in large measure alien to the American solution, genius, and aspirations. Learning from the past, groping for answers in a microcosm of all nationalities, both attempting to be faithful to the vision of the Founding Fathers and pragmatic under the prevailing circumstances, the United States trod a difficult and thorny path toward the implementation of the First Amendment.

Reformer John Calvin was as much an absolutist as Cardinal Alfredo Ottaviani of the Roman Curia in holding that error has no rights. In effect, they would say: "You are wrong because you know we are right."[87] Calvin proposed the utter destruction of cities that serve false gods "with the edge of the sword, destroying it utterly and all therein and cattle thereof," a truly Old Testament curse. Some of his contemporaries viewed things quite differently.

St. Thomas More in his genteel and ecumenical way expressed a contrary fancy: "By my soul I would this world were all agreed to take all violence and confusion away on all sides, Christian and heathen, and that no man were constrained to believe but as he could by grace, wisdom and good works be induced and that he would go to God, go in God's name, and that he that will go to the devil, the devil go with him."[88]

Who was listening to the "Man for all Seasons"? Surely not Henry VIII who declared himself head of the Church, nor Calvin who as chief interrogator ordered Servetus burned at the stake, nor Queen Mary who had a key role in providing John Foxe with his famous list of martyrs, nor her sister Elizabeth I who played a similar role in Catholic hagiography. Centuries later Cardinal Ottaviani could laconically report progress: "We don't burn heretics any more."

By and large, historians, especially the British, told only one side of the story of the relationships of Cross and Crown, bringing the American mind to the conviction that Protestantism meant freedom of religion while Catholicism denoted repression. The media, by and large, have kept this myth alive as have others. The famous expert on Communist repression and persecution, author Arthur Koestler, for example, blithely equated Catholicism and Communism,[89] a theme so precious to the American Nativists.

Most European countries considered the Christian religion an essential support for civic order and public peace. Clergy were given certain privileges and accorded immunities and protections. The Church-State clashes of the Middle Ages, the Renaissance, or of the last two centuries, cannot be judged with twentieth-century eyes; the assertion that the state cannot be ruled by Pater Nosters is a modern cliché.

The *éminence grise*, Cardinal Jean du Plessis Richelieu, who was prime minister of France as well, in 1629 reduced the role and influence of the nobility class, led Catholic France to join Protestant Sweden and Germans against Catholic armies. He became an exemplar of the priest-politician and of the all-but-schizophrenic posture forced upon the hybrid species. Similarly the bishop of Autun, Charles Maurice de Talleyrand, a member of the French Constituent Assembly in 1789, proposed the confiscation of all Church property, only to be excommunicated by the Pope. He served the French nation during the Revolution of 1789, Napoleon, then King Louis XVIII during the Revolution of 1830 — he, a bishop who mastered the art of political survival under sharply contrasting regimes.

The fact of the matter is that no group in America could honestly point to the Old World in its traditions, customs, and laws and claim religious liberty as its pure and disinterested gift to the First Amendment and what it stands for. Most groups, whether Catholic or Protestant, immigrated to be free and often to avoid persecution on religious grounds. It can be fairly asserted that all did contribute in some way, even at times if only by negation, to the First Amendment and its implementation over the years.

Perhaps Protestants might well take initial credit through the two greatest presidents. George Washington called religion and morality "indispensable supports" to political prosperity, "these great pillars of human happiness, these firmest props of the duties of men and citizens. Reason and experience both forbid us to expect that National Morality can prevail in exclusion of religious principles. ... Let us with caution indulge the supposition that Morality can be maintained without religion." Abraham Lincoln called for a day of "National Humiliation, Fasting and Prayer" for March 30, 1863, because of the "awful calamity of civil war." The nation, he wrote, must "recognize the sublime truth, announced in Holy Scriptures and proven by all history that those nations are only blessed whose God is the Lord." He lamented that America had forgotten God: "Intoxicated with unbroken success, we have become too self-sufficient to feel that necessity of redeeming and preserving grace, too proud to pray to the God that made us! ... But we have forgotten God."

The sacred conception of both Church and State, however, held sway until the end of the eighteenth century, not to mention its revival in the Third World of the twentieth century, especially in Islamic nations.

The American Revolution in 1776 and its subsequent Bill of Rights disestablishing the Protestant Churches in the Colonies and enfranchising the free exercise of religion had the support of the minority religious groups, including the American Catholics. These last were not particularly impressed with nor attached to the European tradition of the sacred conception of State or Church in relation to one another. Moreover, the French Revolution of 1789 with its radically secular cast had much more influence than the American Revolution around the Western world.

France went secular with a vengeance, *L'État Laique* (the lay state), inspired by the new rationalism and atheism. Voltaire gave France its rallying cry and slogan: "Écrasez l'infame. Crush that monster religion, and set Western man's spirit free for pursuing his glorious enterprise of raising his culture to Olympian heights." In its bloody history, the Revolution ruthlessly consumed and voraciously devoured its own followers, ending up eventually in military dictatorship but nevertheless leaving a legacy of some great value to Western civilization.

The French Revolution was not, in the judgment of the historian Hilaire Belloc, "a welter of treason on the part of the priests and of massacre upon the part of the democrats . . . (nor) was the Revolution a necessary enemy of the Church nor the Church (the necessary enemy) of the Revolution." Neither the Church in its doctrine nor the French government in its dogma essentially impugned one another, they agreed on the dignity and equality of man; the Revolution on its own tenets could not persecute the Church, neither could the Church on its own tenets excommunicate the Revolution, according to Belloc. However, the bitter and sanguinary conflict that resulted, which was more between theology and political theory, not only perdured beyond the revolutionary time but has persisted to the present day, "worse, in fact, today than in 1789."[90]

Nor was democracy itself and by itself a guarantee of true freedom: democratic forms can be unjust, elections per se do not secure human and civil rights. It was quite understandable that many Frenchmen, like many minority Americans, did not join in and in fact refused to celebrate the two-hundredth anniversaries of the French Republic and the U.S. Constitution.

Numbers, as one observer put it, do not insure justice: "Of this I am most certain that in a democracy, the majority of citizens is capable of exercising the most cruel oppression on the minority whenever strong divisions prevail in that kind of polity as they often must, and that oppression of the minority will extend to far greater fury than can almost ever be apprehended from the dominion of a single sceptre. In such a popular persecution, individual sufferers are in a much more deplorable condition than in any other. . . . Those who are subjected to wrong under multitudes are deprived of all external consolation. They seem deserted by mankind, overpowered by a conspiracy of the whole species."[91]

The French secularity was quite naturally bitterly opposed by the Catholic Church in France, which resulted in a very prolonged and bloody persecution of Catholics with the exiling of bishops, the execution of priests, nuns, and laity on the guillotine. The Catholic Church could not and did not accept the premises of the Church-State relationship, nor its rationale, nor even its institutions, which proclaimed liberty of cult. Defiantly the Church rejected the Civic Oath and the Constitution of the Clergy, a loyalty test. The enthronement of a prostitute in the Cathedral of Notre Dame as "the goddess of liberty" scarcely could commend the Revolution to the Catholic people. As this revolutionary influence and resultant tactics spread over Europe, it was not surprising that Popes Gregory XVI and Pius IX hurled their anathemas against the violent and virulent *absolute* separation of Church and State.

Father John Courtney Murray, the architect of the Church's 1965 answer, saw the popes trying to protect the freedom of the Church; he in turn looked to new constitutional forms in which its freedom and that of all other religious organizations would be secure. However, he opposed the *absolute* separation doctrine, which he judged would subordinate the Church to the state — a view amply verified in the history of not only the French state but of modern states as well.[92]

The famous French "Declaration of the Rights of Man" conceived of the state as uniquely grounded upon human rights, but it revealed "a paradox at the heart of its modern policy: the simultaneous negation and totalization of the state as the guarantor of rights."[93] Only once are "duties" referred to: even the duties for assistance to the poor, for the promotion of public welfare, and other state duties are not so much as mentioned. "Human rights consist in freedom of opinion of religion, of press and of speech. Significantly the only 'sacred' right is the right to property carefully defended against state encroachment."[94]

The state Church, the royal censor, and state-sponsored corporations disappeared. The French Revolution declaration did not recognize freedom of assembly or association, including workers' unions; it is a classical example of the denial of subsidiarity. This atomistic individualism actually left the citizen unprotected against an all-powerful state; it became the basis for the weakening of the family, the abolition of private corporations, and the persecution of the Church in the name of the "citizen."

In the name of public order, the state assumed the right to limit religious opinion, speech, and private property. The state in reality was totalitarian in spite of its façade of true freedom, brooking no rivals to its power. The chief underlying factor in the judgment of the state as totalitarian lies clearly in the identification of society itself with the state, the identification of "we the people" with the organized body called the state. The state and its officers were not the servants of society but its masters.

Finally the French human-rights declaration twice refers to the "sacred"; the deist God, called "The Supreme Being," appears only as the authority behind the deliberations of the Constituent Assembly.

Continental liberalism maintained that human reason was autonomous absolutely and thus subject to no external authority in private life, and consequently the free man could worship or not as he wished. The only divine majesty that liberalism recognized was that of the state. Thus the Church was absorbed into the community, the community into the state, and the state into the party with the one party-state as the supreme spiritual and moral as well as political authority and reality.[95]

The philosophical monism of it all meant not only a separation of Church from the state but a separation of the state from all religion. Continental laicism under the guise of impartiality subverted the underpinnings of the culture of Europe, eroded moral standards, and released on the world the antihuman modern totalitarianism. Those who opposed this modernism were not simply dissenters but "enemies of the state," or rather, "enemies of the people."

This drive toward the exultation and deification of human reason crossed the Atlantic; the Enlightenment attracted its American apostles who sought to promote and even institutionalize a sort of "republican religion": Ethan Allen, commander of the Green Mountain Boys and victor at Ticonderoga in 1775; Joel Barlow, U.S. minister to France, known as the "Connecticut Wit"; Elihu Palmer, organizer of a deist society and publisher of *The Temple of Reason*; and the most famous, Tom Paine.

These aggressive deists had much in common with Benjamin Franklin, John Adams, and Thomas Jefferson, but these latter "did not seek to disenchant the public and disapproved of attempts to do so."[96] Paine especially carried out a virulent and savage attack against all religion but especially Christianity, ridiculing belief in God, in the Trinity, in resurrection, and almost every facet of organized religion, all to the exaltation and aggrandizement of pure reason.

The deists ran afoul of George Washington who was to assert in his Farewell Address: "Of all the dispositions and habits which lead to political prosperity, religion and morality are indispensable supports." While a true son and devotee of the Enlightenment and the Age of Reason, Jefferson was at the same time a practical politician and a farsighted statesman. He would drive religion into the sanctuary and sacristy, privatizing it totally, but his success was not one-hundred percent. He believed in religious liberty but interpreted it to mean an absolute separation of Church and State. His campaign for religious liberty really began in his native state, Virginia, and was embodied in the famous Bill Number 82, the "Virginia Statute for Religious Freedom."

During the years of the Revolutionary War, Jefferson was chairman of a committee to revise the laws of Virginia; the committee report was presented to the state assembly in June of 1779. There were one hundred twenty-six laws: Number 82 was a radical bill for religious freedom. It was radical because it proposed to disestablish the Episcopal Church, take away its tax support, and move all religion outside the public realm over into the private domain.

"No man shall be compelled to frequent or support any religious worship, place or ministry whatsoever. ... None shall be enforced, restrained, molested or burthened in his body or goods, nor shall otherwise suffer on account of his religious opinions or belief; but that all men shall be free to profess and by argument maintain their opinions in matters of religion, and that the same shall in no wise diminish, enlarge, or affect their civil capacities."

Professor William Miller passes this judgment: "Despite the atmosphere of revolutionary ardor, and the eloquence of the preamble and the growing eminence of its author, it went too far."[97]

Meanwhile, South Carolina enacted a provision in its new constitution in 1791 that established not a single church but all Protestant Churches as the expression of religion in the new state. It provided that only Protestants could be legislators and even defined religion, including belief in God, divine retribution, public worship, the inspiration of the Bible, and the duty of every man to bear witness to the truth. In Virginia, the formidable Patrick Henry took his stand in favor of the General Assessment in support of religion as did the Presbyterian Church, which meant a tax support for the established Episcopal Church. It was all the antithesis of Jefferson's judgment and intent.

Many of the Founding Fathers saw religion as the support for public virtue and public morality: "Democracy requires public morality, and that morality requires religion." The moral condition of the Republic in the opinion of such luminaries as George Washington, Richard Henry Lee, Chief Justice John Marshall, and George Mason, needed religion to restrain vice, correct morals, and preserve peace.

Jefferson reacted acidly to his opponents, especially the Presbyterians, but he did not hesitate to condemn the (absent) Catholic clergy whose "priestcraft" had held the minds of men in shackles for centuries. Aided by his close friend James Madison, Jefferson kept up his campaign for "Reason," even while he lived in Paris. Madison carried the torch. Virginia, under his guidance and persuasion, became the very first institution in the Western world to "go all the way to the separation of Church and State."[98]

As he moved into the question of education, Jefferson wanted to strip the churches of their roles as teachers. A state-sponsored system of elementary education would be free and its training in civic virtue grounded in reason. But here he again failed: "The citizens did not want to pay taxes for churches or Christian teachers. But they did not want to pay taxes for secular republican teachers, either."[99]

The bill for the establishment of religious freedom in its final form showed Jefferson's accommodation to the religious and political realities of his time: "Well aware that the opinions and beliefs of men depend not on their own will, but follow involuntarily the evidence proposed in their minds that Almighty God hath created the mind free and manifested his supreme will that free it shall remain by making it altogether insusceptible of restraint, that all attempts to influence it by temporal punishments, or burthens or by civil incapacities, tend only to beget habits of hypocrisy and meanness, and are a departure from the holy author of our religion, yet chose not to propagate it by coercions on either, as was in his Almighty power to do, but to extend it by its influence on reason alone. . . ."

The bill went on to castigate men who would impose their views on others, maintain false religions, compel payments, practice hypocrisy, and those who don't believe "that our civil rights have no dependence on our religious opinion any more than our opinions in physics or geometry. . . ."[100]

He went further to define religious freedom as a "natural right" that prohibits a religious test for office.

Historians would certainly question the assertion that Christianity had been propagated through reason alone; ethicists would as well certainly be loathe to admit that reason alone has been a sufficient sanction for rational behavior in society; and finally all people might easily impugn the gratuitous assumption that religious opinions had no more valence in the commonweal than physics or geometry. Jefferson had said too much and gone too far, but the main substance of his campaign for religious freedom perdured: truth will prevail over error.

The words "We hold these truths to be self-evident. . ." are significant: other generations might have said "ideals" or even later generations "preferences."[101]

Jefferson did not have his way on making the separation doctrine part of the Declaration of Independence nor of the First Amendment of the Constitution. The concept and words of separation simply do not appear and for over two hundred years his letter to the Baptists at Danbury, Connecticut, in which he mentions a "wall of separation," has haunted the Supreme Court ever since coming into full play only in the 1940s.

What did the First Amendment really mean?

Joseph Storey — associate justice of the Supreme Court (1811-45), Harvard professor and author of a series of famous commentaries on the law (including three volumes on the Constitution), friend of many of the Founding

Fathers — explained that the purpose of the First Amendment was "to exclude all rivalry among Christian sects and to prevent any national ecclesiastical establishment which should give to any hierarchy the exclusive patronage of the national government."[102]

The Michigan Supreme Court Justice Thomas McIntyre Cooley (1864-85), another acknowledged expert on constitutional law in 1898, wrote that "by establishment of religion is meant the setting up or recognition of a state church, or at least conferring upon one church of special favors and advantages which are denied to others. . . ."[103]

A contemporary scholar of the Constitution, Edward S. Corwin, provides his definition, consonant with the older and classic interpretations: "The historical record shows beyond peradventure that the core idea of 'an establishment of religion' comprises the idea of *preference*; and that any act of public authority favorable to religion in general, cannot without manifest falsification of history, be brought under the ban of that phrase."[104]

In his book *The First Amendment and the Future of American Democracy*, Walter Berns (1976) laments the Supreme Court's lack of reference to these giants and others in the field "who have written on freedom of speech and religion, or to what the Founders intended with the First Amendment."[105]

Nevertheless, Jefferson remains the chief architect of the concept of religious liberty in U.S. jurisprudence and life itself. It is quite understandable that because he was fighting established Protestant Churches and a firm Protestant ascendancy that he came down heavily on the side of disestablishment, much to the joy of Catholics, Baptists, Jews, and other dissenters in early America. In his zeal for disestablishment, his predilection for freedom of mind, his aversion to unjust coercion, he spelled out religious liberty chiefly in terms of an immunity with much less concern for empowerment. His will to push churches back entirely into the private arena was not only ill-advised and unhistorical, it also opened the door to a totalitarian control by the state of religion and church-believers. The free-exercise clause of the First Amendment was an empowerment of religion that would serve as a balance to the immunity clause.

Perhaps historian John Bennett summed up the question best when he says that there was really a balance in the First Amendment that did not have its origin in the French Revolution of deism: "But it cannot be too strongly emphasized that the American system of Church-State separation was not the result of hostility to Christianity or the desire to put the Churches at a disadvantage. It was the result of the competition of many Churches and the sincere belief of many churchmen that Churches were better off when they were on their own."[106]

Jefferson showed little if any concern for corporate freedom, the liberty in religion that should accrue to groups such as families and the Churches themselves, the right to choice of education, the right to hold public events, to offer its teachings to the public. His insistence that religion was a purely private affair all but precluded his vision beyond individual conscience to empowerments in the field of religious liberty. Again the free-exercise clause of the Declaration of Independence would act as a complementary balance.

Moreover, the American declaration was not truly deist: God was quite explicitly cited as the ultimate source of human rights (as against merely civil rights) as both anterior and superior to the state, rights seen as "in-alienable." Government was perceived not as endowed with the divine right of kings transported to the New World but as servant of society and its people. God was acknowledged in non-deist fashion because He was described as Creator, Divine Providence, and God of Nature.

The tragedy of it all was that in so many American minds religious liberty was a restricted concept: "all" meant, in large measure, all-white Protestants. Jews, Catholics, and other dissenters were clearly in the purview of Jefferson and many others, but the Negroes were not. Not only were they denied religious liberty but all liberty. Jefferson among others held slaves in spite of the noble aspirations and the sublime utterance and majestic rhetoric.

The sacred concept of both Church and State of the Middle Ages was being broken down in favor of the secular state. Society as civil was being differentiated from society as sacred or religious, and their respective functions were being sorted out piece by piece over the subsequent two centuries by Congress, state legislators, and state and federal courts. The Catholic Church in particular at Rome found the adjustment difficult, but the Catholics in the U.S.A. much less so.

People within and without the Catholic Church, however, came to see the Church of the nineteenth century as favoring monarchy and hierarchy while rejecting freedom: economic liberalism, freedom of conscience, religious liberty, and liberty of opinion. Democracy was perceived to be opposed to the divine constitution of the Church. The fact that rationalism and socialism ended up condemned in the American state and American society as well did not ameliorate the image of the Church.

Regrettably the Church did not sort out what was valid in the various revolutions; it did not read the signs of the times that the union of throne and altar was being broken irrevocably in Western civilization, even if not in Eastern. The popes, however, to their credit did correctly read the signs of the times relative to Communism, classic socialism, and the Industrial Revolution as inimical to human freedom and human rights.

Pope Leo XIII, at the end of the century, in prescient fashion steered the Church toward justice for the working man by defending the right to organize into labor unions. Further, he wrote of the two distinct societies, the Church and State, of the order of law and the delineation of powers. He strongly defended the right to private property.

Theologians dissecting his writing in years to follow discerned the basis for an authentic development of doctrine, especially since Pope Leo cited Pope Gelasius I (A.D. 494) as recognizing the two orders of Church and State in society. Writing to the Emperor, Gelasius stated, "Two there are, august Emperor, whereby this world is ruled by sovereign right and sacred authority of priesthood and royal power." Pope Leo XIII thereby was affirming two distinct societies, two distinct orders of law, as well as two distinct powers. Murray called it "the ancient affirmation in a new mode of understanding, an authentic development of doctrine."[107]

Unfortunately for both Church and State the revolutionaries were more enamored by the secular slogans, especially the concept of separation. On December 9, 1905, the Third French Republic enacted the Law of Separation, establishing a new order that meant in fact the pushing of the Catholic Church into the sacristy, stripping it of most of its schools and all universities and relegating it to a virtual silence in public affairs.[108]

Germany had pursued much the same lines under the Kulturkampf and Bismarck; Italy, following Mazzini and Cavour, acted in similar fashion. With the rise of Marxian socialism, other countries followed suit, Mexico and the Soviet Union to name just two that "secularized" their societies. Society as civil was not differentiated from society as religious. What was needed was an affirmation of the freedom of society as differentiated from the state, freedom of people to choose rather than to be dictated to *by* the state in matters religious.

It might not be an unfair historical judgment to make that both Church and State behaved very badly as the new sweep toward a more democratic world was gradually emerging. The state could not be nor expected to be the *Defensor Fidei* (defender of the faith), ironically the title given King Henry VIII by the Pope in the 1520s. Contrariwise, the Church could not be expected to be the guarantor of the state; its purposes were different but not entirely distinct or separate in devotion to justice, freedom, and love among mankind.

With the rise of the secular state, often brutally totalitarian and following the lead of the French Revolution, it could scarcely be wondered that American Catholics and particularly its bishops — led by Cardinal Gibbons, Archbishops John Ireland and John Hughes, among others — judged the American solution quite preferable to the European, even in spite of the sad history of the treatment of Catholics, Jews, and Negroes at the hands of state governments and violent organizations. They could see the state as secular without denying religious liberty; they could see the state as distinct yet fostering the free exercise of religion; they could see the stratagem of the Inquisition whereby the Church theologians and canonists would turn over those guilty of heresy to the secular arm for punishment and execution as contrary to the very nature of the Church, which should have no secular arm as such.

In the American Church's purview, there had to be a legitimate autonomy for both Church and State, a respect for the human person and his conscience, and "a determination of governments never to use temporal force in religion's defense or for its elimination."[109] Such a perception was not shared in important quarters in Rome.

The assessor of the Holy Office, in effect its director, Cardinal Alfredo Ottaviani, threw the gauntlet down to the world's theologians on March 2, 1953, at the Pontifical Athenaeum of the Lateran University of Rome. The author of a standard textbook, *Jus Publicum*, that is, *Public Law*, he catapulted the Church-State question and, in particular, religious liberty into the mainstream of debate in and out of the Church. He had crossed the Rubicon.

And it was at the very time the Vatican was holding negotiations to confect with the Spanish government a new concordat. Ottaviani's speech, entitled "The Duties of the Catholic State towards Religion," defended the Spanish state arrangement of the establishment by law of the Catholic Church in Spain as "a more typical case" of constitutional recognition. Actually the heart of the problem, according to the cardinal, was not the public recognition of the Church as established by law (as in many countries, whether Catholic, Protestant, Muslim, Buddhist, Hindu, or other) — this he took for granted — but the restrictions on non-Catholics with the prohibition of public worship and public propaganda by churches and synagogues.

Pius XII had upheld this provision, but when it was pointed out that Italy itself did not so restrict Protestant sects and synagogues, he replied, "But we are unable to ask of Italy what Spain can and must give."[110] Ottaviani's speech was considered a prologue to the negotiations.

"Only a man who has the truth has the right to religious liberty in professing his religion," the cardinal proposed as his major premise. The minor? "The Catholic religion alone is true; all other religions contain an element of error." The conclusion follows logically that only members of the Catholic religion have a true and proper right to full religious liberty.

Going a step further he affirmed that the state must recognize the true religion, support it, and pay fitting tribute and worship to God. No one, therefore, has a right to propagate error. But what would the cardinal suggest for the non-Catholics in a state?

As successor to the head of the Office of the Inquisition of four hundred years previous, he smilingly said that he would no longer recommend burning at the stake. Non-Catholics were to be *tolerated* in a state where the majority is Catholic, but they were to be confined to the private practice of their religion. Otherwise they would propagate error, and the state must impede moral evil.

He mentioned Spain as the ideal state in practice: when Catholics are in a majority, full religious liberty must be accorded them alone; when in the minority, full religious liberty too with public expression of their faith vindicated.

While Ottaviani did not speak officially, yet his voice and position in the hierarchy was an authoritative one. Monsignor Pietro Pavan, professor of social teaching at the Lateran (later its rector and subsequently cardinal), said openly that Pope Pius XII was very unhappy with Ottaviani's thoughts. It was not long when the Pope himself contradicted the cardinal in large measure. On December 6, 1953, he spoke to a group of Italian jurists in the discourse known as *Ci riesce*.

Pius XII as early as 1942 in his Christmas message had spoken of "the right to worship God in private and in public and to carry out religious works of mercy" as fundamental rights. Now he criticized and rejected the theory that would say that non-Catholics were merely to be tolerated legally. "Political unity may possibly, in God's providence, be the preparation for religious unity." The Spanish "ideal" was not the Catholic universal ideal. The Holy Father did not mention Cardinal Ottaviani at all.

The allocution of Pope Pius XII precipitated a convulsive theological controversy in the U.S.A., a true *odium theologicum*. The chief protagonists were Monsignor Joseph Fenton of The Catholic University in Washington, D.C., and Father John Courtney Murray. Fenton maintained that the terms "Catholic state" and "error has no rights" were consecrated by the Pope and that the thesis that complete separation of Church and State was tenable was in error.

A close personal friend of Ottaviani, Fenton perceived Murray's explanation of the Pope's allocution not only wrong but a personal attack on his friend. He denied that the Pope was trying "to correct" the cardinal; he further denied any true development of doctrine on religious liberty had taken place or was even necessary.

Murray had "inside" information from a close papal adviser, fellow Jesuit Robert Leiber, that the Pope was displeased with the Ottaviani speech. The Pontiff may well have been influenced also by the diplomatic protests of the French, Irish, Swiss, and German ambassadors to the Holy See.[111]

Just one week after a Murray lecture at The Catholic University, Ottaviani wrote to Cardinal Francis Spellman in New York "inquiring about Murray." Spellman in turn cagily asked the Roman cardinal to be more specific as to what was offensive to him and what interpretations were given to the words of the Holy Father. There was no answer.

But it was Fenton who carried the attack on Murray as picturing the Pope as repudiating the teachings of Ottaviani and those who agreed with the cardinal as being in need of reversing their positions. These allegations were, in the monsignor's words, "utterly baseless and incorrect." Those teachings were only traditional, all in the theological manuals and in public ecclesiastical law, Ottaviani being the author of *Jus Publicum*; Fenton claimed that it was all indeed the firm teaching of the magisterium of the Church.

In Fenton's *American Ecclesiastical Review* (as editor), there soon followed an article by Father Giuseppe Di Meglio of Rome who called Murray's contention "devoid of foundation," and what was moving into the affective rather than the cognitive area, "disrespectful."

The pressures from Rome gained in momentum and shortly succeeded in the silencing of Murray. Efforts were made to have Murray's lectures at The Catholic University and at Notre Dame in South Bend canceled. Fenton did not hesitate to put similar pressures on the American Association of University Professors and the International Congress of Historical Science in Rome itself.

Ottaviani secretly sought the support of Father Christopher O'Toole, superior general of the Holy Cross Fathers, who resided in Rome. In 1954, the University of Notre Dame under the auspices of the Holy Cross Fathers published a collection of learned papers in one volume entitled *The Catholic Church and World Affairs*, which contained a contribution by Murray. The cardinal gave no bill of particulars but simply asked O'Toole to force a withdrawal of the book and to keep Murray off the campus and specifically not to mention that he, Ottaviani, had made any request.

Six thousand copies of the book had already been sold when O'Toole asked the Notre Dame president, Father Theodore Hesburgh, to keep the book out of the campus store. Hesburgh replied to his superior that he would resign rather than compromise the academic freedom of the university. Prompted by Ottaviani, the superior general of the Jesuit order, also in Rome, contacted Murray and suggested Murray purchase the remaining five thousand copies. Hesburgh quickly purchased them himself.

O'Toole, however, successfully banned Murray from lectures and retreats in Holy Cross houses. Hesburgh responded by granting Murray an honorary degree at the university.[112]

Murray offered to go to Rome, but his Jesuit superiors saw no point in his contacting Ottaviani who, they said, "has been badly hurt by this affair. . . ." Murray was forbidden to lecture or to write on Church-State problems.

Finally his Jesuit superior in Rome closed the door: "I am afraid you do not know the Rome of today . . . no, we must be patient; some people never forget . . . you must wait. . . . In the end what is correct in your stand will be justified. . . . Clarify your own position and be ready with your solution approved when the opportune time comes. That is not coming in the present Roman atmosphere."[113]

In just two months, Pope Pius XII would be dead and the "interim pope" would succeed to the Chair of St. Peter, Angelo Roncalli, history's John XXIII. Meanwhile America's foremost expert on religious liberty was "benched."

The Catholic Church stood at the crossroads. Was it a closed system in its social and political teachings? Or is it possible to expand on the deposit of faith, to read "the signs of the times" to meet the historical evolutions of modern states? Must the Church choose between repeating the formulas of the past with some application to modern conditions? Or must the Church in the light of modern history — the rise of fascism, Marxism, socialism, and democracy — abandon its premises and contradict its heritage and tradition by denying its relevance to modern civilizations? Is there not a third possibility between repetition and contradiction?

More pointedly, were American Catholics aliens in the pattern of civil and religious thought in their own country?

The declaration of the Council itself in the end gave the answer: ". . . in dealing with this question of liberty the sacred Council intends to develop the teaching of recent popes. . ." ("Declaration on Religious Liberty," No. 2). The answer then was neither repetition nor contradiction but a true development derived from both reason and revelation.

The well-known Protestant theologian and university dean Dr. John C. Bennett legitimately challenged the traditional mainline European position that favored the confessional state. Rightly he asked whether the American Catholics' answer is based on principle or merely expediency. "If Catholics could effectively reassure Protestants on this point, it would be possible to deal more objectively with many of our problems." Bennett proceeded to enumerate a whole laundry list of Protestant grievances when Catholics "are in power": the Catholics would control public schools, cut out non-Catholic teachers, operate public schools as parochial schools "in extreme cases," and show "a tendency to oppose needed bond issues or appropriations for public schools," boycotting the media with "newspapers afraid to publish news unfavorable to the Roman Catholic Church . . . and the behavior of Roman Catholic authorities in other countries, especially Spain and some Latin American countries . . . and the desire to have the U.S. send an ambassador to the Vatican."[114]

That Dr. Bennett had been reading Paul Blanshard could be deduced from internal evidence, but such a deduction was unnecessary. He unequivocally praised Blanshard, who "should be taken seriously even though he writes from a secularist point of view," adding, "The book (*American Freedom and Catholic Power*) is a work of a conscientious and well-informed prosecutor and should be used as such."[115]

Using Blanshard as a reliable source seriously undercut Bennett's credibility. Yet he quite correctly challenged the American hierarchy to make clear their position on religious liberty and the place of the Catholic Church in America. But would Protestants listen to the bishops or even to the American Catholic laity? "I believe their fears (Protestants) are exaggerated but they do have substance and unless Catholics who believe in democracy and religious liberty take them seriously," Bennett concluded, "they will never understand much of the opposition to them. . . ." But who

72

would listen to the American hierarchy? Surely not Blanshard nor millions who thought him an objective observer.

The assertion of Bennett that the traditional mainline Catholic position in Europe favored the confessional state, however, whether Protestant or Catholic, was correct. Among American Catholics it was quite another story. The vast majority of Catholics, no matter what their ancestral country of origin, were never in favor of the confessional state, much less the union of Church and State in the U.S.A. The bishops, from the time of Archbishop Carroll down to the present, defended the American arrangement, even as it was defended by Europeans as a "thesis." The separation doctrine was embraced by only a few countries of Europe.

The Reverend Robert McAfee Brown — a Presbyterian minister who was an invited observer at the Second Vatican Council and a most valued collaborator with the Council Fathers over all four of its sessions — expressed the fear that non-Catholics quite legitimately harbor reservations relative to a Catholic's acceptance of true religious liberty. He summed up the problem succinctly in his excellent volume on Vatican II: ". . . the Catholic Church is not fully trusted on this point. Whether rightly or wrongly, non-Catholics do not believe that the Catholic Church has made up her mind about religious liberty and they are fearful that the church may still espouse a position of intolerance, persecution and penalty for the exercise of a faith not Roman Catholic."[116]

The Reverend Mr. Brown gave three chief reasons for his judgment: first, the past history of the Church images of "Inquisition" and suspicions of expediency rather than principle in granting liberty; second, the present practices in the favorite "whipping boys," Spain and Colombia, as well as repressive measures in other countries against Protestants where there is a Catholic majority; and third, the lack of authoritative teaching by the Church itself, granting some favorable adumbrations, some excellent papal utterances, but no authentic teaching.

He wisely concluded that "it would lay to rest once and for all the fears that non-Catholics have . . . (when) such an utterance (on religious liberty) has become part of the Church's formal teaching."

But not only had the Protestants been eyeing the Catholic Church's response to these challenges, so were many others long before the Council. The Jewish philosopher Will Herberg posed these same penetrating inquiries: ". . . whether the liberal, democratic, pluralistic emphasis of Catholicism in America is for the Church a matter of basic principle or merely a passive counsel or expediency and necessity, motivated by its present minority status. . . . Suppose Catholics were to become an overwhelming majority . . . what then?"

Expressing his admiration for the French Catholic philosopher Jacques Maritain and Father John Courtney Murray he asked simply if they spoke for the Church. "I myself have been warned on more than one occasion (by certain Catholics) against the insidious influence of 'Courtney Murrayism.' ... In short, what are the long range purposes and intentions of the Church in matters so central to the concern of every democratic American, particularly of every American Jew?"[117]

During these years the professional anti-Catholics had not changed their aims or their target, the Church in America. Protestants and Others United for the Separation of Church and State was led by its founder and president, Edwin Poteat, who had warned America of a "clerical dictatorship." He predicted a merger of Church and State with Vatican attempts to break down the barriers between them in America because "a fundamental conflict exists between the ideals of democracy and the political ambitions of the Roman Catholic Church." The POAU lent its support to Paul Blanshard.

A surprisingly large and prestigious segment of the American public — including judges, university professors, journalists, and other thought leaders — was convinced by Blanshard's broadsides against the Catholic Church so much so that many of that segment quoted him in support of their opinions on the Church. Blanshard's bottom-line premise was that there were in the world two major menaces, the Vatican and the Communists. Both suffered from the same anti-intellectualism seeking to practice mind-control.

During the Vatican Council Blanshard visited Rome where he was received graciously by the American priests. He was invited to the American press conferences and even boasted that he was living in an apartment once the home of Pope Pius XII when a student for the priesthood.

But the cordiality masked only a desire to get more information and presumed expertise for yet more unbridled attacks on the Church. He proceeded to write *On Vatican II* in 1966, again warning against the election or appointment of Catholics as judges "unless they repudiate the Roman directives," and advising that both political parties stand for the public school as "the foundation of democracy." He neatly summarized the two issues that would bedevil the U.S.A., namely abortion — "don't listen to the Pope on this one" — and the Catholic school, which "is outside true Americanism."

Will Herberg characterized Blanshard's attacks as pure bias and bigotry that is "pervasive and often quite offensive," displaying "vulgar" anti-Catholicism on almost every page. Countering Blanshard on the school question, Herberg stated that "however great may be the merits of the public school system, American democracy does not grant it a monopoly of education. ... To deny this right (of parents to choose) would be totalitarian statism and would justify defiance in the name of the 'higher law.'

"When Catholics say this they are right, and when Blanshard attacks them for saying it, he simply reveals the totalitarian and statist strain in his own thinking."[118]

74

Where could this authentic teaching come from better than at an ecumenical council of the Catholic Church? The American bishops went to Rome in 1962 carrying the "baggage" of American history and of American experience in religious liberty to the universal council, not at all overawed by the classic history of religious persecution on all sides in Europe. They had had their own experiences in the United States; they were anxious to contribute their perspectives to the other three thousand conciliar Fathers from all over the globe.

John F. Kennedy had been elected President two years before in 1960 and, in the words of historian David O'Brien, "it seemed that at last Catholicism and Americanism had become one and the same." The campaign did reveal popular outbreaks of suspicion among some Protestant leaders, including Billy Graham, who "rehearsed some of the traditional arguments with special reference to the school question."

Kennedy meanwhile in his famous speech to Protestant ministers on September 12, 1960, in Houston, Texas, passed the Protestant litmus test: he affirmed an *absolute* separation of Church and State, pledging himself more American than the Bill of Rights, and he promised opposition to any aid for "parochial" schools. His victory was with a plurality of less than one percent of the votes cast, the smallest in history: 49.753% to Nixon's 49.498%, making him a minority president.

One year later, after an exhaustive analysis of the election returns, researchers at the University of Michigan political science department judged that "there is every reason to believe that (the religious element) was underestimated (as was) the importance of religion in the vote and there was an underestimation of the anti-Catholic vote." The victory was a narrow one not only by the numbers. Catholic politicians were still suspect in many quarters in spite of the Kennedy victory. The razor-thin 100,000 majority and the close electoral vote illustrated, to social scientists, that Kennedy's religion cost him more than two million votes.

With a Catholic in the White House for the first time and a Pope John XXIII in the Vatican, the American bishops descended on Rome with a sense of historical opportunity. They appreciated religious liberty in a pluralistic society both in theory and in practice; they had a message for their brother bishops from almost every nation. Would the ghost that would not die, Nativism, now become moribund? They fervently hoped so.

BOOK 2

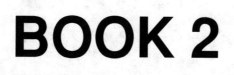

Chapter 5

The Origin of a Conciliar Document

On the Feast of the Conversion of St. Paul, January 25, 1959, the new and "interim pope," John XXIII, dropped a bombshell on the Church and, as it turned out, on the whole world. He stated that he would convoke an ecumenical council, the twenty-first in the Church's history. All the bishops of the world and other selected delegates would come to Rome to St. Peter's in the mode of the great councils of history such as Nicaea, Constantinople, Florence, Trent, and Vatican I.

Even though he gave the homily at the Mass in the great church of St. Paul's Outside the Walls, he did not mention a council. Rather he called the cardinals present to join him in the chapter room of the Benedictine monks who staff the Basilica of St. Paul Outside the Walls (of Rome). Speaking only to cardinals, Pope John informed them not simply of his intention but of his firm decision. Cardinal Ottaviani among the seventeen present was reported to have uttered that it was the Pope's "fifteen minutes of madness" that would take a long time to remedy. How long? "About five hundred years," he is reported to have replied.

Most if not all of the cardinals present were shocked at the Pope's announcement: an ecumenical council had been thought of, discussed, and even considered by a special committee appointed by Pope Pius XII — but the consensus in the late 1950s was that a council was "not opportune at this time." Pope John thought otherwise; many cardinals thought otherwise too but contrary to Pope John's judgment and decision. They too soon coalesced into a "loyal opposition," forming what might be called a sort of fire brigade dedicated to controlling the damage that they foresaw threatening the Church. What was called the Coetus Internationalis, the "international coalition" or the "international connection," came into being.

Its leader was Archbishop Marcel Lefebvre and its supporters included Vatican Secretary of State Cardinal Domenico Tardini, Cardinal-Archbishops Ernesto Ruffini of Palermo and Giuseppe Siri of Genoa, plus many others who saw danger in the future. Ottaviani, although obviously sympathetic, did not openly align himself with the Coetus precisely because he saw to it that he was appointed chairman of the powerful doctrinal commission in preparation for the Council sessions. The first order of business was control by the Roman Curia of the preparatory commissions, which would draw up the agenda and working papers of the Council.

There was no question as to who was in practical control. Ottaviani through his Holy Office had crushed the French priest-worker movement in July of 1959. Official warnings came out of that same office, which cast shadows over the biblical scholars at the Church's most prestigious Jesuit Biblicium in Rome, engendering controversies that did not die down for four years. The tactic succeeded in keeping many of the Church's brightest and best scholars off the preparatory commissions for most of the pre-Council preparations: Henri de Lubac, M. D. Chenu, J. Danielou, John L. McKenzie, Hugo and Karl Rahner, and John Courtney Murray.[119]

Other congregations too, for example, the Seminary and Education, were issuing warnings and prohibitions, aimed chiefly at biblical scholars but spilling over to other fields and areas outside of Rome. American priest-leaders such as Godfrey Diekmann and Gustav Weigel were forbidden to lecture at The Catholic University, presumably at the urging of Archbishop Egidio Vagnozzi, the apostolic delegate to the United States. John Courtney Murray himself was tagged as not only *not* invited to the Council but actually "disinvited." Many blamed Ottaviani; Murray attributed the "disinvitation" to Vagnozzi. One thing was clear: Ottaviani and Lefebvre wanted no part of religious liberty as a topic for the Council.

Meanwhile Murray was being lionized in the U.S.A. and featured as the cover-story for *Time* magazine, December 12, 1960, in a piece titled "U.S. Catholics and the State," implying that after four hundred years in America there was still a problem if not some doubt about Catholics. Arthur Schlesinger, Jr., wrote that John F. Kennedy's basic attitude on religious liberty was wholly compatible with the sophisticated theology of Jesuits like Murray whom he (that is, Kennedy) greatly admired. Murray had been consulted by telephone on the content of Kennedy's famous speech in Houston before the Baptist ministers.

Newsweek added that "Murray demonstrated in theory what John F. Kennedy demonstrated in practice: that Americanism and Roman Catholicism need no longer fear each other."

Both these opinions were misleading. Kennedy bent over backward to assert an *absolute* separation of Church and State and refused to consider Catholic schoolchildren as equal citizens, both points being anathema to Murray as the final Council document on religious liberty made quite plain. Secularism for Murray was a betrayal of the American ethos expounded in the Declaration of Independence. Kennedy espoused these tenets of secularism in the interest of votes; he and Alfred Smith before him were caught in a political bind. He certainly never agreed publicly with the philosophical or theological bases for true religious liberty as secularism denied true freedom.

In the midst of a flowering campaign, *Look* magazine reported Kennedy as saying that "for the office-holder, nothing takes precedence over this oath to uphold the Constitution." This statement of absolutism brought instant response from many on the primacy of conscience, on the loyalty to God over loyalty to the state, and with the added conclusion that JFK was espousing a totalitarianism with unqualified allegiance to the state.

In his precipitate and headlong dash to curry favor, Kennedy wrote off sending an ambassador to the Vatican (which most Catholics cared nothing about, including the American hierarchy), aid to parochial schools, and favored birth control, a calculated response that was described justly as "blunt, flat, direct, explicit, repeated, absolute." Such was the expedient manner in which to counter the stereotype of a Catholic being dictated to by pope, bishop, or priest and hence incapable of truly believing in religious liberty.

He did not respond that such cross-examinations were discriminatory because they were directed solely at Catholics, and not required of Protestants. Historian William Miller concluded: "The joke was that he turned out to be, in effect, our first Baptist president — one, that is, who defended a thoroughgoing separation more characteristic of that group than of his own church. . . . This was, of course, a political necessity in that time and that situation. . . ."

Kennedy never had to face the abortion question,[120] but his harsh precedent became bitter medicine for subsequent Catholic politicians. He did not represent the substance of Catholic thought: the perennial philosophy of natural law and the major institutional opponent of the skeptical, reductionist, relativist, and pragmatic philosophies of modernity. His was not the philosophy rooted in Aristotle, St. Thomas Aquinas, or the tradition of reason, of objective truth; rather it was empirical, skeptical, unideological, and yet with an ideology that Catholics in large measure consider outside the boundaries of good government and a just society, still perpetuating the injustices and inequities of the past.[121] The 1990s would give rise to the question once again: Can a Catholic politician be a full American and fully Catholic? Kennedy only muddied the waters in a "distressing moment in American history, a confrontation of two variant meanings of religious liberty."[122]

The drive for a clarification of religious liberty as seen by the Catholic Church, rather than by its most prominent member in the U.S.A., went on apace. While he was not a member of any preparatory commission for Vatican II, Murray was consulted by Archbishop Lawrence Shehan of Baltimore who was on the preparatory commission that dealt with religious liberty as a possible topic.

Murray was very critical of the drafts, which were entirely pragmatic, lacking a philosophical or theological base. Citizens should have religious liberty, the drafts said, because circumstances dictated it. They left untouched the real question, with Spain the ideal and the Council bowing to expediency rather than principle as in Ottaviani's famous speech in 1953.

Murray was caustic on the "Curial Right," whose position he judged extremely weak and kept in force "only by the power of the Holy Office to shut up anyone who presumes to question it."[123] He concluded that "we have a heaven-sent opportunity to effect a genuine development of doctrine in this matter."[124]

Actually the Church-State problem had been taken off the agenda as "too controversial"; Murray pleaded with Shehan to have it restored. So when the Ecumenical Council opened in October of 1962, Monsignor Fenton, close friend of Cardinal Alfredo Ottaviani, was inside the Council and Father John Courtney Murray was fretting at the Jesuit Seminary in Maryland.[125]

The first session of Vatican II, to no one's surprise, never got to the question of religious liberty at all, but the two opposing mentalities had already clashed. Ottaviani was supported by Fenton, Connell, and especially in the U.S.A. by the apostolic delegate, Archbishop Vagnozzi. In spite of the evident opposition both in Rome and in the United States, Cardinal Francis Spellman of New York, a noted conservative by all accounts, took personal action. He saw to it that Murray was invited as a *peritus* (or expert) for the second session.

Spellman's action could easily be seen to signal one and all that regardless of the theological and philosophical predispositions of the American bishops, the question of religious liberty was in a class by itself. The chairman of the Commission on Ecumenism, Cardinal Augustine Bea, sought some hard data as to the seeming truth of this opinion.

Murray now in Rome at the Council soon sent a four-page memo to each American bishop giving reasons why the topic should be restored to the agenda, and outlining the content he would propose. Cardinal Amleto Cicognani, Vatican secretary of state, had stricken the subject; a letter signed by Spellman in the name of the entire United States hierarchy demanding that religious liberty be on the agenda followed the Cicognani action.

The strong American voice was heeded, as Pope Paul VI ordered the joint commissions headed by Ottaviani and Bea respectively to meet, which they did in plenary session on November 11 and 12, 1963.

Cardinal Michael Browne of Ireland and Archbishop Pietro Parente, both of the Curia, spoke against the text; Bishop André Charue of Namur, France, suggested that the *periti* be heard. Ottaviani called on Father Karl Rahner first and then one or two others. American Bishop John J. Wright asked that Murray speak.

Face to face with Ottaviani and with Fenton sitting at the end of the table opposite him, Murray launched into his theme in defense of the American constitutional system and its guarantee of the free exercise of religion as being quite consonant with the Church's constant teaching on the dignity of the human person, consonant with the recent teachings of the late Pope John XXIII in his encyclical *Pacem in Terris*, so widely and enthusiastically acclaimed across the world. Murray was actually paying tribute to his friend and close collaborator, Monsignor Pietro Pavan of the Lateran University, the commonly accepted ghost composer of that great encyclical.

The encyclical itself constituted Pope John's last will and testament to the world and was addressed to all people of good will. Secretary of the United Nations U Thant, Soviet Premier Nikita Khrushchev, and President John F. Kennedy all publicly praised the encyclical, which laid down certain premises for the Council document.

U Thant read approvingly the Pope's warning against nuclear disaster in a world war; Khrushchev, while rejecting "any religious concepts," accepted the call for safeguarding peace; Kennedy saw Pope John talking "the language of progress and peace across the barriers of sect and creed." But the Pope went much further.

He noted the rise of the working class in politics; the accession of women in public life; and the independence of emerging nations. He praised the division of powers in government, the separation of legislative, judicial, and executive branches of government, and the right of every person "to honor God according to the sincere dictates of his own conscience, and therefore the right to practice his religion privately and publicly."

It therefore came as no surprise that Pavan became Murray's closest collaborator and dear friend in the promotion of the "Declaration on Religious Liberty" of Vatican II.

The Council stood at the crossroads on the subject. The traditionalist called for a repetition of the classical model of the Church-State relationships with modifications to meet modern conditions: "We don't burn heretics any more," again joked Cardinal Ottaviani. Basically it was repetition with a new veneer. Radicals on the other hand would call for utter rejection of the Church's tradition and past to meet modern times. Was there not a third way?

Pavan was already on record as seeing a true development from Leo XIII to Paul VI in a gradual progress but in a straight doctrinal line. There was an objective order, a moral order unchangeable in its essence but with many different gradations in application all rooted in the relationship of God and man. There was also a second theme, namely the central position of the human person in his economic circumstances, in human welfare, in his practice of religion.[126]

Murray and Pavan saw the solution in the time-honored tradition of the development of doctrine — a third way between the two extremes. In the fourth century, St. Cyril of Jerusalem wrote that "as a mustard seed contains hidden within itself the numerous branches to come, so this Creed (the Nicene) contains in germ all the saving knowledge contained in the Old and New Testaments."[127] In the fifth century, St. Vincent of Lerins taught the double authority of both Sacred Scripture and the Church's tradition and also for a recourse to an authority outside these two, namely the Church and in particular the Roman See and ecumenical councils. But he added that there is also room for a development of doctrine if it was indeed a true unfolding and not mere change.

In the nineteenth century, Cardinal John Henry Newman brought to a deeper maturity the thought of St. Vincent without any mention of religious liberty but in prescient anticipation of what such an idea might bring to the Church. He stated: "The development of dogmatic theology was not a silent and spontaneous process. It was wrought out and carried through under the fiercest controversies and amid most fearful risks. The Catholic fact was placed in a succession of perils and rocked to and fro like a vessel at sea."[128]

Time is necessary for the comprehension and perfection of a great idea that "may be interrupted, retarded, mutilated, distorted by external violence . . . and depraved by the intrusion of foreign principles."[129]

Was Newman simply reflecting on Vatican I with its arguments over papal infallibility? Regardless, he was quite accurately laying the groundwork for an appreciation of the idea of religious liberty on the second half of the twentieth century at once the concern of nations and religion.

Aristotle had advanced a canon that said that the nature of a thing must be sought in its full development, its final form — a caterpillar to a butterfly. Was the time ripe for a fuller unfolding of the implicit theology of the dignity of man in reference to religious liberty?

Newman saw the question based in the nature of the Church itself. "Again if Christianity be a universal religion suited not simply to one locality or period but to all times and places, it cannot but vary in its relations and dealings towards the world around it, that is, it will develop. Principles require a very various application according as persons and circumstances vary and must be thrown into new shapes according to the form of society which they are to influence."[130]

With this framework there will be controversy; the bark of Peter will be rocked to and fro; time is necessary for mature thinking; and the Church is Catholic, universal, and must take into account the whole human race. Murray and Pavan sought to promote the sweeping idea of religious liberty, not by way of the repetition of past formulas, nor by way of a facile rejection of the past theology as outdated, but through an analysis and historical perspective of the concept itself in the life of the Church and the life of the twentieth century.

Realistically they added (in Murray's words) a caveat: "It would be idle to deny that the doctrine of the Church (on religious liberty) as formulated in the 19th Century is somewhat ambiguous in itself, out of touch with contemporary reality and a cause of confusion among the faithful and of suspicion throughout large sectors of public opinion."[131]

Two rising tides in modern society were meeting at St. Peter's: the development of doctrine as well as the modern state groping for justice, peace, and true freedom. Thus it was not at all surprising that *Pacem in Terris* was so universally received. How would the Council Fathers reconcile these two tides? The honor of opening up the subject fell to its relator, Emil DeSmedt, the very eloquent bishop of Bruges, Belgium.

Murray described the challenge to DeSmedt: "It was a matter of striking off a sort of story line. It was also a matter of inviting the Conciliar Fathers to improve the Secretariat's text, which is not particularly good, by amending it in the sense of *Pacem in Terris*, which came out after the early text had been composed."[132]

During the preparatory phase of the Council from 1960-62, the central preparatory commission had had before it two schemata: Cardinal Bea's of the Secretariat for Ecumenism and Cardinal Ottaviani's of the Doctrinal Commission. They differed on basic principles, the one beginning with the human person, the other with the objectivity of truth. Could the two texts be fused into one, combining the pastoral with the doctrinal approach?

Bea, the chief protagonist in the Roman Curia and the Council in favor of religious liberty, had not published any text during this phase: on October 22, 1962, Pope John XXIII had raised the secretariat to the same level as other conciliar commissions. The door was opened to prepare and present a text. Bea still wondered just how a text would be received by the bishops of the world, not excepting the Americans.

In February 1963, he had asked to see two American *periti*, Monsignors George Higgins and Mark Hurley (this book's author), to put the question to them at the Brazilian College. How would the American bishops react to a text on religious liberty? The two Americans responded that in their opinion ninety-five percent of the Americans would speak strongly and vote in favor. No doubt Bea had taken other soundings: it was alleged that the Italian bishops would not be in favor, especially since so many had been graduates of the Lateran University, considered the fountainhead of conservatism. Pavan, with some exasperation, declared that over half would vote in favor, and noted that he, the reputed chief architect of *Pacem in Terris*, and Pope John himself were both graduates of this same Lateran. Concurrently, Pavan was still a professor there.

The Vatican Council had reached its Scylla and Charybdis — that is, between a rock and a hard place — on the matter of religious liberty: the development of doctrine within the Church and the rise of the modern state; the paternalistic concept of authority in the Church and the absolutist secularist concept of authority in the state; the two models of history (the confessional state and the secular state, *L'État Laique*); and, above all, the general confusion of the relationship of society and the state that presented the Council Fathers with dilemmas, conundrums, contradictions, contraries, in effect a can of worms out of which must come a coherent and a theologically and philosophically sound solution. The document had to be fair to history as well as to modernity, fair to tradition as well as to Sacred Scripture and the magisterium, the teaching authority of the Church.

The text on religious liberty, which at the time was chapter five in the document on ecumenism, began its tortuous path through the labyrinthine ways of the Council with DeSmedt's *relatio* (presentation), really just an introduction.

In a most eloquent and ringing speech, DeSmedt gave a detailed analysis of the document. There were four basic reasons for producing a text on religious liberty.

First, for the sake of truth: the Church must uphold and defend a true religious liberty because the Church has been commissioned to be a guardian of the truth.

Second, as a defense: the Church must not remain silent in the face of atheistic materialism and totalitarian tyrannies, which are widespread over the family of nations; half of all mankind are living under totalitarian governments and regimes.

Third, for the sake of peace of neighbors: the other half of the human race lives in religiously pluralistic societies of various and diverse religions; the Church must show the way to justice between men, and peace, particularly in the field of conscience.

Fourth, for ecumenical reasons: many non-Catholics nurture the suspicion that Catholics in Machiavellian fashion advocate religious liberty in those places where they constitute a minority but contrariwise believe in denying similar liberty when in majority numbers.

With a rhetorical flourish (in Latin) Bishop DeSmedt concluded: "Our document will be considered for what it is. It is not a treatise but a pastoral decree directed to the people of our time. The whole world is waiting for this decree.

"It will not be impossible, we hope, to complete our treatment of this very short but gravely important decree and approve it before the end of the second session. . . . We shall work day and night."

The Protestant observer of the Council, the Reverend Robert McAfee Brown, who sat in St. Peter's listening to DeSmedt, had had a prior look at the text and had this to say: "I have had a chance to look at the proposed chapter and I think I can report that it says *all* the things that a non-Catholic wants to hear the Catholic Church say on this matter." He added that "it is of course likely that there will be some serious opposition to the chapter in the aula (i.e., St. Peter's) and certain bishops will want to get rid of this or that emphasis within it."[133]

How prescient he was! There was the Coetus Internationalis dedicated to sabotaging the declaration by arguing for postponing consideration to a postconciliar commission. Its members had "parliamentary" rights and strove to derail the document by using the very rules of the Council.

The world's press, kept out of the sessions of the Council, trumpeted some misleading headlines stating that the document had been "rejected," "put aside," or "pigeonholed" by the Council. There was some basis for their fears.

The Council did not have time immediately to debate the subject. Proponents had hoped that there would be a preliminary vote of acceptance of the document as a basis for future discussion. Moreover, it had become clear that many other subjects would never see the light of day from the Council. Many would be relegated to "post-conciliar" commissions, to future papal encyclicals and discourses.

So the document did not reach the heaven of immediate acceptance hoped for by its proponents, nor was it consigned to the hell of perpetual banishment, nor even purgatory, the destination wished for by its doughty opponents. Rather it rested in limbo awaiting resurrection in the third session the following year. The opposition was organized; its principal nucleus was the Coetus, the international assembly.

From the very beginning of the Council process, this quite legitimate caucus — legitimate according to the Council rules — was, as already detailed, dedicated to the defeat of the "Declaration on Religious Liberty." Its guiding star, Archbishop Marcel Lefebvre of Dakar, now took the spotlight.

Addressing the Council in St. Peter's Basilica, the archbishop opposed the granting of full religious liberty to all groups. In some cases, he said, it would condone immorality, since some people make immoral actions part of their religious beliefs. He added a special caution: the Council should not decide the question based on the experience of one country, namely the United States.

Would the document not lead to indifferentism that one religion is as good as another? Would it not lead to subjectivism that as long as a person followed his conscience, it did not matter what religion or church he belonged to? Would it not give sanction to secularism, which would drive the Church out of public life?

These questions were most certainly germane to the problem at hand. The Coetus itself introduced twenty-seven pages of amendments. The text subsequently underwent six major redactions and revisions. There were 120 speeches in St. Peter's; 600 written interventions were introduced with some 2,000 suggestions for improvement.

Interestingly, another French archbishop, Cardinal Joseph Lefebvre, openly took issue with his namesake. The Catholic Church, he argued, has had the great capacity over its history to foster a true development of doctrine. The declaration must be drawn up in light of the "evolution of circumstances through the centuries." He pointed to the two great circumstances of modern history: the simultaneous rise of totalitarian states, whether to the right or to the left, and of democracies.

Here was the true "sticking point." Marcel Lefebvre, Cardinal Ottaviani, Cardinal Ruffini, Bishop Luigi Carli of Segni (who, although a newly consecrated bishop, yet somehow got the floor over senior bishops), Monsignor Joseph Fenton, Monsignor George Shea of Newark, Father Francis Connell, and many others believed they were standing on the solid rock of immutable teachings of the Church, particularly of the popes from the nineteenth century (Pius IX and Leo XIII) or the twentieth century (Pius X, Pius XI, and Pius XII) on matters of religious liberty and Church-State problems. They were defending the solid teaching: the Council could repeat and reiterate and reenforce that solid teaching and could make suitable adaptations to modern circumstances, but it could in no way compromise or contradict this firm tradition.

But Pope Paul VI had not remained quiet on the subject. On September 29, 1963, in his allocution to the Council Fathers, he deplored the violation of the right to religious liberty around the world: "We are grieved when we behold that in some territories religious liberty, together with the other principal rights of man, is suppressed by the principles and acts of those who do not tolerate opinions different from theirs on politics, on races of men or on religion of every kind . . . who would like to profess their religion honestly and freely." His Holiness had supported in advance DeSmedt's second point in regard to totalitarian regimes, whether to the left or to the right. The opposition, however, was not swayed even by the papal utterance.

The opposition to the document had not confined itself to Rome. The apostolic delegate in the United States, Egidio Vagnozzi, sent a letter to Father John J. McGinty, S.J., Murray's superior in New York after the second session. The Archbishop quoted the "new" rules on the activities of the *periti* framed in December 1963 by the coordinating commission of the Council to the effect that the *periti* were "forbidden to organize currents of opinion or ideas, to hold interviews or defend publicly their personal ideas about the Council."

Murray had written an article for the Jesuit magazine *America*, November 30, 1963, to which Vagnozzi took exception. Actually each *peritus* who was appointed to assist one of the ten commissions of the Council took a special oath over and above that of the general *periti* of the Council. Murray was on the Commission for Ecumenism under Cardinal Bea and under that oath.

The matter did not die at this point. Murray privately asserted that Vagnozzi "has elected to be my personal enemy and has made statements about me throughout the country which are libelous. . . . Finally if there should be any trouble in my own case, which is hardly likely, I am sure that his Eminence of New York (Spellman) will stand behind me. He is one of the few American bishops who can be counted on to talk back to the Delegate. And he has — bless his heart — elected to be my patron."[134]

At this time, Monsignor Fenton left The Catholic University to become pastor of a parish in upstate New York. He took a parting shot in defense of the Roman Curia in general and Cardinal Ottaviani in particular as the most important figure in the first session of the Council who was not "hoodwinked by those who dislike the unchanging continuity of Christ's teaching within His Church."[135] The attack on the Curia, he claimed, was a veiled attack on the Holy Father himself.

Both these two stalwart warrior-theologians, Fenton and Murray, suffered from severe heart trouble of which each of them died rather suddenly after the Council.

Chapter 6

The Council Debate on Religious Liberty

The "Declaration on Religious Liberty" had been for one reason or another put off for almost three years, partly because of a determined opposition and partly because of the complexity of the subject. At the outset, it had been chapter five in the document on ecumenism, then an appendix, and finally a separate text all its own.

The Council Fathers recognized the need for a statement on religious liberty for two basic reasons: the Catholic Church could not be silent in the face of repressive totalitarian states that were depriving half of the human race religious freedom; and in the religiously pluralistic societies of modern times, the Church felt obliged to lead the way toward justice and peace, especially in the field of conscience and ecumenism.

Reading "the signs of the times," the Fathers were also aware of the 1948 "Universal Declaration of Human Rights" of the United Nations, which included freedom of conscience and religion in both public and private observance (Article 18). Also during the Council itself, in 1963, Pope John XXIII's encyclical *Pacem in Terris* pointed in the same direction: the Church must speak out.

The encyclical broke new ground for society, elaborating the principles for both a just society and a just state and government. These numbered four: (1) truth, which affirmed the human dignity of every person; (2) justice, which demanded freedom from all unjust coercion; (3) love, which was the motivation that should inform all human relationships; and (4) freedom, which was the bedrock of all well-organized societies and civilized states. Nowhere did it espouse a doctrine of absolute separation and opposed the exiling of God from human society (even as the American Declaration of Independence did not so exile God). *Pacem in Terris* — Peace on Earth — was indeed both a charter and stimulus for the Council Fathers. But not all were converted.

Those conciliar Fathers who were strongly opposed to the document turned to parliamentary maneuvers to relegate the declaration to a post-conciliar commission or a future papal encyclical. The fact that religious liberty was not even considered during the first session was entirely explainable: most subjects, even very important ones, were not either. In the second session, the document was introduced by Bishop DeSmedt as part of the ecumenism document but not voted on even as a preliminary reading of the collective mind of the Council Fathers, thanks in large measure to the fierce opposition from both within and without the Roman Curia.

New York Times reporter Milton Bracker wrote: "Many, probably most, of the Italians refuse to concede that the basic freedom of conscience, as enunciated by Pope John XXIII in his last encyclical, *Pacem in Terris*, does not constitute an invitation to Italians, or at least 'permission' for them, to become Communists."[136] Pavan countered, insisting that at least half if not more of the Italian bishops would vote favorably on the question. However, he and Murray had to overcome what was known as the "French School," which was quite in favor of religious liberty but on classical French lines.

French bishops and theologians were very much in favor of religious liberty but disagreed with Murray and Pavan on its bases. Influenced by the French philosopher René Descartes who insisted on the necessity of a clear idea, the French scholars saw as a very clear idea the fact that conscience should be free and untrammeled. From that fact they deduced that man himself should enjoy freedom in religion and since man was by nature social, then a further derivation would cover freedom in social and political life.

For Murray this reasoning was too subjective, too indirect. Freedom flowed directly and not as a derived right from the fact of creation and the inherent dignity of the human being. Nor was freedom in his social and public life a derived right but rather inherent in his *ipso facto* membership in the human race.

Murray persuaded the French and others that the starting point must be the fact of human dignity, man made to the image and likeness of God, and that it must be nourished and protected in a constitutional form that would limit government in the first instance but also others: private relationships, corporate bodies, and other social groups.

His persuasion carried the day as he became the chief proponent of Bishop DeSmedt's floor presentation to the bishops in St. Peter's. The major debate took place at the third session from September 23 through September 25, 1964.

Cardinal Ottaviani conceded that the Church had always taught that conscience must not be coerced; he cited the priest Tertullian who in A.D. 212 wrote what he considered a principle valid for all time: "It is the right of every human being to worship him in whom he believes. No one has the right either to harm or help the profession of religion by another. Nor is it the task of religion to force anyone to profess any religion: this must be cultivated spontaneously without recourse to force. . . ."[137] The cardinal, however, saw in the text that rights to liberty in the supernatural order were being superseded by rights in the natural order. Supernatural rights take precedence over natural rights, thundered the doughty blind cardinal in fluent and spontaneous flawless Latin. He warned that the sections dealing with proselytism be omitted because they could be used against the Church itself. Why, he asked, should we arm our adversaries?

Palermo's Cardinal Ruffini told the Council that freedom is proper to truth and only truth has rights. He advised tolerance for non-Catholics that must be "patient and kindly." Only the Catholic Church, however, should have full state support.

Cardinal Benjamin Arriba Castro of Tarragona, Spain, asserted that freedom of worship would ruin the Church, for "only the Catholic Church has the right to preach the Gospel." His colleague from Santiago de Compostella, Cardinal Fernando Quiroga, added that the text seemed to have been written for Protestant countries. Cardinal José María Bueno y Monreal from Seville allowed that the text was doctrinally correct in general but weak on the juridical and political level; error, he said, can lawfully be prohibited under certain circumstances. Outside St. Peter's a major secretary of the Council, Archbishop Casimir Morcillo of Madrid confirmed the Spanish opposition, stating that the declaration would break a "contract with Spanish history, literature and culture. . . . The State must keep on being Catholic in religion and Catholic in education."

Again the *New York Times* weighed in against Spain: "In Rome Protestants are 'separated brethren'; in Spain they are damned souls who are still agitating for the right of public worship."

Two aspects of the attack on Spain should be noted: first, the success of Francisco Franco and the Nationalists (with the support of Germany and Italy) over the Loyalists (supported by the Soviet Union and the left-wing forces in the U.S.A.) grated interminably on those who supported the left, like the *New York Times*; second, the attack on Spain made it appear that Spain was really the leading choice and exemplary model of Church-State relationships for the whole Catholic Church.

A scholarly defense of his country was later given by Father Teodoro Jimenez-Urresti of Bilbao, Spain, by way of explanation. Article 6 of the 1953 concordat with the Holy See, in the words of Vatican Secretary of State Cardinal Domenico Tardini, had to be maintained. Pius XII had added, "We are unable to ask of Italy what Spain can and must give." Article 6 was quite explicit: the Church would enjoy official protection and "no person will be molested on account of his religious beliefs or private practice of his worship. Religious ceremonies or external manifestations other than those of the Catholic religion will not be permitted."

The Spanish scholar described the international propaganda campaign as "largely inspired . . . by the Soviet Union which had suffered a major defeat in Spain between 1936 and 1939 — where the struggle between Trotskyism and Stalinism was decided and the future heads of European Communism (Togliatti in Italy, Tito in Yugoslavia, Thorez in France, and Gomulka in Poland) were active despite the burning and sacking of churches and convents, the murder of 6,484 priests and religious, 283 nuns and 429 seminarians."[138]

Kept out of the Marshall Plan with President Harry Truman pointing to

Article 6, Spain was an outcast: "Spain has paid for her neutrality far more dearly than the Axis powers for their defeat." Calumnies instigated by some Protestant pastors — for example, "Not a week goes by in Spain without some member of the Protestant Church being tortured to death" — further poisoned the climate.[139]

Yet Article 6 remained on the books in Spain and found its defenders at the Council. But Spain was not the world nor the Spanish Church the whole Catholic Church. Cardinal Raul Silva of Chile soon made the point. Speaking in behalf of fifty-eight Latin American bishops, he reminded the Council that Spain did not speak for "New Spain"; a wider religious liberty was necessary in Latin America. The United States bishops now moved in as a dominant voice.

Prior to the opening of the third session, Father Murray had done his "missionary work" well. He enlisted the support of Archbishop Karl Alter of Cincinnati, an acknowledged "heavy hitter" of the American hierarchy. Alter said that he always had difficulty with "error has no rights" because the Council was not asked to treat the virtue of religion on the relationship of God to man, but rather the relation of citizen to state and immunity from unjust coercion. Distinguish, he wrote to Murray, "between the free exercise of religion and freedom of conscience."[140]

Murray sent an essay on the subject to every American bishop and to the Dutch Documentation Center in Rome (DOC), which translated it into five languages for distribution to other bishops.

Some considered the first drafts of the "Declaration on Religious Liberty" too abstract. Pavan warned against a too exclusively theological mentality. Murray agreed: "For my part I agree with Pavan that the political-legal aspects are coordinate with, not subordinate to, the theological-ethical aspects."[141]

Murray was inclined for historical reasons to let the Spaniards have their Spanish system, just as the English and Scots their by-law established churches, or as Scandinavian or indeed Islamic nations have their historical prerogatives while insuring in some measure religious freedom. But Spain, Murray insisted, must not be seen as "the ideal"; nor did he wish to present the U.S.A. as "the ideal" either. The Council, he said, must read history!

The Jesuit *peritus* then orchestrated much of the American interventions. He wrote every word of Cardinal Richard Cushing's rousing speech; he proposed that Archbishop Lawrence Shehan treat the biblical and theological foundations; he advised Bishop Ernest Primeau, with whom he lived at the Villanova Pensione in Rome, to expand on the basic fact that internal freedom of conscience also needs external freedom in worship, observance, and education, and to show clearly the distinction of a right both as an empowerment and an immunity.

Bishop John Carberry was asked to speak on the competence of governments in religious affairs, and Archbishop Patrick O'Boyle on government limitations, the common good of society being something quite different from the limited sector of the common good committed to government protection, that is, public order. The First Amendment to the U.S. Constitution, Murray claimed, adequately guaranteed the freedom of the Church as expounded over the century by Leo XIII, Pius XI, and Pius XII. The declaration could then conclude with the proposal that what the Church claimed for itself, it now sought for other churches and other human beings.

On September 21, 1964, two days before the debate, Murray addressed the American bishops at the North American College; in spite of objections by Monsignor George Shea of Newark and Redemptorist Father Francis J. Connell, the American bishops voted unanimously to accept Murray's recommendation of the text of the "Declaration on Religious Liberty."

Murray had become something more than a philosopher and theologian of religious liberty: he had become a lobbyist of the Council orchestrating many of the interventions by non-Americans as well as Americans. The opening words of Cardinal Cushing expressed Murray's personal and professional feelings: "It is most gratifying to us that at long last a full and free discussion on this subject will take place in this Council hall. In our time this is a practical question of great importance both for the life of the Church and for social and civil life. It is also a doctrinal question, for the doctrine of the Church on religious liberty in modern civil society has not yet been declared clearly and unambiguously."[142]

A reporter for *LeFigaro* of Paris, Abbé René Laurentin, described his feelings as Cushing spoke "in the name of all the American bishops . . . a tall, purple figure with white hair (who) spoke Latin, this fabulous man . . . syllable by syllable . . . with enormous effort and fierce concentration. An energy radiated from his whole being, the loud speakers vibrated at the limit of their power. . . .

"I shared . . . the emotion of this fighter defending the cause of liberty . . . this great grey man doing himself violence to defend an idea of which, obviously, he would give his life."[143]

The cardinal had set the tone that this issue was one upon which all U.S. bishops agreed and which they would press for passage at all costs in the interests of the Church Universal. Cardinal Albert Meyer of Chicago was next, affirming the innate freedom of the human person in religious affairs; he was followed by Cardinal Joseph Ritter of St. Louis who acknowledged such liberty "as the innate right of all who come into this world."

Bishop John J. Wright of Pittsburgh, speaking in the name of seventy bishops, rejected any simply pragmatic approach to the question. American Catholics could argue that in regions where religious liberty has been granted in a pluralistic society, the Catholic Church has obviously flourished. Wright called this approach "not worthy of the subject," stressing that religious liberty corresponds to truth, to truth about the nature of the human person but also about the nature of the common good of society itself. He noted that religious liberty "can be worked out even in a state favoring some particular religion for historical reasons — as it does in England where a Protestant Church (the so-called Established Church) traditionally enjoys special privileges but where now, at least, all except the King and Queen (unless I am mistaken) have full religious liberty." He was no doubt referring to the religious constrictions on the royal family, for example, being prohibited from marrying a Catholic. Ireland was a second example he named.

Paying tribute to both England and Holland, he criticized America for "as a matter of fact — and it should be acknowledged openly — religious liberty is often more complete in other countries than it is in America ... with regard to school rights."

Finally he called upon all the bishops of the world to be "the foremost and fearless leaders among the heralds of liberty, because historically we are the heirs of liberty in matters religious acquired almost in every case and almost in every nation only through the blood and tears of our fathers. Thus we know from our own experience (in the U.S.A.) how dear and fruitful liberty is."

The Catholic Church, he was advising the Council Fathers, "never had it so good" in any other country, America with its separation of Church and State as stated in the Bill of Rights.

In a dramatic twist about American support, Auxiliary Bishop Charles Maloney of Louisville, an avowed and noted conservative, spoke for the lay auditors at the Council, most of whom were not Catholic. "Yesterday (they) asked me to announce their unanimous resolution: 'All the auditors of the Council approve the doctrine proposed in the treatise on religious liberty.' Moreover they strongly urged that it be promulgated by the Council."[144]

Cardinal Franz Koenig of Vienna supported the text but deplored its silence regarding nations that have two classes of citizens: (1) those who profess atheism and thus have access to the highest offices in the land and (2) Christians who are excluded from these offices. Such societies, he said, turn the hearts of their citizens against their rulers and make them disinclined to cooperate in achieving the common good. The Council, he concluded, must speak in the name of the entire human race and demand religious freedom behind the Iron Curtain. Koenig never mentioned Communism, which ruled the nations just off his own country's borders; but his chosen target, "so-called scientific atheism," left no doubt of his plea for religious freedom.

The indefatigable Archbishop Marcel Lefebvre strongly opposed the declaration, which granted liberty to those who propagate error and added again that the particular circumstances of one country, namely the United States, should not be the norm for the entire Council. Cardinal Michael Browne of Ireland claimed that Pope Pius XII had set forth a different basis for religious liberty, namely the common good. Archbishop Parente of Italy asserted that the declaration prefers the rights of man to the rights of God; Bishop José Lopez Ortíz of Spain objected that the state has the right to declare itself Catholic when it is the will of practically all its citizens. Similarly, Brazil's Bishop Antonio de Castro Mayer of Campos spoke in opposition, allowing that the state could profess the true faith, which all men must accept anyway.

And so the debate went, back and forth, pro and con, for three days when cloture was called for by Cardinal Leo Josef Suenens of Belgium. One of the last to speak (under the rules) was Archbishop Alter of Cincinnati who rejected the frequent criticism that the declaration jumped too easily from the subjective order of conscience to the objective order of social rights. The Pope's own theologian, Bishop Carlo Colombo, defended the doctrinal character of the text; his position was quickly denied by Father Anecito Fernandez, master general of the Dominican order.

At the American press panel just hours after the last talk in St. Peter's on religious liberty, Murray, in answer to questions, admitted that the concern of the Spanish bishops was quite legitimate because the declaration would indeed change Spain's law of intolerance. He defended the churches established by law in England and Scandinavia; nor did he see any objection to a nation proclaiming that a majority of its citizens were Catholic, Protestant, or Muslim. These were merely statements of fact that people loved their culture and traditions. But where there is legal intolerance under the coercive power of the state, then the declaration will demand change. And what of the U.S.A.?

Murray described the American situation: "In the United States of America the free exercise of religion is governed by the order of society — that is, the public order. This is made up of three civil goods: one, public peace; two, public morality, including the notion of public health; three, harmony in the exercise of civil rights. Religious liberty is subject to the same norms."[145]

Now that the debate was over, Murray had his first chance to work directly on a new revised draft of the text itself. His collaborators were Monsignors Jan Willebrands, Jerome Hamer, DeSmedt, and Pavan. Murray gave first place to Pavan, stating: "Our joint influence has been recognized as 'determinant' of the new doctrinal line. . . . The fact is that I should have had little if any influence except for the fact that Pavan's views coincided with my own. Therefore he deserves 'equal billing' as a matter of justice."[146]

Shortly, however, new roadblocks were erected, in not a none-too-subtle fierce counterattack on the declaration. With the acquiescence of the Pope, a new "mixed commission" was formed to reexamine the document —

"mixed" meaning from both the Holy Office and the Secretariat for Ecumenism. Nominated from the very reactionary wing of the hierarchy were Cardinal Browne of the Curia (an Irishman and Dominican priest), Father Fernandez (the Spanish master general of the Dominican order), and Archbishop Lefebvre, a trio of more extreme views than which could scarcely be chosen and all on record as against the "Declaration on Religious Liberty."

Cardinals Albert Meyer of Chicago, Joseph Ritter of St. Louis, and Joseph Frings of Cologne joined in a letter of protest to Pope Paul who assuaged their negative reaction with the assurance that the text would remain the property and prerogative of the secretariat under Cardinal Augustine Bea, which had already unanimously approved the Murray-Pavan revision.[147] But the opponents had not given up at all. If the "mixed commission" could not successfully erect a roadblock, the Coetus Internationalis and its allies could.

On the next to last working day of the Council, on November 19, 1964, Cardinal Eugene Tisserant, French member of the Roman Curia, announced that no vote would be taken on the document on religious liberty, as promised. His explanation was that there was not sufficient time for the Council Fathers to consider the new text with its many changes. Actually the announcement seemed a breach of faith because just the day before, the secretary, Archbishop Angelo Felici, had told the Council that the members themselves could vote on whether or not they wished to delay the voting.

"Almost from nowhere petitions sprouted like mushrooms around the council hall," said one bishop. In an unprecedented action, bishops left their places, swarming to the transept of the great basilica to sign a petition in protest. Tisserant's invitation to the Fathers of the Council "to submit their observations on the text to the Secretariat before Jan. 31, 1965" was scorned as a placebo pill and a further strategy to kill the document.

Meanwhile DeSmedt was giving his report as the relator of the text; the bishops were applauding him at every turn and when he said that the text would *not* be voted on, the bishops caught the humor of his words and gave him the longest and most prolonged applause of the entire Council.

At the same time Cardinal Meyer and several others, armed with four hundred forty-one signatures spontaneously gathered in dissent against the parliamentary maneuver, left the Council aula and marched up immediately to see Pope Paul. Following the rules of the Council the Holy Father referred the whole matter to the tribunal of the Council. The tribunal in turn upheld the decision of the presidency, led by Tisserant, but the Pope intervened to add that while there would be no vote during the current session, the declaration would be treated "in the next session, and, if possible, before other schemata (texts)."

These events conspired to give the secretariat yet another chance to revise the "Declaration on Religious Liberty"; accordingly a new text and *relatio* were sent by the coordinating committee of the Council to all the bishops and Council members. It was the fourth redaction that even the most aggrieved on either side admitted was an improvement of no mean proportions.

The declaration in its text was at last in possession. Its chief architect was described by an observer as "distinguished at all times by his unique grasp of the subject, his loyalty to the Church, his nobility of mind and his love of truth": Father John Courtney Murray.[148]

Chapter 7

The Council Document: Religious Liberty as Known Through Human Reason

The very title of the conciliar text illustrated at once its main purpose and its severe limitations: "On the Right of the Person and Communities to Social and Civil Liberties in Religious Matters." No attempt was made to present a comprehensive treatment of the theology of religious liberty, of freedom of conscience under God, much less a political document. It was to be a religious treatise with a variety of starting points as was clearly perceived in the debates.

Contrasts both profound and subtle arose from a variety of theological presuppositions, even doctrinal in nature as well as from diverse historical conditions. Bishops spoke from the perspective of nations where there was little or no religious freedom at all; from the perspective of totalitarian regimes, whether to the right or to the left; from the perspective of democratic countries where religion was by law established; from the perspective of secular states espousing complete separation of Church and State. In general, however, there were two main focal points: the totalitarian states where religious freedom was denied totally or in large measure; and democratic states where there was a wide pluralism among the people in matters religious.

The concluding words of the "Declaration on Religious Liberty" itself sum up the matter: "Consequently, in order that relationships of harmony and peace be established and maintained within the whole of mankind, it is necessary that religious freedom be everywhere provided with an effective constitutional guarantee and that respect be shown for the high duty and right of man freely to lead his religious life in society" (No. 15).

How would these words play in such diverse countries as the former Soviet Union, China, South Africa, Sudan, Vietnam, Poland, Uganda, Chile, and Spain? What of the by-law establishments in England, Scotland, Scandinavia, Indonesia, Saudi Arabia, Colombia? And how does the United States measure up against the criteria?

The right to religious freedom has its foundation manifestly in the dignity of the human person. The foundation of this right, its premise, is to be found and to be known both by human reason (philosophy) and divine revelation (theology). Further, there must be a distinction clearly made between this right as a negative and as a positive, that is, negatively as an immunity and positively as an empowerment or entitlement.

The object of religious liberty, its content, consists of, first of all, an immunity from unjust coercion, whether at the hands of individuals, social, fraternal, economic, religious, and political groups, and most particularly governments in matters religious. Since men, women, and children are all by their very nature social and *ipso facto* members of the human family, this freedom must extend to their lives as lived as family members; in a word, there must be corporate liberty. Thus families, sodalities, groups, associations, unions, granges, chambers of commerce, fraternities, sororities, and a host of other fellowships are covered by the same protection of their religious freedom.

This right to freedom from duress and unjust constraint has at least two meanings: no one may be unjustly compelled to act against his conscience, nor may he be restrained from acting in conformity with his conscience. In their histories, Spain and the U.S.A. afforded examples of both injustices: the execution of witches illustrates in the case of America a compulsion, and the laws of intolerance against minorities illustrate in Spain's case a restraint. Moreover, freedom in religious practice must not be allowed simply in the privacy of the home or pushed back into the sacristy. The Council text was clear: "Whether privately or publicly, whether alone or in association with others, within due limits," corporate freedom must be accorded to all bona fide groups.[149]

In *The Height of Glory*, C. S. Lewis told of the consequences of such a denial of corporate freedom: "To make Christianity a private affair while banishing all privacy is to relegate it to the rainbow's end of the Greek Kalends."

While the entire Council agreed that in today's world religious freedom was a necessity, a minority maintained that it should be only a positive civil right, something granted by the state. The majority disagreed, affirming that the right is fundamental and intrinsic to the human person. In other words, it is not the state that confers the right but nature and nature's God and therefore is inalienable. However, it must also be recognized further as a civil right by the state.

This right inheres in a person regardless of his condition or actions. It cannot be inferred, however, that such a right to liberty gives a person the right to be wrong. No one has a strict right to be wrong: otherwise Hitler, Stalin, Pol Pot, Saddam Hussein, the modern barbarians, could claim such a right. The person in error in good conscience enjoys immunity from unjust coercion. Further, no one has a *right* to profess publicly and propagate error, but if in error in good faith he would enjoy immunity in things religious as his right. Still, in the objective order he has no moral right to be wrong.

Each human being must fix his own relationship with God; he is bound by truth, and he must be true to himself. "God made you without your cooperation but he will not justify you without it," wrote St. Augustine. Yet God respects man's freedom: "The truth cannot impose itself except by virtue of its own truth as it makes its own way into the mind at once quietly and with power" ("Declaration on Religious Liberty," No. 1).

Thus an attitude of mind toward those in error is essential; there must be understanding, respect, and tolerance for the person who may be in invincible ignorance and in good faith, even if objectively in error. The virtue of fraternal charity still applies!

In assigning a negative content to the right of religious liberty, that is, "a freedom from," the Council was assigning it to all, even the atheist. Thus the Council was in harmony with the U.S. Bill of Rights in its First Amendment, which also guarantees such immunity. But neither the Council declaration nor the First Amendment implies that a person has the right to believe what is false or to do what is wrong. Such would be moral nonsense. Error and evil cannot be the proper object of a right. There was, however, "a freedom for" in the declaration.

The declaration did not stop with only a negative immunity, whether personal or corporate: all have a positive right to profess their faith alone and in association with others. All others, especially the state, have a correlative obligation to respect these rights. Public expression must be esteemed, but it must extend beyond expression.

Religious communities, according to the conciliar declaration, must have certain entitlements, certain empowerments, in respect to religious freedom. Not only must they be enabled to express their faith and worship publicly but also to select and appoint their own leaders and ministers, to transfer and dismiss them, to communicate with religious authorities abroad, to build churches, schools, and hospitals, to use both the spoken and written word, and the right to private property as necessary for freedom. The Council in the declaration spells out "the right of men freely to hold meetings and establish education, cultural, charitable and social organizations under the impulse of their own religious sense"(No. 4).

Murray had pointed out that the modern concept of freedom was dangerously inadequate because it neglected this corporate dimension of freedom, isolating the problem of freedom from responsibility, justice, order, and law. The original experiment in freedom had also become an experiment in justice.[150]

The Council clearly recognized that things had changed over the past century and a half. Not only had the Church become more conscious of the dignity of contemporary man, but nations and states too had very gradually given more recognition to the dignity of the human person. This consciousness was all the more poignant in light of the judgment that the twentieth century was by far the bloodiest of any in history. There was perceived a convergence on the part of both the Church and State, a historical convergence that cried out for true freedom on earth.

The encyclical *Pacem in Terris*, promulgated between the first and second sessions of the Council (Pope John had died after the first), had great influence on both the Church and many nations of the world.

This masterwork, described in St. Peter's as *the* most important document on religious liberty, set down the lines of solution and along the avenues of history. It enjoined civil authorities "to coordinate social relations in such a fashion that the exercise of one man's rights does not threaten others in the exercise of their own rights nor hinder them in the fulfillment of their duties. . . ."

How then to draw the line between natural rights, specifically the right to religious liberty, and the common good? On what conditions can the public authority intervene? How balance the encyclical's affirmation that "every human being has the right to honor God according to the dictates of an upright conscience and therefore the right to worship God publicly and privately"?

The encyclical continued: "In our time the common good is chiefly guaranteed when personal rights and duties are maintained. The chief concern of civil authorities must therefore be to ensure these rights are defended and promoted so that in this way each one may more easily carry out his duties" (No. 60).

No doubt too the Council had recent history in mind: the "Universal Declaration of Human Rights" of 1948 explicitly affirmed its "faith in fundamental human rights, in the dignity and worth of the human person . . . the right to life, liberty and the security of person . . . freedom of peaceful assembly and association . . . of education . . . freedom of thought, conscience and religion or belief . . . to manifest his religion or belief in teaching, practice, worship and observance."

The Charter of the United Nations, born in San Francisco, had said no less and reaffirmed "faith in the dignity and worth of the human person." The European Convention on Human Rights in 1951 supported the right to "freedom of thought, conscience and religion," and added yet another facet: "This right includes freedom to change his religion or belief," which was simply an echo of the "Universal Declaration" (Article 18).

The leading Catholic neo-scholastic philosopher of great influence on the conciliar document on religious freedom, Jacques Maritain, rejoiced in the United Nations' "Universal Declaration of Human Rights" as a "landmark" and he saw it in relation to the natural law and to the nature of man. Every natural and artificial thing has a nature of its own, but man is endowed with intelligence and thus determines his own ends. He must judge what those ends necessarily demand by his human nature. The second question is: What is the natural law as known? There is at least one self-evident principle on which all reasonable men can agree, to wit, good must be done and evil must be avoided. "Natural law," Maritain wrote, "is the ensemble of things to do

102

and not to do which follow therefrom in necessary fashion."[151] Every sort of deviation is possible, given the nature of human nature; there is much careening and turning and intermittent error. Nations that signed the "Universal Declaration" had quite contradictory notions of freedom of religion, of speech, of assembly, the right to life and to liberty. Yet underneath there has usually been a basic recognition of these rights as valid and necessary.

Nations can come to an agreement on human nature and human rights but only on the foundation of truth. By being human, each person and hence each nation can come to that truth through human intelligence and spell out human rights for all.[152]

The Catholic Church at the Council was not only conscious of these historical developments around the world, especially after the Second World War, but in a very real sense was trying to catch up with human progress in civil rights by searching its own traditions, history, philosophy, and theology. The Church would use its intellect (reason) assembled in St. Peter's and carefully search revelation (both Tradition and Sacred Scripture) to express itself on religious liberty.

While vindicating human rights, including religious, for her own sons and daughters, the Catholic Church was now claiming the same for all other churches, synagogues, temples, and mosques, as well as religious communities, even if not on exactly the same basis: all have equal rights as children of God and by reason of creation; there was a special vindication in the message of Jesus Christ.

The Council was reaching out to all people of good will: men, women, and children of all faiths or of none. As in the other documents the Church had much to say in the field of education to all countries.

The United Nations and the various conventions on human rights had in turn been catching up with the Church in the matter of freedom in education and the rights of parents in the choice of schools for their children. Over the past century the Church had insisted that parents were primary educators over against the claims of the state, totalitarian or otherwise. Popes Pius XI and John XXIII had very explicitly vindicated the respective rights in education of the family, of the state, of society, and of the Church. The Vatican Council took aim at its religious aspects, no doubt encouraged by similar recognition by the world bodies of the family of mankind.

The "Universal Declaration" (Article 16) stated that "the family is the natural and fundamental group unit of society and is entitled to protection by society and the state." It should be underscored that the "Universal Declaration" distinguished between society and the state — we the people and we the government of the people. Both must protect the family: "Everyone has the right to education. . . . Parents have a prior right to choose the kind of education that shall be given to their children."

The Vatican Council was even more progressive and specific; it set up two general scenarios in which it saw unjust discrimination and clear violation of human rights: when children were enrolled in religious schools and when children were enrolled in state schools.

In both cases, "parents have the right to determine, in accordance with their own religious beliefs, the kind of religious education that their children are to receive" ("Declaration on Religious Liberty," No. 5).

In the first case, parents who have chosen religious or schools other than those of the state should have true freedom of choice and not be subjected directly or indirectly to unjust burdens because of that freedom of choice. "The use of this freedom of choice is not to be made a reason for imposing unjust burdens on parents, whether directly or indirectly" (No. 5). In its document on education, the Council used similar language: "The government must see to it, in its concern for distributive justice, that public assistance is given in such a way that parents are truly free to choose according to their conscience the schools they want for their children" ("Declaration on Christian Education," No. 6).

While the Council was speaking to all governments, American members, conscious of the denial of these rights in the U.S.A., submitted their own formula: "The principle of distributive justice demands that the government, in distributing burdens and benefits within the community, should have in view the needs, merits and capacities of various groups of citizens in general. This principle should control the action of the government in the question of the support of schools."[153]

From the general principle the Americans moved to its application: "The principle of distributive justice would require that a proportionately just measure of public support should be available to such schools as serve the public cause of popular education, whether these schools be religious in their orientation or not."[154]

The Council Fathers specifically claimed these rights for all parents, as a matter of natural law, not simply for Catholics. Archbishop George Beck of Liverpool praised the school arrangements in England, Scotland, Ireland, and Holland, which acknowledged the rights of all parents. The Americans were even more careful, asking not for parity and total equality for religious schools but assistance insofar as they serve the "public cause of popular education," a formula that was already in full force in other fields in social work, hospital care, military service, Head Start, the Job Corps, and the like but not for religious schools.

It was the suggested formula in 1912 of Archbishop John Ireland of St. Paul, Minnesota, who had pleaded for support for all schools, public, private, religious or not, making a distinction between paying for secular subjects required by the states and religion as a subject in the curriculum. He suggested Great Britain as a model, especially Scotland. "Let the state pay for the secular instruction demanded by the state. This is not paying for religious instructions."[155]

Not only have the parents, teachers, and students been denied direct aid in religious schools but even much indirect aid as well. Some states legally allow for transportation to school, but very few supply it. The U.S. Supreme Court has allowed textbooks for these schools; in most states they are denied. Some schools receive health care; most do not. The U.S. Congress mandated special classes for handicapped youngsters in nonpublic schools, for remedial work supplied by public schoolteachers to enter nonpublic school classrooms; in effect, they could not be trusted, even though under the complete control of the state school authorities, to maintain the separation of Church and State.[156]

The point is that the religious schools and more particularly the Catholic are constantly being harassed by the state authorities, imposing most inequitable and unjust indirect burdens on parents, teachers, and students.

The U.S. Supreme Court in 1947 ran the gamut of sympathy for the "victims" of the discrimination to the implementation of such discrimination.

Justice Hugo Black had this to say: "The First Amendment requires that a state be neutral in its relations with groups of believers and non-believers; it does not require the state to be their adversary. State power is no more to be used so as to handicap religions than it is to favor them."

Yet another opinion, that of Justice Robert Jackson, read:

> I have sympathy . . . with Catholic citizens who are compelled by law to pay for taxes for public schools, and also feel constrained by conscience and discipline to support other schools for their own children.
>
> No one conscious of religious values can be unsympathetic toward the burden which our constitutional separation puts on parents who desire religious instruction mixed with secular for their children. They pay taxes for others' children's education and at the same time the added cost of instruction for their own.
>
> Nor can one happily see benefits to children which others receive, because in conscience they or their parents desire for them a different kind of training others do not demand. . . . Hardship in fact there is which none can blink.[157]

Two assumptions seem to undergird the U.S. Supreme Court's decisions on nonpublic church schools. First of all, since the schools are church-sponsored, they are to be treated ambivalently by the fifty states. They are schools when it comes to obligations: necessary curricula, health, safety, conditions for graduation, required courses, etc. But they are churches when it comes to benefits from the state and hence are cut off from even a modicum of equal treatment as schools.

The state is perfectly willing to accept the benefits from the schools: educated citizens, eligibility for military service, vocationally prepared workers, and the like, as well as the billions of dollars in savings to the taxpayers and the state budget itself. Do they not serve the public purpose of education as much as government schools? Answer? A school is a church!

Secondly, in the doctrinaire and dogmatic application of the separation doctrine of the Supreme Court, its justification lies in the history of the school question. Consistently the justices have appealed to the nineteenth century, the wretched antipathies between Catholics and Protestants, not to mention Jews and blacks, as a justification for a twentieth-century decision that must keep the churches apart and in their place. Justice Jackson, for example, spoke in light of American tradition that was steeped, as we have seen, in anti-Catholicism, as justification for what he admits are acknowledged hardships and discriminations in the twentieth century against the nonpublic sector. It is just the price parents, teachers, and pupils are required to pay to maintain the dogma of secularism — so says the high court and so say most legislators!

While professing complete devotion to the separation doctrine, Supreme Court majorities have sanctioned aid of many kinds, direct and indirect, to colleges and universities, both religious and secular. What was unthinkable on grade level 12 becomes quite constitutional at grade 13 and beyond: a clear retreat from the separation dogma but a selective retreat aimed mostly at the Catholic school system that had at one time eighty percent of the pupils in religious schools.

Arthur E. Sutherland, a constitutional law professor at Harvard, in viewing this discrepancy wrote: "And indeed one such reader finds difficulty in perceiving a clear line of constitutional cleavage between governmental and to, say, first year instruction in a junior college and similar aid to, say, fourth year instruction in a high school." Yet the latter and not the former is in compliance with compulsory-education laws: parents, teachers, and pupils stand under a second coercion because of their religious convictions.

During the Vatican Council Father John Courtney Murray finished his book *We Hold These Truths*, a classic on religious liberty in the United States. The subtitle perhaps said even more than the title: *Catholic Reflections on the American Proposition.*[158] His work on the Vatican's "Declaration on Religious Liberty" shows a transparent correlation with his work on this book in which he devoted an entire chapter entitled "Is it Justice? The School Question Today."

The American tradition, he wrote, was the basis for solution to problems in dispute, not the least the Catholic (parochial) school question. There has been and must be a development of a judicially enforced Constitution, because the American constitutional law is a living law. Any solution must remain true to the spirit that animates that law, at the same time with due recognition of the changing realities of American life. The McCollum

Supreme Court decision violated both the spirit and realities in America with its rigid dogma of the absolute separation of Church and State.

Madison put it better: the separation of government from religion for "the whole intent of the First Amendment was to protect not to injure the interests of religion in America."[159]

There must be the free exercise of religion; there must be no hostility toward religion, and there must be an "accommodation" in the interests of the people.

"Until the problem (of schools) is solved with all justice and realism, the American ideal of ordered freedom, for which the Bill of Rights stands, will not have been achieved," Murray concluded. And what was good for America, *pari passu*, was good around the world and especially in the Vatican Council.

The theory of state monopoly in education has its genesis in the total identification of society and the state in the belief that the two are coterminous. That theory verges on the totalitarian, whether in the East or the West, the Third World or elsewhere. Under the consequences of such a theory the state, which properly speaking has no right at all directly to be teacher or educator, determines what is truly art, truly science, truly culture, and even truly religious or religion.[160]

"If these schools," Cardinal Spellman stated at the Vatican Council, "serve the public purpose of popular education, the fact that they may be religious in their orientation should not exclude them from a rightful measure of public support."

The state as the servant of society in this case is being politely told not to intrude into the orientation of the school, which, *mutatis mutandis*, is none of its business, just as the orientation of schools for child actors, for tennis players who are minors, for those aspiring to a musical career (which receive state aid as public schools) are not interfered with as long as the basic requirements of the state are met. Parents were being told by the Council to expect support as their right, not in absolute fashion, but insofar as the schools serve a public purpose; hence they may have to pay for any "extras" in the curriculum, religion being one, or tennis lessons, or musical training, or acting lessons, etc.

Somewhere in a viable philosophy of education in the modern state and twenty-first-century society there may be a rising conviction, inchoate and unclear but nevertheless real, that in a pluralistic society there must be a pluralistic answer. Neither the totalitarian state's solution of rigid uniformity, nor even as in the United States the "democratic" solution of the will of the majority alone, secures true freedom of education.

The Protestant theologian Professor John Bennett suggested that the best interpretation of "the nation under God" would mean that "the state is neutral as between traditional faiths, that it is not a secular state or indif-

107

ferent to the religious life of its citizens or to the relevance of their religion to its affairs, that it does not profess a common denominator religion that it is in no sense a teacher of religion. . . ."[161]

So much for the American families, Catholic, Protestant, Jewish, Amish, Muslim, Seventh-Day Adventist, and others that choose to exercise their right of choice — but only at a heavy price unmatched in any other field such as social work, hospital care, military service, prison detention, and other fields.

The second problem in education addressed by the Council concerned students who were forced by law to attend schools that were "neutral" in religious orientation or that openly contradicted the religious beliefs of their families, an uneasy anxiety common to parents, teachers, and pupils all over the world.

Neutrality in education is impossible: values or disvalues are part and parcel of education, especially moral values or disvalues. Each school has a value system, even one that denies moral values.

There are philosophies of education that give first place to the state, with the highest value being the subordination of the individual to the state, a fact clearly perceived in totalitarian countries but also in the U.S.A. where for years Marxism has been presented as a "scientific" basis for higher learning: in sociology, politics, economics, and even literature.

An expert on Karl Marx, Joseph A. Schumpater (who died in 1950), summed up a typical academic's view of Marxism: "Marxism was and is at once a philosophy of life, a religion, an interpretation of history, a theory of social classes, an analysis of economic development, and a blueprint for political and social harmony."[162]

Herbert Marcuse, the late leading German exponent of Marxism, spent years on the California State University system at San Diego propagating this faith. One of his star pupils, Angela Davis, is currently on the California State University payroll at San Francisco as an expert special pleader for Marxism and the priority of the state over the individual, scarcely a tenable thesis since 1988, with the all-but-total collapse of Marxism both in theory and in practice all around the world, save perhaps China where repression still reigns supreme.[163] Not so well-known is a similar subordination which lay at the basis of the philosophy of America's most famous educator, John Dewey: he made society the ultimate value.

In contrast, the Second Vatican Council's "Declaration on Christian Education" (No. 1) affirmed that every man has an inalienable right to an education corresponding to his proper destiny and suited to his native talents, his sex, his cultural background, and his ancestral heritage. As young Christians advance in years, the declaration went on, they should be given a positive and prudent sex education, encouraged to take part in social life, dialogue with others, and work energetically for the common good.

The whole matter of sex education in schools and that which is contrary to parental beliefs has become a clear and pressing concern of Americans and others. The proliferation of obscene literature and entertainment, the transfer of health problems to the schools, the advocacy in schools of contraception, free condoms, and abortion, of homosexuality as an acceptable alternative lifestyle — all of these point to the fact that denial of the moral order or the studied ignoring of moral principles do not add up to neutrality in education.

Schools are, willy-nilly, forming consciences, that is, the judgment of what is morally right and morally wrong. Even as Marxism has served as a basic philosophy of education in totalitarian states of the former Soviet Union, China, Cuba, many countries in Africa, and others, so a secular humanism has been basic to so much American education.

Without judging the rights and wrongs of it all, it is fair to say that these and other ideologies and philosophies of education clearly stand at variance with the convictions of millions of parents.

The Council labels as unjust the compulsory system in which these moral and religious convictions are either contradicted or ignored. Just before the opening of the fourth and last session of the Council, the Ontario bishops of Canada issued a statement that said in part: "We are obliged to point out that even in the practical order, the choice of our province is not between Catholic schools and some form of common religiously oriented schools. . . . The only alternative available to us is schools without adequate religious orientation."

Some Council Fathers warned that when the state took over the Catholic schools, promising to respect their special religious character, once control was assumed by the state the promise was soon forgotten and the government in effect declared itself competent in the field of religion, dictating its common syllabus and courses of study. The Council in effect cautioned against state monopoly, especially where it was antireligious or "neutral" in religion.

The United States did not meet these criteria on either score: with children enrolled in religious schools, or with children enrolled in state schools. Yet the American bishops did not advocate nor ask for complete parity between religious and nonreligious state schools, which they saw as "a dreadful oversimplification of a complicated issue." Cardinal Spellman, as already seen, proposed that "a proportionately just measure of public support should be available to such schools as serve the public cause of popular education, whether the schools be religious in their orientation or not."

It is significant that the Council in its purview kept in mind the rights of all families in education no matter what religion and no matter what country. Parental rights extended as well to parents of no religion, whether atheists, humanists, or secularists. Reason, logic, and common sense should dictate how a nation treats parents, teachers, and pupils in education, which is an essential aspect of religious liberty. Freedom in education was clearly seen as a most necessary and essential component of religious liberty.

Christians, however, have a special mandate for yet a deeper appreciation of religious freedom: it is found in divine revelation. The first half of the declaration made no appeal to religion as such, using human reason, history, and a keen sense of reality around the world. The second half moved to Tradition and the Sacred Scriptures.

Chapter 8

Religious Liberty as Known Through Divine Revelation

The demands of religious liberty, according to the Council Fathers, "have become more fully known to human reason through centuries of experience. Furthermore, this doctrine of freedom is rooted in divine revelation and for this reason Christians are bound to respect it all the more conscientiously" ("Declaration on Religious Liberty," No. 9).

Governments are enjoined to "safeguard the religious freedom of all its citizens in an effective manner by just laws and other appropriate means . . . to create conditions favorable to the fostering of religious life . . . in order that society itself may profit. . ." (No. 6). Governments thus are prompted to include religious freedom in their constitutions. On what basis?

The document repeated Christ's own familiar words: "Render to Caesar the things that are Caesar's and to God the things that are God's," in which He recognized civil authority as legitimate. Further, "He did not wish to be a political Messiah who would dominate by force. . . . His kingdom does not make its claims by blows" but by witness to the truth (No. 11).

The Council and thus the Church placed the right to religious liberty in the fact of creation and the essential dignity of each and every human being; it thereby in effect declared it an inalienable human right. But the Council went further and praised those countries that made it a civil right as well, stating "that men of the present day want to profess their religion in private and in public. Indeed it is a fact that religious freedom has already been declared a civil right in most constitutions and has been given solemn recognition in international documents" (No. 15).

The Christian revelation vindicates the dignity of each human as being far beyond philosophical reasoning. Similar justification was clearly maintained in the U.S. Declaration of Independence where the Creator is endorsed as the source of rights, a reflection of Christianity's description of the human person as made to the image and likeness of God. The citizen is endowed with certain inalienable rights by reason of this dignity on a higher plane and by a deeper foundation than simply being in existence, namely that God is the Source. The state does not give or grant these human rights but must recognize them; nor may it curtail or deny them unreasonably.

The Catholic Church teaches that divine revelation has three factors: Tradition, Sacred Scripture, and the magisterium, which is the teaching authority of the Church. God through Christ has made His will known: when authentically passed down through the ages orally, revelation becomes

Tradition; when recorded in writing, it became Sacred Scripture, that is, the Bible. The Bible contains revelation as a written record; not all in the Bible is revelation, however. A written record can become a dead letter, needing constant interpretation and commentary in succeeding times and epochs. The Church as magisterium is the final interpreter, not unlike the U.S. Supreme Court on the written Constitution.

The Bible most certainly teaches the essential dignity and worth of each human being; it does not in so many words, however, affirm religious liberty. Not so the Church's Tradition; it does reveal Church thinking and teaching on the question of liberty.

To repeat what was pointed out in Chapter 6, the Church Fathers expressed the tradition of freedom of conscience as early as A.D. 212, when the priest Tertullian put the matter quite explicitly as valid for all time and for any age: "It is an inherent human right and a natural faculty conceded to every human being to adore Him whom he wants to believe in. No one can either harm nor help the religious profession of another. It is not the task of religion to force anyone to profess a religion; this must be cultivated spontaneously without recourse to violence, also due to the fact that the offering of the sacrifices requires above all to be the expression of a soul (acting) voluntarily."[164]

Curiously the Council experts and scholars failed to mention Tertullian in their footnotes in support of the Catholic tradition; ten other ancient scholars are cited, including Lactantius, Ambrose, Augustine, and Gregory the Great, as well as several Church councils. Freedom of conscience was "constantly preached by the Fathers," the Council said with some satisfaction, but such was not the whole picture.

The Council frankly admitted that in history Catholics in various countries did not live up to their own tradition, and non-Catholics as well did not either. What was in the collective memory of the conciliar Fathers? Perhaps St. John Chrysostom's anti-Semitism? Pope Gregory's protection of Jews? The Fourth Lateran Council, which prescribed special dress for Saracens and Jews? The Spanish and Portuguese Inquisitions? The savagery against Catholics in the French and Bolshevik revolutions? The Kulturkampf? The persecution of Catholics in Ireland, Japan, Sudan, China, Spain, and Mexico? The exclusionary laws of India? The menace of Islam to freedom of religion? The crass materialism and carnal secularism of the United States? The anti-Catholicism of the nineteenth and twentieth centuries in America? Who can say? Certain errors related to religious liberty, however, were noted and dealt with.

Some bishops worried about a reaction that the Council would be perceived as promoting error, as charged by Archbishop Lefebvre and the Coetus Internationalis. The error of indifferentism that claims that one religion is as good as another so that it really doesn't matter to which one a person belongs, since all are going in the same direction? The error of subjectivism whereby one's religion didn't really matter so long as one followed his conscience? The error of secularism whereby religion has no place in the public forum of any state or nation? These were, of course, legitimate concerns that the Council had to address and do so from the divine revelation entrusted to it by Christ as well as from human reason.

Basing its declaration on the dignity of the human person, the Council acknowledged an awareness of a new consciousness of personal freedom around the world, especially in the face of totalitarianism, and a new political consciousness of the aspirations of the human spirit to pursue its destiny under governments whose powers should be circumscribed by constitutional limitations.

It proceeded therefore in its own words to search the sacred tradition and doctrine of the Church — the treasury out of which the Church continually brings forth new things that are in harmony with the things that are old. The Gospel is permanent; its application fits each era and civilization, and there evolves a development of doctrine to meet the needs of the people.

Indifferentism? The Council text stated: "We believe that this one true religion subsists in the Catholic and Apostolic Church to which the Lord committed the duty of spreading it abroad among all men." Religious liberty does not mean that a person has moral liberty to choose his religion according to personal taste.

As the *Herder Correspondence* during the Council in 1964 made the point: "No one inside the Church . . . has the remotest idea of putting such an interpretation on it." The apostolic commitment to make disciples of all nations to the end of time and "even to the shedding of blood" remained a categorical imperative (No. 14), but first of all by prayer, sacrifice, and witness, respecting the personal dignity of each person and relying on the power of the Word of God and the action of the Holy Spirit.

Subjectivism? The declaration leaves untouched traditional Catholic doctrine on the moral duty of men and societies toward the true religion and toward the one Church of Christ. In plain words, no one has a right to be wrong, but if wrong, one has a right to immunity from unjust discrimination and coercion. Conscience must be free, but it must be aimed at being or becoming a true and informed conscience.

As already mentioned, the Council Fathers did not base the right to free exercise of religion directly on freedom of conscience as the French school had originally proposed. The Council did not want to appear to lend support to the perilous theory that a person may follow his conscience simply because his conscience says that he may act in a certain manner. Objective truth is the true norm of moral action; conscience is not a maker of law or a lawgiver but the faculty for judging the rightness or evil of an action or omission. Nevertheless, immunity against unjust coercion perdures.

Secularism? This is "a view of life that limits itself . . . to the human here

113

and now in exclusion of man's relation to God here and hereafter" (U.S. Bishops' Statement, 1947). Spiritual values, religious truths, and moral absolutes are driven out of the public forum, out of public school education, out of the political forum.

John Dewey was its prophet, the most famous proponent of secular humanism that is atheistic or, as some would claim, "anti-theistic." At any rate it is profoundly antireligious and in the United States anti-Catholic.

The "Declaration on Religious Liberty," contrary to secularism, emphatically rejects an *absolute* separation of Church and State. "Absolute" in effect means driving religion out of public life, "back to the sacristy." The Gospel, according to secularists, is to be preached only within churches and studied in the privacy of the home — if that. The recent collapse of totalitarian governments in Eastern Europe and the former Soviet Union clearly illustrated the role of the Church in preserving the aspirations for freedom among the people throughout almost a century of persecution where religion was relegated to the private realm under the rubric of *absolute* separation.

The Council did not wish to canonize the formal union of Church and State as in Great Britain, Saudi Arabia, Colombia, Sweden, Spain, Iran, and dozens of other countries, and did not sanction such a union but rather accepted it as a historical reality. In a quick step, as though not wishing to vex or disturb the status quo, the Council briefly addressed the question: "If because of the circumstances of a particular people special civil recognition is given to one religious community in the constitutional organization of a State, the right of all citizens and religious communities to religious freedom must be recognized and respected as well." Thus, it did reject the secularist absolute separation while accepting a constitutional separation of Church and State and standing somewhat neutral on state religions but with the rights and obligations of each honored and respected.[165]

Shades of Father Murray who insisted in his debate with Dr. Bowie, the Protestant minister, that secularism was the greatest peril to the welfare and weal of the United States as well as to all religion! Religious people should not be arguing with one another, much less about churches established by law, in the light of the real danger, he maintained.

Are societies and states then helpless in face of the claim of religious liberty? Are there no limitations on liberty? The Council affirmed the right of the state "to defend itself against abuses committed under the pretext of freedom of religion" (No. 7).

These abuses are to be found when contrary to public order, public peace, and public morality, in which case the state has the right to curtail them. But freedom of man must be respected as far as possible and curtailed only when and insofar as necessary (No. 7) and, it might be added, as essential to civilized society. The Council sounded Jeffersonian. Thomas Jefferson stated that a civil magistrate cannot intervene in the matter of the exercise of religious liberty except "when principles break out into overt acts against peace and good order."

Civilization demands for its very existence and the happiness of citizens that there be public order, public peace, and a public morality. Hence there may be limitations on religious freedom as on other rights, for even the right to life is not an absolute. A society cannot simply rely upon self-regulation on the part of people, the principle of personal and social responsibility that is self-imposed. What juridical norms should control a government if it curtails religious liberty in given circumstances? The right to liberty remains inalienable, but at times its exercise may be brought under temporary controls in specific cases.

The Council accepted the principle of public order. The requirements of public order are rooted in justice in which the rights of all citizens are guarded, including providing for peaceful settlement of dissension and the conflict of rights. The order of society is an order of peace, "domestic tranquility" in American constitutional parlance. Finally the order of society is a moral order, which means minimal standards of morality — public morality enforced on all, most assuredly not a sectarian or denomination morality as such. Murray considered health as part of public morality.

Public order is constituted by three values: political, juridical, and moral. "The free exercise of religion may not be inhibited unless proof is given that it entails some violation of the rights of others, or of the public peace or of public morality. In these cases . . . a public action ceases to be a religious exercise and becomes a penal offense."[166]

Wartime affords numerous examples: the prohibition against holding services in a Church where the lights could not be blacked out; the conscription of men and women for service; the prohibition against large assemblies, etc. At times religious processions might be proscribed by reason of an imminent danger — for example, a religious march in Northern Ireland, Israel, or Lebanon. The Council Fathers faced the question of conscientious objection to military service, a moral question at base. The Council merely exhorted countries to give serious consideration to conscientious objectors. Most countries around the world deny such an exemption.

In the field of public morality, which might be called elementary social morality, the state may curtail certain freedoms asserted in the name of religion. The U.S. Supreme Court has so handled diverse cases, local courts myriads of them.

The Supreme Court has judged, for example, that pornography is not protected by the First Amendment; that Indians using the drug peyote in religious ceremonies are not exempt from drug laws; that the handling of poisonous snakes in a liturgy has no privilege in law; and that the refusal of medical treatment by parents to their own children has been adjudicated on the side of the state in various courts as against a claim of religious freedom.

Even in terms of a specific religious morality, every sin is not a crime against society: sin and crime are not coterminous per se but often are related and interact on the religious front. The question was illustrated in one of the most famous cases of the land, that of the Mormons' belief in polygamy, a practice that the federal government tried to stamp out by passing the Anti-Polygamy Act of 1862.

The Mormon Church fought its case through the various courts, showing that its sacred scripture, the Book of Mormon, permitted and even encouraged polygamy among its own members. The matter was litigated all the way to the U.S. Supreme Court, culminating in the Reynolds vs. U.S. case in 1878.

The high court decreed that polygamy was not acceptable in Western civilization, even though it was allowed in Asia and Africa. Polygamy offended public morality in the U.S.A. and was outlawed in all civil codes. Ignorance of the civil laws could not be accepted as excusing cause although ignorance of fact might, the Court added. The decision went even further that in light of the Mormon teaching that a person could even lose his soul if given the opportunity for the practice of polygamy and refused it, the practice still could not be accepted by the Court. The Mormon Church acceded.

The case illustrated that the United States was not and could not be "neutral" in regard to religion just as it could not be in its relationships with the cultural and scientific communities.

The proper stance must be one of encouragement and support, of benevolent neutrality between groups within these communities but approval insofar as they serve the civic and cultural ends of the state and society. The contrast with totalitarian countries is altogether stark.

Customarily in the authoritarian state, whether to the left or to the right, all ultimate power is concentrated and vested in the government. The net result usually is that there evolves a special correctness, a political correctness: official economics, one official political party, one acceptable social life; an official science and a state-approved art and even an official party line for athletics, not to mention a peremptory position on religion, whether theistic or atheistic. Thus the state is at once not a scientist, nor an artist, nor a theologian. The totalitarian state, in the words of George Will, aims not only at state ownership of all cultural institutions, of all industries, of all flow of information, of all public argument, but also the ownership of minds. Intermediary institutions such as schools, churches, clubs, labor unions, and even families "must be pulverized" in the totalitarian state.

It is therefore not the function of the state to decide whether a scientific theory is true or false; it is not the function of the government to declare a work of art a masterpiece or a fake: it is not a judge of artistic achievement. Yet it should not remain neutral either but rather promote, guard, and vindicate personal freedom in scientific research and artistic creation. The general welfare is involved: so it is with religion and churches, synagogues, temples, and mosques. They are not only part of the temporal social order but a sustainer

116

thereof. The state must have a positive policy toward religion insofar as it contributes to the common good and the social order, for in that respect religion sustains not the spiritual order so much as the temporal, which it is the obligation and function of the state to foster and promote for the common good.

The state is not per se a teacher either: it is simply not competent to be a teacher, whether in totalitarian regimes or democracies. In 1859, the much-quoted English economist and philosopher John Stuart Mill in his book *On Liberty* clearly made the point. He advised that parents should control the education of their children "where and how they pleased." The state should content itself in paying the fees, especially of the poor. But state education and the enforcement of education by the state are two different things. If the state becomes a teacher, the consequences are dire.

"A general state education is a mere contrivance for molding people to be exactly like one another, and as the mold in which it casts them is that which pleases the predominant power in the government, whether this be a monarch, a priesthood, an aristocracy, or a majority of the existing generation; in proportion as it is efficient and successful, it established a despotism over the mind. . . ."[167]

Another economist, the famous Thomas Paine, recommended a tax cut for the poor with the savings to go to the education of their children, believing as he did in parental choice.[168]

The American Constitution may well have been a primary influence on this point: man is endowed by his Creator with certain inalienable rights; the state and its laws exist primarily to protect and promote these rights; political authority has no more competence to pronounce judgment in the field of religious truth than in science or in art. The state is simply incompetent in the field of religion but has proper power to judge temporal and earthly affairs. Where this area of the temporal is violated in the name of or under the pretext of religion the state may intervene, since the religious assembly would be illegitimately encroaching upon the rights of the state. The temporal and the religious sphere are bound on occasion to intersect.

Are there no limitations on the state's limitations? There is as much if not more room for abuse on the state's side of the question under the rubric of religious liberty. The Council recommended for the state ideally a constitution that would limit the powers of government.

The constitutional state must regard itself as having no competence to decide the contents, validity, and merits of religious systems for, as has been said already, the state is not a theologian. Thus it has no business to judge whether a religion is true or not or even what is valid therein. Such things are outside its field of competence.

Moreover, the constitutional state has a positive duty to respect the rights of its citizens to religious liberty: to recognize, to respect, and to promote its free exercise in a *positive* way, not merely by neutrality, which often becomes a mild hostility if not outright opposition; and to limit only abuses in the name of religious liberty.

The Council did not take the easy way out in granting that a state may act for the welfare of all its citizens — the general weal and the common good. Rather the Council saw the danger of allowing a state or government to act in the name of the common good, of measuring abuses by a yardstick of the common good. How easy has it been in history for totalitarian and other governments to invoke this concept in justification for repression of religious people, not to mention outright persecution! This criterion, the common good, was judged to be too broad, too vague, too open to manipulation — in a word, too unrestrictive on government and too restrictive on people, both in their individual capacities and in their corporate bodies, their associations and groups. How often have both individuals and groups been declared an enemy of the state! And in the name of the common good?

At the German Press Centre, and perhaps with Germany in mind, Father Murray, while recognizing the need for the state to be concerned with the common good, nonetheless warned against its use as a sound criterion. "An appeal to the common good as a ground for legal restriction on religious liberty can in certain circumstances be nothing more than an appeal to 'reason of state.'"

Such an appeal, he cautioned, could well be a veiled appeal to the right of the majority, even the tyranny of the majority. "The legal protection and promotion of the whole order of personal rights and freedoms that are proper to the human person as such are the primary and fundamental element of the common good. . . . Therefore an infringement of the personal rights of men cannot be justified by an appeal to the common good." Such an infringement would itself be a violation of the common good.[169]

If not an appeal to the common good, to what could a state appeal when citizens in the name of religion violated the state's rights? The Vatican Council opted for the concept of public order, giving the state less leeway and the exercise of religious liberty by its citizens more leeway.

Individual people and social groups are admonished to respect the rights of others and act in the common good of all "in justice and humanity. However, the state has the right to protect itself against possible abuses committed in the name of freedom." There must be "adequate protection of that just public peace which is to be found where men live together in good order and true justice. All these matters are basic to the common good and belong to what is called public order. . . . [Therefore] man's freedom should be given the fullest possible recognition and should not be curtailed except when and insofar as necessary" ("Declaration on Religious Liberty," No. 7).

Public order was a much narrower concept than the common good and hence did not limit the citizen but the state's powers to restrict religious liberty, to limit it in the name of public order as just one element in the concept of the public good. A government would have to show that a given religious practice, which it might quite rightly judge to be no help to or even deleterious to the common good, was indeed inimical to public order before banning it. It would be easier for a state to issue a ban, basing it on the common good; hence the Vatican declaration was more, not less, liberal.

Certain public parades, for example, have engendered just such controversies. In Skokie, Illinois, the Ku Klux Klan marched ostentatiously down the main streets amidst a heavily Jewish population, insulting and outraging the vast majority of its citizens, Jewish and Gentile alike. Scarcely could it be argued that the parade was in the interests of the common good, but could it be banned on that basis? The Council would reply that only if it were against public order. Similarly in San Francisco the annual gay homosexual parade has featured most offensive and heinous sacrileges anathema to Christians directly and indirectly to any decent-minded person. Yet, is the parade violating public order, even if no tenable case can be made for its promotion of the common good, and even if a plausible pleading could be made that the parade with its bizarre antics, blatant nudity, and obscene posturing and gesturing violated public morality?

The public authorities in these cases judged that they could keep public order, but they admitted that they were skating on thin ice. In athletic jargon, they had to make "judgment calls" that the courts at all levels have been trying to sort out, often only case by case. The U.S. Supreme Court has indeed seen the necessity for upholding public morality: polygamy is proscribed; pornography is not protected by the First Amendment; even nude dancing was, in June 1991, declared contrary to public morals and hence illegal.[170]

The Council, however, was in effect instructing states to confine the necessary restrictions on religious liberty and religious activities to a minimum, yet conceding that restrictions may be necessary lest every action be deemed exempt from the authority of the state simply because someone throws the mantle of religion over it or claims freedom of conscience.

Pacem in Terris was the first papal document that used the term "religious freedom." Unfortunately it did not deal with the relation of religious liberty and what is commonly called "religious toleration."

Tolerance is the acceptance of a situation that cannot be justly changed. Many describe religious liberty as tolerance, meaning freedom from coercion in the practice of religious duties. Thus the tolerant person pictures himself as somewhat broad-minded because he is indulgent, lenient, and benevolent as regards what he considers people in error: it is the broad-minded fantasy of those who believe that they hold the truth and that society itself is open as opposed to closed. In fact, toleration is only one small facet of true religious liberty, only a first step.

The Council viewed religious liberty from the point of view of the human being, its subject and possessor of the right to such freedom and applied to each and every person. It was a positive conception, with both the immunities and equally the entitlements and empowerments, with the personal right not only freely to profess but to propagate his religion. Thus the declaration moved far beyond mere toleration.

Its rejection came from the conviction that the principle of toleration could be stretched to mean the tolerance of intolerance as a principle of an accepted fact.[171] The word toleration implies only that compulsion is absent; it says nothing positive about living together with mutual respect and recognition of values. Contrariwise, the Council declaration implies a positive communication of values. It is precisely here that the state must foster the free exercise of religion not primarily as a religious matter but as a temporal one, that is, for the common good. Its power to restrict is based on the temporal welfare, not the spiritual.

On certain occasions the state actively seeks the support of the Churches. The 1991 Gulf War is one example where the U.S. government sought the advice of religious leaders precisely as to the moral and spiritual implications of declaring war in the given case. President George Bush even invited the Reverend Billy Graham to stay several days in the White House while he pondered his decision. The Catholic bishops publicly spelled out the conditions they saw as necessary to be fulfilled before armed conflict was justified.

Similar circumstances arose in connection with prohibition; with the rights of union labor to organize and to bargain collectively; with the plight of farm workers, migratory workers, illegal aliens, and other causes.

The religious contribution was clearly in the interests of the temporal welfare of the Republic, not to mention the spiritual. At the same time, these events provided occasions for the Church (Catholic, Protestant, or otherwise) at times to intrude on the rights of the state within its own legitimate sphere, by unwarranted sallies of religious leaders, clerical and lay, into partisan politics.

Society, the state, and the Church must always opt for the common good. The Council called for liberty insofar as possible within public order, public peace, and public morality, certainly considerations in the history and purview of not only the American people but especially in its courts of law. No one doubted that there was an American flavor about it all at the Vatican Council both as to method of promoting a text and in its content as clearly perceived by Archbishop Lefebvre.

Such was the document submitted for the final debate and vote. True to Pope Paul's promise the Council took up the question at its opening sessions in September 1965. Sixty-two Fathers of the Council spoke, revealing that the do-or-die minority still hoped to scuttle the document.

Eight cardinals spoke the first day, with three in opposition: Ruffini of Palermo, Siri of Genoa, and Arriba Castro of Tarragona, Spain. Francis

Spellman of New York and Richard Cushing of Boston were supported by Urbani of Venice and Bernard Alfrink of Utrecht in the Netherlands. During the following days bishops from all over the world showed themselves in substantial agreement. Cardinal Lorenz Jaeger of Paderborn, Germany, in the name of one hundred fifty bishops noted that the situation of the Middle Ages had disappeared: it was time for a good modern document. Cardinal William Conway of Ireland noted that his country had suffered religious persecution for "two hundred years (sic)" and now had religious freedom in its own constitution. Not to be outdone, Cardinal John Heenan of London asked for a clear and unanimous voice of the Council in favor of religious liberty. But there remained the irredentist minority whose power would soon be tested in the ballot box.

On November 5, 1965, in a most notable address on Vatican Radio, Archbishop Robert Dwyer of Portland, Oregon — noted as an articulate, eloquent, and intelligent voice of the "right wing" of the American hierarchy — stated that the most important document of Vatican II was the "Declaration on Religious Liberty," which was "epoch making" and "one of the great landmarks of religious history."

The Church has at last gotten rid of the dream of the Two Swords, which Dwyer called the "theory of the crutch" wherein there prospered "the illusion of a Christendom where religion and politics were merged into one and where the interests of the Church were hopelessly entangled with the interest of the state. . . . Its worse effect has been the limitation of religious freedom by the imposition of political, economic or social sanctions upon any species of non-conformity."

A sharp distinction must be made, he continued, between liberty and license, between religious freedom and religious indifferentism. "Freedom absolves no one from his personal responsibility to truth nor does it dispense him from the search for truth which God has revealed to mankind . . . in Jesus Christ.

"The whole document is monumental. Surely in time to come, men will say of the Second Vatican Council that it wrote a Charter of Man's spiritual freedom as a child of God."

Nowhere was the hope that the declaration — so unanimously supported by all Americans at the Council: bishops, priests, religious, laity, and non-Catholics as well — would give birth to a new era in religious liberty in the homeland. Doubts as to where the Church and especially the American Catholic Church stood were cleared up and dark shadows dissipated.

On December 7, 1965, the final working day of the Council, the "Declaration on Religious Liberty" was accepted with 2,308 votes aye, 70 nay, and 7 null. It was a fair presumption that the American bishops voted unanimously or almost so in favor.[172]

121

BOOK 3

Chapter 9

The Taney Contradiction

People of good will on all sides on the American scene took for granted that the Council's document would go a long way toward eliminating the old prejudices and the incipient neo-Nativism in the American psyche. Simultaneously the election of President Kennedy was seen as a confirmation in action, in harmony with the Council. Such, however, was not the case.

The noted American historian Daniel J. Boorstin wrote that "the election of John Fitzgerald Kennedy to the Presidency in 1960 signaled a new era in American history. . . . Catholics, although the largest single religious group in the United States, had suffered some of the disabilities of a minority. . . ." After the defeat of Alfred E. Smith in 1928, "it had been widely assumed that to be a Catholic was to be disqualified from election to the nation's highest office."[173]

Only someone purblind and irredentist would deny that the election of President Kennedy opened new doors and new vistas for Catholics in relationship to the political order and aspiration for high office. In his speeches and legislative positions, however, he implicitly affirmed an absolute separation dogma, one that would tempt succeeding aspirants who were Catholic to assume a similar stance. The litmus test then was the nonpublic school question but soon to be augmented by the abortion controversy that would move the Church out of the mainstream of popular morality as measured by polls and into a minority and countercultural stance. Where would men and women who were Catholic stand, given the fact that the litmus test worked both ways?

In his public philosophy and statements, President Kennedy was not an exemplar of religious liberty in detail and as pronounced by the Vatican Council. To the contrary, he stood in direct opposition to some of its basic tenets, most especially in his espousal that the separation of Church and State must be *absolute*; he spelled out that philosophy in his strong opposition to any kind of assistance to nonpublic schoolchildren contrary to what was clearly enunciated in section five of the conciliar text on religious liberty, not to mention section six of the Council's treatise on education.

The assumption that the President and the Council were in basic agreement and that his election had put a finishing touch on Nativism proved to be an illusion. The President publicly and indeed genuinely praised the Council's work but held to certain reservations, unfortunately seen as dictated by political expediency rather than principle. But a new element came into the public forum, one that he did not have to address, namely abortion.

The school question continued to fester over the ensuing years, but the abortion question overtook it after the sudden Roe vs. Wade decision of the Supreme Court in 1973.

As early as 1868 thirty-six states had passed laws against abortion, reflecting the majority Protestant ethic. The Justice Harry B. Blackmun opinion, supported by five other justices, came as an unexpected shock, even to pro-abortionists. Chief Justice Warren E. Burger lamely rationalized his vote: "Plainly the Court today rejects any claim that the Constitution requires abortion on demand." As for the Blackmun opinion dividing the question and its solution by postulating three trimesters, investigative reporters Bob Woodward and Scott Armstrong laconically wrote: "It left the Court claiming that the Constitution drew certain lines at trimester and viability. The Court was going to make a medical policy and force it on the states. As a practical matter it was not a bad solution. As a constitutional matter it was absurd."[174]

Described by Justice Byron R. White as an exercise in "raw judicial power," it was a direct challenge to all moral principles, one that the Catholic Church and others could not evade. Some have even called it the most divisive, emotional, and intractable altercation since the Dred Scott decision, which re-legalized slavery. Perchance it played out, much like the Roe vs. Wade case. Chief Justice Roger B. Taney rendered the former decision.

Roger Brooke Taney was the fifth chief justice of the United States, born of Catholic parents in a family of Maryland's landed aristocracy. He married Anne Key, a sister of his own famous classmate, Francis Scott Key. Their only son died in infancy and their six daughters were reared as Protestants in the religion of their mother, Taney himself remaining a practicing Catholic.

As a private matter, he manumitted his own slaves and, although a true Southerner, he was very instrumental in freeing others and promoting projects for African colonization. But when the highly charged question was moved into the public forum, Taney, in the eyes of his contemporaries, delivered a moderate opinion on slavery, states' rights, and white supremacy. The 7 to 2 decision, in 1854, however, caused violent reaction among abolitionists, especially in the North, and is usually listed as one of the true causes of the Civil War. Seen with twentieth-century eyes, it was arguably the worst Supreme Court decision ever rendered, leaving Afro-Americans in slavery in the Southern states and semi-slavery elsewhere.

Quite clearly Taney's private opinion, his moral judgment, his personal ethical persuasions, did not follow him into the courtroom but rather were parked at the door of the chamber of justice.

The keen observer of the American scene and featured editor, columnist, and TV celebrity Charles Krauthammer coined the expression "the Taney contradiction" and applied it to current Catholic politicians, in particular Governor Mario Cuomo of New York. Taney had shown that he was personally opposed to slavery but did not want to "impose" his personal convictions on others, especially on a majority favoring slavery. Hence "the Taney contradiction."

Taney and his fellow jurists were not so singular, so eccentric, nor so different from their patriotic forebears and Founding Fathers. These American founders propounded advanced principles of equality that were ahead of their time. The abolitionist Frederick Douglas argued that slavery was only the scaffolding that would be removed when the building was complete; Lincoln saw the Declaration of Independence as announcing the right to equality, the enforcement of which would come about when circumstances permitted. "Thus by articulating progressive principles, even though failing to live up to them in practice, an argument can be made that Jefferson and Madison were champions of human liberty and equality."[175] But in the last decade of the twentieth century?

Politicians who are Catholic frequently held to the Taney contradiction in the 1990 elections. The California attorney general running for governor, John Van deKamp, put the matter plainly: "I am a Catholic. . . . I practice my religion, that's a personal matter. . . . But let no one doubt that I am irrevocably committed to freedom of choice. . . . I have always supported Med-Cal funding for abortions."

The implications were quite clear: private morals must remain private, yet in spite of personal conviction the politician will not only support abortion but will support using taxpayers' money to support the killing of the unborn, euphemistically termed "terminating a pregnancy" or simply "exercising a choice."

To many, the Catholic and other politicians want their cake and want to eat it too: it is the Taney contradiction, not on slavery, but on abortion.

The legislatures in Idaho and Louisiana passed laws designed to restrict abortion, both with an eye toward the Supreme Court in the U.S.A. and a possible overturning of the 1973 Roe vs. Wade abortion decision. Idaho's Governor Cecil Andrus and Louisiana's Buddy Roemer — the former in a state with a large Mormon population, the latter with a large Catholic population — both pictured themselves as strongly anti-abortion. Yet each vetoed his legislature's bill, moving many to see in their action the syndrome "I'm personally opposed, . . . but": the Taney contradiction.

The legislature of Guam passed an anti-abortion law unanimously; the local Catholic archbishop was reported to have threatened excommunication for legislators who opposed. The *Washington Post* and the *Los Angeles Times* weighed in heavily with the point that Guam is "90% Catholic" and "twenty out of twenty-one senators (of Guam) are Catholic." No word on the Idaho law as "that of the Mormons" — whether *New York Times, Los Angeles Times, USA Today, Washington Post*, and other dailies, even though Mormons constitute a large plurality of voters and are anti-abortion.

The national spotlight, however, focused more brightly on New York where its governor, Mario Cuomo, took the lead in defense of the Taney contradiction. He stated quite plainly that as a Catholic he accepted the teachings of the Church, but as a state governor he left his private convictions at the door as he walked in (his own words). He deplored the phenomenal growth and the trauma and tragedy of abortion, the thought of 1.6 million deaths a year "sobering," he said.

The governor framed the abortion issue in his own terms, namely that he believed in the separation of Church and State and that while affirming the Catholic bishops' right to speak out, he could not accept as governor what he believed as a Catholic, to wit, that abortion in the words of the Second Vatican Council is an "unspeakable crime."

"My position is very simple, I think I'm the governor of all the people. It is not my place to try to convert all of them to Catholicism and insist they live the way I privately believe I should," said Cuomo. He thereby furnished the basis for two major assaults on the Catholic Church, both on the grounds of being un-American. Columnist Bill Reel of the *New York Daily News* called this paragraph of the governor "swill." While not naming Cuomo, Lutheran Pastor Richard Neuhaus of New York said that politicians who solemnly renounce private morality are common political cowards with "expertly guided anguish."

The pro-abortionists and their allies for their part denounced the bishops for speaking out on this issue as an assault on the First Amendment, a violation of the separation of Church and State. Catholic bishops as such and the Church became special targets.

Professor of History Arthur Schlesinger, Jr., led this crusade, he who had been a close personal adviser to President John F. Kennedy. Accusing Cardinal John O'Connor of New York of "pursuing a weird course," he berated the American bishops as seeming to do their best to verify the fears long cherished by the Know-Nothings of the 1850s, the Ku Klux Klan in the 1920s, and a succession of anti-Catholic demagogues that the Roman Catholic Church would try to overrule the American democratic process.

"They seem to be doing their best to prove the case that Catholic politicians will not be free to act for what a majority regards as the general good."

Schlesinger invoked the professions of faith in the *absolute* separation of Church and State of Alfred E. Smith in 1928 and John F. Kennedy in 1960, stating that they would take no dictation from Rome, nor for that matter from Protestant sources either.

The liberal establishment led by Schlesinger presented themselves as champions of the First Amendment, specifically of the absolute separation of Church and State; tackling the abortion question, not on an analysis of what abortion is or is not, but rather appealing to various public polls (the majority makes morality and right); suggesting none too subtly that Catholics cannot be trusted, if truly convinced in their faith, fully as Americans; and claiming that Catholics do not really believe in the democratic process.

This position was not historically accurate at all. The emancipation of black Americans, with its origin clearly in the churches, came about largely contrary to public opinion. It was not until 1954 that the "separate but equal" doctrine on segregated public schools was overturned by the U.S. Supreme Court, a doctrine devoutly affirmed in the great universities such as Columbia and the University of California, Berkeley, to name just two, and until 1964 on equal voting rights. These came not from popular referenda but from the Supreme Court.

Similarly, Governor Cuomo, a fervent opponent of the death penalty, successfully blocked the death penalty in New York by veto, even against the overwhelming public and legislative approval of his constituents. His personal conviction in this case was not left at the gubernatorial office door. Incidentally the American Catholic bishops, quite conscious that their own Catholic people shared the general public's approval of the death penalty, yet voted to approve a statement against the death penalty.

Some of the press pundits frolicked in Cuomo's contradictions. Noting that the governor had allegedly patterned his public life on the "Man for All Seasons," St. Thomas More (lawyer, England's first layman lord chancellor, and martyr to Church-State relationships), they pointed out that while More did not impose his convictions on others, he did follow his conscience even to the chopping block. More significantly, St. Thomas professed a superior sanction for himself: ". . . unto the oath that was offered me, I could not swear without risking my soul to perpetual damnation."

He acknowledged that a majority of the masters of the realm, reading like a who's who of the British elite, had taken the oath, a fact that gave him great pause: "I would sore be afraid to lean on my own mind alone against so many." The great council of the realm stood against him, counseling acceptance of the oath. Was it not the Gallup poll of his day?

There was, St. Thomas wrote, yet even a greater council on his side, namely "the great council of Christendom." Was this not Vatican Council II?

So the chancellor of the realm did not park his Catholicism at the door of the chancellery; nor did he feed his mind with the placebo pill that as a Catholic he was personally opposed to the Oath of Supremacy but as chancellor he favored it; nor did he feign amnesia about the Church's teaching on who was the head of the Church; and he specifically noted that his eternal salvation was involved in the choice he had to make.

Today, as in More's time, politicians who are Catholic are being subjected to an unfair and unjustified litmus test, the single-issue syndrome that the media so vehemently deplored in other instances.[176] This inquisition is the modern loyalty oath. In the 1930s, the cry arose against Catholic professors in many American universities to please park their Catholicism at the classroom door, not, mind you, Marxism, or secular humanism, or scientism, or atheism, or agnosticism. Today, sadly, it is the politicians' turn, not to abjure the primacy of the Pope nor the throne or government as head of the Church, but on something more important: the very right to life.

The governor's jousts with two New York ecclesiastics, Cardinal John O'Connor and Bishop Austin Vaughan, attracted national attention and brought into focus not only the matter of conscience but also the actions of Catholic bishops in the marketplace.

Mark Shields, a columnist for the *Washington Post*, reviewed some of the more notable interventions of Catholic bishops in American history. In 1886, Cardinal James Gibbons supported striking transit workers, bringing down the wrath of the *New York Times* for meddling in non-Church affairs. The bishops opposed President Reagan on military aid to Central America, on some economic policies, on the nuclear freeze, on expanded Medicare, and on funding for AIDS. These positions were applauded by the media for the most part and especially by the liberal establishment.

Shields might have gone back to the first Catholic bishop, John Carroll of Baltimore, who was asked by the Continental Congress in 1776 to accompany Charles Carroll (his cousin and signer of the Declaration of Independence), Samuel Chase, and Benjamin Franklin to Canada to woo it to the U.S. side.[177] Shields, however, concluded that the whole matter was not one of principle at all but simply a matter of whose ox was gored.

The media, nevertheless, applied a double standard, or rather turned a blind eye toward clerical intrusion into the political process. The unspoken word, the hushed-up question that haunted the presidential campaign of 1988, concerned the candidacy of two Protestant ministers, the Democrat Jesse Jackson and the Republican Pat Robertson. Could Protestant ministers run for public office without the charges of "imposing morality," of being undemocratic, of violating the separation of Church and State, while a Catholic layman could not?

These and other Protestant ministers (such as Mayor Andrew Young of Atlanta and Representative Walter Fauntroy of the District of Columbia), with quite open abandon, have made the churches across the land the anchors of their partisan political campaigns. Without any scruple or hesitation they register communicants inside the churches; they deliver clearly partisan political "sermons" in the sanctuaries; they form clergy groups in partisan support and quite unabashedly collect money in and through the churches.[178]

The point at issue is not the rightness or wrongness of these purely partisan campaigns but the almost total acquiescence in them by the government (particularly the Internal Revenue Service), the media, and "patriotic" and other organizations. Whether the question be abortion or equal rights for

Catholic school teachers, pupils, and their parents, the Catholic Church has become a special target.

Keen observers saw a resurgence of a more subtle but nonetheless very real Nativism. The Taney contradiction served to illustrate a double standard by dragging in the issue of the separation of Church and State and in a very precise way: with the threat of the denial of tax exemption enjoyed by churches and other organizations.

Nat Hentoff, a commentator for New York's very liberal *Village Voice*, calling himself a "Jewish atheist," surveyed the various dissensions in American society in broad terms. He disagreed with the bishops on contraception, the use of condoms and their relation to the AIDS epidemic: "It's not only dumb, but it further weakens the authority of the bishops because few Catholics will take such silly advice." He continued:

> On the other hand, there are Church positions ... that are far more relevant than the economic views of the Democratic Party, and of course that other trickle-down party. The Catholic bishops have also been ahead of the rest of the country ... in [opposing] nuclear arms, [questioning] policies in Central America ... [opposing] capital punishment ... and in [voicing] support of union organizing.
>
> No one on the left has complained about the Church imposing those religiously based positions on the rest of us.
>
> But whether their positions are foolish or admirable, the Catholic Bishops have a First Amendment right to advocate whatever they want to. And in so doing they do NOT (sic) violate the separation of Church and State.

As far back as 1978 the Internal Revenue Service decreed that the Catholic press could not run the voting record of members of Congress if it implied approval or disapproval. Nor could the Catholic papers concentrate on one issue, to wit, of course, abortion. In questioning a candidate, "the questionnaire in content or structure (must not) evidence a bias or preference with respect to the views of any candidate or group of candidates." The Catholic bishops were similarly put on notice when the threat of the loss of tax exemption was dangled over their heads.

The same IRS in 1985 warned the Catholic bishops that religious organizations may not intervene in a political campaign, directly or indirectly, on behalf of or in opposition to any candidate. The regulation and subsequent rulings forbade "one-issue" campaigns or concentration "on a narrow range of issues."[179]

There was only one issue and only one target: abortion and the Catholic Church. The other Churches (with some exceptions in the Evangelical, Pentecostal, and "right wing" groups) and synagogues could espouse special interests with impunity from the government as well as the media. There was no problem when the synagogue councils stressed to Congress in no uncertain terms the one issue of Israel, for example. While the U.S. Catholic bishops do not and did not endorse partisan candidates for office, the case in both the Protestant and Jewish communities was quite different.

The Protestant Churches have never hesitated to support publicly many candidates openly as groups, nor hesitated to espouse single issues, for example, affirmative action. The presidents of the Orthodox Rabbinical Council of the Conservative Assembly and the Reformed Central Council — covering all three branches of Judaism — in 1984 endorsed the candidacy of Walter Mondale and wrote to their congregations asking them to do likewise. Such was blithely reported by the *New York Times* on October 18, 1984.

Just four weeks earlier this same *Times* had editorialized: "It might as well be said bluntly . . . the Catholic bishops' effort to impose a religious test on the performance of Catholic politicians threatens the hard-won understanding that finally brought Americans to elect a Catholic president a generation ago."

Lutheran Pastor Neuhaus answered the *Times*: "While the statement does have limited merit of bluntness, permit me to suggest that it invites the prospect it decries and advances bigotry in the name of tolerance. Recent editorials and op ed pieces suggest that the *Times* is reviving the anti-Catholic bigotry that many thought had been laid to rest in the last several decades."

But was it laid to rest?

It was this same area into which Arthur Schlesinger, Jr., intruded: "For years the bigots have said the Church would not hesitate to impose its will upon the general populace or to tell Catholic politicians how to act. . . . Then Al Smith and John Kennedy said — and showed — that Catholics in politics are as free as any other American citizens to base their judgments on the national interest and the democratic process, and most Americans have come to believe them."

Schlesinger went on to say that New York's Cardinal O'Connor and Bishop Vaughan were changing that image of Catholics as true citizens, free to be true politicians in the American tradition.

"I thank heaven that Bishop Vaughan and Cardinal O'Connor were not holding forth in 1960. If they had spoken then as they speak now, John F. Kennedy would not have been elected President."

In a trenchant reply, Charles Krauthammer challenged the thinking of both Cuomo and Schlesinger. He noted that Cardinal O'Connor had questioned whether politicians could "have it both ways, Taney-like on abortion," accusing the "liberal constituency" of not arguing the merits of the case but rather focusing only on the propriety of bishops entering the fray as an assault on the separation of Church and State. To the Schlesinger assertion that the bishops "would try to overrule the American democratic process," Krauthammer responded that "this idea of overruling is outright nonsense. The Catholic Church is in no way compelling anyone to do anything, let alone interdict the will of the majority." Moreover, "If it does manage to persuade a majority of Americans that abortion is wrong and ought to be banned, how is that different from any group persuading a democratic majority to ban, say, polygamy or drug-taking?"

The commentator moved to the other "liberal complaint" that since the Catholic position on abortion is religiously derived and becomes law, then religion has been imposed. "This argument," he contended, "is nonsense too," precisely because under American pluralism it makes no difference where a belief comes from.

Krauthammer went on: "Whether it comes from church teaching, inner conviction or some trash novel, the legitimacy of any belief rests ultimately on its content, not on its origin. If pro-abortion, deriving its position from Paul Erlich's doomsday scenario, be legitimate, why is an anti-abortion position derived from scripture a violation of the First Amendment? The liberals did not protest Martin Luther King's invocation of scripture nor the Catholic bishops invoking St. Augustine in opposition to nuclear warfare; no one said these violated the Bill of Rights."

Finally making the same point as the Reverend Mr. Neuhaus, Krauthammer suggested that Schlesinger, in coming forward "to warn darkly that such outspokenness risks stirring up anti-Catholic bigotry," may be contributing to the resurrection of that very thing. "On the face of it, I would say it already has," concluded Krauthammer.

Actually presidential candidate Kennedy did not have to face the abortion question, since abortion was illegal in every state at that time. However, he did tackle the question of assistance to nonpublic schools: he came down hard against all aid, all assistance, all relief, and, in the opinion of some educators, simply bent over backward to garner votes from the Baptists and from the National Education Association constituencies.

Several Catholic bishops publicly mentioned that they could excommunicate Catholic politicians for their stand on abortion, that is, that politicians could be personally opposed as Catholics but yet vote to fund abortion with tax monies (the Taney contradiction syndrome). Bishop René Gracida in Texas did excommunicate several; a few called for denial of Holy Eucharist to those holding the Taney contradiction. The U.S. bishops once again, in 1990, unanimously opposed abortion, even in the light of the firestorm it was sure to arouse.

Governor Cuomo,[180] in the words of the *New York Daily News* columnist Bill Reel, was playing a "deft bit of politics" and his position "never made any sense and still doesn't." He went on, "If you think about it, there is really only one good reason to oppose abortion, personally or otherwise, and that is because abortion kills a tiny human being. A bishop or an atheist can see that." Cuomo, in Reel's opinion, was "devious and hypocritical on the abortion issue."

In a bit of sardonic humor, the columnist finished his piece by stating: "Just once I'd like to hear a politician say, 'I personally think abortion is murder, no question about it, but I'm strongly in favor of it anyway because otherwise I can't get elected.' There would be an honest politician."

Unfortunately the problem of a necessary plank on abortion in a candidate's platform in order to get elected lay just below the surface. In his biography on Mario Cuomo, Robert McElvaine offers the following observation: "During the early stages of his political career, Cuomo was more willing to try to legislate private morality than he has been since the late seventies. During his 1974 campaign for the Democratic nomination for lieutenant governor, for example, Cuomo stated that 'had he been a member of the Legislature he would have voted against the 1970 law that relaxed abortion curbs in the state.' "[181]

Senator Edward Kennedy took a similar position at the Liberty Baptist College in 1983, but was, according to McElvaine, "less concerned with theological questions than is Cuomo. Cuomo takes Catholic moral teachings very seriously."[182] Senator Daniel Patrick Moynihan was also seen as holding views similar to Cuomo's, but "as a practical as opposed to a practicing Catholic, Moynihan said with a grin in 1986, 'I have made it my business not to know so much about Catholic doctrine that I know when I am in error.' "[183]

Catholic politicians in large numbers took the stance similar to the governor's "as a matter of political convenience. The evidence strongly suggests that this is not the case" with Cuomo, according to his biographer.

Cardinal O'Connor in June 1984, a few months before the national elections, made a statement in a televised interview that "I do not see how a Catholic in good conscience could vote for a candidate who explicitly supported abortion." He named no politician. The interviewer continued asking if Cuomo should be excommunicated. The cardinal did not answer. The governor, his son, Christopher, and his wife, Matilda, were watching the program; she recalls that "Mario got so white, so pale, and he stands up and leaves the room. They hit us like a hammer in the head."[184] Cuomo said later that official Church people would not ask Catholics to vote for or against candidates on their "political position on abortion." "We learned," he said, "that the impression was not accurate." Some bishops, however, took a similar stance: privately they would support or oppose a candidate but never officially. The bishops as a national body, nevertheless, have not and it seems certain would not take a collective decision of support or opposition to any single candidate.

The governor and other politicians (for instance, 1984 vice-presidential candidate Geraldine Ferraro), however, compounded the moral problem by not only acquiescing in the performance of abortion as public officials while holding to a disclaimer as private citizens but also by favoring the use of tax money to promote abortions. Their cooperation in the financial promotion of abortion became more proximate and thereby weakened their argument of personal private opposition and of purely passive acceptance of the law of the land. The Taney contradiction would not lie down and die.[185]

The president of the National Conference of Catholic Bishops in 1984, Bishop James W. Malone, added: "It's absurd to say, I am against murder but I will not impose my views on anyone else. The entire question revolves around the fetus: is a fetus a living human being? Pragmatic arguments such as a mother's right, overpopulation, welfare costs, unwanted children and the like have no valence if the answer be in the affirmative. The Church does impose excommunication on those who procure abortion such as a doctor but the U.S. bishops have not judged politicians as procurers nor invoked the formal excommunication penalty."

The question of a Catholic bishop's right or the right of the Church to cut someone off from communion with the Church, that is, excommunication, took on a life of its own. Again the liberal establishment jumped on the bandwagon, claiming vociferously that excommunication was a violation of the freedom of religion. However, several commentators pointed out that that same establishment had lauded Archbishop Joseph Rummel of New Orleans when he excommunicated years ago a leading politician, Leander Perez, and two other Catholics because of their racist and segregationist policies.

At the same time in June 1990, Representative Barney Frank — Democrat of Massachusetts, openly homosexual, involved with male prostitutes in his District of Columbia home, and reprimanded in Congress for "fixing parking tickets" for a prostitute — was formally excommunicated by the High Rabbinical Court of New York for "bringing disgrace upon the high office of Congressman . . . and [for being] a blatant promoter of moral depravity."

The press all but ignored this excommunication, but Rabbi Joseph Friedman of New York did not, saying: "Since a number of people have asked us about our position concerning John Cardinal O'Connor's recent statement of excommunication (which he did not assert), we can only comment that from the standpoint of his religion, the Cardinal is obviously correct . . . religion is not a democracy. Either one accepts or rejects its authority. If one accepts its authority, then it is not proper to pick and choose only the things one likes and finds easy and convenient."

Former New York Governor Hugh Carey, a Democrat, weighed in, labeling his coreligionist politicians as "Cafeteria Catholics" who "pick and choose until they get to the pro-abortion check-out counter when they dump their tray of beliefs." Another illustration of the Taney contradiction!

Nor was he the only Catholic layman to express criticism. William F. Buckley, Jr., in his *National Review* of November 1989 challenged the stance of the three most prominant Catholic politicians: "The positions of Mario Cuomo, Daniel Patrick Moynihan and Edward Kennedy remind us that the temptation to be guided by political considerations not only shapes our public declarations but tends to calcify our consciences."

What influence these litmus tests for Catholics and the resulting alienation in the Catholic constituencies, which number approximately twenty-five percent of the U.S. population, have had on politicians who are Catholic is difficult to estimate. What influence the whole question of abortion had on Governor Cuomo's decision not to run for President in spite of his highly favorable position in the Democratic Party is open to conjecture. It could not be ignored or passed off as inconsequential or irrelevant. It surfaced in too many places and on too many occasions to be dismissed.

The abortion question on the American scene sharply divided (and continues to divide) the American public; the Catholic Church, with its consistent opposition, became the chief target of proponents. It was not enough to keep to the questions at issue: abortion and assistance to nonpublic schools; rather it became a broader occasion for a latent anti-Catholicism to rear its ugly head, a neo-Nativism.

While the anti-Catholics are not coterminus with Americans who are genuinely convinced that the Catholic Church is in error on these issues, the venom of the crackpots, ideologues, and fringe groups has been matched by many leading, respectable citizens, recognized groups, and associations. Particularly slanted and one-sided were the media of the U.S.A., which, surely contrary to expressed intent, have contributed significantly to the resurgence of Nativism.[186]

Chapter 10

The Church in the Public Arena

It must be stressed at this point that a political or educational stance against the Catholic school or for abortion and abortion "rights" does not mean these positions are per se anti-Catholic or an expression of Nativism. Good faith may be presumed in many if not most cases. Responsible people, good and fair-minded citizens, are ranged along opposing lines, and their patriotism is not at issue. Two areas, however, must be explored: first, the opponents not of the radical fringe, whether to the right or to the left, and second, not the fact of opposition, but its manner.

Nothing would be more simple than to compile a whole volume of virulently anti-Catholic materials in drama, music, newspapers, pamphlets, books, radio, and television. The U.S.A. is bristling with the likes of Tony Alamo and his twentieth-century Holiness Tabernacle Church, which specialized in pouring out pamphlets of the nineteenth-century variety that would do justice to the APA's, the KKK's and the Know-Nothings in venom and noxious viruses that have never died in the United States.

Alamo's picture of Pope John Paul II as "A Catholic Nazi World War II Criminal" and his accusation that the Holy Father sold cyanide gas to the Nazis for use at Auschwitz "for the extermination of millions of Jews . . . worse than all the kings of earth . . . (the pope of Catholics who believe) that the imbecilic pope is god."

Some TV evangelists such as Jimmy Swaggart have spiced their sermons with anti-Catholic sentiments; fringe Seventh-Day Adventist groups (not official) preach that the Catholic Church is the whore of Babylon. The free speechers are silent.

Similarly when the National Endowment for the Arts came under fire for using tax funds to support a number of offensive paintings, photos, and plays — deeply offensive to all Christians (for example, urination on Christ and grossly pornographic use of Christian symbols) — the press rose in righteous wrath against censorship. Yet when in 1988 the *Red Base* magazine published an issue on Palestine, the B'nai B'rith protested its anti-Israeli stance and the National Endowment for the Arts responded by ordering the publication to return the $4,483 grant from tax funds.

The dean of the Simon Wiesenthal Center in Los Angeles, Rabbi Abraham Cooper, bitterly complained that the pop singer Madonna was propagating dangerous anti-Semitic words that could incite hatred against the Jews. It was, he said, "dangerous and an insult to every Jew." The center asked that the compact disc be removed from store shelves.

The ACLU was silent; the press was sympathetic. The episode illustrated that freedom of speech can and indeed must be judged, not simply for its exercise but for its content: some songs by Madonna and others are outrageous and often sacrilegious. Here again there is a double standard.

Over and over again the media have exploited anti-Christian and anti-Catholic assaults, featuring, for example, a gay Christ with a crown of thorns and an American flag for a loincloth, clearly sacrilegious, without a whimper from the free-speech advocates. In the case of an insult to Catholics, the content of the message does not count, but curbing that same freedom of speech, outrageously racist, somehow does not violate the First Amendment and reduces the free-speech advocates to silence.

The secular humanists, the agnostics, the atheists, the liberal (so-called) intelligentsia, and the media, both print and broadcast, have often coupled Catholics and the Catholic Church with the Fundamentalists because of some overlapping agreement on such issues as abortion, contraception, pornography, and homosexuality. "Bluenose" and "Puritan" are hurled uncritically at Catholics as if they were Fundamentalists, which — given their doctrine — they simply cannot be. The implied symbiosis between the two is a false charge.

There is no need to dredge up these twentieth-century anti-Catholic types, anti-Catholic tabloids, anti-Catholic literature; they constitute the fringe that can be passed over. Rather examples do come from "mainline" Americans, if that be a fair adjective, of the normal respected press and broadcast media. The thesis that anti-Catholicism is alive and well comes as a studied conclusion from the facts. Catholic and non-Catholics alike had thought that such ghosts had been exorcised from the American psyche. The evidence rests not on the fact of opposition to Catholics and their positions but clearly in the very selective manner at which problems of religious liberty are met and basic reasons given in respectable society for its uneven and often contradictory treatment; in a word, a double standard.

In 1990, a major daily, the *Philadelphia Inquirer* (part of the extensive McKnight-Ridder chain of papers), published an article by David R. Boldt, its senior editor. The headline read: "The Bishops Return to a Darker Era in U.S. Politics."

Boldt was applauding an offensive cartoon by Tony Auth who enjoys a reputation for absurdity and offensiveness. But he went further: "Their efforts (i.e., the bishops') reflect a lack of understanding as to just how delicate the balance between Church and State is in regard to the Catholic Church in America."

He continued, "The Roman Catholic Church, it needs to be remembered, is quite literally an Un-American institution . . . not democratic . . . (and) sharply at odds with those that inform the laws of American secular society. And its principal policies are established by the Vatican in Rome." This is 1990, not 1890!

Quite expectedly this outburst drew intense fire from Catholics. William B. Ball, a Pennsylvania attorney who has argued freedom-of-religion cases successfully before the U.S. Supreme Court (for example, in favor of the Amish), caustically pointed out that in U.S. history religious bodies publicly proclaimed their faith even when there were adverse political effects: anti-slavery before the Civil War, the Prohibition movement, the civil-rights marches, the support of Israel, and the plea to protect the unborn. Ball rhetorically asked if Boldt would have stopped the Reverend Martin Luther King, Jr., as he spoke out against unjust laws.

Finally Ball quoted the U.S. Supreme Court's decision, Watson vs. Jones, which he said should be required reading: "The right to organize voluntary religious associations to assist in the expression and dissemination of any religious doctrine, and to create tribunals for the decision of controverted questions of faith within the association, and for the ecclesiastical government of all the individual members . . . within the association, is unquestioned.

"All who unite themselves to such a body do so with the implied consent to this government and are bound to submit to it."

The Court was saying that if one joins freely, he submits freely or he leaves freely.

Boldt concluded by saying that for two centuries a fine line had been drawn but in a direct warning to Catholic bishops: "The balance achieved only holds steady as long as Catholic prelates conform to the role portrayed by John Kennedy and refrain from using their spiritual authority in the political arena." The underlying tenor of Boldt's thrust was that Catholics could not be treated exactly like other religious Americans and that America was secular and not religious — recalling Father John Courtney Murray's warning that all religious citizens should quit squabbling among themselves and face the real enemy: secularism. Secularism would push the bishops and priests (and rabbis, ministers, and imams) back into the sanctuary and off the streets and public forums of America.

Was the Catholic Church (along with its communicants) expected to muzzle itself in sheer gratitude that the electorate had voted a Catholic into office? Was challenging politicians to protect the unborn by using democratic means to do so, unpatriotic and un-American?

The main point was that the media lavishly praised other religious leaders for doing exactly what the Catholic bishops were doing but only on issues with which they agreed. The content did matter.

Describing the bishops as "desperate men," Boldt invoked the very goblins and demons that he said he was interested in exorcising: "There's room to wonder whether the bishops fully understand the risk they run of reawakening all the old religious prejudices and fears that once inflamed American politics and which John Kennedy had sought to extinguish. The bishops would revive them by giving them substance."

Then in an extraordinary conclusion he wrote: "They (the Bishops) intend to show that, as the organized bigots used to say, Catholic officials take orders from Rome." This not from the lunatic fringe or the lurid tabloids but from a mainline paper by a mainline editor!

The stereotype was clearly drawn: bishops do not speak for themselves as Americans should.

Boldt claimed that he was just following up on the Auth cartoon that pictured the bishop of Camden, New Jersey, shouting to the Catholic governor of New Jersey who flip-flopped on the abortion issue: "Thou shalt take our doctrine on abortion and thou shalt shove it down the throats of thine constituents."

Bishop James T. McHugh of Camden, Philadelphia's neighbor, obviously vexed, deplored passivity, saying: "It is time that Catholics publicly rebel against the arrogance, bigotry and outright exclusivism of the pro-abortion forces in this nation. . . .

"*America* magazine (Jesuit) had it right; people will indulge in this kind of bigotry because they think they can get away with it and the sad truth is that they can."

That Philadelphia's *Inquirer* in 1991 could be accused of Nativism was an atavistic reversion to 1844 when that city became notorious as a hotbed of Nativism where the Nativist charged that "a set of citizens, German and Irish, wanted to get the Constitution of the U.S. into their own hands and sell it to a foreign power." There followed the burning of St. Augustine's and St. Michael's Church and St. Charles Seminary.[187]

Could Catholics, laymen and laywomen, not just priests and bishops, enter the public forum on matters of human rights, of justice, and of charity, with obvious implications in the political order, very often on the tax structure, and be accepted as loyal Americans? Were the bishops and priests not guilty over the years of engaging in partisan politics? Was it not possible to qualify public forums as to whether they were partisan or nonpartisan?

By and large, and in sharp contrast to many leaders in religious communities — Protestant, Mormon, Muslim, and Jewish alike — the Catholic bishops held the line against priests engaging in party politics or accepting political office. History had taught them the lesson of a Cardinal Richelieu in seventeenth-century France or a Monsignor Jozef Tiso, Slovak prime minister, hanging from the gallows after World War II, a devoted pastor but failed politician. Moreover, the canon law of the Church, in its 1917 code and in the newest of 1983, prohibited priests from accepting partisan or administrative public office.[188] On the national level there were, however, a few exceptions in the two hundred years of the Republic that might be said to prove the rule.

Father Gabriel Richard of Michigan in the nineteenth century, Father Robert F. Drinan, S.J., of Massachusetts, and Father Robert J. Cornell of

Wisconsin served in the U.S. Congress, the latter two in defiance of canon law. The most famous case, however, was that of Father Charles E. Coughlin of Detroit. A gifted orator he took the lead in the 1930s against the Roosevelt administration with an eloquence that fascinated millions on his weekly Sunday broadcast, and other millions with his publications. He stormed against the international bankers, he attacked President Franklin Roosevelt as a liar, and he was a leading voice in what turned into an anti-Semitic crusade. While he did not run for office, he led the formation of a third party, which entered a candidate for President against the Democratic and Republican nominees. To his credit, when he was ordered to cease his public intrusions into the political arena Coughlin obeyed his archbishop and retired to his post as pastor of the Shrine of the Little Flower in the archdiocese of Detroit.

There were a few priests too who ran on partisan local tickets such as Father Louis Gigante in New York City, but they created only a tempest in a teapot locally. Clericalism, which is the unwarranted interference of the clergy in the affairs of the laity, is a seductive temptation for a few priests and very few bishops.

Yet in 1990 the Catholic Church in America — the Church that historically supported the First Amendment to the Constitution perhaps more than any other single religious group because it had more to lose and more to gain; the Church that had fought so hard to drive Bible reading out of the public school; the Church that supported union labor through its formative years against charges brought by Nativists; the Church that fought prohibition as a religious intrusion into the public weal; the Church that denounced slavery prior to the Civil War and desegregated many schools south of the Mason-Dixon line prior to the 1954 Supreme Court decision; the Church that was and still is a haven for the immigrant (in a word, the Church that has a proud human- and civil-rights record) — this Church was once again labeled un-American.

The *Catholic Encyclopedia* states that "World War II destroyed anti-Semitism as a political force in American life." It has been widely stated that the Kennedy election did the same for Catholics in the midstream of America; *de facto* anti-Semitism lives on in America in the *extremist* milieux; not so anti-Catholicism, which has again surfaced in *mainstream* America.

The implication has been all along that Kennedy's stance on Church-State relations was somehow acceptable to the Catholic Church. In large measure, it was; but on the two controversial problems of the 1990s, it was not. Kennedy bent over backward to appease the anti-Catholic school groups in denying any kind of assistance to Catholic school youngsters. He did not have to face the abortion question precisely because abortion was illegal in the U.S.A. Kennedy's acceptance of an *absolute* separation of Church and State went beyond even what a restrictive Supreme Court had judged. Similarly the "impregnable wall between Church and State" was another analogy that did not stand close analysis even by the same Court. These analogies hid more than they revealed.

Political considerations were, quite understandably, paramount in one seeking votes, although no one would disagree that there were limits. President Kennedy had really only one Achilles' heel in the eyes of Catholics: his opposition to parochial school assistance, the time-honored anathema in American history. No sooner was he elected than he sought, not to mend fences with the Catholic segment who had supported him with over seventy percent of its vote (albeit disappointed on the school matter), but rather to strengthen his ties to the Protestant constituency wherein he had been a loser to candidate Nixon.

Within weeks of his occupancy of the White House, JFK invited Billy Graham and sixty-two Baptist missionaries to a prayer breakfast at which the Reverend Mr. Graham extolled the new President who "traded quips" with the Baptists, the session lasting six hours at the White House itself, complete with reporters and photographers in attendance for maximum media attention.

Graham had worked himself into something of a pretty pickle when he told *Time* magazine shortly *before* the election that religion was "a legitimate issue. A man's religion cannot be separated from his person; the religious issue is deeper than in 1928. People are better informed today." Protestants, he added, might hesitate to vote for John F. Kennedy because the Roman Catholic Church is "not only a religion but a secular institution with its own ministries and ambassadors." Two weeks later Graham, with some feeling, told *Time* (September 19, 1960) that it was legitimate to ask a Quaker about pacifism, and a Christian Scientist about medical aid, and "a Catholic's views on the secular influences of the Vatican." He concluded that he deplored all forms of bigotry.

Graham was seen publicly at functions where presidential candidate Richard M. Nixon, then vice president, was guest of honor. Whether intended or not, Graham was widely perceived at the time to have sent a message to Protestants to stop, look, and listen before voting for a Catholic for President.

Pierre Salinger, Kennedy's assistant, met Billy Graham on a train in Indiana during the campaign and asked him if he would sign a statement with other Protestant ministers calling for religious tolerance during the election. On the train Graham agreed but the next day reneged, saying that he should not interfere in an election. Yet later he participated in rallies in behalf of Nixon.[189]

Professional anti-Catholics such as C. Stanley Lowell of the POAU (Protestants and Other Americans United for the Separation of Church and

State) said, "We are extremely pleased with President Kennedy," while Paul Blanshard predicted JFK's reelection in 1964. It was, in reporter Fletcher Knebel's words, "The Protestant clergy of America, led by Catholic John F. Kennedy, versus the nation's Roman Catholic hierarchy, led by Francis Cardinal Spellman of New York."[190]

The main issue was "the demand of the Roman Catholic hierarchy for Federal loans to parochial schools." Kennedy complained: "The bishops never took that position during Eisenhower's eight years and now they do it to me." Knebel judged that "with the exception of the integration dispute, perhaps no domestic question of the modern era so inflames people."

Kennedy and his aides believed that the bishops "never approved his candidacy and timed their political acts to create maximum embarrassment for the new President even after the election." What were these hierarchial actions that were dubbed political?

In 1959, Kennedy opposed the U.S. sending an ambassador to the Vatican and allocating federal funds to aid nonpublic pupils. "Whatever one's religion in his private life might be, for the office holder nothing takes precedence over his oath to uphold the Constitution and all its parts — including the First Amendment and the strict separation of Church and State."

Kennedy is reported as being "bewildered by the vehemence of the Catholic reaction," and his assistant Ralph A. Dungan "coached Kennedy on the Catholic creed."

The President was both wrong and right: wrong that the American bishops reacted so strongly about the ambassadorship to the Vatican. Most could not have cared less, since there was no call for it by the American hierarchy. He was correct, however, in believing that the bishops and the Catholic people did feel deeply aggrieved by the patent discrimination against Catholic school children, teachers, and parents. Neither were they impressed with Kennedy's very sweeping precedence posture: "Nothing takes precedence." Nothing?

In November of 1959, two hundred Catholic bishops condemned the government's use of tax money to promote artificial contraception as recommended in the Draper report. Again the issue had nothing to do with Kennedy, who was on the verge of announcing his candidacy; the bishops had gotten together as usual in their annual November meeting and issued their dissent.

During the primary campaign in Oregon on May 20, 1960, the Vatican newspaper *L'Osservatore Romano* declared in Rome that the Catholic hierarchy (no country was named) had the right and duty to intervene in politics and to expect dutiful discipline from Catholics. The hierarchy alone, it said, has the right to judge whether the higher principles of religious and moral order are involved in political issues. This article was "an incendiary bomb" and fed Protestant opposition with ammunition that a Catholic would have to take orders from Rome.

The Vatican paper was entirely out of line in both its timing and as eventually, it was proved, out of touch with the Catholic people and hierarchy of the world. Vatican II's 1965 document on religious liberty thoroughly rejected *L'Osservatore*'s theology and practical politics. At the very time that it was by implication casting doubts on presidential candidate Kennedy, it was doing the same on Father John Courtney Murray. American Protestants were not the only ones confused.

Cardinal Spellman's predilection for Republican candidates was well-known and his selective treatment caused dismay in the Kennedy camp. He was not alone among the hierarchy, yet the best educated guess would still be that a comfortable majority of bishops voted for Kennedy over Nixon, as did the Catholic people at a rate of 7 to 3.

Perhaps the worst misunderstanding arose from an episode in Puerto Rico where Archbishop James P. Davis of San Juan signed a pastoral letter forbidding island Catholics to vote for Governor Luis Muñoz Marín's Popular Democratic Party. Knebel described the scene: "Editorial skyrockets burst in the Protestant press. If the bishops of Puerto Rico — U.S. soil — could give parishioners orders on how to vote . . . what was to prevent bishops in the 50 states from doing the same? Kennedy was stunned. . . . The incident hurt badly."

Actually Muñoz Marín was reelected; Archbishop Davis did not have Kennedy or anyone else in mind when he opposed what he considered the immoral policies of the Muñoz Marín government. In restropect, he said he did not care what Kennedy or anyone else thought.[191]

Finally Kennedy resented Cardinal Spellman's "jumping the gun" on January 17 by blasting the new administration's discrimination against Catholic schoolchildren: he believed that the hierarchy had changed its stance because there was a president in the White House who was a Catholic.

Here again Kennedy was dead wrong: the school question was always and continues to be a burning question because it entails a true grievance, a discrimination on religious grounds. The timing had little or nothing to do with Kennedy's candidacy, except that he came out in opposition to the call for equal justice. It was a question argued from the very beginning of the Republic. Actually Kennedy in 1950 as a member of the House Labor Committee had sponsored a $300 million federal aid-to-education bill that included transportation funds for parochial school pupils. "He had a different view then," said Monsignor Frederick Hochwalt, head of the National Conference of Catholic Bishops' department of education, according to the Knebel report.

Kennedy continued to believe that these and other events were more than mere coincidences; the bishops continued to believe that their collective mind on education rights preceded Kennedy by more than a century and would be carried on until justice is done, no matter who the President was.

Knebel concluded: "Whatever the final outcome of the school-aid fight — and it may go on for many years — history will note that the country's first Catholic President fought side by side with Protestant leaders against the clergy of his own church. It may also note that the Kennedy-Protestant alliance forged a powerful political weapon for Republicans to cope with in 1964."[192] However, most of the Catholic laity who would vote for Kennedy sided with the bishops on that question.

Father Charles M. Whelan, a law student and later professor of law at Georgetown, called Kennedy's statement in his message to Congress on February 20, 1961, "erroneous, inopportune and unnecessary." One year later *America* in its editorial pondered "the dilemmas of the first Catholic President. The distinction lies between clear understanding, on the one hand, of the political circumstances and contingencies which might make it personally expedient for a Catholic president not to be in the reviewing stand at a St. Patrick's Day parade — and, on the other hand, failure to understand and refusal to countenance a positive act of discrimination."[193]

While clearly condoning Kennedy's reluctance to be photographed in the Oval Office with the Vatican's secretary of state in December 1961, *America* added that "photographs of the President with Protestant spokesmen like Evangelist Billy Graham . . . are pure 14-karat gold, to be laid away at five-per cent interest till the day of reckoning in 1964 . . . a tight-rope walking in the field of religious public relations, (which) causes no appreciable adverse reaction among his (Catholic) coreligionists."[194]

Immediately after the election the editors of *America* speculated on how Catholics would view President Kennedy: "They (have) a certain natural pride that he happens to be a Catholic. But there is no gloating in the Catholic attitude. Catholics look for no special preferments or special favors, and they will get none. They would be disappointed in the President if he ran things in any other way.

"But they do want justice, particularly with respect to their schools, and they want the President and the Congress and the country at large to think hard about giving it to them."[195]

One year later *America* said it would not change one word of that statement. The one great exception, perhaps the one that proves the rule, was still the school question.

"We shall continue," *America* pointed out, "to press the reasons why in justice Federal aid to the nation's schools should not be allotted in a way calculated to put harsh economic sanctions on millions of parents, who, in the exercise of their religious liberty, choose to educate their pupils in parochial schools.

"Surely no one who is not misled by the charged rhetoric of such assorted commentators as Mr. Blanshard and Co., the editorial writers of the *New York Times*, Drew Pearson and *Look* correspondent Fletcher Knebel can fail to see that Catholics could not in conscience have done other than protest the undeniable discrimination of such public laws as would effectively deprive them of their rights guaranteed under the Constitution."[196]

Perhaps the Irish columnist for the *London Times*, Conor Cruise O'Brien, illustrated the thinking of many American non-Catholics: "An American Catholic is a Protestant who goes to Mass. The name of John F. Kennedy comes to mind." This acerbic comment is a calumny on President Kennedy but may well express the litmus test for Catholics who are candidates for public office.

The Kennedy equation balancing Church and State is usually reported only in part. Actually he added a great deal more than an *absolute* separation doctrine when he said: "But if the time should ever come — and I do not concede any conflict to be remotely possible — when my office would require me to either violate my conscience or violate the national interest, then I would resign the office, and I hope any other conscientious public servant would do likewise."

Kennedy's sister Eunice Shriver took issue with the advertisement in the *New York Times* by the National Abortion Rights Action League, NARAL, which distorted the President's position by cutting off these additional words. She wrote that "President Kennedy believed and practiced the value that America should offer a free marketplace for all views, even those of Catholic bishops. He would have resented his words being distorted to confuse and obscure that view."[197]

This episcopal typecasting continued right into the 1990s. During the August 1991 anti-abortion sit-ins at Wichita, Kansas, led by the non-denominational Operation Rescue, Judge Patrick Kelly, in sentencing some of the many hundreds arrested, described himself, quite correctly it seems, as "a Catholic." The *New York Times* characterized him as "a lifelong Catholic" but "a JFK Catholic," quoting a lawyer who said that "Pat is a Catholic. But like John F. Kennedy who was a president first and a Catholic second, Pat is a judge first and a Catholic second."[198]

The *Catholic Encyclopedia* confidently asserted that "Kennedy's death probably destroyed anti-Catholicism as a force in American life." The adverb "probably" was well chosen and cautious, but the judgment has had to yield to contrary evidence.

To attempt to exonerate the Church from entering into partisan politics, when the Church is identified only with bishops and priests, would be vain. To point to the Catholic Church's history in support of freedom of religion in the U.S.A.; to underline the official teaching on religious liberty from the Vatican Council; to underscore canon law's prohibitions against priests assuming elective office; to repeat the U.S. bishops' official statements in these matters — all of these did not suffice to allay suspicion in seemingly open and liberal quarters.

Since there are some three hundred seventy-five bishops and over fifty-two thousand priests in the United States, policing such members is a daunting task. Some did move into the partisan field in some elections: some directly, others indirectly.

Cardinal Spellman, for example, was quite willing to appear publicly with General Dwight D. Eisenhower when he visited New York City as a candidate; the cardinal found it just as expedient to be "out of town" when Adlai Stevenson appeared. Similarly, just prior to the elections, Cardinal John J. Krol (who supported Nixon in 1968 and 1972) had no qualms about appearing publicly with Ronald Reagan; Archbishop Pio Laghi, the Vatican's apostolic delegate, took it upon himself to fly all the way from Washington, D.C., to California "to advise the President" in a photo session shortly before the November elections. Cardinal James F. McIntyre of Los Angeles played the same game of not being home for Democratic candidates when he personally favored Republicans.

Some bishops appeared to apply a litmus test on abortion to Gerald Ford and Jimmy Carter. The vast majority of Catholic bishops, however, took no public stance in partisan political elections, convinced that Catholics, like so many other citizens, do not want to be told how to vote.[199]

The 1984 election brought out into the open a Catholic who took a hardline pro-abortion stance, the Democrat candidate Geraldine Ferraro. Bishop James C. Timlin of Scranton publicly took a position against her election in what could rightly have been seen as an unwarranted partisan intrusion into the public forum.

The case of Cardinal O'Connor *vis-à-vis* Mrs. Ferraro was quite different, although attracting massive media attention. She, as the *Boston Globe* columnist David Farrell put it, thought that her public record began in San Francisco when she was nominated for vice president. Actually, two years earlier she had as a congresswoman allied herself with Catholics for Free Choice, CFFC, in the hope that the arguments she (and others?) espoused would diffuse abortion as a political problem. These arguments were mailed to every member of Congress with her covering letter claiming "it will serve as an indispensable aid . . . (as) a concise sourcebook of pro-choice thought. . . . They show us that the Catholic position on abortion is not monolithic and that there can be a range of personal and political responses to the issue."

It was this claim of "the Catholic position" that the cardinal took exception to. Farrell was even more caustic: "If Ferraro was not referring to the church's position, why didn't she simply use the phrase 'the position of Catholics' instead of the 'the Church's position'?" He called her tactics in trying to move away from her CFFC position a transparent sham: "Her problem is she never dreamed she would be a vice-presidential candidate or that the battle over abortion would reach such proportions."[200]

Cardinal O'Connor said that the Ferraro letter created a mistaken impression that the Church teaching was "open to interpretation." He became an easy target for much of the media who accused him of meddling in politics, of violating the separation of Church and State, and of taking dictation from Rome.

Two weeks before a California state election in 1989, Bishop Leo T. Maher forbade a candidate, who was a Catholic, to receive Holy Communion precisely because she was blatantly pro-abortion in the public media, complete with billboards. To have chosen the time just prior to the election was a tactical blunder on the bishop's part, a blunder that became national news and was used as one example of partisan episcopal meddling in an election. The case was, however, unique and quite atypical but furnished opponents of the Church an example to be exploited, perhaps for years to come.

The alluring temptation to sally into the political thicket of partisan politics — which, Vatican II counsels the clergy, should be left to the laity — proved too much for Father Richard McBrien, who had invited Governor Cuomo to Notre Dame. Clearly stung by Patrick Buchanan's success at the voting booth and Cuomo's failure as a write-in, McBrien graced the pages of the *New York Daily News* on March 1, 1992, with an impassioned contrast of the two "practicing Catholics, formed and nurtured in the same pre-Vatican II Church."

Buchanan was painted a devil, Cuomo a saint, both disciples of Francis: the one of Francisco Franco; the other, Francis of Assisi. The one was pictured as "anti-communist, anti-foreigner, anti-feminist, anti-gay, anti-Semite, anti-black and anti-poor"; in a word, a Nativist. The other was depicted as nurtured on "honest hard work, concern for others, love of family and openness to all."

While invoking the weight and prestige of Vatican II, theologian McBrien neglected to compare or to contrast the two politicians on the two most vexing problems facing Americans and especially American Catholics, namely abortion and justice for schools, for which the Council rendered quite explicit judgment.

The point here, however, is not the McBrien lampoonery and hagiography; had it been the reverse, with Buchanan the saint and Cuomo the devil, the conclusion would be the same: the priest in partisan politics inviting the same charge of clericalism.

NARAL took out a full-page ad in the *New York Times* on April 22, 1990. Its lurid headline in large black type read: "Who Decides? Bishops? Politicians? or You?" The ad was an exercise in bishop-bashing: denouncing the bishops' advertising campaign; accusing the bishops of turning religious teaching into public policy and using its tax-exempt status to do so. The separation of Church and State is at stake: "Should the Bishops decide for you? . . . We will stand up to the Bishops. . . ."

This expensive advertisement asked for contributions but noted that NARAL is *not* tax-exempt but that the NARAL Foundation is and that checks could be made out to the latter as a "charitable contribution."

The June 1990 issue of the *Village Voice* accused NARAL and NOW (National Organization for Women) of a double standard that while asserting their own right to free speech, they wanted to deny the same to the pro-lifers. The First Amendment, it went on, proscribes the *state* from certain actions; the Catholic bishops are not the state.

In August 1984, Bishop James W. Malone, president of the U.S. bishops' conference, had issued a statement trying to explain that not every position taken by the Church is taken simply because it is consonant with Catholic teaching. The Church endeavors to share moral convictions in a pluralistic society in public-policy debates. He listed three areas where such convictions were based not on Catholic theology or doctrine as such but on criteria surrounding human rights known to most people regardless of their religious orientation or tradition.

> When we oppose abortion in that (public) forum, we do so because a fundamental human right is at stake — the right to life of the unborn child.
>
> When we oppose any such deterrence policies (e.g., nuclear bombs) as would directly target civilian centers or inflict catastrophic damage, we do so because human values would be violated in such an attack.
>
> When we support civil rights at home and measure foreign policy by human rights criteria, we seek to do so in terms all people can grasp and support.

The Church's position on these three subjects is not precisely a religious one, dependent on religious sources (for example, on the Old or New Testament); rather it is available to human reason and to human insight. Because a subject has religious backing does not mean that it is per se religious.

The Declaration of Independence is a document whose origin lies heavily in the Judeo-Christian tradition, but it is not exclusively from a religious tradition: thou shall not murder, lie, steal, perjure, defraud workers of their wages, cheat widows and orphans, etc., can at once be quite "religious" and quite "American" and do not constitute an imposition of a sectarian religious doctrine into public policy. Public policy is often supported by religious sources and nourished by its traditions.

Vatican II made the same point concerning the autonomy of earthly affairs: ". . . created things and societies themselves enjoy their own laws and values. . . . For by the very circumstances of their having been created, all things are endowed with their own stability, truth, goodness, proper laws and order."

Are the very "religious" words "All men are created equal . . . with unalienable right to life, liberty and the pursuit of happiness" to be negated by a supreme or other court on the grounds that the words are "religious"?

The fact that the people and especially the media and politicians readily accepted the interventions of the American hierarchy in the debate on public policy on the deterrence of atomic warfare and on civil rights without accusing the bishops of meddling, imposing their will, or violating the separation of Church and State, illustrates the inconsistency when abortion becomes the subject matter.

That the Catholic bishops perceived the work of the media alleging un-Americanism as anti-Catholic came as no surprise. Bishop James McHugh of Camden, the target of much of the criticism, was very direct: the media in their "news analysis, cartoon and editorial commentaries, failed in terms of accuracy and objectivity and led to further distortion and dishonesty." The bishop saw the matter widely regarded as anti-Catholic.

Lutheran Pastor Richard Neuhaus was much more direct: he questioned the press's tactic of holding up President Kennedy and Governor Cuomo as "Catholics who pass the test." Neuhaus dryly added, "Since 1960 it has become more evident that John Kennedy was, to put it gently, not a very conscientious Catholic, and since the Webster decision (of the Supreme Court tightening abortion laws) Governor Cuomo has abandoned 'personally opposed but' and come out flatly favoring the right to abortion. In the view of the *New York Times*, the only good Catholic is a bad Catholic.

"The editors are saying that there is a great deal of anti-Catholic bigotry dormant in America, and that they would not be adverse to rousing it from its fitful sleep. None too subtly the editorial observes that excessive aggressiveness in the political arena could pose a risk to the Church's tax-exempt status."

In a word, "Blackmail," the Lutheran pastor concluded.

Charles Krauthammer took even a wider view, like Father John Murray, seeing the deeper issue, the secularization of the United States, with religion driven back into the sacristy and out of public life. His particular target was the ACLU, with its paid staff of sixty attorneys and two thousand volunteer lawyers who were "on manger patrol": out with Christmas cribs, out with the name of God on coins, out with "In God We Trust," out with military, hospital, and veterans' chaplains, out with tax credits and vouchers for nonpublic school clientele, out with the teaching of monogamy, out with prayers by a football team, out with the symbol of fish on logos of companies because they are Christian.

In *America in Perspective*, 1986, a solemn judgment was made on the triumph of secularism in American society in surprising agreement with what has obtained in totalitarian states, whether to the right or to the left: "The great cultural significance of religion has been neutralized in the central areas of modern society. ... In the worlds of science, technology and bureaucracy ... religion has become peripheral and private."

There has resulted, it went on, in a cleavage between what is public and what is private: "Religion can flourish and has flourished in the private sphere — but only there — so that the private sphere acts as a harmless play area for faith as a leisure-time pursuit."[201]

This generalization has the ring of truth about it. Science and technology have indeed been cited as "proof" of the irrelevancy of religion, but the case fails both as to history and to current events. Martin Luther King and his followers, Cesar Chavez and his workers, Lech Walesa and the Polish people, the tenacity of faith under monolithic Marxism, and the search for the high moral ground by presidents and politicians in war and scandals scarcely point to religion as purely private: "a harmless play area for faith as a leisure-time pursuit." Neither does the proffered debate on abortion. But secular humanism would if it could push religion into the sacristy.

Churches and religion are private matters, and the separation from the state must be absolute; the *New York Times* put it thus: "Every religion has the right to set its own doctrine without interference . . . but when the doctrine affects public health, that's everyone's business." Neuhaus, commenting on this dictum, said: "The implication is that the rights of religion end at the edge of the public arena."

Nothing could be a clearer definition of the place of religion in American society according to the secularists than the above: chase religion back into the sanctuary and sacristy. Nothing could be sadder than to witness mainstream America succumb to the prejudices of the nineteenth century and keeping them alive into the twenty-first. The ghost of racism had been routed at least in law and greatly reduced in the marketplace. The ghost of Nativism of the nineteenth century did not die in the twentieth.

Chapter 11

The Revival of Anti-Catholicism and Nativism

Writing in the Catholic laymen's magazine *Commonweal* on June 1, 1991, the state senator of Rhode Island, featured columnist David R. Carlin, Jr., noted Bishop James McHugh's charge against the *Philadelphia Daily News* cartoon, which pilloried Catholic bishops: "Yes, I am for choice in education. I am for the state giving your tax money to parents to give to me so I can teach their kids to be against choice in abortion." McHugh called it "mockery and contempt" and added, "I think it's high time that Catholics mobilized themselves to reject bigotry and insult."

Carlin responded that he was "particularly opposed to gross anti-Catholicism," but he added that he was not aware of any significant bigotry against Catholics in present-day America. "Tell me where Catholics are discriminated against in housing, employment, admission to schools and colleges, access to government services, etc.

"I haven't noticed it. Perhaps I lead too sheltered a life," he concluded.

Carlin claimed, justly it seems, that "writers, politicians and academics bite their tongues lest their words be misunderstood and they find themselves accused of racism, sexism, anti-Semitism, homophobia, etc.

"Let's not," he went on, "toss the charge of anti-Catholicism about too casually." To which may be added, "Amen."

Carlin, however, like so many others, left out in his litany, "religion," unless it be included in the word "etc."

Robert Jordan of a Catholic coalition made a similar distinction: "There's a big difference between Guido Sarducci and someone taking a Host and breaking it and stomping on it on the floor of St. Patrick's (Cathedral in New York), scarcely a casual matter, whether based upon the First Amendment guaranteeing free exercise of religion, the right of assembly, free speech and free press."[202]

The case, however, was desecration not only in New York but on both coasts. Carlin felt that he had to explain himself further. Unfortunately he was much more concerned about Catholics being liberal than attacking anti-Catholicism. He castigated those Catholics "who refuse to debate their critics, who instead try to stifle criticism by charging their opponents with bigotry. I said I hoped Catholics would not pick up this illiberal virus." Again, "Amen!"

Citing a *Los Angeles Times* article, Carlin listed the people who believe that anti-Catholicism is a significant problem in the United States today, with but one or two exceptions: Catholics who have been usually identified as belonging to the "right wing." He noted that the *Los Angeles Times* cited him as warning against hypersensitivity.[203]

Carlin then, it seems here, distinguishes the problem into a nothingness: prejudice versus discrimination, the former involving attitudes, the latter action; hence unless there's action, don't "get overly anxious about it." The second distinction: personal versus institutional anti-Catholicism. There should be nothing to worry about if Catholics are "disliked" as a class, which is "deplorable but not particularly worrisome"; however, hostility to the Church as an institution because of its ban on abortion, for example, is within the bounds of dissent in a pluralistic society but does not constitute bigotry. The third distinction: anti-Catholic versus antireligion. There is, he concedes, a religion of secular humanism hostile to religion in general and hence to Catholicism, but "it is somewhat less hostile to Catholicism than to fundamentalist Protestantism," which is a gullible assumption, given the controversies over both abortion and euthanasia. The Catholic Church is seen and denounced as the enemy: clearly, unequivocally, and directly.

Carlin concluded that "outright anti-Catholic discrimination is exceedingly rare." Quite rightly he pleads that "the critic should always be presumed innocent of bigotry until proven guilty." Again, fair enough. He ended his feature article with: "My earnest prayer is that Catholics not jump on the phony and already overcrowded 'anti-bigotry' bandwagon, which is one of the most illiberal developments on the American scene today."[204]

The historical record and the lineup of Catholics of the liberal persuasion charging blatant discrimination, institutional prejudice, and bigotry from the intelligentsia, the liberal left, and the secular humanists would tend to argue rather cogently that while Carlin's warning against hypersensitivity is well taken, sensitivity on the matter of anti-Catholicism is not out of order nor the prerogative of either the conservative right or the liberal left.

Another professedly "liberal" Catholic, Father John Courtney Murray, pointed out that Catholics and Protestants distrust each other's political intentions just as many of both groups distrust the secularist. The Protestant has claimed a unique identity with American culture, both historical and ideological, with an addition of a secularist vagueness about individual freedom. The secularist in history chose as his chief target and enemy the Catholic Church, which holds that there is a higher authority than the state and thus is antitotalitarian, and that the temporal is subordinate to the spiritual, to wit, that a human being has a dignity anterior to the state itself.

Murray draws the conclusion in these cogent words: "The result has been Nativism in all its manifest forms, ugly and refined, popular and academic, fanatic and liberal. The neo-Nativist as well as the paleo-Nativist addresses to the Catholic substantially the same charge: 'You are among us but you are not of us.' "[205]

The bone of contention here is very important because those whom Senator Daniel Moynihan calls the "best people" in the Catholic camp are the most resistant to the implications of the manifest historical record of anti-Catholicism and Nativism down the twentieth century, these "best people" who do not wish to admit that American Catholics are suffering injustices that should be redressed. These people espouse many causes but "become increasingly embarrassed at asserting their own (Catholic) interests and claims."[206] Father Andrew Greeley agrees with this assessment that these "best people" are resistant to facing the facts.

Perhaps fighting anti-Catholicism is not yet "politically correct." The current record (which must be documented in detail) illustrates rather the opposite, not simply that anti-Catholicism is alive and well in the U.S.A., and not simply among the fanatical fringes of society but in high circles as well as in the marketplace.

Often it is said that a person cannot truly appreciate unjust discrimination and bigotry unless he or she is in the target group. Ask an Afro-American what it means to be black; a Mexican to be brown; a Jew to know anti-Semitism; a homosexual to be in the closet; a woman to be female. Why would not a similar criterion be true for Catholics? Does a Nativism stripped of most of its racial overtones but concentrating on Catholics subsist in American society?

Senator Moynihan tells us: "More and more I come to believe that Nativism will prove to be the last and most persisting of American bigotries. . . . Anti-Catholicism is one form of bigotry which liberals curiously seem still to tolerate."[207] A Harris poll in 1979 of community, corporate, and thought leaders, including blacks, concluded that "the feeling (of the leaders) that . . . Catholics [are] not being discriminated against, or not being the victims of prejudice, does not hold water."

While the major point must remain "Nativism in mainstream America," the zany, illogical, unreasonable, and self-contradictory anti-Catholics must not be cavalierly brushed aside. They are organized, they command votes, and they make a profit all the while. It makes Catholic blood run cold to note that even Supreme Court justices not only read the literature of the fringe groups but even have the temerity or naïveté to cite them in their published opinions.

The Chick Publications, for example, trades profitably on such bon mots that the Pope is the anti-Christ; Rome is the "Harlot of the Apocalypse"; Hitler is made to say: "I can see Himmler as our Ignatius of Loyola; all the various cults playing the U.S.A. are really just various forms of Roman Catholicism."

Like the poor, these crackpot types like Chick, Alamo, and company, will always be with America: anti-black, anti-Mormon, anti-Semitic, anti-Asian, anti-Mexican, anti-foreigner, and anti-Catholic. No one would expect Fundamentalist televangelist Jimmy Swaggart, nor San Francisco State University's Marxist Professor Angela Davis, nor atheist Madalyn Murray O'Hair, nor Secular Humanist Society's President Paul Kurtz to call for equal treatment for Catholics. They too have their influence and stand not very far from mainstream America.

The extremists of the far right view Catholics, if they are knowledgeable on the Church's social teachings, as socialist at best and Marxist at worst; the extremists of the far left, on the other hand, judge Catholicism as an ideology, with its votaries forcing its sectarian dogmas into public affairs and public debate. Both extremes would gladly relegate the Church and religion to the happy isolation of the sanctuary. But the extremists are not the major problem.

According to the Catholic civil-rights watchdog: "The American Civil Liberties Union, the ACLU, and the American Jewish Congress, the AJC, have argued for years that Catholics have no right to bring their religious and moral principles into public policy making."[208] With their incessant threats of lawsuits and actual filed lawsuits, many in defense of First Amendment rights to their glory, yet they too have proved nicely selective, openly contributing to the suspicion against Catholics as full-fledged Americans.

American universities too have been in the throes of trying to balance the right to free speech and the censorship of speech when racial bigotry, insult, slur, and contumely are propagated in word and other forms of expression.

The problem of the balance between free speech and insulting racism was clearly exposed by William A. Henry III in an April 1991 edition of *Time*. He charged and presented evidence that even the universities of America, those bastions of free speech and inquiry, have been restricting free speech by labeling it "unacceptable behavior" and on that basis dismissing students, censuring faculty, and emasculating curriculum, even to the point of impugning Shakespeare as "racist, sexist and classicist." Racial equality as well as women's and gay rights are promoted in "political correctness." Henry explains that "dozens of universities have introduced tough new codes prohibiting speech that leads to, among other things, a 'demeaning atmosphere' and some have suspended students for using epithets toward blacks, homosexuals and other minorities, not only in classrooms but in dormitories, in sports or even off campus altogether."

Tackling the problem of hate speech on university campuses, Father Robert Drinan, law professor and ex-congressman, pointed out that the U.S.A. is the only country in the world without a law restricting speech aimed at "stirring up animosity towards persons or groups because of their race or ethnic origins." Contrasting the ACLU'S absolutism allowing almost any speech and the American Jewish Congress's suggested "group libel law," Drinan stated that the 5 to 4 decision of the Supreme Court seems to support the latter, forbidding demonstrations "designed to stir up racial prejudice." He then expressed the hope that education and dialogue would cure "anti-Semitism, racism, sexism and homophobia."[209] There was no mention in his litany of antireligion much less anti-Catholicism, even though religion is clearly listed in the human rights covenants approved by the United Nations.

The implication was quite clear: anti-Catholicism, in Father Drinan's opinion, simply does not exist on university campuses or even in society alongside the other areas of bigotry and prejudice, at least not enough to warrant a passing reference. Neither was any criterion suggested to judge hatred based upon religion; it was simply ignored on most campuses, not the least in the San Francisco area, with its more than two dozen colleges and universities.

The caustic wrangling over "political correctness" has caused widespread apprehension, of all places on the Berkeley campus of the University of California, that bastion of free speech and its vanguard. Other university campuses report the same problem: Can speech be divorced from its content? Is freedom of speech an absolute, no matter its ingredients?

The response of the universities, including Berkeley and Stanford, has appeared to be uniform, namely that they have regulations "that prohibit the use of language that is overtly abusive, either racially or sexually." And what is new about this condition on campus? Vice-Chancellor Russell Ellis of the University of California put it this way: "Now, the content of conformity has to do with race and gender."[210]

Race and gender but not religion!

To their credit the California legislature and the governor in 1991 did include "religion" along with race and gender as pivotal points in judging "hate crimes."

President John Silber of Boston University complained that a person, speaking quite rationally and reasonably against abortion on most campuses in the U.S.A., will be shouted down and not allowed to be heard precisely because of not being "politically correct."[211]

Ron Austin, writer and producer of such TV shows as *Mission Impossible, Charlie's Angels*, and *Matlock*, himself a Catholic, averred that "anti-Catholicism is alive and well in Hollywood if for no other reason than the Church's stand on sexual issues that's not 'politically correct.' "[212]

In a case that went far beyond simply "political correctness," Steven Mosher was expelled from Stanford University and denied his degree because after many months in China, he wrote a thesis that exposed what he found in the world's largest country. Communism was, he said, romanticized; forced abortions were the everyday rule; one child per family was *de rigueur* and infanticide a common practice.

These revelations have been common knowledge for years, attested to by hundreds of firsthand observers. But the Chinese consulate in San Francisco filed a protest and Stanford took note that the Chinese government supported hundreds of Stanford students. What was politically correct? What happened to the First Amendment?

On April 30, 1991, the CBS regular news television service featured a piece on the U.S. universities and PC, that is, what is "politically correct." It centered its focus on Harvard where a young lady had draped a flag of the Confederacy from her dormitory window. Some students, especially blacks, took umbrage at the display; in counterattack one black young girl displayed a homemade flag, complete with the Nazi swastika, attempting to make the point that free speech was not absolute and that the content thereof did have something to do with public order, public peace, and public morality.

The liberal Harvard Law School professor Alan Dershowitz was brought into the picture, but he gave no clear answer at all, merely pointing out that there was a conflict: When does free speech insult people sufficiently to curb it? The Confederate flag-raiser clearly spelled out her belief that free speech was an absolute even if it be insulting "to blacks, homophobics and women."

Again at no point whatsoever did anyone from TV anchorman to reporter to performer give even a hint that religion might also be a field for gross insult and outrageous contumely. Universities and those associated did not show the slightest interest in that possibility.

Neither have the various courts of the land done much to resolve the problem. When Rabbi Gutterman, for example, gave a traditional invocation and benediction at a high-school graduation in 1991, during which he prayed for America, for the students, and for life, the lower courts in Rhode Island and the First Circuit Court of Appeals declared such prayers as violating the establishment clause. The next move has been taken to the Supreme Court.

What happened to freedom of speech? The U.S. bishops' conference intervened, declaring that the state of mind of both speaker and listener was beyond the competence of the government to control. The merits aside, the bishops' brief pointed out the "unjust dichotomy" whereby the courts afford scrupulous constitutional protection "to those who criticize and demean religion" within the compulsory confines of a public school classroom and yet restrain anyone who has a reverential word for God or about God, even at public voluntary functions. The conclusion: "These contradictory results . . . defy common sense . . . and any definition of justice."[213]

Within this conflict lie the seeds of a secular humanism that uses freedom of speech to excise religion from the public arena, while denying the freedom of speech and the free exercise of religion in public, both protected in the First Amendment.

Whatever the merits of these conflicts as illustrated by a major weekly magazine and an equally major network, it is noteworthy that they, like the universities, have confined their investigative reporting to race, women, gays, and lesbians, and to "initiatives for race and gender enrichment." It seems assumed that free speech, while under fire on one question, is yet un-assailable on the other: the grossest of calumnies against religion are forms of free speech and but instances of freedom of expression, no matter who is offended.

"Congress shall make no law respecting the establishment of religion or prohibiting the free exercise thereof; or abridging the freedom of speech, or of the press, or the right of the people peaceably to assemble and to petition the government for a redress of grievances."

Is the clause on religion less potent legally than the other clauses? Must freedom of religion take a back seat to freedom of speech? May Catholics and other religious groups be vilified, with the perpetrators enjoying an im-munity resting on these other clauses? But racial bigotry does not yield to freedom of speech?

When both clauses on religion and on speech are converted into absolutes, into doctrinaire formulas, and into indisputable dogma, the resulting con-flicts of interest usually lead to injustice, whether in the one case or in the other.

Sociologist Father Andrew Greeley in 1978 took dead aim at the assump-tion that all was well: "The problem of growing anti-Catholicism, indeed anti-religious environment in America, especially in the Federal Govern-ment, faced the bishops who were assured by Fr. Brian Hehir that there was no such anti-Catholic or anti-religious conspiracy: 'It is complexity not conspiracy' the bishops were so assured at their national meeting with the euphemism." On the contrary Greeley maintained that "the federal bureaucracy has turned viciously anti-religious in the last several years, and Catholics and Protestants are the principal targets of this viciousness. . . . It is pervasive."

Research proposals on Catholic schools is a case in point. Black staff members in the National Institute for Education stated explicitly that Catholic schools are segregationist; the head of the U.S. Department of Health, Education, and Welfare (HEW) pictured these schools as enclaves of wealthy segregationists. Add "the Council of Churches, the American Jewish Committee, the NAACP [National Association for the Advancement of Colored People], and the National PTA [Parent-Teacher Association] whose officials are all anti-religious and anti-Catholic to begin with." The Internal Revenue Service and the new left have as their targets Catholic schools and Catholic newspapers, according to Greeley.

These beliefs, as they should have, did not yield to contrary evidence that Greeley was only too anxious to supply. The charge of anti-Catholicism is easily documented, but the further judgment that it be Nativism is somewhat more difficult to prove. Greeley calls it just that: "This neo-nativism can be beaten. It does not represent a substantial segment of the American popula-tion. It is rather limited to a small group of intellectuals and bureaucrats, many of them self-anointed spokesmen for 'minority' groups who really don't reflect the feelings of those for whom they claim to be spokesman.

"But anti-Catholic and anti-religious elites do happen to have certain key positions in the national media, the universities and the federal bureaucracy."[214]

What makes anti-Catholicism Nativism? Surely opposition to the Catholic position on abortion or on Catholic schools — much less to the bishops' condemnation of capital punishment or its favor of a nuclear freeze and a host of other concerns — does not render one a member of the anti-Catholic persuasion. But the regurgitation not only of anti-Catholic arguments, condemnations, appeals to fear, the involving of old symbols and nineteenth-century rhetoric — all to the central point that Catholics cannot be trusted to be full-fledged Americans — is most certainly Nativism in its most virulent form and sadly to be found in the highest places of the state, the government, and in society in general as it was in the previous century but in more sophisticated forms.

A Harris poll showed that ninety percent of American non-Catholics do not believe that anti-Catholicism is a serious problem, and deny any such prejudice. Yet thirty-five percent agreed that Catholics tended to be narrow-minded, virtually the same percentage holding negative stereotypes about Afro-Americans, Jews, and Hispanics, "clear evidence of a real but unrecognized prejudice."[215] Studies show a special prejudice against Catholics on university faculties. Louis Harris concluded his study with these words: in spite of a historical record that shows anti-Catholicism to have been one of the most bitter and long-lasting prejudices in the history of our nation, "Catholics have suffered discrimination" because of their religion.

The uneducated do not hold these prejudices with blatant religious and racial bigotry. It is among the elite where the melody lingers on. Columnist Alexander Cockburn could write: "John Paul II is plainly enslaved by barbaric superstitions. ... Why should we rest until the last Pope has been strangled with the entrails of the last Commissar?"[216] The Harris poll gives evidence that the more sophisticated were more likely to harbor anti-Catholic attitudes than the poor and less educated.

While the national issue of Catholic schools has always been the focal point, the 1990s' drive for abortion has brought anti-Catholicism and indeed Nativism out of the closet. The Nativist bases his opposition on alleged un-Americanism in the Church and school, buttressed with unholy visions of the foreign potentate the Pope ready to direct American citizens from Rome if not from the White House.

Nativism, according to Professor John Higham of Johns Hopkins University, is a habit of mind, a deep and instinctive impulse in the American psyche, "a generic need to hate." Aliens are seen as threats to national unity; there remain both a racial and a religious peril. These Nativist traditions "over a long period of time have not changed conceptually as much as historians of ideas might suppose."[217]

The great act of faith that Nativism had really died out — at least in mainstream America since World War II — has not been realized. Catholics have become the surviving target as the historic victims; Jews and blacks have fallen into a racial category that has enjoyed strong protection in the marketplace and in the media, especially since 1954.

There was no deep and long tradition of anti-Semitism in seventeenth-century America, largely because there were only about two hundred fifty Jews in the Colonies at that time. In the nineteenth century, they were seen as providers, community builders, lovers with the Protestants of the Bible.[218] Charges of nonproductivity, because Jews were not farmers in agrarian society, were ideologically anti-Jewish, not on religious grounds, but economic.

Discrimination against Jews was immediately branded as altogether un-Christian and un-American. The Know-Nothings ignored the Jews, and Higham concludes that in the 1890s, while the Midwest of the U.S.A. seethed with antagonism against Catholics and Mormons, there was "not a trace of anti-Semitism."

The twentieth century, however, ushered in anti-Semitism, iniquitous and nefarious, its palpable symbol the lynching in Georgia of Leo Frank, a wealthy Jewish businessman, stemming from a "biological racial determinism," hence racist.[219] By 1920 the Jews in America were suffering severe persecution, pictured as monied, Bolshevik, immigrant, radical, and, of course, not fit to be full-fledged Americans. Henry Ford caricatured the "international Jew" and the "money-changers of Wall Street," at once Communist and capitalist. Jewish students were subject to quota systems in the universities and schools of medicine; some hotels, whether in Miami or Dallas, had signs reading "Gentiles Only"; Father Charles Coughlin exacerbated the problem with his attacks on the money changers in the temple, and even the *New York Times* advertised for help "for Christians only." Many employers called for Anglo-Saxons only.[220]

On November 14, 1942, the American bishops as a body denounced the persecution of the Jews as "satanic": "We feel a deep sense of revulsion against the cruel indignation heaped upon the Jews in conquered countries and upon defenseless peoples not of our faith. ... (We protest against) despotic tyrants who have lost all sense of humanity by condemning thousands of innocent persons to death in subjugated countries as acts of reprisal, by placing other thousands of innocent victims in concentration camps and by permitting unnumbered persons to die of starvation. We cannot too strongly condemn the inhuman treatment to which Jewish people have been subjected in many countries."[221] Surely it was a timely and explicit description of Stalin, Hitler, and others of their ilk.

THE AMERICAN RIVER GANGES.

The *Supplement to the Catholic League Newsletter* (Vol. 13, No. 8), where this cartoon was reproduced, tells the reader: "This famous anti-Catholic cartoon by Thomas Nast appeared in an 1871 issue of *Harper's Weekly*. Note the Vatican and Irish flags on Tammany Hall, . . . the 'Political Roman Catholic Schools' on its right," and the teacher protecting the public schoolchildren from the mitered crocodiles. **[See page 25.]**

The cartoon above, one of many distributed by the Ku Klux Klan in 1928, was reproduced in *The Shadow of the Pope* (by Michael Williams). © 1932 by Michael Williams. Published by Whittlesey House, a division of the McGraw-Hill Book Company, Inc. The one below was reproduced in the *Supplement to the Catholic League Newsletter* (Vol. 13, No. 8), with the caption reading: "An anti-Catholic cartoonist in 1928 imagines a cabinet meeting if Al Smith were elected President. The pope and bishops run the country while Smith, dressed as a bellhop, keeps them supplied with booze." **[See page 30.]**

ENTHRONED – CARDINAL BONZANO – ITALIAN
KNEELING – GOVERNOR SMITH – AMERICAN

This handbill, scattered throughout the South and Midwest during Al Smith's presidential campaign, was reproduced in *The Shadow of the Pope* (by Michael Williams). © 1932 by Michael Williams. Published by Whittlesey House, a division of the McGraw-Hill Book Company, Inc. **[See page 30.]**

This cartoon from *The Rail-Splitter* was reproduced in *The Shadow of the Pope* (by Michael Williams). © 1932 by Michael Williams. Published by Whittlesey House, a division of the McGraw-Hill Book Company, Inc. [**See page 32.**]

Pope Pius IX and the American Connection

This *Harper's Weekly* cartoon by Thomas Nast was reproduced in *The Shadow of the Pope* (by Michael Williams). © 1932 by Michael Williams. Published by Whittlesey House, a division of the McGraw-Hill Book Company, Inc. The caption reads: " 'TIED TO HIS MOTHER'S APRON STRINGS.' *U.S.* 'Allow me to Sever you from your Foreign Mother Church. You are as able to take care of yourself as your Brethren of other Sects." **[See page 38.]**

This Thomas Nast cartoon depicts Vatican Council I, with the pope, surrounded by corpses, facing a "Christian knight." Note the phrases "No Discussion Allowed" and "I Am Infallible." This cartoon was taken from the *Catholic League Newsletter* (Vol. 13, No. 8). **[See page 40.]**

This cartoon from *The Menace*, illustrating the revival of Nativism, was reproduced in *The Shadow of the Pope* (by Michael Williams). © 1932 by Michael Williams. Published by Whittlesey House, a division of the McGraw-Hill Book Company, Inc. [**See page 159.**]

This cartoon, which appeared in *USA Today*, is an example of the way many major daily newspapers ignore common decency regarding their treatment of Catholicism's sacrament of the Holy Eucharist, not to mention the church schools. (Cartoon by David Seavey. © 1983 *USA Today*. Reprinted with permission.) [**See page 186.**]

The swimming pool analogy of the American Federation of Teachers, the AFT. The relevant question is: "But is swimming compulsory?" (Cartoon by Herblock. Reprinted with permission. © 1978 by Herblock in the *Washington Post*.) **[See page 186.]**

The Doomsday Scenario

This cartoon appeared in the *Courier-Journal*. (Cartoon by Hugh S. Haynie. © 1982, The Courier-Journal and Louisville Times Co. Reprinted with permission, Hugh S. Haynie.) [**See page 214.**]

The Doomsday Scenario

"...IT FOLLOWED HER TO PRIVATE SCHOOL ONE DAY WHICH USED TO BE AGAINST THE RULE... BUT NOW THE WHITE HOUSE SAYS OKAY TO FLEECE THE PUBLIC SCHOOL."

This cartoon appeared in *The Plain Dealer*. (Cartoon by Ray Osrin. © 1982 *The Plain Dealer*, Cleveland.) [**See page 214.**]

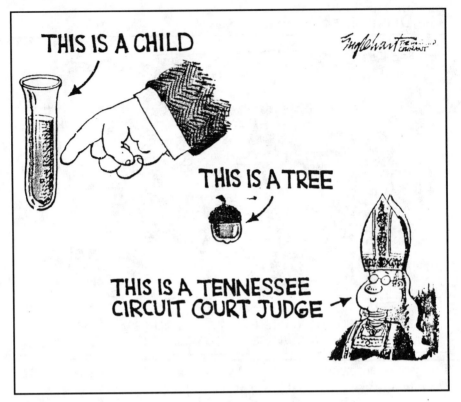

The judge, however, is an anti-abortion Southern Baptist. (Cartoon by Bob Englehart, *The Hartford Courant*. Reprinted with permission. © 1992 Robert Englehart.) **[See page 243.]**

The nun theme. (Cartoon by Jim Boardman. Reprinted with permission.
© 1992 King Features Syndicate.) [See page 250.]

THE OMNIPOTENT POWER FACING THE CHURCH ON SUPREME COURT JUDGMENT DAY. . .

The Catholic Church must retreat to the sacristy. (Cartoon by Wiley. Reprinted with permission from the *San Francisco Examiner.* © 1987 *San Francisco Examiner*.) **[See page 256.]**

"Rich" private schools versus "poor" public schools? (Cartoon by David Seavey. © 1982 *USA Today*. Reprinted with permission.) **[See page 263.]**

This cartoon, which was reproduced in the *Catholic League Newsletter* (Vol. 16, No. 2), "was representative of the press reaction to Governor [Tommy] Thompson's May 1988 voucher proposal which included parochial schools." (Cartoon by Bill Sanders. Reprinted with permission. © 1988 *Milwaukee Journal*.) **[See page 265.]**

Professor Arthur A. Cohen, an expert on pluralism in the U.S.A., perceived a reciprocal distrust between Jews and Catholics based on reasons other than religious: "Catholic anti-Semitism is directed at the secular image of the Jewish people. . . . This perhaps is as it should be. . . . The modern anti-Semite is only incidentally Catholic. The Jew, by contrast, is suspicious of the Church . . . centered (not on the individual Catholic) . . . but on the real and imagined power of the Church.

"It should not surprise reflective Catholics to discover that Jews are by and large suspicious — if not openly hostile — toward the Catholic Church. Assuredly it does not surprise Jews to acknowledge the general, however tranquillized anti-Semitism of most Catholics."[222]

Greeley calls explicitly for real research on "anti-Catholic feelings among Jews and blacks." It is widely assumed that anti-Catholicsm has disappeared and "only a freak would question it," which Greeley dubs "a secret to be kept."[223]

By and large, the dialogues, debates, and even controversies between American Catholics and American Jews have been free of the vocabulary and language of Nativism in that neither side declares that the other could not be fully American. Rabbi Arthur Gilbert illustrates the point cogently: "If we are to get along with one another in this country we must first agree — as all the evidence indicates — that there is no conflict whatsoever between religious commitments entailed in any of America's major faiths and our responsibilities as American citizens. We act in the best interests of America when we declare our allegiance both to the Constitution, and, above that, to a free conscience under God. . . ."[224]

The protective mantle of antiracism, however, was spread over both the Jews and the Afro-Americans in the 1950s, offering quick redress in law. Similarly when the sharp controversy arose over abortion, the media conveniently isolated only the Catholics and the Protestant Fundamentalists, treating the latter as a fringe of mainstream society, Orthodox Jews being largely left out of the controversy.

In 1962, according to opinion polls, only one percent of Americans viewed the Jews as threats to the country. Irving Greenberg *(Jewish Identity In America)* in 1967 described Jews as "quintessential middle class, secularist, saturated with the hedonistic ethos of mass consumption and mass culture society," the leading disseminators of urban morality. The Nativism against Jews had greatly diminished and anti-Semitism stood outlawed.

It is also commonly accepted that the 1954 lynching of Emmet Tell in Alabama "set (the U.S.) on the road to the civil rights movement." Racism was *de jure* dead, even if not *de facto*.

The Center for Media and Public Affairs in Washington, D.C., summarized the point in these words: "In many respects the problem of anti-Catholicism parallels that of anti-Semitism in America . . . in suspicion of an alien religious tradition allied to ethnic prejudice ... against successive waves of European immigrants ... with the canard of a dual loyalty to Rome or Israel.

"Ultimately, though popular stereotypes of Jews are linked to their shared ethnicity. By contrast, Catholics of all ethnic and national backgrounds are defined by their adherence to a shared faith."[225]

Higham concurs in that judgment: "No other xenophobia functioned in so highly a way as anti-Romanism," starting in the 1890s with special ad hoc committees, fraternal orders, and secret societies. After 1910, Nativism became "Anglo-Saxon." "The new religious xenophobia contained all of the traditional ingredients: ex-priests lecturing on the moral iniquities of the confessional and convent, warning about Catholic political conspiracies." "No popery" proved itself long-lived and persistent down the years of the twentieth century even as Catholics became "non-xenos."[226]

The theme of "Americanization" captured not only the headlines but also the new immigration laws of the 1920s. Congress appointed the Willinghaus Commission to study the problems of immigration; the result was an attempt to close the doors against foreigners, especially those coming from the Mediterranean area and southern Europe, largely Catholic. But the Poles were not from that area and yet they came under the anathemas of the commission, which concluded that Poles and Italians were poor prospects for "Americanization."

"Polish civilization had lacked some of the qualities shown by nations farther west. ... The absence of family life which is so conspicuous among southern and eastern Europeans in the United States is undoubtedly the influence which most effectively retards assimilation." Italians were labeled in worse fashion: "Certain kinds of criminality are inherent in the Italian race."[227] The significant correlation with Catholics and Catholicism is unmistakable.

America in the 1920s was a happy hunting ground for the ideological defense of caste, a caste system almost exclusively white, Anglo-Saxon, and Protestant, WASP, "which now (1964) prevails within the American upper class which began to develop at the turn of the century in response to the flood of impoverished immigrants from Southern and Eastern Europe. . . ."[228] One's club and one's educational affiliations rather than family position or accomplishment alone placed a person in the establishment position in both the corporate and urban social world. The tide of newcomers brought into life the disenchantment of the native American establishment. The case of T. S. Matthews may illustrate the point.

He was born in Cincinnati in 1901, son of an Episcopal bishop, a tenth-generation native on his father's side, and a third-generation on his mother's side, she also a very wealthy family member of the Procter and Gamble Company. Like his father, he attended the proper schools at St. Paul's,

Princeton, and Oxford. He worked as editor for the *New Republic* and *Time* magazine where he was very successful. Yet he moved to England, somewhat alienated because of the deterioration he saw in the "American way and dream."

The new Republic had lost its way: "Once America badly needed cheap labor, and rationalized its need by declaring a limitless capacity for making American silk purses out of any old European's sows' ears. The need fulfilled, the United States will now accept only a strictly limited quantity, grading its quotas by an arbitrary assessment of quality — northern and western Europeans are better stuff than southern Europeans, and Orientals almost unusable."[229]

Another Brahmin in New York was John Jay Chapman, a mixture of Puritan New England and aristocratic Manhattan, and a descendant of John Jay. During the 1920s he fought "a twilight battle with the present." His emotional anchorage was violent anti-Catholicism and anti-Semitism, his family roots traceable to the Huguenots of France and the St. Bartholomew's Day massacre. He saw America wrestling with corruption and "rocking with Bolshevism in every form: and threatened by the Jewish peril." This tragic flight led him to support the *Ku Klux Kourier* to which he contributed poetry that depicted the aliens as the Master Pirates, Old Europe's nation-wreckers being aided by the U.S. citizens — "the Jesuit and the Jew." He concluded that "the decay of life, mind, and character of the American has got on my brain and has come out in the form of anti-Catholicism" and, it might be added, identifying Catholicism as anti-American. E. Digby Baltzell describes Chapman as violently "anti-Catholic, anti-Irish, anti-immigrant and anti-Semitic," a not-too-untypical WASP but of the antebellum period.

Elated by Chapman's diatribes, his friend Madison Grant, "probably the last of the Brahmin racists," asked the *Forum* magazine "to get some Protestant to take the position that the Catholic Church, under Jewish leadership, and the Jews and the Communist Labor Party are all international organizations and as such are hopelessly irreconcilable to the principles of Nationalism upon which modern Christendom is founded."[230] He found that the Jews from Russia were by far the most dangerous.

Baltzell passes the comment that "it is hard to believe that an educated man could have written such a fantastically inaccurate diagnosis of the ills of his time. But perhaps he was only carrying to its logical conclusion a proposition held by most proper Anglo-Saxon Protestants in the so-called mongrelization of their previously homogeneous society."[231] Grant's book *The Passing of the Great Race in America*, published in 1916, became "the bible of some 16,000 purchasers in the course of several editions."

At the same time in the space of ten years, 1920-30, there appeared on the market over one hundred twenty publications plus forty-four Ku Klux Klan periodicals devoted to anti-Catholicism. These featured lurid accounts of the Church by ex-priests and ex-nuns, by fake ex-priests and fake ex-nuns, by traveling patriots and antipopery groups. While these came in large measure from the underclass, its influence reached into the highest echelons of American society.

In 1922, for example, a midwest Masonic magazine, *The Square and Compass*, castigated the more widely distributed Masonic monthly, *New Age*, for its virulent assaults on Catholics. It complained that "the Rite is slowly and insidiously educating the craft to believe that the end and aim of Masonry is to fight the Catholic Church."[232]

The point at issue is not that there was an elite that opposed immigration of foreigners, most especially Catholic, but that its aversion to Catholics was based upon a platform of what an American truly was. This elite's stereotyping of Catholics as not quite American did not and has not yielded to evidence to the contrary.

The election of John Kennedy struck a major blow against anti-Catholicism except within a new aristocracy, a would-be cultural elite. Survey data show a clear increase in anti-Catholicism since 1960 while anti-Jewish and anti-Protestant feelings have decreased. Catholics are commonly thought of as blue-collar workers, traditionally Democrats in politics, with unhappy priests deserting the Church, against abortion, and increasingly declining to support Catholic schools. Research data show this picture to be false and "the existence of a systematic integrated and vigorous stereotype of American Catholics that perpetuates and is perpetuated by bigotry. The American cultural elite has a well-developed image of American Catholics which is false from beginning to end despite a good deal of evidence (to the contrary)."[233]

Sociologist Greeley broadly asserts that the emerging Catholic intelligentsia suffer the most as a price for societal status in "the university, the press, and the foundation." In an acerbic yet very perceptive remark, he suggests that the old sign of the past now reads "No practicing Catholic need apply" as a symbol of "the persistence of elite Nativism."[234]

In 1919, the American hierarchy somewhat prophetically tried to head off and perhaps anticipate the antipathy of so many Americans toward the Church and its schools.[235] Noting that the Catholic population had been "pitilessly" tried during the First World War, suffering a "rude test so drastically applied, the bishops judged it opportune to restate the principles which serve as the basis of Catholic education."

They called for an education that unites intellectual, moral, and religious elements as the best training for citizenship. "Since the child is a member not only of the family but also of the larger social group, his education must prepare him to fulfill his obligation to society. . . . (The school) bears a responsibility to the whole civic body."

Moving to Church-State relationships, the bishops contended that "the spirit of our people is in general adverse to state monopoly . . . (which)

164

would mean the end of freedom and initiative. . . . With great wisdom our American Constitution provides that every citizen shall be free to follow the dictates of his conscience in the matter of religious belief and observance. While the state gives no preference or advantage to any form of religion, its own best interest requires that religion as well as education shall flourish and exert its wholesome influence. . . ."

And the schools? "Our Catholic schools are not established and maintained with any idea of holding our children apart from the general body and spirit of American citizenship . . . (but) are an example of the use of freedom for the advancement of morality and religion."[236]

It seems that the hierarchy and indeed the Church believed that its loyalty had been clearly vindicated in the crucible of war. The 1920s, however, set the stage for a cruel revival of Nativism, especially among the upper classes, the intelligentsia, and thence into the media. While the target was ultimately the Catholic Church itself, the special target was the Catholic school, not per se as school, but as an instrument for promoting un-American values. The campaigns against the schools lasted the rest of the twentieth century. Church-State problems and the political activities attendant thereunto were exacerbated and aggravated, with only a brief respite during World War II.

World War I was over: it was now open season, hunting season on the Catholic schools; there were plenty of hunters, especially in California.

Chapter 12

The Nativists Lay Siege to the Catholic Schools

Presidents, governors, legislators, and politicians seeking advancement commonly make solemn pronouncements that they stand for the education of "all American children," for equal treatment of America's future: its youngsters, "its most precious heritage."

During the election campaigns of 1988 one presidential candidate, Senator Paul Simon of Illinois, was asked where he stood on tax aid for non-public schools. His answer was neither an affirmative nor a negative; rather he said that "our first obligation is the public schools. . . . Before we help non-public schools we really have to care for our own backyard first and we are a long way from doing that."

What backyard do the youngsters of the voluntary school belong in? Are they not American? Entitled to equal rights or even a modicum of benefits? What is meant by "our backyard"? By "our own"? Are there second-class citizens? It would seem so!

At the same time Congress, under the leadership of Senator Daniel Inouye of Hawaii, appropriated eight million dollars to build a Jewish school in France.[237] France gave President Nixon a special award because he initiated tax credits for Americans who contributed to the maintenance of French museums in France. But tax credits for nonpublic school youngsters were anathema for most senators, their vote to the contrary notwithstanding.

Much as the words that the politicians used in the nineteenth century that "all men are created equal" meant all but blacks and Catholics, and later Jews, so the current vocabulary of sworn equitable treatment for school-children has an ironic ring in the ears of the parents of about ten percent of the nation's elementary and secondary pupils. Yet, given the social statistics, not to mention the academic, with drugs, teenage pregnancies, crime, gang wars, rape, and the rest, the American people are beginning to ask further questions. What values are the schools teaching? Are they consonant with parental choices?

Increasingly, it has become apparent that all schools, like families, do teach values or perhaps disvalues. There is no such thing as a valueless education, whether it be in the subject matter taught, in the attitudes inferred, or the habits encouraged. The only real question is: Whose values and what values are to be inculcated in the curricula in the 1990s and onto the twenty-first century and in a modern pluralistic society?

The nineteenth century witnessed the transfer of education from the

Church to the state, especially on the elementary and secondary level.[238] Only four Protestant Churches along with the Catholic Church sought to implement the traditional role. Since 1975, however, Protestant Church schools and Hebrew day schools have increased in rising numbers while the Catholic schools have experienced a precipitous decline. The changes in the religio-social structure of America have profoundly modified the understanding that nineteenth-century America had of itself: those changes have resulted in a new pluralism and a new view of the role of the public school.

Father John Courtney Murray judged that America's new self-understanding of religious pluralism has invalidated four concepts upon which the nineteenth-century public schools were built: (1) the public school was understood to be vaguely Protestant; (2) it was purely secular in its atmosphere; (3) it was a vehicle for the inculcation of "democracy" as a quasi-religious ideology; and (4) it existed for the transmission of spiritual and moral values in some nonsectarian sense. Murray concluded that "none of these four concepts fit with the present facts of American life. American society is neither vaguely Protestant, nor purely secular . . . its religion not democracy . . . not (a) generalized faith in values."[239]

The dual pattern in nineteenth-century education with the public school alone tax supported and the nonpublic barred from support as a "historical pattern" is outmoded, an anomaly in our present pluralistic society. It is a relic of the past surviving in the present on the momentum of ideas and social facts that time itself has left behind.[240] It is a pattern of segregation: of religion from public school premises and of the religious school from public support.[241]

Speaking to the National Convention of the American Association of Public School Administrators in 1961, Father Mark J. Hurley (this book's author) made bold to say to them that "20th Century America has not solved its educational problems in a pluralistic and free society. The 19th Century patterns have been found wanting in several serious respects. Some men are trying to apply the old patterns to the new cluster of problems, but what is really happening in America is that there is going to be a reexamination of the old solution in its application to the new pluralistic patterns of the second half of the 20th Century.

"Neither a European model nor the original American model has met the needs of large segments of the American population whether the question be religion, race, or cultural and social minorities; 19th Century legislation has not solved the 20th Century problems in education."[242]

If American society has changed in the twentieth century, why not the pattern of public education? The system, particularly in the matter of "choice," is retrospective rather than progressive, especially in the area of values.

The key questions relative to moral and spiritual values are the same for

167

the United States as they were for the Vatican Council: the segregation of religion, even in a pluralistic sense from public school premises, leaving the compelling impression that religion has no place in either education or life itself in America; secondly, the segregation of religious schools from all public assistance, as though they were outlaws or at best pariahs in the field of education.

To oppose assistance to Catholic schools is not per se un-American nor anti-Catholic; nor does this judgment automatically make one a Nativist. But when the schools are opposed precisely as un-American, then the stamp of both anti-Catholicism and Nativism cannot easily be ignored or rationalized. Moreover, it can confidently be asserted that American thought leaders have not recognized that nineteenth-century solutions so fervently held during the twentieth — with its cruel discriminations based on both race and religion — no longer fit modern times.

The public schools have contributed mightily to the progress of the U.S.A. and will continue to be a prime factor in its future. The monopoly position of these schools, however, has been challenged by the alterations in the pluralistic structure of American society.[243]

"The American government today," Murray concluded, "is not reckoning fairly with the diverse educational needs of the pluralistic community which it is supposed to be serving."[244]

It may well be, as Murray says, that the treatment of nongovernment schools (only below grade 13) is both out of date and at variance with justice. Who then persists in preserving the status quo? Quite naturally the public school establishment strives to keep its near monopoly, not only in positive ways seeking support but in negative ways opposing any soupçon or scintilla of assistance to those who do not choose to send their children to them.

Over the years the public school establishment has been forcefully and actively anti-nonpublic school and, given the size of the Catholic schools, openly and bitterly anti-Catholic.[245] The establishment accepted the active support of none-too-visible organizations, some as pure fronts to avoid direct confrontation, and others as "friends." Many public school superintendents, administrators, and teachers descended into a vicious Nativism, proclaiming, as late as 1991, that the only truly American school was the public school.

The most potent and virulent front for the public schools has been and is Scottish Rite Masonry, which, with other Rite Masons' groups too, has assumed the mantle of prime promoter and protector of the common schools. Over the years the Masonic lodges tried to shut down the Catholic schools entirely and right up into the second half of the twentieth century.

The ordinary American simply does not want to believe that such a prejudice really exists. He knows many fine Masons; he knows that they are neither anti-Catholic nor Nativist; he admires the works of charity in the more than two dozen Shriners' hospitals; he sees them as good jolly fellows who dress in Islamic costumes, carrying out rituals in secret. It's all just good fun and certainly acceptable in a pluralistic society. He tends to reject any "witch hunt" or "McCarthyism," all of which is a fair presumption.

Presumptions yield or at least should yield to contrary evidence, and that evidence is overwhelming. Moving into the records of the twentieth century, much arcane data come into the light of day.

One Colonel J. Arthur Peterson, for example, Grand Master of the California Vigilant Association, describing (in 1920) his organization as "guardians of constitutional democracy," said: "We are very strong for the public schools and we contend that all people should be compelled to send their children to the public schools, and no person should be permitted to teach or hold any office in the schools who is in any way not a product of the public schools and who does not send his or her children to the public schools."[246] But if Peterson could be dismissed as "an old APA," which he was, his concept of American education found fertile ground in the economic elite.

The Masonic Orders of the nation took up the cudgels and carried on an unremitting assault on the Catholic schools. The California Freemasonry's *Trestleboard* had just such a history. In November 1892, it asked the rhetorical question: "Shall Romanism Invade Our Schools?" The "Romish priesthood (forces) Catholic teachers into the public schools. Think of it! Forced to allow their immaculate pure women to sit down in a hotbed of vice and boldface vileness and teach in the public schools." Here again the religious test for office reared its ugly head.

Through the years Catholics were accused of the assassination of President Lincoln; there were also lurid tales of escaped nuns and the Pope was constantly vilified. Yet the *Trestleboard* reflected not the tabloid fringe but top-level Freemasonry in California, not the lunatic fringe. The Masonic Order of California claimed its own educational program through the public schools, "with ramifications in every city, town and hamlet in California."[247]

Praising the Masons of Michigan who have placed on the ballot a constitutional amendment to close all nonpublic schools, the *Trestleboard* called for that bright day when every state in the Union will close these elementary schools, for "only thus can we be assured of a thorough Americanization of the growing generation . . . in order that children's minds may no longer be poisoned with doctrines of un-American institutions, . . ." and thus settle "the irrepressible conflict between Roman Catholicism and Freemasonry."[248]

In the California legislature in 1923, two measures were introduced: to regulate the building of nongovernment schools and to allow only "100 percent Americans" to be principals of them. Assembly Bill No. 1285, dated March 20, 1923, going even further, would close all the nongovernmental

elementary schools. This bill was practically identical with the one introduced in Michigan. But where the anti-Catholic school lobby failed in
California and Michigan, it succeeded in Oregon.

The Oregon Compulsory School Bill was passed on November 7, 1922,
by the entire electorate. On March 31, 1924, a federal injunction restrained
the state from enforcing it; on June 1, 1925, the U.S. Supreme Court
declared it unconstitutional. Justice James C. McReynolds delivered the
judgment, saying, among other things, that "the child is not the mere creature
of the state; those who nurture him and direct his destiny have the right,
coupled with the high duty, to recognize and prepare him for additional
obligations."

The harassment of the Catholic schools continued. California had imposed property taxes on nongovernment schools, the only state to do so. In
January 1869 the California Supreme Court decreed that the schools were
subject to property tax; the legislature followed: "All property of any kind
and nature whatsoever in this state shall be subject to taxation." These
measures meant the destruction of almost every Protestant school and the
closing of many colleges as well. Catholics kept their schools and in fact increased their numbers rather substantially.

Tax exemption was pushed through the legislature and approved in the
electorate in November 1900 for Stanford University and for it alone. Here
again Freemasonry played a significant role, enlisting not only the Knights
Templar and the California Masonic lodges but also "the Commander of the
United States, Reuben H. Lloyd, and the Grand Lodge of California." But
the Masonic participation was to be kept secret: "It was agreed by the Grand
Officers of the Orders involved that no mention should appear of the trans-
action in any of their records" and that the signers' names not be made
public during their lifetime.[249] An 8,670-acre campus plus other properties
of well over ninety thousand acres of land were given special treatment;
power prevailed over justice and equity and indeed over principle.

In 1914, the state exempted all private colleges and universities from
property taxation; but, unlike Stanford, their exemption was limited to one
hundred acres. Next the electorate voted tax exemption for all churches and
cemeteries (the Masonic orders owning dozens of them). Efforts to extend
the principle to elementary and high schools failed in the election campaigns
of 1926 and of 1933 after earthquakes had severely damaged schools in
southern California. The problem became acute when the assessors of the
state, who had been appraising the schools as "one-purpose" buildings, now
decided to fix the price at full market value, which in effect meant the confiscation of the private schools via taxation.

Commander Reuben Lloyd had a worthy successor in Henry Clausen, a
San Francisco lawyer and the leading light of the Scottish Rite in California.
He had been a student at the Jesuit University of San Francisco in the class

of 1927-28, worked as a military lawyer with the rank of lieutenant colonel in the Army, married a devout Catholic, allegedly separated from his wife and daughter over the question of baptism, and has devoted his time and talents "to cause any harm that he can cause to Catholics in any way, shape, or form. He has been a vigorous anti-Catholic and in my judgment, a very unfair man in his dealings with Catholics for many years."[250] It was he who spearheaded the opposition to Catholic schools in two bitterly fought election campaigns and litigation before the California courts of law.

Since Freemasonry operates as a secret society, material as documentation is not readily available; most American lodges do have a gag rule on religious discussions. Most Masons will say in good faith that they have never heard an anti-Catholic statement in their local lodges. Anson Phelps Stokes makes the point: "I do not think symbolic or Blue Lodge Masonry as a whole is anti-Catholic anywhere in this country. . . . The Southern Jurisdiction of the Ancient and Accepted Scottish Rite of course has been for a long time very definitely anti-Catholic, (and) in its political activities against Catholic schools. . . ."[251]

In 1951, the California legislature passed the Laughlin-Waters Bill exempting nonpublic schools from taxation: 75 assemblymen voted aye, 5 nay; in the Senate 37 out of 40 voted aye. The overwhelming majority of signers were Protestant and many members of the Free and Accepted Order of Masons. Governor Earl Warren (future U.S. Supreme Court chief justice, from 1953 to 1969) of the Scottish Rite Thirty-third Degree, "highest of all degrees in Masonry," signed the bill into law.[252] But the Scottish Rite under Henry Clausen hired Joe Robinson, a professional signature gatherer, to circulate petitions to put the measure on the 1952 ballot.

Charles E. Chapel, a Mason, took note: "Joe said he did it to protect California from the Roman Catholic Church and the Pope of Rome . . . though his front organization composed of innocent people solicited funds from Protestants, especially from California Masons. . . . He has received more than $304,000 in contributions. . . . I don't know how Joe got the membership roster of our Masonic Lodges. . . . Incidentally, revealing the membership of Lodges is a Masonic offense."

Chapel concluded with the innocent and perhaps naïve statement that "Masonry as an organization does not take part in political campaigns. . . . Joe Robinson has mailed out millions of pieces of literature on Proposition 3 asking for a 'no' vote."[253] But the assemblyman did not reckon with Henry Clausen.

Proposition 3 garnered 2,441,005 votes in favor and 2,363,528 against, winning in favor of tax exemption in 24 counties but losing in 34. The slim margin solicited yet another attempt to impose full property taxes, and in effect confiscate the schools; the temptation remained burning in certain men's minds.

After their razor-thin rejection, 50.8 percent to 49.1 percent, the proponents of Proposition 3 decided that the front organization, the California Taxpayers Alliance, having served its purpose, should be dissolved in favor of "a completely new organization . . . Constitution Advocates," which had already gone to court to negate the results of the election. Its lawyer of record was Clausen, the petitioner Alfred J. Lundberg, and also the officers of the new organization were almost all Masons. Constitution Advocates sought contributors for "the long and costly litigation" and would respect a contributor's wish "to remain anonymous." The umbrella of anonymity was held over many organizations in the years to come.

Writing in *The Christian Century*, Harold E. Fey in a bitter attack on the Catholic Church frankly claimed that Protestant and Jewish sources opposed tax exemption for the schools as did Lloyd Wilson, "president of the San Francisco Rotary Club and a prominent Mason." He made the further point that the California contest is of national interest because it brings the Church-State issue to focus on the tax question.[254]

The president of the Northern California Council of Churches, Holland F. Burr, in a press release deplored "the setting up in California [of] a system which we believe is contrary to true American principles."[255] The Protestant Church Federation of Berkeley echoed the thought: "It is destructive of the American tradition. . . ."[256] Fifteen Scottish Rite organizations contributed $65,000 out of $344,000 collected. Lundberg himself wrote to the public schoolteachers of the state.

The famous Commonwealth Club of San Francisco recommended a NO vote as did the Education Society of San Francisco. The National Education Association (NEA) denied that forty-seven states granted such tax exemption, which was a plain lie. The Northern California-Nevada Council of Churches told its minister members to speak from the pulpit, issue church bulletins, and "to resist the pressures being applied by the hierarchy."[257]

That there was confusion over the campaign was clear from the disclaimers. The illustrious potentate, Paul Morrison, assured that his Shrine Temple, Aahmes of Oakland, "did not give, collect, or solicit funds for the mentioned campaign, nor the Imperial Council in Chicago or Islam Temple in San Francisco as far as I know."[258] There is no reason to doubt the good faith of Masons like Morrison; the lid was kept on the work of Clausen and his supporters. Many members of the lodges did not know what their leaders were doing, but there could be no doubt that those in the public school establishment, though officially silent, were in strong support of Clausen's initiatives.

A three-judge court in Oakland on September 24, 1953, found Proposition 3 "valid in all respects." Three years later the California Supreme Court heard the case, again with Clausen as attorney of record. There was a strong and quite surprising intervenor.

The ex-governor of California, Culbert L. Olson, intervened in the case seeking to reimpose the taxation. He dusted off all the old spurious charges against the Church. Appealing to the members of the California Supreme Court, he said directly: "Without intending any offense to any member of this Honorable Court, a majority of whom were the writer's appointees as Governor of California, I must say that the great political power and influence of the Catholic Church and its activities directed from the Vatican State through its priesthood here in California and elsewhere is so strong that it succeeds in getting through the legislators' acts 'to the benefit of its schools and a destruction of the separation of Church and state,' this powerful enemy of our public school system." Olson then said that he had sent a copy of Paul Blanshard's book to each member of the court.[259]

The Supreme Court, however, sustained the lower courts with the slim majority of 4 to 3, Chief Justice Phil S. Gibson rendering the decision on June 15, 1956. Thus the stage was set for yet another attempt to cripple the schools, which in fact meant "Catholic," even though others would suffer as well.

If there were any question about the nature of the 1952 campaign, there was absolutely no doubt in 1958.

During this period the Masonic fraternity of the Scottish Rite deluged their membership with anti-Catholic and anti-Catholic school propaganda. While the craft's Supreme Council entered its disclaimer, "This Supreme Council neither makes nor permits to be made in its publications any criticism of any religious faith or church" (this on the cover of its official publication, New Age), the disclaimer was entirely disingenuous and patently dishonest.

New Age, the official magazine of the Scottish Rite (not to be found in public libraries), constantly attacked the Catholic Church, accusing priests of inciting murder in Colombia, South America, caricaturing Catholic schools as "primarily instruments for proselytizing and the spread of Vatican propaganda which should not be supported by any nation that values either its integrity or its safety." The periodical asserted, according to William J. Whalen, that the Vatican was "a foreign political entity . . . one of the foulest and most pernicious pressure groups" in the world, an avowed enemy of the U.S. Constitution and the Bill of Rights.[260]

New Age questioned the appointment of William J. Brennan, Jr., to the U.S. Supreme Court in 1957 because his religion demands "blind obedience to Papal doctrine"; Catholic officials should be questioned "on their attitude towards the pronouncements of Pius XII" on how they might solve "the conflict between their oath of office and their religious obligation." Again it was in the manner and mode of nineteenth-century Nativism making the Catholic faith and Church a religious test for public office.

Whalen concluded: "We believe that any impartial observer must agree 'that the evidence from the official organ of the Scottish Rite Southern Jurisdiction' fully demonstrates the animosity of that Masonic body to Catholicism.'[261] Furthermore, "Masonic opposition to parochial schools whether Catholic or Protestant is clear-cut." The Rite claimed over a half million members, a who's who in America.

A research study of *New Age* reported that the magazine had published 288 articles in 1949, 32 percent of which were anti-Catholic; in 1950, 305 articles with 27 percent anti-Catholic, without ever a single favorable word for Catholics: "Communism and Roman Catholicism are identical twins . . . seeking to control the governments of the world. Both harbor radicals, both are perverts — one perverts democracy, the other religion."[262]

Almost any issue of *New Age* was replete with articles on Catholicism, with an almost pathological fixation on the Catholic school. The Sovereign Grand Commander, John H. Cowles, Thirty-third Degree, the top Scottish Rite Mason in the world, showed his true colors and displayed the classic Nativism of the unreconstructed WASP. He defended segregation, denying that God created all men equal:

> My opinion is that human blood . . . does not imply oneness of the races. God made skins of various colors . . . and He placed them in various parts of this planet. . . .
>
> Today we find various races wanting to assimilate with the white race but experience shows that whenever opposite racial strains intermarry, the resulting offspring does not inherit the best in each race, but rather produces the worst element in each racial strain. . . .
>
> Segregation leaves each racial group free to pursue its own customs and culture. . . .[263]

Could there be a better illustration of Nativism in a very high place in America?

A typical sample of the stereotyping of Catholics was published under the title "Is Democracy Threatened?" Taking Paul Blanshard's thesis, the article declared that "the activities of both the Roman Catholic Church-State and communism in the United States are a great threat to the democracy we cherish."

It continued: "They are not competitors. They are really rivals struggling for control of all world governments.

"Roman Catholics are not really citizens of the countries in which they reside."

The author then gives the solution for Catholics. "When the individual Roman Catholic gets courage enough to tell his hierarchy what he wants done — and makes them do it — instead of groveling under fear and threats of the Church, then the individual Catholic will find himself welcomed by his fellow citizens as a part of true American society and democracy."[264]

Whalen quite properly points out that the vast majority of American Masons do not subscribe to the venom of the Scottish Rite and other Masonic groups. "Most discount the crude anti-Catholicism and Nativism of the Southern Scottish Rite. . . . They regret the alliance between the Rite and the KKK in Oregon and in some Southern States."[265] But even outside the Rite there was similar antagonism. One Mason could disclaim any prejudice and yet write: "In free America, there has never been any opposition to Catholicism as a religion insofar as Freemasonry is concerned. . . . The Church of Rome (is) one of the most pernicious and dogmatic institutions ever born into the world under the guise of religion."[266]

Hiding behind front organizations and doing so in the name of friendship for the public schools, the Masonic organizations devoted time and money toward the suppression of the Catholic schools. California afforded the best chance because of its history of imposition of property taxes on the schools, literally with power to destroy. The Masonic fraternity, led by Clausen, made an all-out drive to crush the Catholic schools with yet another referendum to the voters in 1958.

There was no mistaking the purpose and intent: the Protestant or Jewish schools were simply not considered, only the Catholic. The disclaimers that the Masonic fraternity did not engage in politics or in religion was easily abrogated this year as in the past when the Catholic schools were involved. Yet many prominent Masons bitterly opposed Clausen's crusade and publicly repudiated the campaign as quite contrary to the principles of Masonry as well as the Bill of Rights. But the leadership of the craft prevailed and a million-dollar campaign was mounted, with money collected in the lodges as a membership assessment, the membership at large to the contrary notwithstanding.

Grand Master L. Harold Anderson in 1957 addressed his fellow Masons at a Hollywood breakfast: "We have in California 235,000 members with a strength of 500,000 Master Masons. . . . Masonry has asserted a tremendous influence by its support of the free public school system . . . in support of bond issues, the careful screening of candidates for their Boards of Education . . . and assert diligent attentions and vigilant protection to public school curriculums, faculties, school-boards and every facet of public education."

Then he added another facet of "public" education, calling anti-Catholic school legislation a matter of "proposed public school legislation"; he deplored the California Supreme Court's decision in favor of tax exemption, and the U.S. Supreme Court's refusal to hear the case. "It becomes at once a cause of alarm and a challenge." The Masonic craft must look to a front organization to shield its behind-the-scenes political action.

"To meet this challenge there has been formed an organization of public school minded taxpayers, called 'Californians for Public Schools' . . . for instruction . . . that makes (our children) loyal American citizens.

"Your Grand Lodge has examined the membership and aims of 'Californians for Public Schools' and heartily subscribes to its purpose and program. ... Lodges (not just Scottish Rite) of California will soon receive a communication from me which will advise them how Masonry can join others ... to preserve fundamental American freedom of complete separation of Church and State."[267]

The following message was sent to individual lodges: "Your officers of Fellowship Lodge were recently summoned to a meeting with our Most Worshipful Grand Master, Leo Anderson. . . . Our leadership at the top is the best. Our Most Worshipful Grand Master and others are making 20 to 25 speeches per month in support of Proposition 16 (to deny tax exemption). . . . The lodge has voted that a check be sent for an amount equal to two dollars per member to the Grand Lodge for our fight in support of Proposition 16. This amount was considered a minimum sum. We ask you to send your check for as much as you feel you can."[268]

The campaign was not confined to California: the Masonic craft solicited funds nationwide. As of September 25, 1958, almost two months prior to the November election, "Californians for Public Schools" reported that 959 lodges in California had contributed along with 58 out-of-state lodges a grand total of $276,707.40. From the Washington, D.C., headquarters came a check for $20,000.[269]

Sovereign Grand Commander Luther A. Smith weighed in from the District of Columbia headquarters with a reprint used in the campaign. All the American Churches and Jewish synagogues, he wrote, accepted the "New Order" of the Founding Fathers with religious freedom and independence, "all except the Roman Catholic Church." All Catholic Church property belongs to the Pope "with absolute legal title" and the "most authoritative book ever written on this subject is *American Freedom and Catholic Power* by Paul Blanshard."

His appeal was not only anti-Catholic — a check on legal titles in any county seat would give the lie to the claim on property — but it was clearly Nativist: Catholics were not to be trusted as full citizens.[270]

Henry Clausen dusted off his legal brief and, expanding upon it, published a very long four-page attack on the Church that was reprinted for the 1958 campaign, again featuring a protracted list of charges from the nineteenth-century Know-Nothings and the APA's and their ilk.

The Supreme Council of the Thirty-third Degree from Alexandria, Virginia, warned about "one sect, which by its own figures, owns and operates parochial schools out of all proportion to the others, about 90%, more than the rest combined." It commended the Scottish Rite as the strong arm of Freemasonry: "One Grand Lodge has enacted Masonic legislation to the effect that matters of statewide public school impact are not taboo under the euphemism of politics or of religion, but may be discussed in Lodges, committees formed and finances furnished."[271] Quite expectedly, given its source, the battle in California was mentioned in detail, boasting that "Californians for Public Schools" obtained over half a million signatures to force the matter once again onto the California ballot.

Nor were the ladies neglected. The Grand Chapter of California Eastern Star (female equivalent of the male craft but not professedly Masonic) wrote a letter to its membership "to repeal the Parochial School Tax Exemption," enclosing appropriate materials to be passed on to family and friends, with plenty of spare copies if requested.[272]

At the George Washington National Masonic Memorial Temple in Alexandria, Virginia, the Scottish Rite national headquarters, plain sheets of paper were given out to casual visitors with the by-now transparent line of argument, "You won't out-breed them but you can out-vote them." It continued: "On election day repeat to yourself the pledge of allegiance to the United States of America and then let your conscience (not the Pope) be your guide as you vote."[273]

Along these lines *New Age* had also encouraged Masons as Masons to get into public life and public office. One Los Angeles lawyer, Walter F. McIntire, for example, in 1924 had complained, "Since Richardson has been governor of California, he has appointed fourteen judges in this section of the state, and everyone of them has been either a thirty-second or thirty-third degree Mason. He appointed one Jew, also a Scottish Rite Mason. So it goes."[274]

The Scottish Rite, however, did not confine its work to California. Year after year as bills came before Congress, the Rite sent its front man to campaign against the Catholic schools. No less than the Sovereign Grand Commander, John H. Cowles, testified on a federal bill in 1949. Calling his Supreme Council "the mother supreme council of the Rite over the world, with lodges in 33 states and all the territorial possessions of the U.S.A.," its membership, he boasted, consisted "of distinguished businessmen, publishers, and lawyers some of whom have served on the Federal Courts, State Supreme Courts, the Congress of the United States, Chief of Staff of the United States Army and one in the cabinet of the late President Wilson"; he expressed his support for public schools, opposition to federal aid to education, and concluded with a long detailed attack on aid to nonpublic schools, which are "asserting that their schools are part of the American school system."[275]

He warned of the grave medievalism and ecclesiasticism of a church opposed to a republican-democratic government, which would control "the world mind through the control of world education. . . . The Roman Catholic schools are not in a true sense either American schools or partners in American education"! He even invoked "shades of Hitler and Mussolini" and rehashed all the Nativist canards against the Church amounting to over sixteen thousand words printed in the congressional hearings report. Elmer Rogers, assistant to Cowles, told the committee that his appearance was the twentieth in twenty-five years and that the Scottish Rite had spent five-and-a-half million dollars in that time with publications reaching 318,000 members. One Rite publication submitted to the Senate in 1945 was a treatise to show that crime and religious education were correlated, Rogers reported. No mention was made of Protestant or Jewish "parochial" schools.

Not only was this and similar presentations over the years anti-Catholic and anti-Catholic school, they also illustrated without any question the persistence of Nativism in the most favored economic class in the U.S. and precisely Nativism because it was based on charges of un-Americanism against the Catholic population.

Another regular testifier in the same mold was Major General Amos A. Fries, of the "Friends of the Public Schools." He gave the same line year after year: anti-Catholic and Nativist. But when asked who supports the Friends, he evaded the question by saying that it was private people who believe in public schools. Yet when pressured to identify who gave the largest check in the year previous, Fries admitted it was the Scottish Rite.

Of course, there were other groups against the tax exemption. Protestants were divided, with a Protestant minister protesting that some Protestant ministers were taking the attitude "If it will hurt the Catholics, I'm for it." Rome, he concluded, is definitely the decisive issue.[276] The Synod of the Presbyterian Church, the California Conference of Methodists, and some leaders of the Congregational and Baptist Churches came out against the exemption, which "in principle" they accepted for their own colleges and universities. San Francisco's Civic League and Improvement Clubs, a unit resurrected only for elections, called for a "yes" vote, as did the state PTA. Curiously this last group stated that it was not supporting Proposition 16 "fully" but still advised its members to cast a "yes" vote. Yet it forbade its members in their meetings to discuss the question "fully," keeping, as it said, to the words of the executive board.

While some other groups could be dismissed as fringe, yet such literature was passed out by the "Californians for Public Schools," and accepted, no matter how vicious. One piece was entitled: "Too Many Catholics Spoil the Political Broth, It Seems," so "there can be only one policy followed. . . . In the coming elections never vote for a Roman Catholic."[277] The POAU claimed the support of "citizens, Masons, Free Living Christians."[278]

At the same time the prestigious Protestant magazine *The Christian Century* anticipated that the proposal to tax the schools would go down to defeat and with its blessing.[279]

The wider picture perhaps was summed up in *Commonweal* by an on-the-spot observer: "While it is true that the Inspector General (Clausen) of the Scottish Rite has for years sparked the campaign in California against schools and foisted on members the scurrilous literature attacking Catholics in POAU style, yet clear distinction must be made between head and members; so too for the Protestant clergy.

"Citizens . . . against taxing schools have the active support of prominent Masons, of Protestant bishops and clergy, and of Church members in impressive numbers and prestige; not all of course not even a majority, but large numbers all the same. The front organizations 'Constitution Advocates,' 'Friends of the Public Schools' and the 'California Taxpayers Alliance' . . . are not for any schools; (they) are simply anti-Catholic, but not necessarily co-terminus with the Scottish Rite or the Protestant clergy or any other group."[280]

Nevertheless, there were cozy arrangements; the California Teachers Association took no position on Proposition 16 while it did on five others. It presented its members with the ballot arguments. Similarly the black newspaper *The California Voice* and the *Oakland Tribune* as well as the NAACP. One member complained that NAACP members were giving the impression that the organization was in favor of taxing the schools.[281] Franklin Williams, a national Afro-American leader, took no position but had his wife join the pro-private school group.

The electorate of California repudiated the drive for the repeal of tax exemption 3,446,829 to 1,686,122, with the winners reporting campaign receipts of $1,355,764.67 and the losers $471,635.02. Actually, competent observers checking the facts of the campaign — the number of members of the crafts, some 250,000, for example, who were assessed a minimum of two dollars each, and the outside contributions — estimated that since all indirect contributions were not required to be reported, the Masons and their allies spent at least a million dollars. By the same token, two million dollars was a more realistic figure for the supporters of the private schools, particularly the Catholic Church of California.

Thus 643 Catholic, 390 Protestant, and 43 Jewish schools stood truly free from taxation of their properties for the first time since 1868. But the campaigns revealed more than numbers.

The National Fair Campaign Practices Committee, with headquarters in New York, chaired by Charles Taft, concluded that the 1958 campaign was more than "twice as dirty" as the 1956 one, with smears based upon race and religion more than doubled and with "the Roman Catholics becoming the prime targets in this area." Even before the election, the NFPC judged that there was "campaign poison in California." Its executive director, Bruce Felknor, reported to the National Conference of Christians and Jews that "California editors have called last fall's elections the dirtiest in the 108-year history of that state. Much if not most of that dirt was thrown in the campaign for Proposition 16. It transgressed virtually every bound of decency and good taste, even asserting that many of the deadly Mafia gangsters recently charged with controlling the dope, prostitution, some labor, gambling rackets in the U.S.A., are Catholic and some presumably Catholic educated." He added that there was also some anti-Semitism outside California.[282] President of the San Francisco Board of Supervisors Francis McCarthy termed the campaign "just about the filthiest, dirtiest elections in California history." The editor of Oakland's *Observer* described it as "A Hymn of Hate — a Chorus of Hate for the Roman Catholic Church."

In spite of the almost universal judgment of the fact of anti-Catholicism, the American Civil Liberties Union saw no reason even to study the case. Characteristically when Catholics are oppressed, the ACLU customarily evades the question with the worn-out cliché "We subscribe to the proposition that 'Though I hate what you say I will defend with my life your right to say it.' " The opinion was unanimous that "the matter did not warrant intervention by the ACLU,"[283] as reported by Ernest Besig, director, in northern California.

In a review of the campaign under the title "Bigotry in California" in the liberal Catholic magazine *Commonweal*, Lawrence T. King rendered a long analysis. While he gave examples and deplored the vicious charges against Catholics that "flooded the state in leaflets and pamphlets," he failed even to mention the sources, except "Californians for Public Schools," which was nothing more than a front for the Masonic and the public school establishment through its CTA, its administration association, and others who worked behind the façade.[284]

King, it seems, is a case in point. Catholics, particularly of the intelligentsia, often shrink from accusing people of being anti-Catholic, even when obviously they are, or to call a spade a spade where, for example, the Masonic crafts are concerned. It was simply incredible that he could have not looked deeper than the front organization, the evidence being overwhelming.

Further, the campaigns not only in 1958 but over the many years before have revealed anti-Catholicism not primarily among the fringe groups, the marginal population, the dispossessed, but rather within the highest levels of government, of professional and business leaders, the universities, and the media. It is not a question of being against Catholics or against Catholic schools nor against the Catholic position on abortion or contraception; rather it is very much the question that when Catholics take such positions in the public forum, they are accused of being un-American and not fully to be trusted with public office. This vile strain runs through so much of American history that it can scarcely be ignored nor glossed over.

One other factor was evident as well. Hundreds of Freemasons — among them leaders such as U.S. Supreme Court Chief Justice Earl Warren and leaders in Church and State — openly repudiated their own lodges and the campaign forced upon the membership. Catholics alone could never have carried the election, much less by a two-thirds vote.

Henry Clausen was soon promoted to the very top post, to the Thirty-Third Degree, and chosen to be the Sovereign Grand Commander of the Scottish Rite, with his headquarters in Alexandria, Virginia, where he continued his lifelong crusade against the Catholic Church and its schools.

Catholics and others were saddened over the years by what the campaign revealed, even if the ACLU was not.

The president of Columbia University (from 1902-45) in New York, Dr. Nicholas Murray Butler, told how he was "sorrowfully surprised" to find how widespread anti-Catholic attitudes were in circles quite remote from the Ku Klux Klan. His fellow educator, the president of Harvard University, Dr. James Conant, provided a pertinent example: "The greater [the] proportion of our youth who fail to attend public schools and who receive their education elsewhere, the greater the threat to our democratic unity."

Conant's attack, correctly seen at the time as undisguised anti-Catholic school, was clearly disingenuous, since a high percentage of the students at Harvard matriculated from elite private schools on both the elementary and secondary levels. Most of the U.S. presidents had not attended the public common schools at all, even those who were Harvard alumni.

Nor did Dr. Conant have any scruples or doubts about accepting public tax money in support of his own private institution. "Any attempt to try to lump together all private institutions in one category is a great mistake. The arguments in favor of public schools as an instrument of democracy do not apply to colleges and universities."

Blithely he pointed out that compulsory education laws don't apply above grade 12, an argument, it would seem evident, that calls for precisely the opposite conclusion in the interests of true freedom of choice. Colleges, he continued, draw from all sections of the nation and are "nearly as significant as the public." Private schools, conveniently below grade 13 to exclude Harvard, "would lead to a fragmentation of our public schools as instruments for strengthening our democracy. The same doesn't apply to education beyond the high school, for our colleges already enroll a large percentage of our youth."

Nor was the Nativist approach missing: "I have always been one of those who is strongly opposed to the use of taxpayers' money for private elementary and secondary schools (whether church-connected or not), because I believe it would lead to a fragmentation of our public schools as instruments for strengthening our democracy."[285]

He had no scruples in calling for more money for private universities (read Harvard), which moved into hundreds of millions of federal dollars and direct funds for teachers in higher education. What was sauce for the goose was clearly not sauce for the gander.

Conant's arrogant assertion that universities were entitled to tax money, even though they are private corporations, on the basis of the numbers enrolled, was ridiculous on its face. The nonpublic schools had over seven million enrolled in elementary and secondary schools, a good deal more than the private universities. He exhibited how a principle is not a principle, how "Americanism" can be two-faced; how minorities can in the name of liberty still be treated as second-class citizens. And there was no question that Conant had the Catholic schools in particular in his gunsights.

Charging foul play by Conant and his allies, Monsignor Matthew Smith, the editor of the *Register*, a national Catholic paper, pulled no punches. He noted that before a meeting of public school administrators in Boston, the leaders were propagating fables about the Catholic schools, "spread by secret society leaders as an excuse for their aim of the absolute secularization of all schools ... (which) is proclaimed in every issue of the Scottish Rite Bulletin of the Supreme Council, 33rd Degree, Southern Jurisdiction at Washington. . . ." He did not hesitate to see beneath the fronts of the public school establishment.

"By no means are most American Masons religious fanatics . . . but (there has been) an unending flow of anti-Catholic attack on our Church, its dogmas, and its schools. . . .

"The Scottish Rite, however, did not invent the charge which it inspired the president of Harvard and others to utter at Boston. . . ."[286] No, even the illustrious Protestant preacher Dr. Norman Vincent Peale is quoted as using "every anti-Catholic shibboleth in Nativist vocabulary."[287]

Indeed he had not exhausted the anti-Catholic rhetoric, for it was to be found in yet other respectable quarters. *The Wall St. Journal* (August 25, 1950) reported a meeting of public school administrators at Teacher's College, Columbia University, which declared that "private secondary schools are wasteful and inherently undemocratic and the expansion of a duplicate school system constitutes a very grave threat to the continuing progress of the democratic school system." The *Journal* predicted a battle by public school educators to abolish the private school. It went on to say that "when a rich man sends his son to prep school, it might be dismissed as snobbery. But when middle-class income families already hard pressed by high local school taxes are willing to take on the burden of paying private school tuition also, then the public school administrators cannot dismiss the matter so easily."

Again it was a cozy position: Columbia is a private school accepting millions of taxpayers' dollars in direct and indirect aid. Before 1950 a majority of American students were in private colleges and universities; by 1950 they were about even. But since then less than thirty percent attend private institutions like Columbia. Who then are being divisive? If at one level, why not another?

The problem is not pluralism in education but unjust discrimination born of a Nativism, the ghost that refuses to die, even in America.

Historians in more scholarly fashion have drawn some incisive conclusions as they have surveyed American history. Did Nativism die with World War II or with the election of John Kennedy? Are American thought leaders at long last free of such a morbid syndrome? Impartial scholars have passed judgment, not on the nineteenth century, but on the twentieth.

Baltzell has concluded that "the average American intellectual tended to be pro-Semitic and at the same time rigidly anti-Catholic," so the average member of the country-club set was naturally anti-Semitic.[288]

Katz concurred, saying that the no-aid provision (for Catholic schools) was "associated with successive waves of anti-Catholic feeling."[289] Otto Kraushaar judged that "these (same) prohibitions owe their origins to times past when anti-immigrant or anti-Catholic sentiments were rampant."[290] However, they had not died nor disappeared as attested to by lawyer Leo Pfeffer, the most successful enemy of the Catholic schools in the twentieth century, who said: "Most of these provisions were placed into State constitutions in the 19th Century when anti-Catholic bigotry flourished and because they were generally applied in the Courts against Catholic schools."[291] Yet Pfeffer spent many years in litigation to maintain these very provisions conceived in "anti-Catholic bigotry" as he said.

While Higham's judgment was that no other xenophobia functioned in so highly organized a way as anti-Romanism in the nineteenth century, he also judged that it remained a strong strain in societies and fraternal organizations. He even went so far as to couple anti-Catholicism with the anti-Catholic school movements and draw the conclusion that "the most luxuriant tenacious tradition of paranoic agitation in American history has been anti-Catholicism."[292]

It was the American Catholic experience that neither anti-Catholicism nor Nativism was dead, nor even moribund as had been hoped.

Chapter 13

The Catholic Schools and the Judiciary

While abortion has become the litmus test for Catholics in the political field, given the two-hundred-year history of Nativism in the United States, it is a very recent test. Until the past quarter of a century, Protestants and Jews as well as Catholics were in large majorities anti-abortion, a fact reflected in the laws across the land that proscribed abortion as a felony. Modern medicine chipped away at the medical obstacles, followed by the legal profession on the legal plane. Such has not been the case in reference to Catholic schools: the problem has been perennial.

All through American history, a Catholic in favor of equal justice and hence equal treatment in education was often criticized as holding an un-American position. To be anti-Catholic school does not imply anti-Catholicism as such, but to be anti-Catholic school on the premise that these schools are un-American and that the public school (always below grade 13) is the only true American school smacks of Nativism. A pro-Catholic school citizen, it is alleged, does not really believe in the First Amendment and the separation of Church and State. The matter in dispute cannot cavalierly be dismissed as minor.

U.S. Supreme Court Justice Lewis F. Powell, Jr., designated the question as "of the greatest importance"; Justice William H. Rehnquist agreed that it contained "some of the most perplexing questions to come before the Court." Justice Byron R. White added: "We can only dimly perceive the boundaries of permissible government activity in this sensitive area of constitutional adjudication." He went on to say that there can be no *a priori* solutions because of the "sparse language of the First Amendment," nor from history, nor even from U.S. Supreme Court precedent. Chief Justice Warren E. Burger, Jr., wrote that solutions must come "more on experience and history than in logic." Justice Antonin Scalia was even more candid: "Supreme Court jurisdiction concerning the establishment clause in general and the application of that clause to government assistance for religiously affiliated education in particular is in a state of utter chaos and unpredictable change."[293]

The controversy over the meaning of the separation of Church and State "comes to a head in the area of the relations (in) education. Today it is the most troublesome and baffling in all American thinking about the separation. . . . I deal with it with no little 'fear and trembling.' "[294] So wrote the Protestant theologian John C. Bennett.

184

The "Catholic" school issue is the proper appellation, rather than non-public or private school, which includes Protestant, Jewish, Muslim, and others precisely because usually the treatment of the nonpublic sector in education is distilled down to a "Catholic question," not only in the media but surprisingly also in the Court decisions and legal obiter dicta on the litigation. An egregious instance was offered by the daily *USA Today* at its very birth.

The enterprise known as *USA Today*, a worldwide media communications giant, began its quest for its place in the sun on September 15, 1982, with the words of its founder, Allen H. Neuharth, setting the tone: "*USA Today* hopes to serve as a forum for better understanding and unity to help make the USA truly one nation." Fair enough!

Its first editorial surveyed the field in which "better understanding and unity" were in its purview: employment, crime, the economy, tuition for college education, health, the price of crops and loans, social security, the environment, nuclear war, interest rates, and the opportunity to compete. No doubt it was a formidable field for future exploration, a diverse and variegated garden of choice topics for any newspaper to begin with. So what issue was chosen for the very next day? One not even mentioned in the litany of problems "to help make the USA truly one nation."

The very next issue of *USA Today* on September 16 chose as its editorial a single problem and initial target: the "private school." Its attack was iniquitous precisely because it portrayed the "private school" as elitist, thereby encouraging segregation; and, it went on, any government assistance, even in the form of help to parents by way of tax credits, is inimical to the public schools, clearly inferring that any support would imperil the democratic way. "America is built upon the premise that equality is the essence of democracy," the journal assured; "public schools are the property of all the citizens, private schools are not. Any such relief would contribute to the decline of public schools whose quality has declined alarmingly in recent years."

Accompanying the editorial was a tendentious cartoon showing a stark contrast between the public and the private school, the former depicted as a poor bedraggled beggar, tin cup in hand, with the label on it "public schools," where as the latter was pictured as a lady rich in furs and jewelry holding out a cup labeled "private schools."

There are understandably many "private schools" funded by rich people, but subsequent issues of the journal made it quite clear that it had the very largest group in mind, the Catholic schools, again by way of editorials and vicious cartoons pillorying the religious Sisters, mocking the place of religion in the schools, and suggesting none too subtly that these schools do not walk in the American tradition — clearly whiffs of Nativism.

Opinions were published both pro and con, but the highest priority given to the school question and in terms of Americanism and democracy left no doubt where the new publication stood and more importantly the premises upon which it opposed Catholic schools.

Two perennial anti-Catholic school drumbeaters were cited. Senator Ernest Hollings wrote that tax credits "would turn our nation's educational policy on its head . . . and destroy the genius of our system of public education." Doomsday scenario!

Also joining the senator with his usual cliché, Albert Shanker of the national public schoolteachers' union, the American Federation of Teachers (AFT), said that if people were pro-choice, let them pray for it: "There is no more reason to pay for private education than there is to pay for a private swimming pool for those who do not use public facilities." Whether this "let them eat cake" was original with the union leader working always for a monopoly in the schools, the swimming pool analogy found its way in congressional debate through Senator Lloyd Bentsen, who stated: "While no one is required to swim in the public swimming pool, taxpayers should not have to finance a person's private pool. The right of choice is inherent in everything we stand for in this nation." The senator evidently did not see that freedom of choice in schools was contingent upon ability to pay and that while swimming was not compulsory, school attendance was. The shallowness of their position seemed to have escaped them.

The president of the National Education Association, Willard McGuire, saw the matter also as something that would destroy the nation's public schools. He assured the readers of *USA Today* that tax credits were unconstitutional, violated the separation of Church and State, and were inimical to democracy.

While two commentators wrote in favor of tax credits — Senator Robert W. Packwood of Oregon, and Phil Hudgins, an editor from Georgia — there was no mistaking the bias of the fledgling paper in its maiden voyage and its subsequent editions. With every right in the world to oppose tax aid to Catholic schools, *USA Today* — by isolating Catholic schools as the real target, by describing them with mordant ridicule, and by fomenting opposition based upon democracy and "true Americanism" — could scarcely be distinguished from those promoting old-time Nativism. Sadder to relate, the Supreme Court of the United States, through some of its justices, showed the same tendencies to isolate the Catholic school and not other private and religious schools as "the problem" and to attack on the basis of patriotism, with an impugning of both motives and good faith. As a wag put it: "The Supreme Court reads the papers and the polls."

The Court decisions and the varied opinions of its members since 1947 give an ineluctable impression that the school question is almost exclusively a Catholic problem, in effect denying equal treatment and protection under the law. It reads like a persistent mantra: "nonpublic schools virtually all of which are Roman Catholic." Justice Powell showed a special predilection for this approach to the "private schools"; nor were Justices William O. Douglas and Hugo Black to be outdone. When writing of the "private schools," they used as a chief source the professional anti-Catholic school lawyer Leo Pfeffer who boasted orally to the Court that he had fought "parochiaid," a code word for "Catholic," for thirty-three years. The Court noted, for example, that "in 1840 there were 200 Catholic schools; in 1964 sixty times as many." No other statistics were given, either as to the growth of the Catholic population in the one hundred twenty years, or as to the numbers in other religious or private schools, just a "sixty times" gain like the growth of a monster! Scarcely ever were the statistics and growth of Protestant and Jewish schools cited.

Justice William J. Brennan, Jr., gave the most attention to history, using what he perceived as the controversies of the nineteenth century between Protestants and Catholics as illustrations of confusion and violence. Powell wrote that "a page of history is worth a ton of logic," a position directly challenged by many historians as to the use of history in the school cases. Father John C. Murray, as already noted, disagreed with the imputation of nineteenth-century history on the twentieth century as if things had not changed substantially.

Worse, the high court frequently based its decisions on a "hypothetical profile" of what a Catholic school is, a profile having its origin in clearly anti-Catholic sources: Henry Clausen, Sovereign Grand Commander of the Scottish Rite and author of *How to Pauperize Your Public Schools*; Paul Blanshard; Professor Ellwood P. Cubberly of Stanford University, author of the widely used text on educational administration; C. Stanley Lowell of Protestants and Other Americans United for the Separation of Church and State, the POAU; Bishop Eugene Carson Blake; and one Loraine Boettner. This last, who was several times cited in Court opinions as an authority on Catholic schools and a reliable source for the "hypothetical profile," was the final straw.

She spewed Nativism in almost every sentence in her blatantly biased book on the Catholic Church: "It is fast beyond challenge that Protestant countries of Europe and the Americas have been comparatively strong, progressive, enlightened and free, while Roman Catholic countries have remained relatively stationary or have stagnated and have had to be aided economically and politically by Protestant nations.

"The lesson of history is that Romanism means the loss of religious liberty and the arrest of national progress."

She proceeded into the field of morals, citing the Church's aggressive policy in infiltrating governments, schools, press, radio, etc., with its lax moral code.[295]

In a congressional debate on tax credits for schools, Senator Daniel

Patrick Moynihan of New York took vigorous exception: "Here we see a Justice of the Supreme Court citing this (Boettner's book) as sociological, educational information.

"I suggest there is an insensitivity associated with such citations and that it portrays a mindset which has been insensitive for a very long time. It would be inconceivable to my mind that a comparable citation from the Ku Klux Klan or the Protocols of the Elders of Zion would pass unremarked in the public press."

The senator concluded: "I would not mind had Justice Douglas cited a determined secularist saying that there should be no religious teaching in school, but the Justice cited the passage that said the Catholic schools teach the wrong religion. No doubt that is the view of many people, but it scarcely is the stuff of a Supreme Court decision."[296]

Moynihan's objection concerned Douglas's use of Boettner's contention that a Catholic school's purpose is "not so much to educate but to indoctrinate and train, not to teach Scripture truths and Americanism but to make loyal Roman Catholics."[297] Justice Black, incidentally, agreed with Douglas.

There is presented no comparable "hypothetical profile" of a Protestant, Jewish, or Muslim school, only "Catholic" throughout the many cases.

It was a very short step from the concentration on the Catholic schools to point to them as some justices did, as the ones that would get the most benefit out of any tax relief or assistance. Chief Justice Burger, with Justices White and Rehnquist, disagreed, saying that constitutional determination should not be based on whether 5 percent, or 20 percent, or 80 percent will benefit from legislation and must not "vary with the number of churches benefitted," adding that "I fear the Court has in reality followed the insupportable approval of measuring the effect of a law by the percentage of recipients who choose to use the money for religious rather than secular education."[298]

While USA Today and other media, especially in their cartoons, pictured the private schools as affluent and rich, and since many of the justices of the Court reduced the matter almost exclusively to Catholic schools, it was not surprising that they countenanced the Nativist attack on the "wealth" of the Church, which on its face included all churches but, in its application, chiefly the Catholic Church.

Justices Douglas, Black, and Thurgood Marshall cite Boettner that Church and school monies are not separate; the people have no say; the bishop owns the schools personally "as an individual" who is appointed by, who is under the direct control of, and who reports to the Pope in Rome. They further invoked as an authority Presbyterian Bishop Eugene Carson Blake who warned of the mounting wealth of churches by which "churches ought to be able to control the whole economy of the nation within the predictable future." C. Stanley Lowell is also given as an authority prompting the justices to see the Churches in this light, namely "the extent to which they are feeding from the public trough in a variety of forms is alarming."[299]

Lowell, the professional anti-Catholic, is cited in documentation that the Churches have over $140 billion, with an income of $22 billion. The conclusion was clear: since the Catholic Church is so rich, and church and school monies were interchangeable (the single-budget theory), the schools had no need for assistance.

Refusing to accept this line of reasoning, Justice White pointed out that in 1972 there were 18,000 Church schools, 12,000 of them Catholic, and 3,200 nonsectarian private schools; the Catholic schools were concentrated in 8 industrial states and were losing 6 percent of their number each year, projecting a loss of 1,416,122 pupils in a few years. (Actually by 1990, some 2,100 Catholic schools had closed and its school population reduced by 3,100,000.) He recognized the chief cause to be financial and saw a direct relationship between the Catholic school loss and the serious financial problems of the public schools because the Church schools saved hundreds of millions of tax dollars. Thus, he concluded, these schools were positive contributors to the welfare of the state schools.[300] Chief Justice Burger also spoke of the savings to the public as "enormous."

One after the other the Supreme Court justices expressed their sympathy for the Catholic school system, its teachers, parents, and pupils. Douglas expressed no lack of respect for parochial schools but voted against them "out of a feeling of despair that the respect which through history has been accorded the First Amendment is this day lost."[301] Jackson claimed "sympathy with Catholic citizens" who have to pay double taxes for education. Too bad, Justice Wiley B. Rutledge said; it was just the price of religious liberty where some had to pay a greater price than others. Douglas and Black assured one and all that they did not think that they were dealing with "evil teachers but zealous ones who may use opportunity to indoctrinate a class."[302]

In 1985, for example, the Supreme Court voided a shared-time program in Grand Rapids, Michigan, 4 to 3, and a community education program 7 to 2. A shared-time school offered remedial math and reading programs by full-time employees of public schools, the second drama, arts, and crafts for both adults and children taught by part-time school employees. While granting that the programs had a clearly secular purpose, yet they were struck down because of association with "the parochial school system." More importantly the Court stated that state-paid teachers may subtly or overtly indoctrinate students in particular religious tenets at public expense, show state support for religion, and would take over a substantial portion "of the parochial schools' responsibility for teaching secular subjects."[303] The Court acknowledged that there was no such abuse in the programs. The bottom line, which appears in other cases too, is that Catholic school employees cannot be trusted and even public schoolteachers cannot be trusted when on Catholic school premises to uphold the Constitution of the United States.

With perhaps a touch of the sardonic, Burger remarked: "However sincere our collective protestations of debt owed by the public generally to the parochial school systems, the wholesome diversity they engender will not survive on expressions of goodwill."

The majority on the contrary pictured the Catholic schools and attendance at them something to be tolerated, something while not evil was yet not quite good. The implication persisted that to encourage people to choose these schools would not be a good thing. Throughout the Court dicta the recurrent assertion appears that to assist Catholic and other schools would "render it more likely that children would attend sectarian schools" (Powell). The theme is constant, which says in effect that the public schools are the only truly American schools and that it would be bad for the commonwealth if these "sectarian" schools prospered. These were in law thereby schools of and for "second class citizens"! Monopoly must be protected but only at the elementary and secondary levels.

The economist Milton Friedman attributed this type of assault as coming from the educational establishment, which has not hesitated to use schoolchildren to bring propaganda home to their parents that prophesied "the end of the public schools system" in Oregon in 1990 if aid were given in any form. The administrators' and teachers' unions, which are among the largest contributors to the campaigns of the politicians, preach the "doomsday scenario" for the public schools.[304]

As the state of Pennsylvania legislature wrestled with the question of the same modicum of assistance to the nonpublic school sector, the president of the Eaton Area Education Association, Pennsylvania, Jack Grier, descended to the true nadir: "The enemy of public education in Pennsylvania is the Catholic Church. If the Catholic Church were to cease today, it would be better for all of us."[305] At the same time *U.S. News and World Report* asserted that "the Nation's faith in its public schools is fading fast," a sentiment reported even in Saudi Arabia in the *Riyadh Daily*. The doomsday scenario was not caused by the Catholic schools nor the private schools. However, the public school establishment attacks any assistance, even meager, to them, all the time swallowing tax credits and tax advantages for many segments of the economy, whether business, labor, commerce, the arts, sports, or science, swallowing the camel and straining out the gnat.

These private schools, as Justices White and Burger stated, are actually contributing to the financial welfare of the public schools, with savings to the taxpayer being "enormous." The National Catholic Educational Association estimates that the Catholic schools alone saved the taxpayers three *billion* dollars at the secondary level and eight *billion* dollars at the elementary in 1990.

That the nonpublic schools have been an embarrassment to the public school establishment can scarcely be denied. The vast majority are not, as alleged, rich and elitist. They operate on only a fraction of the budget and even a much smaller fraction of capital outlay, with smaller staffs, and far less administrators and bureaucrats, and with results quite acceptable to the families involved. The charge that these schools are not controlled by "the people," as presumably the government schools are, falls flat in the face of the fact that parents have the simple and unalloyed option of withdrawing their youngsters to a school free of expense; they have the power of the purse in a way not available to parents with children in government schools.

In vain have the Church schools affirmed that they were "American" historically before there were any public schools; Harvard, Princeton, University of California, and many public elementary and secondary schools all started in churches, a pattern in many areas of early America.

The attempt on the part of members high in the educational establishment to denigrate the Catholic schools has fallen on deaf ears for the most part.[306] People do want the nonpublic schools for various reasons but in vast numbers of cases cannot afford them. Why? They see results in not only what might be considered learning, scholarship, and intellectual achievement but also in the education for moral and spiritual human values. They reject the notion that these last must be the concern solely of the home and church divorced from schools and education; they believe the secularist dichotomy is utterly unrealistic.

Socialists James S. Coleman and Thomas Hoffer, both not Catholic, in 1987 published a research study in which they concluded that the Catholic schools of America constituted a form of "social capital" of enormous value, importance, and worth in American society.[307]

Coleman found that private schools did provide quality education, are not elitist or segregationist, and "the tuition barrier to private schooling as it exists now is almost certainly harmful to the public interest, and especially harmful to those least well-off."

In a review of the Coleman report, Father Andrew Greeley — himself a sociologist at the National Opinion Research Center, University of Chicago — concluded that "there are few if any other institutions in our society that have such an effect on those who are caught in the blind alleys of deprivation. The Catholic schools will never be able to help all those in the United States who are deprived. But they do a very good job of helping some of them, better than other available institutions do.

"The schools are not only the most effective weapon the Church has in its fight against poverty; they are, on the basis of unquestionable evidence, the most effective institution in the country in overcoming the effects of poverty (physical or spiritual) on the poor." Perhaps Judge Clarence Thomas is a prime example of this conclusion.

The public school establishment from coast to coast is lamenting over-crowded classrooms, shortage of qualified teachers, low salaries, and budgetary woes, all salient points. The fact that 3.1 million students (and more) have been thrust into the public school sector simply has put a very larger burden on them. The public school establishment does not care, its attitude being: protect our jobs, crush the nonpublic schools, especially the Catholic ones, and secure a monopoly in elementary and secondary fields, regardless of the price paid. After all, it still argues, it conducts *the* American school.

The media have undertaken to feature "the failure of the public schools," "the collapse of public school education," "the drastic drop in SAT scores." Much of the criticism is grossly unfair. American society does not accord the American teachers the respect and support they deserve; the wide gap be-tween money spent in affluent districts as opposed to poor and minority areas also cries out for solution. Unfortunately the public school estab-lishment and its allies do not see the private schools as cooperators in the field, always small in comparative numbers and always so destined to be. In other fields such as health care, social service, government chaplaincies, and other areas, there is such cooperation between the public and private sector to everyone's benefit. But the schools are not accorded a similar position in American society. The public schools have a good case, but why does it have to be solved by the unfair burdening of Catholic and other schools, of parents, of pupils, of teachers?

The Brookings Institute, the Washington-based think tank, has called for a new system of education in the U.S.A. based on parental choice, competition among schools, and reduction of bureaucratic influence because it found the system "fundamentally flawed." The institute judged the private schools to be "freer, more autonomous, more liberal in decision making about person-nel, curriculum, instruction and discipline . . . and as a result more organized, ambitious . . . with a clear sense of purpose."[308]

Actually the American Constitution, unlike probably any other national constitution in the entire world, does *not* mention education at all. The theory of the Founding Fathers was that centralization and huge bureaucracies would be deleterious to education and consequently the schools should be close to the people and answerable at local levels. But the Supreme Court has hampered effective implementation. Parental choice would seem to fit that pattern comfortably and could scarcely be attacked as "un-American." Yet it is!

Senator Edward Kennedy, Democrat, introduced an education bill on January 21, 1992, that was to foster freedom of choice for parents to choose a school for their youngsters, targeted for poorer families, but he excluded the nonpublic schoolchildren. Senator Orrin Hatch, Republican, introduced an amendment that included all children and all qualifying schools. At the same time in California there was being circulated for signatures an initiative to amend the state constitution to allow true choice in education, with a state-supported voucher redeemable in any bona fide school under special restrictions and safeguards as to race, family income, religion, etc.

The Hatch Amendment, after a debate described as "heated," was voted down 57 to 36. The American Federation of Labor and Congress of Industrial Organizations (AFL-CIO) in the person of Albert Shanker of the AFT mounted an expensive campaign of lobbying the senators; a brochure sent to each member allowed for choice among public schools but invoked the "doomsday scenario" against the nonpublic schools. The Kennedy position would exclude poor children even from experimental demonstration schools if religious. Ironically, the senators who were most vociferous for choice in abortion on the premise that the poor could not afford abortions that the rich could, became the most antagonistic for choice in education denying to the poor the choice that the rich can afford. Most of the senators who list themselves in the *Congressional Reporter* as "Catholic" voted the straight Democratic party line, including Moynihan who wrote lamely that "the issue of school vouchers raises strong feelings on both sides. I respect the views and good will of all concerned."

The Catholic and other voluntary schools are not a threat either in theory or in practical numbers to the public schools of the nation. But they do have another key role in American society. Jewish theologian and author Will Herberg evidenced an appreciation of diversity and pluralism inherent in the private religious schools and praised the Catholic Church in particular for its constructive role in the social agenda of race, of class, and of labor, and "particularly in education."

He explicitly seconded the testimony of Protestant theologian Reinhold Niebuhr that the Catholic Church in America is democratic in two special senses: "It resists the claim of the state to enforce uniform education. (It argues) in the name of the rights of parents, the right to give their children an education according to their convictions. . . . It is also democratic in the sense that a Christian viewpoint emphasizes the true dimension of the individual as having his ultimate authority and fulfillment above the political community and social process in which he is involved."[309]

Catholics are not alone in such an interpretation of rights in education, a true pluralism, and healthy competition. The former president of the Synagogue Council of America, Rabbi Walter Wurzberger, in 1981 came to similar conclusions and advice for the Jewish community.

> In some instances the Jewish community went overboard in opposing measures which would actually advance their own religious interest. Because of a one-sided preoccupation with the Establishment clause, until this day many Jews persist in their opposition to tax credits for tuition payment to parochial schools.

This position hardly makes sense, especially in view of the fact that no objection is voiced to the granting of tax exemptions to religious institutions.

I find it difficult to understand why this state should not be permitted to reimburse expenses incurred by religious schools in the teaching of secular subjects. . . .

Rabbi Wurzberger added yet another dimension: "We must also avoid falling into the trap of identifying our interests with those of secular humanism. . . .

"Separation must not mean privatization of faith. . . . Judaism insists religious attitudes and beliefs engender moral perceptions which have a bearing on public policy. It would be unconscionable to disenfranchise religion by restricting its impact solely to the personal sphere. . . ."[310]

Again shades of Father John Courtney Murray who had warned of the same danger many years previously of syphoning "all government aid simply and solely towards the subsidization of secularism as the 'one national religion and culture' "!

Dr. D. Elton Trueblood, a Protestant, had this to say about the school question:

> It is commonly supposed in our country today that the Constitution of the United States proclaims the principle of "separation of Church and State." As a matter of fact it does nothing of the kind.
>
> Establishment (of religion) and separation are radically different ideals. . . . We have never experienced either separation or establishment.
>
> We desire not separation, which would always favor atheism but religious freedom that permits us to cherish connections between life of the spirit and the life of the state.
>
> (This) is a middle system. . . .[311]

Is America then officially secular even if by reason of Supreme Court decisions? One of the most secularist of all the justices (Douglas) wrote for the Court a remarkable answer:

> We are a religious people whose institutions presuppose a Supreme Being. We guarantee the freedom to worship as one chooses. We make room for a wide variety of beliefs and creeds as the spiritual needs of man deem necessary. We sponsor an attitude on the part of government that shows no partiality to any one group and that lets each flourish according to the zeal of its adherents and the appeal of its dogma. When the state encourages religious instruction or cooperates with religious authorities by adjusting the schedule of public events to sectarian needs, it follows the best of our traditions. For it then respects the religious nature of our people and accommodates the public service to their spiritual needs. To hold that

it may not would be to find in the Constitution a requirement that the government show a callous indifference to religious groups. That would be preferring those who believe in no religion over those who do believe. Government may not finance religious groups nor undertake religious instruction nor blend secular and sectarian education nor use secular institutions to force one or some religion on any person. But we find no constitutional requirement which makes it necessary for government to be hostile to religion and to throw its weight against efforts to widen the effective scope of religious influence.[312]

Many justices in dissent later quoted Douglas against himself. Rehnquist, for example, cited the above passage at length, noting that he (Rehnquist) was "disturbed as much by the overtones of the Court's opinion as by its actual holding," meaning, it seems, that the high court embraced Douglas's eloquent expression of a nation based on belief in God and violated it in application as though the state were entirely secular, the separation dogma absolute, and the wall of separation impregnable.

The separation doctrine, however, has not been as crystal clear as the secularists (read ACLU, POAU, American Jewish Congress, etc.) would wish; but in the field of education below grade 13 the courts have since 1947 clearly favored the exclusion of the religious schools from almost all state assistance. Only in 1990 did some courts even admit that there was any such thing as secular humanism, in spite of the fact of nationwide groups and associations formed as nonprofit corporate tax-exempt entities, under the law.

Describing his fellow Jews, author James Yaffe claimed that "their political behavior can be predicted more easily than any other ethnic group in America. There is definitely a Jewish vote."[313]

It is interesting that he described Jews in terms of ethnicity rather than religion, a block of voters with "an inviolable tenet of Jewish liberalism in America (as) the strict separation of Church and State, . . . including opposition to government aid to parochial schools," while admitting that his belief had no basis in Jewish religious tradition which favored theocracy: "The farther you go from the heart of Judaism the closer you get to the belief in separation."

Rabbi Arthur Gilbert corroborated Yaffe, writing that most Jews believe in "a wall of separation" and favor the separation of not simply the Church but religion from the state and "vigorously resist help for parochial schools." Citizens, he insists, must have the right of freedom from religion as well as freedom for religion. Paradoxically, however, Gilbert concludes that "we must not strengthen or encourage secularism as the implicit value system communicated by the state."[314] The rabbi clearly supported a value system of secularism and curiously did not mention the Hebrew elementary and secondary schools of the country, which stand contrary to secularism.

Neither did the National Council of Jewish Women, which testified in Congress that "the passage of any bill containing provisions which would permit public funds to be used for the support of non-public schools is a danger to the basic principles on which this country was founded." Max Lerner wrote that he supported federal aid to raise the levels of our democratic education. "But if it means betrayal of separation of church and state . . . it is a Trojan horse which will disrupt and destroy the citadel of American life."[315]

But that citadel, according to many Jews, is based on secularism, which is so anathema to Catholics. Where does that difference lead?

Greeley asserts that there is a strong anti-Catholic feeling in the Jewish community and that "the empirical evidence shows it."[316] It does not seem to be Nativist, however, and Murray makes a similar judgment: "There is the ancient resentment of the Jew, who has for centuries been dependent for his existence on the good will, often not forthcoming, of a Christian community. Now in America, where he has acquired social power, his distrust of the Christian community leads him to align himself with the secularizing forces whose dominance, he thinks, will afford him a security he has never known."[317]

A Reform rabbi, Jacob J. Petuchowski, testified to the secularist cast of Judaism: "The fact of the matter is that Reform Judaism in America, has, somewhere along the line, lost its religious moorings. . . . (Its) leaders can also be counted on to make common cause with the ACLU and assorted atheists and secularists in fighting for the removal of the last vestiges of the presence of religion in American public life.

"I shall always remember the big display in the (Reform) temple foyer, urging me to write to my Senator with the plea that he block the appointment of Judge Bork. . . . Post cards were supplied on the spot. So this is what Reform Judaism means by the 'separation of church and state,' a cause so much closer to its heart than some of the provisions in the 18th chapter of the Book of Leviticus. . . . Reform Judaism's development is first and foremost a 'Jewish' form of the institutionalized secularism. . . ."[318]

Yaffe further noted that "this solid front on separation has begun to crumble in the last few years."[319] Milton Himmelfarb, one of the American Jewish Congress's leading intellectuals, advocated a relaxation on the aid-to-schools question, the AJC being the most doctrinaire and militantly secular of all Jewish groups.[320]

Finally Yaffe put a label on the matter: he called it the Jews' "Lay Religion." From his treatment two things emerge: there is such a thing as a secular religion that can be quite dogmatic, doctrinaire, and rigid; and opposition to government aid to "parochial schools" is very high on its agenda.

Taking sharp issue with the POAU, David Zwiebel, general counsel for Agudath Israel of America, accused it of injecting "red herrings" on the

196

question of "school choice." The Supreme Court, he wrote to the *New York Times*, upheld a state law conferring tax benefits on those who incur expenses for the education of their children, even in parochial schools. The critical point is that no imprimatur of state approval can be deemed to have been conferred upon any particular religion or on religion generally whenever aid to religious schools is available only as a result of decisions of individual parents.[321] He was, in contrast to others, defending the Jewish elementary and secondary schools. The Jewish community — just like the Catholic, Protestant, and others — had no qualms about accepting federal and other tax monies for colleges and universities religiously controlled and oriented. The contradiction of principle had its birth in the courts and remains for resolution even yet in the Supreme Court.

Insofar as what may be either anti-Catholic or anti-Catholic school, it is not thereby automatically Nativism; insofar as it is argued, however, that those who oppose this secular religion or favor such aid are somewhat less than fully American, it manifestly savors and smacks of Nativism. Nor are these straw men and chimeras. A mainline Protestant viewpoint, as distinguished from Evangelical or Fundamentalist, was given by Dr. John Bennett: "It is impossible to separate what is purely secular in the field of education from that which has religious implications." If religion is left out, then "this itself is a negative form of religious teaching; it strongly implies that religion is peripheral and dispensable as a matter of human concern."

People may object to religious dogmas being brought into the classroom; but what about secular dogmas? Then there are some who would promote a "religion of democracy," an instance of the danger spoken of by Justice Douglas "of preferring those who believe in no religion over those who do so believe.[322]

Calling attention to the perceived injustice in education, the Protestant leader Dr. F. Ernest Johnson stated that "personally I should like to see a national policy adopted that would permit a wide range of local experimentation with courts standing guard and ready to intervene only when there is a 'clear and present danger' that some violation of religious liberty will occur."[323]

Most of the justices had no trouble finding "clear and present danger" where the Catholic schools were involved. Three patent contradictions beggared explanation, whether in history, in experience, or in logic.

Justice Rehnquist pointed out the gross contradiction whereby the U.S. Supreme Court sanctioned the loan of textbooks used by the public schools to nonpublic school pupils. At the same time it disallowed instructional materials and equipment such as maps, charts, test tubes, balances, and other laboratory equipment. Thus a child could be lent a textbook with maps in it, say for geography, but could not be lent a map, the Court all the time conceding that these materials "are self-policing in that starting as secular, nonideological and neutral they will not change in use."[324] Similarly bus transportation to and from school was constitutional, but bus transportation to a museum or zoo was not.

If Rehnquist thought the Court's handling of the matter was deficient as a matter of process and insupportable as a matter of law, the nonpublic school people saw it simply as mental gymnastics treating them as second-class citizens.

Similarly when the Court decreed that the aid legislated by Congress for disabled youngsters to be taught in nonpublic schools by public school-teachers, usually at the end of the school day, was not permissible because even the public schoolteachers could not be trusted to keep sectarianism out of their work simply because they were in a Catholic school where presumably even the walls speak out, it was indulging a useless distinction without a proportionate difference. Furthermore, after ten years of implementation of the program in New York state, there was not on the Court record one instance of abuse by anyone.[325] The result has been utterly ridiculous.

The money appropriated by Congress had to be diverted to the purchase of mobile classrooms or vans that were not allowed to be moved even onto the playground of the school. They had to be parked at the street curb, requiring the disabled pupils to dress in winter, brave the wind and rain, exit their empty classrooms, and proceed to the curbside class. A truly ridiculous spectacle carrying the same message: second-class citizens not able to get equal service as public school disabled youngsters do in order to uphold a doctrinaire, dogmatic, and abstract theory of the separation opinion of the majority of the high court, in reality a religious test for equal treatment.

The Middle Atlantic Regional Director of the American Jewish Committee, Dr. Murray Friedman, calling himself something of a pragmatist, said: "I come at this from the vantage point of the social justice role of religion as well as the spiritual role. . . . I would like to see the possibility of (a Black mother in Philadelphia, in failure-prone or crime-ridden areas) being able to send her child to a Catholic parochial school . . . and to use a portion of her tax money to be able to avail herself of that opportunity, the opportunity that so many of us have in the middle class or upper middle class backgrounds.

"I find it appalling that you would remove various forms of aid to disadvantaged children because the service is delivered in a parochial school. So what do you do? You put the buses a few feet outside the parochial school. That's under the law and presumably under the Constitution. But pragmatically it makes no sense to me. . . ."[326]

It made sense, however, to the American Civil Liberties Union even as late as 1989. Its spokesman, Barry Lynn, testified before Congress on a child-care bill: "How can we expect to have three-year-old children in childcare on one floor of a Presbyterian or Roman Catholic Church not to be

198

aware and quite likely influenced by overtly religious activities occurring around them on every floor? They will see religious symbols on the edifice itself, will hear religious music through the walls, will routinely encounter persons in religious garb in the hallways or the play area."327

In spite of the Supreme Court's dictate, some lower courts seemed to entertain modifications. In a case originally brought against the disabled youngsters by the POAU in Missouri in 1985, the District Court allowed the parking of mobile vans off school property. On appeal the Eighth Circuit Court on May 21, 1991, affirmed the constitutionality of using mobile class-rooms, no matter where they were parked.

The decision was one step in retreat from the ridiculous spectacle of empty classrooms and mobile vans face to face at taxpayer's extra expense. It was also a new step toward a review by the Supreme Court.328

The third example, more egregious than the others, illustrated the seman-tic contortions and procrustean legal gymnastics by which the Court was able to justify direct and indirect tax assistance to private and religious col-leges and universities and, under the same conditions, deny it to elementary and secondary schools. Equitable application of principle is difficult to find: Justice Powell said in effect that he would use history rather than logic. The logic, to put it mildly, was quite elusive.

Universities and colleges professedly religious were allowed to accept government aid for the construction of buildings and the fashioning of spe-cial projects by purchasing state revenue bonds at rates more favorable than in the open market. The monies were to be kept in separate accounts and subject to state review. The Church lower schools, especially the Catholic, the Court said, don't qualify because: "The school is an organism living on one budget. . . . What the tax payers give for salaries of those who teach only the humanities or science without any trace of proselytizing enables the school to use all of its own funds for religious training."329 It was the "one budget transfer theory" but not applicable everywhere.

The lower schools had only one budget and could transfer funds from one department to another, thus effecting indirect and incidental help to religion. How many budgets did a university operate under? And could not the funds be similarly transferred?

The high court dreamt up another distinction: private universities could receive state aid based on student enrollment if the monies were kept in separate accounts and subject to state review. But even if monies to religious elementary schools were kept in separate accounts subject to state review, the "principle" does not apply because it would involve too much state en-tanglement.

The Court plowed on: institutions of higher learning that granted *only* theological degrees (read seminaries) could not receive assistance; but if they granted theological *and* other degrees (read Harvard, Yale, Princeton,

The Catholic University of America, Notre Dame, etc.), then they were eligible. The Catholic Church and other churches did not object to the exclusion of seminaries and welcomed the exclusion of universities practicing racial discrimination.

Thus, tax aid that would manifestly at least be of indirect aid to the teaching of religion in the universities like Harvard and Yale somehow got lost as a principle or even as a practical norm when devolved down to the schools.

What about aid to hospitals? It was, the Court assured, no problem: "The government may of course finance a hospital though it is run by a religious order, provided it is open to all people of all races and creeds. . . . For the hospital is not indulging in religious instruction or guidance or indoctrination."[330]

If it were objected that hospitals financially support chaplains and chapels, minister directly to patients according to their free choice of religion — most Catholic, Jewish, Seventh-Day Adventist, and Protestant hospitals welcome the priests, rabbis, and ministers and clergy of all denominations to visit and to assist patients directly without any undue fuss or disturbance — what happened to the "single budget" test? What of some hospitals with restrictive dietary practices derived from religious beliefs — and that operate on a single budget and hence are open to a "transfer of funds"? The Court blithely answered that they don't "indulge."

Moreover, teachers and administrators at the university level can be trusted with the First Amendment whereas those in religious lower schools cannot, regardless that the official Court records do not in any case support the presumption.

The record shows, the Court said, that a Baptist college has no "religious qualifications for faculty membership or student admission and that only 60% of the college student body is Baptist, a percentage roughly equivalent to the percentage of Baptists in that area of South Carolina."[331] That the lower schools could meet a much more stringent standard showing a much larger percentage of faculty and students not of one faith was dismissed as irrelevant. The Court would accept the record for one but not for the other.

The Baptist Joint Committee on Public Affairs had no qualms about testifying in opposition before Congress on a bill to assist child development, asserting that no grants or contracts should be awarded "pervasively sectarian institutions" because it would be extraordinarily poor public policy.[332] Coming from one of the most sectarian of all mainline denominations, and one with no reservations about accepting funds for colleges with compulsory chapel as well as compulsory Bible courses and Baptist conduct codes, their position never seemed to bother either congressmen or Supreme Court justices, at least in majority numbers.

Over and over again the Court affirmed that university professors could be trusted, while others could not. Patronizingly, Justices Douglas and Black in Machiavellian mode revealed their own basic distrust: "Those who man these (lower) schools are good people, zealous people, dedicated people. But they are dedicated to ideas that the Framers of our Constitution placed beyond the reach of government." Is it not the obvious implication that these are not full-fledged Americans? Dedicated un-Americans? Justice White responded: "Nor can I imagine on what basis the Court finds college clerics more reliable in keeping promises than their counterparts in elementary and secondary schools ... since within five years the majority of teachers ... will be lay persons with many of them being non-Catholic."[333]

If these constraints on the lower schools did not make sense, then it would be necessary to invent new barriers, not to the higher echelons, but to the lower: so was born the "excessive entanglement" theory selectively applied.

While, the Court said, Catholic schoolteachers could be trusted with state-issued textbooks, they could not be trusted with maps, charts, TV sets, test tubes, computers, and other equipment because they might use them in support of religion. Moreover, to supervise them, the state would become "excessively entangled." University professors and administrators, however, would not have the same problem.

But the high court, as we have seen, went even further: public school-teachers under public school administrators could not be trusted to uphold the First Amendment in a Catholic school when teaching the handicapped.

Yet the Court's own record of the absence of complaints was rejected in that case but accepted when applied to universities.

What then was the rationale? The Court stated that at the university level entanglement was "substantially diminished." In the "hypothetical profile," college students are less impressionable, there is a "limited chance to be sectarian," and "many" (sic) of these universities seek to evoke free and critical responses from students. Catholic universities, it continued, admit non-Catholic students and faculty, require theological courses, but don't proselytize or indoctrinate. Even rabbis teach in these universities; nor was there compulsory attendance at religious services. What the U.S. Supreme Court omitted was a hypothetical profile of Protestant and Jewish universities, the direct influence of religion in Brigham Young, Brandeis, University of the Pacific, and hundreds of other denominational colleges and universities. But all passed legal muster, even where chapel attendance was compulsory.

Justices Douglas, Black, and Marshall took direct exception while relying on the same hypothetical profile by Boettner of "parochial schools," even though the case concerned universities. At any rate these justices invoked logic in their opposition, calling the distinction between Catholic universities and lower schools a "sophistry." Using the same criticisms — "sectarian purposes," "enmeshed" teaching between secular and religious, need for surveillance, the operation under one budget, making money available for other purposes, required religious observances, the wealth of the Churches, the vast real-estate holdings, and the departure from James Madison's *Remonstrance* (the whole litany, much of which was clearly a somewhat refined species of Nativism) — their opinion was defeated at the university level but prevailed in most of the decisions at the lower levels.

Thus the same set of circumstances and tortured reasoning supported "parochial schools" (the justices' term) above grade 12 at the university level but rejected "parochial schools" below that magic level.

From a legal point of view, perhaps the most contradictory exercise of jurisprudence lay in the acceptance of the "hypothetical profile" of the "parochial school" from anti-Catholic sources and the reaching of quite opposite conclusions. Justices Warren Burger, John Harlan, and Potter Stewart could assert: "We cannot, however, strike down an Act of Congress on the basis of a hypothetical 'profile.' "[334] So the Court rejected the profile for "parochial school" universities but accepted it for the lower schools. In Justice White's own words: "What appeared to be an insoluble dilemma for the States (to grant aid), however, proved no inseparable barrier to the Federal Government in aiding sectarian institutions of higher learning by direct grants for specified facilities."[335]

Over the years the Court has sought to establish criteria by which legislation in favor of nonpublic schools could pass muster as constitutional or could be rejected as unconstitutional. Early on, the metaphor of the "wall of separation of Church and State" — with the imprimatur of Jefferson's letter to the Baptists, scarcely a legal document, and not found in the First Amendment — proved an inadequate barrier.[336] Consequently, new tests were fabricated.

Legislation should neither promote nor inhibit religious activities of a school: its primary purpose must be secular; and there must be no excessive entanglement between Church and State: it was called the Lemon test after the Supreme Court case.

Some state courts made their own application of the Lemon test. Applying the three-pronged test, the Fourth Appellate District Court of California defended as constitutional invocations and benedictions at public high-school commencement exercises. The graduation ceremonies were "secular," so the prayers had a secular purpose of solemnizing the occasion; the primary effect was to give special importance to the ceremony, with any religious effect remote or incidental, and there was no excessive entanglement because the prayers were not tax supported nor part of the daily educational process.

California Associate Justice McDaniel concurred, saying that the Lemon test was itself flawed and called for a dramatic shift in the interpretation of the First Amendment.

"Just as *Brown v. Board of Education*, . . . represented the triumph of the

202

realization that 'separate but equal' yet represented a denial of equal protection, I earnestly entreat any who will listen that the crisis of irresponsibility now threatening to engulf the nation in anarchy can be laid in part at the door of a wholly distorted view of the establishment clause which a century of well intentioned but misguided decisions has spawned."

Arguing at length that efforts to eliminate all vestiges of religion from society had resulted in the destruction of ethics and morals as well, Justice McDaniel concluded: "The Founding Fathers, for the most part deists, were highly moral and responsible persons; otherwise, the notion of humankind's divine origins are made clear in the Declaration of Independence. What the Founding Fathers were staunchly opposed to was not the practice of religion, but the yoke of a state-imposed religion. In other words, while the framers, in drafting the Constitution, saw as an unmitigated evil the establishment of a state religion, at the same time under the precise language of the First Amendment, they fully expected if not encouraged, unfettered practice of religion as part of the daily lives of the population. Thus, the pronouncement that there be no proscription placed upon the free exercise of religion provides the basis for a sound legal argument that voluntary unprescribed religious observances and activities within the educational framework which do not unduly impinge upon the sensitivities of others are to be protected from a tyranny of the minority and not condemned as impermissible."[337]

Justice McDaniel put his finger on a very key point: the "tyranny of the minority" whereby nothing religious can be allowed in public that offends anyone at all, allowing, as he does, for "an unduly" impingement. He was speaking in December 1989 and obviously not for the U.S. Supreme Court.

Justice White, while accepting the tripart test, took issue with the interpretations of the words "purpose" and "excessive." He protested that "the test is one of primary effect, not any effect." The Court makes no attempt at that ultimate judgment necessarily entailed by the standard "which was previously invoked by the Court." He continued, "It seems to me, preserving the secular functions of these schools is the overriding consequence of these laws and the resulting, but incidental, benefit to religion should not invalidate them. ... It is even more difficult for me to understand why the primary effect of these statutes is to advance religion." The Court had no difficulty in distinguishing primary from incidental effects when favoring government actions.[338]

The National Labor Relations Board had asserted jurisdiction over the nonprofessional staff of a Catholic "Boys Town," Archbishop Hanna Center in Sonoma, California. The U.S. Supreme Court in sustaining this jurisdiction quite readily distinguished the primary effect of the NLRB position and a secondary one while conceding some incidental restrictions on the free-exercise clause of the First Amendment.

"If prohibiting the exercise of religion ... (is) not the object of [the government regulation] but merely the incidental effect of a generally applicable and otherwise valid provision, the First Amendment has not been offended."[339] The high court was in effect sustaining an appellate court's decision that there was only "a minimal showing of impact on religious belief or practice" by governmental regulation of a labor contract.

Thus the state could enforce its laws on collective bargaining and union representation even when they infringed on religious liberty, that is, upon the free-exercise clause, if the enforcement amounted to only an "incidental restriction" and was not the primary purpose or effect. Why was the converse not allowed, that is, that a mathematics class had primarily a secular effect and did not have a primary purpose of advancing religion, even though there might be an incidental or minor effect of helping the student in a religiously oriented school? And to help the student is incidentally to help the school!

If the Court could make such distinctions, why could they not be applied to schools: the teaching of secular subjects like mathematics, science, reading, writing, speech, which manifestly do have primarily a secular purpose, with "only a minimal showing of impact on religious belief or practice"? "Primary purpose" and "minimal impact" and "merely the incidental effect of a generally applicable and otherwise valid provision" would go a long way to solve the school question without offending the First Amendment.

Until 1970 the Supreme Court used only two tests; then the third, "excessive entanglement," was introduced, and finally yet a fourth test: religion as a divisive force in the political order. Coming from a Court out of a liberal tradition, this last was quite astonishing. In effect, it said that legislation must be politically correct.

"Ordinarily political debate and division, however vigorous and even partisan, are normal and healthy manifestations of our democratic system of government, but political division along religious lines was one of the principal evils against which the First Amendment was intended to protect. The potential divisiveness of such conflict is a threat to the normal political process."[340]

This dictum was in obvious contradiction to the previous Walz case, which said that "adherents of particular faiths and individual churches frequently take strong positions on public issues. We could not expect otherwise," the Lemon case Court replied; the Walz case was "for the benefit of all religious groups," whereas the case before it would benefit "a relatively small" group in the religious sector, that is, the Catholic.

This excursion into the field of political correctness really boiled down once again to the "relatively small groups," which without question in the case meant "Catholic." That this judgment is not imagined or invidiously imputed to the Court, its very next section piously added: "Finally, nothing we have said can be construed to disparage the role of church-related elementary and secondary schools in our national life." But it concluded that religion must be a private matter. Thus it was the nineteenth-century judgment: push religion back into private life, into the sacristy. And this from a professedly "liberal court."

Some scholars, liberals among them, have seriously questioned the Court's use of history, especially by Rutledge and Brennan. Paul Freund, a Harvard law professor and certified liberal, raised the point: "The accuracy and sufficiency of Mr. Justice Rutledge's examination of history which produced the First Amendment has been questioned by scholars, theologians, polemicists and judges." Rutledge took an absolutist position that the state could not assist any religious activity or church. Law professor Edward Corwin protested also: ". . . the question arises, how far a court is entitled to indulge in bad history and bad logic without having its good faith challenged."[341]

Accusing Justice Rutledge of manipulating James Madison's *Memorial and Remonstrance* to read as a denial of all aid to religion as such and to infuse this meaning of the First Amendment, Corwin commented: "All in all it is fairly evident that Justice Rutledge sold his brethren a bill of goods when he persuaded them that 'the establishment of religion' clause of the First Amendment was intended to rule out all governmental 'aid to all religion.' "[342]

Also questioning the strained employment of early American history, Dr. Alexander Meicklejohn asserted that "in the interpreting of our spiritual beliefs is a public enterprise of the highest order. . . . The shift in meaning of Jefferson's 'wall of separation' is a striking illustration of the change from the organic to the mechanical interpretation of a figure of speech. . . . But men who claim to follow him have transformed his figure into one of mechanical divisions and exclusion. They speak of his wall as if it were made of brick or stone. . . . They make private a matter of supreme 'public importance.' "[343]

The widely disparate and curiously anomalous treatment of the teachers, parents, and pupils of religious schools stands in contradiction to all true liberalism. If the question in abortion is to live or not to live, the true liberal *a priori* would stand on the side of life; on assistance to minority students; on the side of liberality; on the right to protest; clearly against anything that savored of political correctness; on the side of pluralism rather than monopoly; on the rights of individuals *vis-à-vis* the state.

Nor have the conservatives in the political order followed their own dicta favoring private enterprise, less government, a full and open competition in the market place (for example, in education), family rights, subsidiarity, and the like. The only President to date who has publicly spoken out unequivocally in favor of equal rights for all pupils has been Ronald Reagan. True, he did not translate his position into effective action, yet his voice was enunciating a basic principle that needed to see the light of day. George Bush moved in the same direction in January 1992 in proposing "choice" for all parents.

Over the years many members of Congress have fought for equal rights in education, notably Congressman James Delaney of Brooklyn. But they did not receive sufficient support even from the Catholics and others who had a real stake in the question. The situation has not changed appreciably. Two members of Congress have, however, championed equal rights in education.

Republican Senator Robert Packwood asked the Library of Congress to answer two questions: (1) whether state aid to private Church-related schools was a fairly common practice in the United States at least during the first half of the nineteenth century, and (2) whether such aid violated relevant federal constitutional safeguards. The answer was "yes" to the first and "no" to the second. The Library of Congress added that "in America from 1770 to 1820 . . . all or almost all the schools . . . were private, religious and public supported, that is, denominational schools received public school funds."[344]

The latest barrier has become, however, political correctness. Democrat Senator Daniel Patrick Moynihan pleaded for equal justice: "This has not been a matter of educational quality. . . . In the main the nonpublic schools are just as good, and, in the main, startlingly cheaper.

"It has been a matter of ideology, of legitimacy. It is not enough to say that public schools provide the basic educational resource to the republic. . . . It became necessary to stigmatize the other schools as 'foreign' or 'elitist,' or threatening."[345]

Moynihan spotted Nativism in the public debate: the un-American "ideology" of allegiance to a foreign potentate; "illegitimate" because the Catholic schools were not accepting the First Amendment; of "foreign" origin and currently devoted to an alien pattern; and a wealthy "elite" besides.

The high court was seen to erect ever newer barriers, whether appealing to history, logic, or political correctness. Constitutional lawyer William Ball of Pennsylvania, who had successfully pleaded the U.S. Supreme Court Yoder case in favor of the Amish people in their choice of schools or even school at home, summed up what he perceived as the "new doctrine."

He said: "Freedom of religion, the first of what the Court once called the 'conjunctive freedoms of the First Amendment,' is seen in somewhat a different light by the Supreme Court. One aspect of this is seen in the Establishment Clause cases involving aid to religious schools, or better put, to parents choosing religious schools. Under the absolutist views expressed in these cases, religion necessarily becomes a suspect force. So secularized must our institutions be if a parent is to be aided in the enrollment of his child in such a school, religion must not be allowed to 'seep in' — to borrow a curious phrase of the Court — to programs and activities. But a deeper root of the unwillingness of the Court to go all out for religious liberty comes from an insistent view, never universal with the Court, but never universally disavowed by the Court, *that religion is a divisive force.* This was most frequently expressed in Lemon v. Kurtzman. In Lemon v. Kurtzman's interesting essay on political entanglements a more bizarre and censorious doctrine was never dreamed up by the justices than the notion that a statute adopted by a legislature may be invalidated on the ground that it will cause 'religious division along political *lines*'. . . this doctrine originated in Lemon — an aid to religious schools case"[346] — "no aid to religion" has no roots in Colonial America. It is a twentieth-century construct lifted from the 1947 Everson case.

During the debate on Senator Kennedy's education bill in January 1992, the research division of the Library of Congress rendered a "constitutional analysis" of an amendment that would provide parents with a "choice" in education.

"Any government assistance to private religious schools involves a constitutional risk that in so doing government will promote religion. But notwithstanding that risk, not all such assistance is forbidden. . . . The proposed amendment for choice at least on its face does not seem to offend the Establishment Clause. The secular purpose and the non-preferential character wherein both public and non-public school youngsters are targeted do not have 'the primary effect of advancing religion.' "

But what of entanglement? Excessive entanglement "is a matter of degree, and, thus, is highly fact specific." If inextricably intertwined, then direct assistance even to secular functions is forbidden. What then of indirect assistance?

Two programs were struck down; two were upheld. Indirect assistance was validated if *all* parents of school-age children were included who made their own private choices, that is, "genuinely independent" and "no significant portion of aid" flowed to religious education. Thus the Library of Congress Research Service pointed out the two avenues of progress: "breadth of the beneficiary class and the element of genuine choice"; such would not have the primary effect of advancing religion contrary to the establishment clause.[347]

This new doctrine of excessive entanglement, with its ever-increasing barriers, presented the religious sector with what Justice Rehnquist perceived to be an insuperable contradiction, a Catch-22 situation of damned if you do and damned if you don't: "The Court thus creates an insoluble paradox for the State and the parochial schools. The State cannot finance secular instruction if it permits religion to be taught in the same classroom; but if it exacts a promise that religion not be so taught — a promise that teachers are quite willing and on this record able to give — and enforce it, it is then entangled in the 'no entanglement' aspect of the Court's Establishment Clause jurisprudence."[348]

Is there a way out that will do violence to neither the establishment clause nor the free-exercise clause? Constitutional lawyer Dr. Edward S. Corwin suggested a solution that the courts might take a better look at the First Amendment's words "respecting religion." He argued that the phrase "laws respecting religion" should act as a two-way sword, meaning that the state may pass no laws that "disfavor" as well as "favor" an establishment of religion.

If tax aid, for example, were denied on *a priori* grounds, the denial would be unfair and positively hostile to the free exercise of religion; it would not be "respecting" religion as the literal word is used in the First Amendment. Similarly, if the state can enforce laws that only incidentally and in an indirect and minor way infringe on religious liberty but still respecting it, why does it not work the other way, which it already does at the college level, for the religious schools with the secular purpose being secure and inviolate but with minor side effects?[349]

With what seems almost a sigh of resignation White, with Burger and Rehnquist, wrote that "no one contends that he can discern from the sparse language of the Establishment Clause that a State is forbidden to aid religion in any manner whatsoever or, if it does not mean that, what kind or how much aid is permissible.

"And one cannot seriously believe that the history of the First Amendment furnishes unequivocal answers to many of the fundamental issues of church-state relations. In the end the courts have fashioned answers to these questions as best *they* can. . . ."[350]

Since 1947 the U.S. Supreme Court has rendered many decisions that address the two areas delineated in Vatican II's "Declaration on Religious Liberty": the freedom of religion within government schools and the freedom of choice to parents and to pupils who wish to attend nonpublic schools.

One series of decisions effectively secularized the public schools. As William Ball put it: "The Court in its 1963 decision in the Schempp case told the country that it was not — but its banning of Bible reading and the Lord's Prayer therein, and by implication all religious observances — establishing a religion of secularism; but that in fact it did."

Ball added: "Nature abhors a vacuum. Take theistic religion out and other religions will flow in. The Court in 1961 in the Torcaso case told us about such other religions, naming secular humanism as one of them."[351]

Shades of the abortion decision when Chief Justice Burger affirmed strongly for the media that the Roe vs. Wade decision did not allow abortion on demand, only years later to admit that it did! His own words were: "Plainly the Court today rejects any claim that the Constitution requires abortion on demand." It was true that abortion was not compulsory but contrary to his intention, as he later stated with regret, the decision effectively promoted abortion on demand. Roe vs. Wade had a companion decision, Doe vs. Bolton, which defined a mother's health so broadly that it negated completely the trimester theory of Justice Blackmun. In June 1983, the Senate Judiciary Committee reported that the two cases left "no significant barriers" to abortion at any stage.[352]

The point here about schools is similar. In spite of the protestations of some justices that they are not favoring irreligion or even antireligion in the schools, they most assuredly are. Secular humanism is atheistic, anti-religious, basically antifamily, with its own votaries organized into tax-exempt groups, recognized in law and at the same time its ideology supported by fellow travelers in the schools and media.

Heavily values-loaded programs that are contrary to the religious and moral convictions of parents have been introduced into public schools. The invasion of familial privacy by the introduction into the public schools of deeply offensive, thoroughly loathsome, grossly vulgar, and morally repug-nant teachings and practices has appalled millions of Americans, no matter their religion or beliefs.

Under the umbrella of "health" education and care, planned parenthood types have imposed clinics on the schools that teach a libertine philosophy of sex, complete with the free dispensing of contraceptives, the advocacy of "free but safe sex," referrals to abortion clinics, and experiments in sex education and practices usually imposed in those schools that serve minority populations. Homosexuality is defended as an acceptable alternative life-style, even in the early grades. "Just Say No" programs are enthusiastically endorsed when alcohol and tobacco are at issue but not sexual activity, which is condoned openly "if safe."[353] Undergirding these programs lies a basic secular humanism.

Quite contrary to the allegation that Catholic and other parents are against sex education rather than against the usual type propagated in many of the common schools, the Vatican Council explicitly taught, in respect of family and human nature, that in "the harmonious development of their (the pupils') physical, moral, and intellectual endowments . . . with a mature sense of responsibility . . . toward authentic freedom, as they advance in years, they should be given positive and prudent sexual education" ("Declaration on Education," No. 1). Parental objections may well extend to more basic ideologies than the "sexual revolution"; secular humanism as an ideology encompasses more than sex and appears on the scene in many varieties.

Programs (for example, the New Age, the Magic Circle, the Untouch-ables, the Quest, and Skills for Adolescents), groups based on Eastern mysti-cal mind-control systems, and a plethora of clubs and gangs — sometimes elitist and rich, steeped in segregation and exclusivity, sometimes grossly trespassing the limits a family would wish for its youngsters — are promoted in and out of schools.

The point, of course, is not so much the validity of any one or all the criticisms but rather — given the fact that parents of whatever persuasion find willy-nilly their moral and spiritual sensibilities outraged — what recourse do parents have? The bottom line is that secular humanism has gotten a foothold in many school systems; parents as well as childless taxpayers are required to support them. The alternative could be a nonpublic school, but for the vast majority the choice has too big a financial price.

Most democratic countries around the world do afford parents some freedom of choice, some alternative to government schools. Voluntary schools, including religious ones, are accepted as bona fide cooperators in education, a field of primary importance needing the support of all society.

Neither the U.S. courts nor its legislators stand in conformity with a worldwide judgment on the matter of free choice in education.

The "Universal Declaration of Human Rights" of 1948 of the United Nations was explicit: "Parents have the prior right to choose the kind of education that shall be given their children. . . . Education shall be free at least in the elementary stage" (Article 16). The European Convention on Human Rights asserted that "everyone has the right to freedom of thought, conscience and religion. . . . The States shall respect the rights of parents to ensure such education and teaching (be) in conformity with their own religious and philosophical convictions" (First Protocol). The Inter-American Convention on Human Rights affirmed that "parents . . . have the right to provide for the religious and moral education of their children . . . that is in accord with their own convictions" (Article 12).

It should be carefully noted that no attempt has been made here to differentiate among the many opinions, concurrences, and dissents of the justices of the Supreme Court. Rather the attempt was to show the diversity of opinion, the tenor of thinking, and the attitudes that encompassed the Court as it wrestled with the "school question." Even those opinions and dissents that did not translate into *res judicata*, aside from other considerations, are very important and influential in the education of the American people in social, political, and religious areas of life, not to mention the lower courts and legislatures.

Perhaps it should be left to Chief Justice Burger to have the last word: "One can only hope that at some future date the Court will come to a more enlightened and tolerant view of the First Amendment's guarantee of the free exercise of religion thus eliminating the denial of equal protection to children in church-sponsored schools and take a more realistic view that carefully limited aid to children is not a step towards establishing a state religion — or at least while this Court sits."[354]

Chapter 14

The Acquiescence of the Media

The Irish-born statesman Edmund Burke paid a compliment to the power of the press when he told the British Parliament that while there were three estates present — the King, the nobles, and the commons — yet "in the reporters' gallery there sat a Fourth Estate more important than them all." This observation was seconded in a negative way by Theodore Hook: "A reply to a newspaper attack resembles very much the attempt of Hercules to crop the Hydra, without the slightest chance of ultimate success." Hook ignored the fact that Hercules, after many attempts, did ultimately succeed. But the same point was made by the president of the American Newspaper Publishers Association in 1936: "The daily press has more power in the shaping of public opinion than any other force in America." In the 1990s, he would surely add both radio and television as does Alvin Toffler.

This best-selling author and observer of modern civilization pointed out that "without even intending it, Murdoch and Maxwell, Turner and Mohn, Berlusconi and other new media magnates are creating a powerful new tool and placing it in the hands of the global community. But that hardly scratches the surface of what is happening."[355] Toffler included talk-show producers "who depend on fax, computers, word processors, electronic typesetters, digitized imagery, electronic networks, satellites and other interlinked technologies . . . which endow the media system as a whole with an enormously enhanced power that permeates the planet."[356]

Often the media are charged as blameworthy — quite unjustly — because they report either bad news or news with which one disagrees. The presumption must always be that the mainline media, as distinguished from the narrow, biased special pleaders in both print and electronic, are genuinely interested in being fair, objective, and equitable, with a professional disinterestedness in both reporting and editorial comment. But as in law, presumption yields to contrary evidence.

The question here then is not so much whether the media have shown themselves in certain narrow circumstances to be anti-Catholic but that such anti-Catholicism has contributed substantially, given the acknowledged power of the media, to a modern Nativism. Here the facts must speak for themselves.

Over the past two decades the media have accorded excellent coverage of the bishops' meetings and messages on a variety of subjects such as nuclear war, the economy, peace in Central America and the Middle East, racial justice for the Hispanic and black U.S. populations, and many other topics. Further they have provided Americans with an insight into the Catholic

Church's worldwide relief efforts on all continents with a ringside seat at major events in Rome and during papal journeys.

However, the record shows that the media in general seem to lose their sense of balance when the two issues of the nineteenth and twentieth centuries, namely the place of Catholic schools in American education and the matter of abortion, are broached. There are many causes wherein the media moguls and pundits may well and do disagree with the Catholic general public: prayer in the schools, ambassador to the Vatican, contraception, pornography, nudity in public, and so forth. Many Catholics disagree also in some of these causes. But these disagreements do not escalate into Nativism as do the two mentioned above precisely because the patriotism, loyalty, and the integrity of Catholics as citizens are clearly and manifestly impugned.

The American media — TV, radio, and print — guilelessly proclaim their impartiality in reporting the news and their balance in editorial opinion. After World War II they moved in ever-increasing crescendo against unjust discrimination, at times simply following the Supreme Court, at other times taking the lead against the various forms of racism ahead of the courts. Blacks, since they were the most aggrieved, attracted the most attention; Jews — who are at once a people, a nation, and a race — garnered protection under the rubric of race; and Hispanics and Asians gradually attained similar protection in the media.

Noting that much progress had been made in the field of race, historian John Higham added that "except for the subject of race (and related forms of anti-Semitism) the kind of accusations which nativists leveled against foreign elements remained relatively constant. Anti-radical and anti-Catholic complaints in the 20th Century sounded much like those bruited in the 18th."

If Jews, Afro-Americans, and the newly-arrived refugees from Southeast Asia and the migrants from Mexico and Latin America met hostile and indeed un-American bigotry and unconscionable opposition, the basis was race. Catholics, on the other hand, met opposition not because of race but because they "wanted state aid (for schools), ... wanted the Bibles out of schools, and [wanted] equality of treatment with the Protestants in the fields of health, charities, social work and the like."357 Things had not changed essentially from the nineteenth century except that the Catholic Church among others wanted to keep the public schools, where most of their children attended, free from the secular religion. Perhaps it all came down to a definition of Americanism and who was American.

For example, the German Kaiser (during World War I) and then Adolf Hitler (during World War II) replaced the Pope as the *bête noire* of the Western world — but only temporarily. The point was well-taken: America had gradually and painfully expelled *de jure* racial discrimination from its laws and taken giant steps to eliminate *de facto* discrimination. Could the same be predicated about Catholicism, since the rubric of race would not apply: Catholics were not a people, a nation, or a race? Evidently the same protections did not apply.

The media to their everlasting glory carried the banners of equality of treatment and of social justice, especially in reference to race.

The protestations of innocence, of impartiality, of evenhandedness by the media — that they have indeed exorcised the devil of anti-Catholicism in their works and pomps — never were very convincing to Catholics who were suffering what they perceived to be both *de jure* and *de facto* discrimination.

The never-ending opposition of most of the major dailies to even a modicum of benefits for the voluntary school pupils, teachers, and parents, most often directed at the overwhelming majority of whom were Catholic, often pictured as robbing the treasury, always violating the First Amendment, the public schools being hailed as "American," leaving a la Conant the others in a limbo; vicious anti-Catholic school cartoons by Nobel Prize winner Patrick Oliphant and many others; the solid wall against even a soupçon of pupil assistance by the *New York Times*, the *Washington Post, USA Today*, and other monarchs of the dailies never aroused either the public or the Catholic to a realization of the unfairness and inequities in the education scene. Nor were they seen for what they really are: the media in support of those powerful organizations intent on ridding the U.S. of the Catholic school.

The unconscionable attacks on the Catholic schools by Albert Shanker, president of the AFL-CIO's American Federation of Teachers, were duly printed week by week in the *New York Times* as paid advertisements, the same *Times* that refused to accept paid advertisements in favor of a play entitled "How to Make Love to a Negro without Getting Tired." Blacks and the black media found this production deeply offensive, and rightly so. The civil liberties groups such as the ACLU kept their peace: no freedom of speech involved, no First Amendment here.

The *New York Times*, which had such a scruple about "one-issue campaigns" (abortion), had no such scruples about Shanker and his diatribes against Catholic schools. Quite properly he had the right to oppose measures that would help nonpublic schoolchildren with tax credits and tax vouchers as proposed by Senators Moynihan and Packwood in 1982. But he called for a single-issue treatment of legislators, that is, on this one issue they would vote him or her up or down. The public school role as instruments for national unity, respect for democratic institutions, and for free and disciplined inquiry were in jeopardy by tuition tax credits, he wrote constantly. If there were any doubts that Shanker was flirting with Nativism, his conclusion left no room: "There can be no doubt that tax credits will mean more and more students in nonpublic schools, Catholic schools, fundamentalist schools, Jewish schools, black schools, Ku Klux Klan schools, a handful of Marxist schools. . . ."[358]

But when Catholics found several plays on stage, in the movies, and on TV equally offensive, with attacks on convent life, the ridicule of the Virgin Mary, a sodomized Christ, the scorning of the birth of Christ, Catholics were un-American to protest: the American Civil Liberties Union and allies said so and the media, by and large, supported the ACLU and its followers. The First Amendment, of course!

The ACLU has been most selective in its professed devotion to due process and evenhanded justice. The author of *The First Freedom*, Nat Hentoff, wrote trenchantly on the cases where helpless, disabled infants were allowed to die without even normal care: "Not once has an ACLU affiliate spoken for the infant's right to due process and equal protection under the law. Indeed when the ACLU has become involved, it has fought resolutely for the parents' right to privacy. . . .

"Along with my fellow civil libertarians, most liberals strongly support parents and only parents in those situations. It is hard to imagine anyone more powerless than a handicapped baby . . . but to my knowledge no organization of liberals nor civil rights group has ever said a word about the rights of Baby Doe. Nor has any feminist group, even though the civil rights and liberties being violated in these infanticides are not only those of males."[359]

When Catholics and other Christians, usually Fundamentalists, complained about the obscene art being exhibited with tax money — grotesque sex, urination on a crucifix, rape with a cross, etc. — they were pilloried as Puritans and bluenoses "reciting from a common liturgy of intolerance" but, worse, as "un-American." Not all the media nor all editorialists condoned these "artistic" atrocities, but the preponderant majority of the major news services did. There was no equality of treatment.

The media have long persisted in maintaining certain myths: first, that the Roe vs. Wade decision put trimester limits on abortion, which in fact it did not in practice; second, that the pro-lifers were interested only in seeing a child born but then deserting them; and third, that the Catholic schools were taking money out of public school coffers and, in effect, books out of the hands of pupils.

The admission of the effect of abortion on demand by Chief Justice Burger who admitted his mistake should have dispelled the first myth. Since Catholics are in the vanguard of pro-life they can point to almost 20,000 parishes, 640 hospitals, 1,350 specialized homes, 197 orphanages, 749 day-care centers, 1,701 social-service centers, 235 universities and colleges, 1,421 high schools, 7,517 elementary schools, 105 schools for the handicapped: scarcely a record of neglect after birth! Yet as late as January 29, 1992, columnist Ellen Goodman repeated that myth.

The taking of money from the public schools is a deceptive charge. It is true that if a youngster attends a nonpublic school, the government school will not be paid for that child's nonattendance. But the money is not out of the public school budget as the media allow people to believe. Actually it is the taxpayers who benefit, even if a tax credit or voucher should be granted by the state because the great disparity in cost is borne not by the taxpayer but by the family. Justices Burger and White called the savings "enormous" and a savings of money to the public school itself, as already noted.

But the media, by and large, repeat these myths as gospel and beyond debate, much less subjects for analysis. The litany goes on.

The media customarily identify pro-lifers as Catholics, Evangelicals, Fundamentalists, fanatics, or members of the "radical right." Pro-abortionists, on the other hand, are never labeled as left-wingers, Protestant, Jewish, or atheist, even when such a label was relevant. CNN's owner, Ted Turner, called the pro-lifers "bozos" and "idiots."

Time reported that the Oak Park, Illinois, City Council halted a local hospital from putting up a cross on its own building (which was privately owned) "because some people would be offended," asserting the secularist creed that religion should be private only and without any thought of the patently obscene and offensive displays supported, not by private funds, but with tax money.[360] The ACLU kept its usual selective silence as did most if not all the nation's editorialists who profess such devotion to the First Amendment but scarcely to its free-exercise clause.

The foul-mouthed comedian Andrew Dice Clay was quite rightly castigated as "racist and sexist" by the media but not as anti-Catholic or antireligious. The TV critic for the *New York Times* wrote that Clay had crossed a "revulsion threshold" in his attacks on gays, women, and various ethnic groups. Evidently the *Times* had no "revulsion threshold" for attacks on religion in general and Catholics in particular. When New York columnist Jimmy Breslin called a Korean-American reporter "a yellow cur" and "slant-eyed," he was censured and fired by the *Daily News* and soon moved over to *Newsday*. Michael Levi, a New York City college professor of philosophy who teaches that blacks are "intellectually inferior," was lambasted by black Mayor Dinkins for "poisoning the minds with racism and bigotry." The New York media applauded the mayor; the freedom-of-expression groups again remained silent.

When baseball executive Al Campanis of the Los Angeles Dodgers on the Ted Koppel show made a remark about black athletes' lack of ability in the executive areas of baseball, he was fired from his job. When sportscaster "Jimmy the Greek" (Dimitrios Synodinos) gave a similar opinion on TV he was forthwith dismissed; when Victor Kiam impugned the objections of a white female reporter who had entered his football team's locker room, he was pilloried from coast to coast as an antifeminist and threatened with boycotts of his company's shaving products. Racial and feminist slurs rightly are no longer acceptable in the U.S.A.

In an interesting judgment of the Gulf War of 1991, with its one hundred thousand dead, *Time*'s ace columnist Lance Murrow (in the April 1, 1991, issue of the magazine) deplored the taking of life and the callousness with which people dismiss killings, particularly of those they do not like. In something of a peroration, he declaimed: ". . . to kill a snake, a roach, a pest, a Jew, a scorpion, a black, a centipede, a Palestinian, a hyena, an Iraqi, a wild dog, an Israeli . . . it's OK?"

Notice that he conveniently omits two categories: he shows no conscience on the killing of the unborn, surely as much a concern as the killing of a roach or a snake; similarly he does not include religious prejudice but only racial and environmental concern. He very conveniently picks and chooses while appearing to be consistent and principled.

Happily race has come to enjoy equal protection not only under the laws but has been given the same protection by the media; religion evidently has not. While obloquy, calumny, and detraction against religious groups and churches do not enjoy nearly the shield of protection in the media equal to that enjoyed by races, the slightest slip of the tongue about Afro-Americans or Jews has cost prominent men their jobs. Can the same be said of anti-Catholic utterances, for example, of cartoonists Patrick Oliphant, Mike Peters, or Taylor Jones?[361]

The revival in 1990 of the very popular Dick Tracy of comic-book and broadcast-media fame was aborted immediately when Japanese Americans objected to the slant-eyed characterizations; the same thing happened when Mexican Americans protested the sleepy stereotypes, depictions that were tolerated fifty years ago along with minstrel shows. Rightly these revivals were condemned as insults to racial groups; the content did count and is not irrelevant in America. Again there were no outcries of censorship by the ACLU; no one in respectable quarters cried out that no one was going to tell him what to read or what to see or how to make up his mind for him. Prejudice against a racial group was no longer acceptable tender in America either *de jure* or *de facto*.

Similarly the media generously responded to the National Organization for Women, NOW, when it bitterly protested a popular song of the recording star Holly Dunn. The title "Maybe I Mean Yes" and the text were seen as provocative to rape, playing on 134 radio stations across the country. Again there was no charge of censorship as in the case of a church protest; there was no strident affirmation of free speech, the ACLU silent instead of invoking the First Amendment. The conclusion in this and a myriad of similar cases was clearly that it mattered greatly who was protesting.

While Protestant Fundamentalists and Evangelicals along with Catholics have suffered much abuse because of their positions on pornography, public profanity, and other lesser issues like crèches at Christmas and prayer in the public school, it was the Catholic Church in its position on abortion that brought the historical battles out of the woodwork: a neo-Nativism.

Was there no limit? Professor David H. Bennett in 1988 went so far as to write incredibly that neo-Nativism is really a tool of the new right, that Nativism died with restricted immigration. Further he identified both Catholics and Communists as enemies of the far right. What of the far left? "The men and women of the Left can be pictured as heroic losers; persevering but not prevailing in the struggle for justice and equality, fighting to help the poor, the powerless, the alienated; those on the Right often appear only as the deranged or malevolent enemies of American freedom."[362]

Yet in spite of this inverted history and rosy description, the identification of Catholics with the far right has become a club to isolate the Catholic community from mainstream America while its members who profess to be "pro-choice" are acceptable. As already pointed out, Catholics and Fundamentalists do intersect in a very few instances, and markedly so on abortion along with Mormons, Orthodox Jews, Muslims, and others. Editorially many papers insist on extending the identification far beyond the facts. Fundamentalists and Evangelicals are easier targets. Perhaps the old cliché applies here: "Politics makes strange bedfellows." To report the facts is one thing; to use them as a club and smear tactic editorially is quite another.

All the tired arguments of the nineteenth and early twentieth centuries have been taken out of mothballs, dusted off, and hurled relentlessly against the Catholic Church and its members. It was un-American to be anti-abortion; it was a violation of the separation of Church and State; it was taking foreign dictation from that long arm of the potentate in Rome. The media, supported in "respectable" circles, even including some Catholics, had their issue (abortion) and their target (Catholics, especially the bishops). Abortion and the Church became inseparable; Nativism had its new yet old target.

By a strange twist of logic the Pope appeared in cartoons as the world's leading murderer by keeping babies alive to starve later; U.S. Cardinals John O'Connor and Bernard Law and the Catholic bishops were depicted as enemies of the people. For twenty years since 1970 the media in majority numbers lost all pretense at objectivity in the matter: many reporters became special pleaders; columnists, with some exceptions, champions of the "choice" to kill; and editorialists, utter partisans. The nineteenth-century menace, the Catholic Church, was propelled into the same role as the twentieth- and even twenty-first-century menace. And it was isolated in the media.

Very rarely, if ever, was there identified the Jewish position on abortion partly because there was no one position. Yet large sections of Jews, especially Orthodox and Conservative, had an ancient tradition against abortion. The Alexandrian school taught that a life for a life applied to the fetus. Philo made distinctions between formed and unformed fetuses; if the fetus was formed (usually forty days), then killing it was a capital crime. Maimonides, one of the three greatest Jews named Moses, applied the law even to the

Gentiles: "A son of Noah (i.e., a gentile) who kills a person, even a fetus in its mother's womb, is capitally liable . . . so that society will not corrupt itself." Similarly Rabbi Unterman in 1940, in the face of the thalidomide deformation of the unborn, asserted quite emphatically: "This seems to me very much like the laws of Lycurgus, King of Sparta, according to which any blemished child should be killed. But to do it (by abortion) for fear of what might be the child's lot — the secrets of God are none of (our) business. We have no law which permits us to deny life to one who is wounded."[363] In spite of the time-honored tradition, rabbis of the Orthodox conservative communities tended to remain silent while the Reform rabbis in large numbers became vociferous proponents of abortion.

The isolation of the Catholic Church, specifically its hierarchy, as a lone voice in the question, became the *modus operandi* of most of the media. That Jews and Mormons in theory and practice might agree with Catholics on abortion was never, if ever, mentioned in the media. Catholic bishops were pictured as antediluvian, out of touch, unscientific, irrelevant, insensitive, celibate, and thus isolated, all un-American, all in shades and tones not dissimilar to those used in the nineteenth century.

Dr. Bernard Nathanson, who conducted the largest abortion clinic for some years in New York and who was a co-founder of NARAL, the National Abortion Rights Action League, was treated as a pariah by the media when he changed his mind and became a spokesman for the other side.[364] His videocassette *The Silent Scream* was proscribed by almost all American TV stations — without a word from the ACLU or People for the American Way, both dedicated to free speech, they say. He even admitted that when asked how many deaths there were in America from illegal abortions, he made up a figure of ten thousand per year "out of whole cloth." He has labeled the abortion organization NARAL as virulently anti-Catholic: he witnessed its operations from the inside. Nathanson's second cassette on abortion was also turned down by most TV stations: "Too controversial, too hot to handle, un-American."

"The secular media," the doctor said, "are very biased towards pro-abortion. The *New York Times*, for example, refused to review *Aborting America* (his book) but even refused to handle a piece I co-authored for the *Times* op ed page — which is the mark of a third rate, small town newsrag, not a great newspaper of the sort the *Times* presumes to be."[365] He added his own identification: "I'm Jewish in the sense that I have a Jewish heritage and traditions, but I don't believe in God."[366]

Similarly the media gave little or no attention to Rabbi Yehusa Levin, a thirty-seven-year-old associate rabbi at Congregation Beth Isaac in Brooklyn. For years he has led the opening invocation at the March for Life and has been arrested with Bishop Austin Vaughan and Randall Terry of Operation Rescue. As an Orthodox Jew Levin affirms that there is no question that the Talmud considers feticide a capital crime. As a minority within a minority the Orthodox are often discouraged in the public forum while quite successful in maintaining Jewish identity. "We must oppose (secularists). The liberal elements (of Judaism) are definitely guilty of overkill and have definitely done a lot of harm. It is not in our interest, as Orthodox Jews, to make it more difficult for people to be religious," the rabbi affirmed in a news interview.[367]

The Charlotte Observer of North Carolina published a cartoon showing Christ holding a plate with a loaf of bread and saying: "Take this all of you and eat it . . . unless you're pro-choice or divorced or gay or on birth control." The title was: "If Jesus were a Catholic bishop."[368] The blasphemy on the Last Supper was quite evident, the question of abortion primary, and the villain was the Catholic bishop.

All around the country feminist groups as well as organized gays disrupted Catholic services, harassed the clergy and laity, and vandalized church buildings. During 1990 and into 1991 six churches in Los Angeles were broken into, paint sprayed on their walls, and damage done to fixtures. San Francisco's Cathedral of St. Mary was similarly vandalized. People attending Mass were threatened and intimidated. The special target, however, was Cardinal O'Connor and St. Patrick's Cathedral in New York City. Peaceful picketing and freedom of expression was one thing; invasion another.

The cardinal's Mass was disrupted by militant feminists and gays; the Blessed Sacrament trampled on and desecrated, even to being taken outside the Church "in triumph," the Church decorated with condoms, and venomous demonstrations continued outside.

To its credit the press condemned the invasion as a violation of freedom of speech and assembly; however, in the words of *Newsweek* reporter John Leo, the media "tut-tutted the desecration of the Host but praised the 'peaceful demonstration' outside." Leo continued: "It was a classic hate rally, very likely the most bitter anti-Catholic one conducted since the heyday of the Know Nothings."[369]

In defiance of a court order, again in December of 1990, another consecrated host was gleefully held up as booty outside the cathedral. In both New York and San Francisco, the gay parades featured Christ in ridiculous and obscene costume carrying a cross, men in drag dressed as nuns, "bishops" in paper miters, publicity for an off-Broadway poisonous monologue entitled "The Cardinal Detoxes," to which people were offered free admission if they came dressed as priests or nuns. It was a straight-out hate campaign. A catalog featuring an AIDS show, partly funded by the National Endowment for the Arts, tells that "Cardinal O'Connor is a fat cannibal in skirts, his Cathedral a house of walking swastikas." The media, in most cases, featured these hate orgies. It was one thing to report them, quite another to remain "neutral" editorially.

The fact having been established, the point should not be missed. When Catholics or bishops or others move into public policy they must expect response, and where abortion is concerned as well as homosexuality, there is bound to be heated reaction. The point rather concerns the media forming public opinion.

Let John Leo, a man of impeccable liberal credentials, make the point: he noted that columnist Sydney Schanberg of *Newsday*, for example, couldn't find any disrespect in what happened; "not one columnist or editorial writer showed any awareness of the intense campaign by gays against the Roman Catholic Church"; the drowning out vocally of a Mass in Boston's Cathedral of the Holy Cross was described in the *Boston Globe* as "colorful, loud and peaceful," without mentioning the pelting of people with condoms.

"The media are having unusual trouble describing gay attacks on Catholics, much more trouble than they have with outrages toward other minorities. Famous newspapers and commentators who scour language for the faintest hint of insensitivity to gays, blacks and women showed little interest in this footstomping bigotry.

"The anti-Catholics, since they are covered by the racial or minority category, are instantly listened to by the media," commented John Leo.

The desecration of the Holy Eucharist and the storm-trooper invasion of the New York cathedral were preserved by a video sponsored and produced by the very perpetrators of the outrage, the gay coalition named Act Up. The production of the TV programs called *Stop the Church* was judged too offensive for national viewing by PBS (Public Broadcasting System) but not by its Los Angeles affiliate Station KCET. In September 1991, it ran the venomous, malicious, and spiteful piece over the vigorous protests of the local Catholics, clergy, and laity alike as did other stations around the U.S., including KQED of San Francisco.

Exasperated Catholics were described by William Bennett, the former U.S. secretary of education and later anti-drug czar, in this light: "Sooner or later Catholics were bound to say: 'Look, we're tired of being an easy target. We've had enough Catholic-bashing.' "

Where was the coverage by the media? Why was this attack not reported nationally? Much less, why is a gratuitous and vicious attack, no matter what side the media take, not reported in full measure just by way of information as much more obscure attacks on race readily become national news — for example, graffiti on cemetery walls, locker-room gossip, and the like?[370]

Of course, *all* minorities of any kind deserve fair and equitable treatment in the media. *Commonweal*, the liberal Catholic weekly, asked: "Is there another group in the country which, if similarly assaulted, would be treated in this fashion?" Leo concluded: "But where is the revulsion threshold for similar attacks on Catholics?" [371]

But abortion, not homosexuality, remained the key issue and the media still targeted the Catholic Church in a fashion not noted for either fairness or objectivity.

Prior to 1990 it can be fairly concluded that those in the media, by and large, closed their eyes to the anti-Catholic tilt in the abortion question and stubbornly refused to present "both sides" for people to judge. By 1989 even many in the media had second thoughts about their record of fairness.

Ethan Bonner of the *Boston Globe* wrote that "opposing abortion, in the eyes of most journalists . . . is not a legitimate civilized position in our society" because the matter is "dominated by religious crazies." He further noted that the press in support of abortion had failed "to identify some sources . . . as if they were impartial" when they clearly were extreme advocates such as Planned Parenthood, the Guttmacher Foundation, and other allied groups. These groups used Dr. Nathanson's figure of ten thousand illegal abortions as gospel; the Center for Disease Control put the number at thirty-nine, *before* the Roe vs. Wade decision of 1973.

The *New York Times* and the *Washington Post* along with the three major TV networks quoted, over a period of time, the two leading women pro-abortionists seventy-six times; the two leaders against abortion twenty-six times. The media refused to publish photos of fetuses being killed as "in bad taste" while at the same time showed Ethiopian children dying horribly from starvation. TV Station KQED in San Francisco even petitioned the courts to allow it to televise an execution in San Quentin's gas chamber.

Television programs extensively monitored between January and October of 1989 prompted the conclusion that "the networks treat no other group with such bigotry — not Jews, not blacks, women or even homosexuals. Yet they make no attempt to hide their bigotry towards Christians and Christianity."

The PBS nightly news, the *MacNeil/Lehrer NewsHour*, is perhaps the exception that proves the rule. It usually succeeds in getting responsible and informed advocates on both sides of a controversial issue, including abortion, unlike the talk-show hosts who reek of bias and prejudice in advocacy of prurient sex devoid of morality and decency.

The Catholic Church often takes its bumps on these programs without even a chance for rebuttal even to the grossest gratuitous assertions. The assumption of a "fairness doctrine" is alien to these and others of their ilk.

A movie, much rerun on TV, gives a clue to the selective mentality if not morality of television executives. In *Attack on Terror: The FBI versus the Ku Klux Klan*, a drama replete with sermonizing and moralizing on the bigotry of the KKK against "Negroes and Jews," no mention whatever is made of the classic target, Catholics. The KKK is reduced to racial, not religious, prejudice, a denial of its history.

Relatively recent political elections illustrated the point as well. When pro-abortion candidates won against anti-abortion candidates, the result was trumpeted in the press as a great vindication of common sense, and just as often called a victory over the Catholic bishops. When anti-abortion candidates defeated their contrary rivals, the results were not reported in light of that one issue.

Pro-life candidates in California in the 1990 primaries, for example, defeated their pro-abortion rivals in eight out of nine contests, including the Republican candidate, a woman, for lieutenant governor, and two Democrats. The press ignored them while featuring the pro-abortion winners, even where the question was not an issue in the contest.

In an ironic note in the race for the California legislature in 1991, one Republican candidate named B. T. Collins, a self-declared atheist, when confronted with his pro-abortion stand, replied by asserting that he was "a typical lapsed Catholic." He was indeed defining the dilemma of any Catholic seeking public office, to wit, that he would be accepted if lapsed, since lapsed would imply not accepting certain teachings.

In reporting the results of the election, the news service told how Collins won as an easy victor over an anti-abortion candidate, and how on the same day Mickey Conroy won in Orange County without a mention that he won an anti-abortion platform against a candidate supported by Governor Pete Wilson.

When reporters joined in the pro-abortion march in Washington, D.C., against all journalistic rules, they were reprimanded; one secretary (not a reporter) who joined the anti-abortion march was fired. The American Newspaper Guild endorsed the pro-abortion cause, judging that eighty-two percent of its membership were pro-abortion.

The Media Research Center of Alexandria, Virginia, reported in 1990 that ninety percent of the journalists who work for the *New York Times*, the *Washington Post*, ABC, CBS, and NBC are pro-abortion. (Less than half said that adultery was wrong.) A similar survey also disclosed that ninety-seven percent of producers and writers in films and TV favor abortion (ninety-three percent admitting that they seldom went to religious services). These percentages are clearly out of synchronization with the general public. But would such an imbalance be allowed or condoned on the question of race in the 1990s?

The *Chicago Tribune* attributed good faith to the pro-abortionists, if in error: admittedly, it said, there is "an unwitting double standard at play." Not so charitable was the *Washington Post*'s own ombudsman.

The *Washington Post* is "institutionally pro-choice," said Richard Harwood, a charge vehemently denied by his editor, Leonard Downie, Jr. Yet during the pro-abortion rally in the nation's capital, the *Post* published maps, road closings, parking areas, subway services, lost-and-found department, plus first-aid and general-information sources. Front-page treatment with 12 articles, a 6500-word cover story on the date itself, and 5 more stories with photos the next day, with several staffers joining the march itself, illustrated the *Post*'s judgment that pro-abortion was national news. Not so the other side.

The anti-abortion march was relegated to the metro section, a judgment that its large rally was local, not national, news: one story, one photo on the date; one photo with two stories the next day. More space and more importance were given to much smaller marches celebrating Earth Day and Animal Rights.

Harwood drew the conclusion that "this affair has left a blot on the paper's professional reputation . . . the ultimate and undeniable proof of the paper's bias."

On August 13, 1990, *Time* magazine published the story that the editor of the *Washington Post*, the same Leonard Downie, sent "a stiff memorandum" to his staff, objecting to their joining in a pro-choice abortion rally as compromising objectivity, and he sent "an uncharacteristically stinging memo to his top editors charging that the *Post*'s coverage of the abortion issue had been lopsidedly biased against the pro-life side." *Time* said this call to objectivity "also aroused some resentment in the newsroom."

All America applauded when Congress passed the Racketeer Influence and Corruption (or RICO) laws, which were aimed at organized crime, dealers in illegal drugs, assorted Mafia and other criminal types. The *Los Angeles Times* called for a repeal of the RICO laws when they were invoked against white-collar criminals. But when these same laws were applied to the anti-abortion pickets, the press kept its silence, the ACLU and the left-leaning civil rights groups and those devoted to "privacy" kept their peace, although some commentators, as already detailed, did not: Nat Hentoff, Charles Krauthammer, Mark Shields, Fred Barnes, Cal Rossi, Bill Reel, and others. Clearly what was sauce for the goose was not sauce for the gander.

In his classic study, David Shaw wrote in the *Los Angeles Times* that most media paid no attention to the discovery by Bob Woodward in 1989 that two U.S. Supreme Court justices who were key in the 1973 Roe vs. Wade decision in private memoranda conceded that they knew they were "legislating policy and exceeding (the court's) authority as the interpreter, not the maker of law."[372] Only *Newsweek*, in the national media, mentioned the discovery because as Woodward said, "There are more people in the news media than not who agree with the (Roe) abortion decision and don't want to look at how the sausage was made."

Perhaps the most devastating ploy of the media was their refusal to call the "pro-life" organizations by their name but arbitrarily labeled them "anti-choice." Pro-abortion groups were hidden under the title of "pro-choice" without allowing a description of what the choice was really for, namely the destruction of human life up to birth.

Whether wittingly or not, the media, which claim to have come to a more balanced presentation, have done a great deal of damage to the U.S. Catholic Church for over twenty years. Media that claim they report the news impartially have not had such a record. The abortion issue could not be ignored by the Catholic Church as well as by others, but as the largest religious group in the U.S.A. by far, with nearly sixty million members, and by reason of its doctrine on the sanctity of human life, a partisan, unequal, and even prejudiced attack on the pro-life people almost invariably became an attack on the Church. And even when the media were not attacking the Church by name, they were wittingly or otherwise fanning the flames of Nativism and encouraging the Catholic Church haters to come out of the closet.

The concept of just what happens at an abortion and the way it is described have a proper place in the exercise of freedom of speech. Ignorance of what an abortion is cannot be the basis for free speech on the subject. Yet when the pro-life proponents insist that abortion be defined in its very lowest denominator as the taking of life and a killing, the media renege and often accuse the proponents of imposing not a biological or physical fact but a religious dogma. The time-honored testing of ideas in the marketplace is conveniently ignored in the media.

When Episcopal Bishop Paul Moore of New York publicly favored abortion, he was applauded in the media and escaped being charged with mixing religion and politics, of imposing his moral standard on others, of being divisive in the state and in society. Not so when the Catholic archbishop of New York took the opposite position. The one is hailed as a true American, the other as not quite fully so.

When a *New York Times*-CBS poll found that fifty-seven percent of the people believed abortion is murder, and a 1989 *Los Angeles Times* poll found the same statistic, about fifty percent still stated that women should be allowed the choice, presumably to commit murder. Where were the columnists? the commentators?

By 1992 there was more balance in reporting. Polls repeatedly revealed that there was an almost evenly divided public on the abortion question: supporters for and against "is evenly split overall," reported the *USA Today*-Gallup poll on January 6, 1992: those with a college degree and higher income (especially of over $50,000 per year) and those who seldom or never participate in religious practices move significantly into the pro-abortion camp, while those whose income fell into the category of the noncollege graduate, the middle class, and the poor as well as those who participate in religious practices tend to accept anti-abortion positions, leaving exceptions for the life of the mother, rape, and incest.

The pro-abortionists turned the presidential campaign into a one-issue contest, with the Democratic hopefuls, the five major candidates, appearing at a NARAL dinner in Washington, D.C., on the anniversary of Roe vs. Wade, January 22, 1992. Candidate Paul Tsongas announced that President

224

Bush (who spoke favorably that day to the pro-life demonstrators, numbering some seventy thousand) predicted that "now he's going to pay the price."[373] The 1991 fall election in Washington state showed an almost even split on the issue of whether to make Roe vs. Wade state law, with a handful of votes tilting the scales toward the affirmative.

Orthodox Judaism has centuries of history against procured abortion; the Mormons also oppose, as do many of the Protestant Fundamentalist sects. But the media usually trashed only the Catholic Church and especially its bishops in their attack.

Rather than treat the issue itself — what an abortion really is — the media often reverted to a defense of "the American way," a regurgitation of Nativism in twentieth-century models.

The giant daily paper in New York, *Newsday*, trumpeted the party line: "O'Connor Steps Over the Line, Church Doctrine Has No Place in State Law or Policy." Get back into the sacristy! Not everyone, however, agreed, but not on the grounds of agreeing or disagreeing with Cardinal O'Connor but precisely on the grounds that the media were applying, once again, a double standard.

Former New York Mayor Edward Koch pointed out that many laws of the Judeo-Christian tradition are found in the laws of the United States. "Thou shalt not kill" and "Thou shalt not steal" are good examples, he wrote. *Newsday* was hypocritical because it did not tell New York's Episcopal Bishop Moore to retreat to the sacristy when he openly campaigned in favor of abortion laws and gay rights. Nor was Rabbi Balfour Brickner of New York, board member of the Planned Parenthood organization and most vociferous proponent of abortion on demand, ever called to heel by this same *Newsday*, concluded Koch who himself is pro-choice. It was clearly another case of a double standard that escalated into a none-too-subtle Nativism.

When Cardinal Humberto Medeiros of Boston spoke out against abortion, he was denounced by *New York Times* columnist Anthony Lewis "for mixing religion and politics"; the *Boston Globe* ran thirty-three articles in three weeks bashing the cardinal directly and indirectly. The case was typical around the whole country: bishops were advised to stay out of politics.

Yet it was this very same Church in its canon law that specifically forbade priests to accept political office. They were (and are) forbidden to be magistrates, judges, mayors, governors, or legislative officers. As far as the U.S. Congress has been involved, only three priests, as pointed out in Chapter 10, have served as legislators in the two hundred years of its history.

The first was Father Gabriel Richard, one of the founders of the University of Michigan, who served as its vice president and professor, and who was elected delegate (Michigan was not yet a state) to Congress in 1823. A French missionary, he had a reputation both for learning and devotion to the cause of rights for the Native American Indians; he had been a prisoner of war of the British in the War of 1812. He lost reelection, reportedly because of the opposition of some of his own parishioners.

Contrary to canon law in the 1970s two priests sought political office and were elected to Congress: the Jesuit Father Robert F. Drinan of Boston and the Norbertine Father Robert J. Cornell of DePere, Wisconsin. The former served ten years; the latter four; both were of the Democratic Party. Both needed specific approval from their local bishops, which neither even bothered to obtain. The National Conference of Catholic Bishops of the U.S.A. passed a resolution against these candidacies but took no concrete action. That came from Rome and the Pope, unfortunately and rightly seen as a reaction to Father Drinan's support of abortion laws rather than his defiance of canon law.

But the media again employed a double standard, denouncing the Church, its Pope, and its bishops for interfering in U.S. politics but supporting Father Drinan because of his advocacy of the liberal agenda. Father Drinan was the darling, Cardinal O'Connor the devil.

Monsignor George Higgins issued a caveat that would tend to bridge the gap: "Many Americans ... conclude that (the Church) wants priests to withdraw not only from partisan political activity but from political activity of every kind and is opposed to all forms of clerical activism, even non-political activism in support of justice and human rights." The Church thus would stay out of partisan politics but not out of the field of human rights, no matter the political implications.

The American bishops, as already alluded to, have over the years as a body issued statements on a wide variety of subjects: nuclear war, racial discrimination, integration of schools, armaments for foreign armies, anti-Semitism, capitalism, Communism, public responsibility in the electoral process, capital punishment, hostages, social security, housing, farm workers, and a host of other topics — all without being accused of treason to the Bill of Rights. But when they have touched equal treatment for independent schools and abortion, then they are pilloried as un-American, wishing for an establishment of religion, seen as enemies of all separation. It has been the same old whipsaw!

Protestant clerics turned politician, and their number is legion; rabbis becoming legislators and a few other clerics as well do not usually arouse media opposition. But the bishops who have no designs on running for public office and who have not given permission for their clergy to do so are yet portrayed in word and cartoon as somewhat less than American.

Anecdotal evidence, of which there is a profusion and wealth of instances, has been supported by several studies of the media in very recent times in reference to the abortion question and the Catholic Church.

A very limited study by the Center for Media and Public Affairs (CMPA), a nonprofit nonpartisan research organization — restricted to only eight months' coverage, January 1 to August 31, 1989, and only to the *New York Times*, the *Washington Post*, NBC, CBS, and ABC — concluded that the pro-abortion side dominated the debate over Roe vs. Wade, with the most quoted individuals being Kate Michelman of NARAL 42 times, Molly Yard of NOW 34 times, Faye Wattleton of Planned Parenthood 10 times, whereas the pro-life side benefited from John Willke of the National Right to Life 16 times, and Randall Terry of Operation Rescue 10 times. There was a relative lack of in-depth treatment, especially by television, which devoted much more time to pro-abortion demonstrations. The *Washington Post*, "in a departure from its normal policy of identifying groups as they wish to be identified," calling the pro-abortion side "pro-choice" as it wished but naming the pro-life side as anti-abortion as it did not wish, was followed by the TV and radio media, the survey showed.

The pro-choice group "dominated the legalization issue" while pro-life was more effective in all media on the necessity of overturning the Supreme Court decision of Roe vs. Wade and fared better on the issue of morality and when life begins. Women reporters and editorialists overwhelmingly were pro-abortion while men were about evenly balanced.[374]

Two years later the CMPA studied the coverage of the Catholic Church, this time with a more extensive purview. It studied three five-year periods: 1964-68, 1974-78, and 1984-88, and focused on the *New York Times* and the *Washington Post*, *Time* magazine, and the CBS evening news.

The CMPA noted that only one to two percent of the media journalists were practicing Catholics.[375] "The Church came out on the losing side in almost every controversy, except ecumenism, [and] was usually portrayed as divided between hierarchy on one side and an unwilling clergy and laity on the other. The bishops were pictured as conservative, authoritarian and anachronistic, with heavy concentration on dissidents. During the 1970's most published statements favored the Church's position on Roe vs. Wade, which changed in the 1980's with women's rights and status at issue. The result was that the Church was depicted in [the] media as oppressive with little reference to the modern world."

On the matter of Church-State relationships this study found that in the 1960s public opinion (58 percent to 42 percent) supported the Church's stance with the state; in the 1970s it fell to 55 percent, and in the 1980s to only 40 percent. The study unfortunately did not delve into the basic reasons nor try to weigh the opinions against the Church. Abortion was not in the first ten topics in the 1960s; it was third in the '70s, and fifth in the '80s. What in the '90s?[376] An eighteen-month study, reported in the *Los Angeles Times*, revealed that "abortion bias seeps into news" and that the claim of anti-abortionists that "media bias manifests itself in print and on the air almost daily . . . confirms that this bias often exists."

In a detailed analysis running some twelve thousand words, *Los Angeles Times* reporter David Shaw concluded that "responsible journalists do try to be fair, and many charges of bias in abortion coverage are not valid. But much coverage is manifestly unfair, with TV more vulnerable to the charge." He cited many examples.

Los Angeles Times reporter Karen Tumulty denied that the media had given "people the information they need to make up their own minds"; *Chicago Tribune* writer Barbara Brotman said that the abortion issue had been reported "only as a political matter without examination of its personal, moral, ethical, medical and even legal ramifications. . . .[377] With rare exceptions we have never gotten beyond the surface." We, she concluded, have covered the question "like we're covering sports." NBC's Lisa Meyers wrote that, excesses aside, "I do believe that some of the stories I have read or seen have almost seemed like cheer-leading for the pro-choice side."

Shaw maintains that the statistics on illegal abortions before Roe vs. Wade that claim "thousands of women die every year from back-alley abortions" do not square with the Center for Disease Control that the number was thirty-nine in 1972. He pointed to the admission of Dr. Bernard Nathanson that he invented the figure of ten thousand abortions.

The psychological effects of abortion should be studied, he went on; if capital punishment contributes to a climate of violence, would abortion not have similar effects?

The *Washington Post* is "institutionally pro-choice. Any reader of the paper's editorials and homegrown columnists is aware of that . . . (and) news coverage has favored the pro-choice side," wrote Richard Harwood. One of the worst tactics? "Even now 17 years later some in the media wrote about Roe in terms that suggest it legalized abortion only during the trimester: The *New York Times, Los Angeles Times, Milwaukee Journal* and *Louisville Courier-Journal.*"

The *New York Times* after the June 1990 elections headlined a story: "Each Side Cites Primaries as Evidence of Strength on the Abortion Issue." Only three weeks later did the *Los Angeles Times* publish the fact that in California anti-abortionist candidates won seven our of eight state legislative races where abortion was a significant issue.

Lutheran Pastor Richard Neuhaus hit the nail on the head: "The *New York Times* wants the bishops to help people sin safely while the bishops want to help people not to sin. . . . If pleasure is permitted where he now is, Paul Blanshard must be pleased." In the *Times* purview, the "only good Catholic is a bad Catholic." He hoped "that the *Times* will put Mr. Blanshard back to rest and call off its anti-Catholic campaign, for it is really a campaign against the role of religion in public life." After all, he added, no one is forced to be a Catholic and no one who contradicts the Church's teaching has a "right" to be a Catholic in good standing.

Reporter Shaw found the same objections as detailed already in this book: frequency of citations, maximizing one side and minimizing the other, nomenclature, selective coverage, one-sided commentary, even on news reports. But he also found the seeds of Nativism: "Abortion opponents are sometimes identified as Catholics or fundamentalist Christians, even when their religion is not demonstrably relevant to a given story; abortion rights advocates are rarely identified by religion." When Catholic bishops spoke out, there were media lamentations about their intrusion into the political arena, a violation of the separation of Church and State. Shaw ironically noted that when these same bishops opposed the nuclear arms race or the Reagan administration's policies, "no such criticism was levied at the bishops." He might have added that the media accepted the pro-abortion interventions of Protestant bishops, Jewish rabbis, and other clergymen without a murmur about Church and State.

The *Los Angeles Times* reporter summarized his study in these words: "Careful examination of stories published and broadcasts reveals scores of examples, large and small, that can only be characterized as unfair to the opponents of abortion, either in content, tone, choice of language or prominence of play. . . . Television is probably more vulnerable to the charges of bias on abortion than are newspapers and magazines. The time constraints and the ratings chase intrinsic to most television news programs often lead to the kind of superficiality and sensationalism that results in bias. . . ."

The Wichita episode became yet another example of both the control of news and "the kind of superficiality."

As the confirmation hearings for Judge Clarence Thomas for the Supreme Court approached, Operation Rescue led a sit-down type of protest at Wichita, Kansas, in August 1991, and afforded yet another opportunity for the media to report objectively and fairly about still another controversy revolving around the question of abortion.

Founded in 1987 by Randall Terry (who, incidentally, is not a Catholic), Operation Rescue is a nondenominational organization dedicated to taking direct action to impede and, if possible, to prevent abortions by picketing abortion clinics *en scène*. Part of its tactic is physically to block the entrances of the abortion facilities and for its members to grow limp when accosted by police and to accept arrest, clearly a strategy adopted from the civil-rights marches of the 1960s and other movements that were billed as nonviolent civil disobedience.

Father James Burtchaell, a University of Notre Dame professor, published a lengthy article that has as its focus not the rights or wrongs of the Wichita saga but rather the treatment of it in the media. The headline given to the Pacific News Service piece was, accurately, "When No News is Bias."

Burtchaell underscored the necessity of viewing the Wichita episode within the context of the civil disobedience movement, which included the freedom marches of the 1960s, the raiding of selective service files in the 1970s, the attack on ICBM hardware in the 1980s, and the blockading of the South African embassy in 1984. These were all done in the name of non-violence and a higher law than the legal restraints on the lawbooks. Yet there was a startling difference, "a remarkable antipathy with which the (pro-life) protests have been reported."

"The press, the broadcasters and our national essayists had steadfastly held the exertions of the civil rights and anti-Vietnam and nuclear disarmament and anti-apartheid demonstrators before the conscience of the nation. Yet there is a strange reluctance to report on Operation Rescue at all."[378]

Civil-rights sit-ins since 1960 resulted in 3,600 arrests; in 4 years pro-life sit-ins have been the occasion for over 65,000 arrests; in Wichita, 84 clergymen of various faiths were arrested in 1 day, whereas the 14 clergy in Milwaukee, 9 in Catonsville, and even 7 in Chicago "became nationally famous." From jail the Wichita clerics issued a statement, reminding Americans of Martin Luther King's "Letter from a Birmingham Jail." The secular media were silent on the national level.

The accounts of physical abuse of the pro-lifers arrested have met with little or no response. A seventy-two-year-old bishop in West Hartford, Connecticut, "was seized, cuffed behind his back and then lifted from the ground by billy clubs between his wrists. In a Pittsburgh jail, according to Congressional testimony describing the scene, 17 female college students had their clothes ripped off and were forced to walk in the nude, in some cases crawl. Some of them were sexually assaulted."[379]

The brutality of treatment by public officers, the gratuitous use of Mace in Sacramento, with rough manhandling of women in Atlanta, where a priest was put into solitary confinement for celebrating the Eucharist; in Los Angeles, in Wichita, and "in several cities nunchakus (two clubs chained together) were used against protesters . . . one man's arm being broken (in Los Angeles)": these events were not newsworthy in the minds of most editors.

The judiciary's record was equally spotty. The famous movie actor Martin Sheen was given three hours of community service for his eighteenth conviction for antinuclear protest, whereas a pro-lifer was sent to prison for twenty-one months for a first offense. The Act Up militants who desecrated St. Patrick's Cathedral and, like storm troopers, disrupted Mass were fined $100; pro-lifers, on the other hand, $450,000. Judge Patrick Kelly in Wichita ordered bail of $100,000 for the three pro-life leaders, and the jailing of them for being unable to pay, only to be reversed by the appellate court to "explain the high bail," while upholding the judge's decision to prevent the blocking of abortion clinics' entrances. The judge released the three leaders from jail and revoked the bail. Sadly he was reported to have said that he would no longer attend church as long as the Catholic Church had such an obsession with abortion.

Allegations of this kind (hundreds of depositions exist) ordinarily make good copy when they come from Montgomery, or Soweto, or Lubianka. "Why," Burtchaell queried, "have they been edited out of the media's reporting on the anti-abortion demonstration?"

There have been legitimate protests against and just criticisms of some of the pro-life activists. The isolated bombings of an abortion clinic, with few casualties, were denounced by bishops and pro-life organizations, these tactics standing in stark contrast to respect for life. Other methods used went beyond passive resistance: there are the long-suffering police who had to control crowds in favor of public order and public peace; the harassed jailers who faced a sudden avalanche of passive boarders in already overcrowded facilities; and the cornered judges who were caught on the horns of many dilemmas, whether they involved the right to life of the unborn, free exercise of religion, freedom of speech, or freedom of assembly. Even irrational zeal in a just cause can be counterproductive and self-defeating. The point here, however, is that the media were suppressing legitimate news regardless of the conduct of public protesters.

Over the years, the evidence conclusively shows, both in reportorial and editorial sections, that the media did not treat the burning question in even moderately balanced fashion: whether it be the true nature of the Roe vs. Wade case or the companion Doe vs. Bolton, which insured abortion on demand; another example would be the manipulation of the estimates of crowds (even in one January 1992 pro-life march in Washington, D.C., one report told that although the pro-life and pro-abortion groups' marches took place several blocks apart at the Capitol Mall, the figure of seventy thousand was attributed to *both* sides — a renewal of a long history of such treatment). There was similar biased treatment across the U.S.A.[380] The record continues.

The *New York Times* editorially dismissed the pro-life protesters in this vein: ". . . on one side, an evangelical Christian minister and a have-protest-will-travel group of 100 people crusading against baby-killers; on the other the abortion providers, a group of committed feminists who say they will not be intimidated by 'fanatics.' "[381] It reported that the locals in Wichita and Burlington, Vermont, were tired of the protesters. Yet in Wichita the very next day twenty-five thousand gathered in a local stadium in a rally, which received a news flash on TV on some networks but not on others, illustrating Shaw's conclusion on the superficiality of TV news.[382]

The coverage of religious leaders has been different too. Martin Luther King, Jr., Ralph Abernathy, Jesse Jackson, Andrew Young, Abraham Joshuah Heschel, Eugene Carson Blake, Philip and Daniel Berrigan, William Sloan Coffen, Jr., and Desmond Tutu: "They spoke from Isaiah and Luke and Paul, and nobody wrinkled his nose at it."

On the contrary, the Operation Rescue clergy are described as "authoritarian Catholics or wacko evangelicals," clutching Bibles or rosaries. The Wichita rally had a full stage of clergy from many denominations, but only the Reverend Pat Robertson was reported to be in attendance. The local Catholic bishop of Wichita, Eugene Gerber, addressed the rally but was not shown in the national media: neither the national news services nor television networks.

The media leaders, given the results of the polls and studies of editors, feature writers, and reporters, simply have closed their eyes to the pro-life question and have a selective morality that extends to racism but not to anti-religious bigotry in the same way, particularly when they identify, correctly, the Catholic Church with pro-life. As Burtchaell concluded: "The point-at-issue is not that Catholics and evangelicals are pro-life and mainline Protestants and Jews are pro-choice but that abortion somehow becomes a point of moral outrage when people of whatever allegiance make faith their source of moral wisdom."

The headline writer summed up the point all too well: "When No News is Bias." On the other hand, it should be conceded that the press was willing to publish the Burtchaell complaint on more than a purely local basis. In general, since 1991 the coverage of the abortion question has been much improved, again perhaps owing to the press's flagrant controlling and managing of the news previously on this difficult and controversial problem in the United States, which is gradually reaching the consciousness if not the conscience of the general public.

Perhaps believing that no news is good news, the national media, not to mention the civil rights activists, the ACLU, etc., chose to ignore yet another storm-trooper tactic at the National Shrine in Washington, D.C. On the eve of the annual pro-life march on January 22, 1992, the homosexual advocacy group called Queer Nation disrupted the Vigil Mass and Cardinal O'Connor as he spoke from the pulpit. The fifty members staged a mock crucifixion on the front steps of the basilica and formed lines to heckle the worshipers.

The *Washington Post* was silent on the disruption of the Mass and once again labeled as biased on its reporting the march of seventy thousand pro-life partisans to the nation's Capitol. "The *Post* went out of its way to give biased reporting ... and seemed determined to avoid objectivity in [its] reporting," according to Bishop James McHugh of Camden who was a con-celebrant of the Mass and present at the march. "It was an outrageous insult to Catholics to invade the sanctity of worship," he concluded.

The *New York Times* quoted George Bush's talk to the seventy thousand but found it quite difficult to admit the number, saying that there were two groups several blocks apart pro and con and both totaled seventy thousand together, a gross distortion and dishonest reportage.

Congressmen Chris Smith and Robert K. Dornan, Republicans, took the occasion to advise the American public to vote for Bush and to denounce the

Democratic congressmen who were both Irish and Catholics, especially Senator Edward Kennedy for voting for legal abortion.

The same *New York Times*, anticipating the march on Washington, D.C., published an editorial on January 22, 1992, which perpetuated the myth that Roe vs. Wade put restrictions on abortion, not to mention Doe vs. Bolton, and castigated the pro-lifers for their opposition. After all, it said, "in place of Roe's reasonable restraints in the interests of health and late pregnancy development" the anti-abortion crowd should not be trying to change the law. One cannot help wondering on what planet the editorial writer lives. Even the most ardent pro-abortion advocate, as well as Chief Justice Burger, as already cited, knows full well that Justice Blackmun's trimester dodge was a dud and utterly unworkable and in fact promoted abortion on demand. To find such an opinion so late in the game in 1992 is to find total blindness, self-delusion, and a strong suspicion of pure prejudice that outweighs even a soupçon of objectivity.

Yet another element entered the picture that was grist to the mill for the media: politics.

Both political parties, with their devotees in the press, radio, and TV, have taken pains to earn political capital on the emotional controversy. The Democratic Party's platform is unabashedly pro-abortion, including tax support; the Republican platform was anti-abortion in 1988 and promises to be less so in 1992, with the declaration that the party has a very broad tent covering divergent views. As mentioned earlier, the five major Democratic candidates for President toed the party line totally, appearing together on January 22 at a National Abortion Rights Action League dinner; President Bush affirmed his own anti-abortion stand at the January 22 pro-life rally in Washington, citing Jefferson who wrote into American wisdom the compelling legacy that all are created equal, not born equal.

The question of assistance to nonpublic schoolchildren, the Senator Kennedy bill, ran along similar lines, with Democrats in most cases against any assistance and Republicans in favor. These two bones of contention have become for many Catholics their own litmus test for their support at the polls.

George Will of ABC TV posed the question about the Republicans and the President: "How about aid to give educational choice beyond public schools for inner-city parents of poor children? (Bush) is for that. But not enough to fight for it, or to raise a ruckus when the Senate last week defeated it on essentially a party line. . . .

"Abortion? Once every January on the anniversary of the 1973 Supreme Court decision, he waxes ardent on the subject. But there is no follow-through."[383]

Democrats complain that this one-issue politics ignores their record on race, poverty, labor relations, and social justice; they further aver that the Republicans speak in terms of support but never translate it into action and give only lip service.

Catholics and others face the dilemma: Which is better to support? The party that outright denies the right to life and justice in education? Or the party that gives a satisfactory answer at least publicly?

The bottom line for all Americans inevitably must be: Just how fundamental in the matter of human rights are the right to life itself and, secondarily, the right to justice and equity in society's, the state's, and the family's education of the new generation?

The *Commonweal* in May 1991 quite rightly warned that "to the extent that there really is Catholic-bashing in the media, media-bashing by Catholics will do more harm than good. . . . On occasion, practically all groups — Italians, doctors, Blacks, Jews, Arabs, southpaws, Baptists, the rich, farmers, cops, lawyers — feel slighted or scorned or smeared by the media and sometimes they're right. . . .

"Though Catholicism as religion and the Catholic Church as institution are indeed often misperceived in this country, how much mileage is to be gained by efforts to show Catholics as a powerless and picked-on minority?

"How respond? An organized anti-defamation campaign is one answer. . . ."

The Catholic magazine properly warns against Catholics being "too thin-skinned" but perhaps misses the point that the bias and prejudice documented are found in mainstream America and go to the heart of religious liberty and human rights. To suggest an anti-defamation league as one answer seems to contradict its own word to the wise that Catholics are, by and large, too "thin-skinned."

Why not let the record speak for itself? Is not the evidence compelling? Compelling enough to evoke public protest from the liberals as well as conservatives of unquestionable credentials? Or are the *Commonweal* editors proving themselves part of that intelligentsia, "the best people," in the words of two certified liberals, Senator Patrick Moynihan and Father Andrew Greeley, who do not wish to admit that American Catholics are suffering severe deprivations that should be addressed, who believe that Nativism in its Catholic form is a ghost that died?

To its credit *Commonweal* did publish, just a month later, an article by R. Bruce Douglass, co-editor of *Liberalism and the Good*, which pinpointed the secularist attack on all religion: "For the same people who are so concerned about the offense that is given by public expressions of piety generally couldn't care less about sensibilities that are injured when piety itself is abused . . . as in the display of the crucifix in a beaker of urine. . . .

"Those offended are told to be 'broadminded' . . . (not) the responsibility of the one giving the offense . . . which is quickly dismissed as 'repressive.' "

His conclusion goes right to the heart of the media bias: "These days it is more than all right to be concerned, for example, about the quality of our speech with respect to race and gender but not with respect to religion. . . .

Race and gender (are assumed to be) a matter of greater urgency in our public life than religion."

Douglass was responding to an article in *Sports Illustrated* that took a very hostile view of athletes saying prayers on the fields of athletic contests.

The editor of a large prestigious Catholic publishing house, after reading the draft of this book, made the following criticism: "Your manuscript, as always, is well-written and your theme cogently argued. Those of us who read it, however, seriously doubt the effectiveness of your approach. We feel it smacks too much of victimology, something Blacks and other minorities get accused of in today's social debates.

"We feel it is better to argue Catholic positions on their powerful intellectual and moral merits rather than from the context of past injustices or slights."

It can be well argued that the past injustices have not disappeared; that the blacks and minorities got nowhere on "intellectual and moral merits," and that the Vatican Council's "Declaration on Religious Liberty" had its origin with most powerful intellectual and moral merit, which did not overwhelm even the Catholic intelligentsia.

Whether bringing out the record past, present, and the assumed future on the deepest injustices regarding abortion and equal opportunity in all schools is "effective," remains to be seen. The editor may be correct; this book stands in disagreement with his assessment.

If a quite contemporary author could publish the following, which comes from a major publishing house, it does not seem credible that Catholics are objecting to simply "past injustices or slights"; Lawrence Lader furnishes yet another example: "If power corrupts, the increasing power of the Vatican has not only corrupted its religious mission but produced a rebellious constituency. Catholic power, allied with fundamentalism, has threatened the American tenet of Church-State separation and shaken the fragile balance of our pluralistic society."[384]

And what is the hope for the future, according to this worthy successor of Paul Blanshard, whose nine books are virulently anti-Catholic, even if using references and interviews of Catholic priests and nuns, and who candidly admits that "it could be too easily assumed that this book is slanted against the Catholic Church," and who also wrote that "one organization, Catholics for a Free Choice, stands above all and Frances Keesling, its head, deserves a special tribute"? He sees a solution: "Meanwhile radical Catholicism, aligned with mainstream Protestantism and Judaism, remains the best hope for holding extremism in check, and preserving American pluralism and the separation principle against its enemies."

To be pro-abortion does not make one an anti-Catholic. But to base hostility to the anti-abortion position on false or even scurrilous charges, to identify the anti-abortion cause with the Catholic Church, a perfectly legitimate inference, as an un-American exercise against the First Amendment — such a stance is quite another matter. The wrapping of oneself in the American flag, following the "American way," preempting the true faith of the Republic — these not only savor of Nativism but smack of what was once known as "McCarthyism." The doomsday scenario — whether in the abortion question or the school question (the two litmus tests) — often reeks of anti-Catholicism and in many instances Nativism.

Such dogmatism from a secular humanist segment of the population espouses a secularism that would relegate religion to the private arena only, a dogma worthy only of a totalitarian state that would do violence to the free-exercise clause of the First Amendment as well as the various declarations of human rights of the Helsinki agreements, the United Nations charter, and the European and other international and national affirmations, not to mention Vatican II.

That pervading bias, however, is not confined simply to the pro-life or anti-abortion camps. Inevitably and inexorably it had to spill over directly onto the institution most visibly identified with it: the Catholic Church in the U.S.A. That Church is a well-defined, visible, and stationary target and one that conjures up not only awe but alarm in the American populace.

All other issues aside, the Catholic Church in the United States has inspired fear, perhaps because of its history, especially in Europe, perhaps more because of its large size in the U.S.A. Americans tend to distrust big government, big industry, big military, big labor, precisely on the basis of size. Why not big church, with nearly sixty million members?

The *Village Voice*, New York's liberal paper, asked the same rhetorical question: "Why is the Catholic Church the primary, perennial target of those who profess to guard the wall of separation? In part the Church is made a pariah because of the venerable American tradition of anti-Catholicism."

Cardinal John O'Connor, perhaps in something of a whimsical mood, wrote his parishioners to expect to be scapegoats when objecting to certain disvalues proposed by school boards, to TV programs inimical to marriage and family, to some movies. He added: "Expect it when columnists and editors who are censured for ethnic slurs or attacks on virtually any other people, can romp all over the place at the expense of Catholics who dare publicly to uphold their faith, without a murmur from publishers or owners."[385]

Was John Higham correct when he concluded that "the most luxuriant, tenacious tradition of paranoid agitation in American history has been anti-Catholicism"? Is it the ghost that will not die? In the media at least?

Chapter 15

Into the Political Arena

"No religious test shall ever be required as a qualification to any office or public trust under the United States" (Article VI, No. 3).

This article of the U.S. Constitution was not formally extended to the several states until July 28, 1868, with the passage of the Fourteenth Amendment. Many of the states did require religious tests for office, with the U.S. Supreme Court gradually mandating the extension of the Fourteenth Amendment. Yet it was not until 1961 that the Court, in the Roy Torcaso case, ruled that a person in an office of trust under the United States did not have to profess a belief in God. In tracing this progression down through the years, perhaps it could be concluded that in "the American experiment" there was a firm constitutional principle that eventually would be capable of development, much like the Vatican Council's development in the same area of religious freedom, particularly as an immunity from unjust coercion. Circumstances change; people grow and solutions can be faithful both to a valid principle and to the sociological transformations.

One of the lesser-known Founding Fathers but quite famous in his own right, Edmund J. Randolph, delegate to the Constitutional Convention of 1787, argued against any religious test for public office: "If it was in favor either of (sic) congregationalists, presbyterians, episcopalians, baptists or quakers, it would incapacitate more than three quarters of the American citizens for any public office."

He went on to say that he was sure that those appointed to public office would be "sincere friends of religion and that Americans should take care to choose such persons and not rely on 'cobweb barriers as test laws are.' " Otherwise, he concluded, with perhaps a tongue-in-cheek witticism, the political scene would resemble that in England, where every politician "must be a saint by law or a hypocrite by practice."

American Catholics are constantly being accused of medievalism, of turning the clock back, of being against progress, and of being inimical to a true development of law in the Republic. Yet it is their secularist opponents (read Planned Parenthood, NOW, NARAL, ACLU, the American Jewish Congress, etc.) who use the tactic both ways. They do not hesitate to cite the Bill of Rights, which turns the clock back to 1791, when it suits their purposes (which is a doctrinaire ideological interpretation) and at the same time to invoke modern conditions that negate the basic concepts of the Declaration of Independence and the Constitution.

They are both right and wrong. Modern America cannot be held simply to a literal interpretation of the intentions and words of the Founding Fathers.

They enunciated the truth that all men are created equal but did not mean Afro-Americans or Asian Americans.[386] A century later the Supreme Court in the Plessy-Ferguson decision upheld racial discrimination in education with "a separate but equal" doctrine, which was taught to school administrators and teachers for another seventy-five years in the leading universities, including Columbia, Michigan, and California in Berkeley.

The seed of equality was sown in the Bill of Rights; a simultaneous return to the principle and a recognition of historical progress that demanded a growth, a true development, has greatly improved the solution to the problem of race relations that has bedeviled the country throughout its entire history. A doctrinaire interpretation of the First Amendment — for example, that it mandated secularism, or an absolute separation of Church and State, or the relegation of religion to the privacy of the sanctuary ("in the closet," in other words), and a refusal to face the developments in the life of Americans who believe that there has been a true development in freedom of religion that should be accepted and recognized in both law and custom — this interpretation is the basis for Justice Scalia's remark that the field is "in chaos."

The secularists want it both ways: invoke the 1791 Bill of Rights and the changes in modern society as it suits their purpose, all the while accusing the Catholic citizen and some others, on the one hand, of wanting to run the clock back and at the same time not facing modern conditions, modern history. When the Catholic quotes the Declaration of Independence on its explicit wording of a God-given right to life, he is accused of turning the clock back. When he asks that the children in religious schools be accorded equal rights in education, even the Supreme Court has justified the present set-up on historical grounds that in the nineteenth century Protestants and Catholics could not resolve their antagonisms about education. There has been no thought of true developments as were the cases on racism, separate-but-equal schooling, poll taxes, and similar questions.

Under this same doctrinaire interpretation of the First Amendment, politicians who are Catholic must choose to be "fully American *or* fully Catholic."

Prominent and distinguished Protestant Americans pointed out what they considered the key questions facing Catholic aspirants to public office. Stringfellow Barr suggested that "it is simply a brutal fact that the American non-Catholics are afraid of the Catholic Church and its behavior in certain countries. . . . Fear is a bad basis for communication and breeds a kind of cold war."[387] The well-known theologian Martin E. Marty looked across the Atlantic: "More realistically, involvement in dialogue might force the Roman authority to a more clear statement of its American application. . . . The only real impasse is the issue of authority."[388] Robert McAfee Brown also cast his eyes over to Rome: "If a Catholic in either party should receive the presidential nomination, (there will be) the assumption that Catholics 'in power' would gradually do away with the rights of dissent and impose their practices as the law of the land." And on the home front: some of these charges are due to tactical blunders of Catholic spokesmen in high places.[389]

There was, of course, just such a nomination and election. Recalling the victory of John Kennedy, New Jersey's *Catholic Star Herald* editorialized: "His brief term of office seemed to prove once and for all that there was nothing un-American about being Catholic and that Catholics could be trusted to discharge their public duties in such a way as to keep their conscience intact and their citizenship uncompromised. It was refreshing to learn that millions of little Catholic boys and girls did not lose their chance to be president on the day of their baptism."

Recent years have certainly called that "refreshing" opinion into question. The cases are multiple on city, county, state, and federal levels.

One of the principal victims of the new Nativism offered on the altar of sacrifice to a commonly accepted Americanism must be the politician and the eager aspirant to public office, whether elective or appointive. May he follow his conscience as a committed religious citizen and still pass the litmus tests imposed by zealous inquisitors? May a Catholic man or woman claim to be at once fully Catholic and fully American?

The test, alas, is not satisfied by his or her publicly and solemnly taking the oath of office to uphold faithfully the Constitution of the United States and its laws. Rather the first litmus test of the 1990s demands support for abortion under the guise of pro-choice under penalty of heavy financial and vocal opposition by Planned Parenthood, the ACLU, NOW, NARAL, and less vigorous disapproval from the AFL-CIO, the American Bar Association, the American Medical Association, the NAACP, and others.[390]

Many Catholic politicians simply have acceded to the threats and acquiesced — the Church's Vatican Council, the hierarchy, the religious, and the laity to the contrary notwithstanding. Others avoid the problem test by describing themselves as "lapsed Catholics" or "non-practicing Catholics."[391]

The question here is not the merits of the various stances. Rather men and women who hold to the Church's teaching are attacked as suspect in their oath of allegiance to the First Amendment. The inquisition by these "super-Americans" is at once cruel and malevolent, and at the same time self-serving and in many cases venal.

In *U.S. News and World Report*, John Leo laid bare the difference between anti-Catholicism and Nativism: "I am not talking about normal political opposition to Church policy on condoms, AIDS, or abortion. The bishops have entered into the political arena on these subjects and can take their shots like anyone else. I am talking about a straight-out hate campaign."

Nativism is not simply anti-Catholicism but anti-Catholicism with a plus that impugns loyalty to the United States, just as Nativism is anti-Jewish, anti-black, anti-Asian, anti-immigrant, with the same plus.

Among the myriads of cases that would illustrate the quandary and dilemma faced by politicians who are Catholic, two have captured the attention of the media and general public across the nation as being egregious and paradigmatic, both involving the highest political offices in the Republic: the presidency and the Supreme Court.

Few people would contest the judgment that perhaps the most eloquent and articulate politician in the United States is Governor Mario Cuomo of New York. Many familiar with the Aristotelian, Platonic, Scholastic, and new-Scholastic philosophies, with their logic, epistemology, and metaphysics, cannot help but see their influence on this public servant, reflecting quite directly his education in Catholic schools right through St. John's University and Law School. Combined with his God-given talents, his education has given the Republic a welcome relief to the fuzzy philosophies and protean political theories of some of the Ivy League mavens and their upper-society millionaire candidates for public office. Yet he faces a test much more severe than Kennedy ever did in Houston.[392] The abortion question is much more fundamental than the inquiries of the Protestant clergy on that signal occasion which were most concerned about the separation dogma as it applied to Catholic schools in particular. Abortion is much more personal and emotion-laden.

He made his apologia, his defense, of his position as a Catholic and politician at Notre Dame University in September 1984.

The governor of New York rightly maintained that he is a practicing Catholic. Other politicians have sidestepped the inquisition of the pro-choice people by assuring that they are "lapsed Catholics" or "non-practicing," information sufficient to assure the inquisitors that an auto-da-fé is not necessary. By maintaining "the Taney contradiction," however, Cuomo cast a dark shadow upon his judgment.[393] His analysis of the Church-State problem, however, has tended to move the national debate along lines very compatible with the expressed thinking of the American bishops.

A staunch defender of the bishops' right to speak out, he argued that a Catholic public official must allow others to sin and that Catholic morality in all its details may not be imposed by law: "On divorce and birth control, without changing its moral teaching, the Church abides the civil law as it now stands thereby accepting — without making much of a point of it — that in our pluralistic society we are not required to insist that *all* our religious values be the law of the land."[394]

He warned, on the other hand, that just because something is taught by the Church in the field of morals does not disqualify it from being reflected in law nor per se "require its acceptability either."

On the separation doctrine, the governor endorsed the prudential opinion of the American bishops: "It is the judgment of the bishops and most of us Catholic lay people that it is not wise for prelates and politicians to be tied too closely together. ... This consensus (is) an extraordinarily useful achievement."[395]

In something of an apologetics for his fellow Democrat candidates for public office and most specifically the Reverend Jesse Jackson and dozens of Protestant, Jewish, and other clergy, he accepted sufferance without endorsement, tolerance without approval. "The American people will tolerate religious leaders taking positions for or against candidates, although I think the Catholic bishops are right in avoiding that position."

On the question of abortion he conceded that it had a "unique significance" but not a "pre-emptive" one precisely because it is not only abortion that involves life and death but also "nuclear weapons, hunger, homelessness and joblessness." Herein lies the basis for the Taney contradiction. If death, then to whom? If only potential life — the phrase defined as "existing in possibility not actuality" — then there can be no real death but only potential death, or at best, death to a potentiality.

"I can if so inclined demand some kind of law against abortion not because my bishop says it is wrong but because I think the whole community, regardless of its religious beliefs, should agree on the importance of protecting life, including life in the womb, which is at the very least potentially human and should not be extinguished casually.

"No law prevents us from advocating any of these things; I am free to do so."

The governor's response becomes even murkier when measured against the facts: Can he sustain the killing of the unborn right up to birth, of viable babies up to nine months in the womb — "only" one and a half percent of legal abortions are "late term," which translates to over fifteen thousand per year in the U.S. — with due respect to the Dr. Edelin and the Dr. Waddell cases in Los Angeles and Boston, these doctors convicted of homicide in trial courts for deaths at birth and freed on appeal under the Roe vs. Wade philosophy?

Frequent recourse in this debate is made to public opinion via the opinion polls. Essayist Roger Rosenblatt of *Time* and the Public Broadcasting Service reported in August 1991 that seventy-eight percent of the public supported the people's right to choose and then added what many polls show, that sixty percent of the people believe that abortion is murder. Rosenblatt tried, very unsuccessfully it seems, to reconcile the two positions. As a Catholic, the governor did not have the luxury of willfully befogging the debate in America by accepting the "choice for murder" as reported in poll after poll.

While insisting that he was free to do so, that is, to advocate a change in the laws, "if I were inclined," Cuomo obviously was not so inclined, rather just the opposite. As already described in Chapter 9, he held to the position that in spite of his personal convictions against abortion, yet he could in good conscience not only support abortion laws but use his great power of office to fund abortions.

As further proof of his passing the second Nativist test for his Americanism, he has been a consistent foe of any substantial support for the nonpublic schools. His concern that poor women need tax money so that they can get abortions just as well as the rich women does not translate into a "choice" in education wherein poor families, who would like to choose schools other than the public schools, do not enjoy the choice available to the rich. The same logic somehow gets lost and is compounded by the governor's vigorous action to help students above grade 12 no matter the college or university, all of which illustrates the fact that principles at times cede to expediency.

The governor entered a complaint: "Approval or rejection of legal restrictions on abortion should not be the exclusive litmus test of Catholic loyalty." Granted; but should it be the exclusive litmus test of American loyalty? Is abortion truly a unique case? So fundamental that it cannot be tolerated? The Church through its teaching authority answers clearly in the affirmative.

The Church has faced all sorts of evils in society, whether divorce, artificial contraception, artificial insemination, prostitution, abuse of drugs, unjust working conditions, hunger, war, discrimination based on gender or race. It has worked to remedy these evils within and without the legal system, at times quite successfully, at times not. Cuomo is quite correct to complain that as Catholics "we may rationalize our own laxity by urging the political system to legislate on others a morality we no longer practice ourselves." But is abortion different?

The Church says yes, precisely because the most fundamental human right is at stake: the right to life. Not only procured abortion but active euthanasia fall under the same concern for life. How can there be toleration or compromise on this most fundamental right? How can any American actively deny that right to life, once it exists? Is there an equivalency when a politician says he is against divorce but supports the law and says he's against abortion but supports the law? The bishops would respond that there's a deep if not intrinsic difference; there is not simply a difference of degree of gravity. Furthermore one cannot choose among the commandments: obey all but the fifth (against murder), or all but the seventh (against stealing). There is an integrity demanded.

In his peroration, Cuomo alluded to Nativism at least obliquely: "The Catholic Church has come of age in America. The ghetto walls are gone, our religion no longer a badge of irremediable foreignness. . . . This newfound status is both an opportunity and a temptation."

In the question period following Cuomo's *apologia pro vita sua*, he was challenged on seeming contradictions. Why had he consistently vetoed a bill in New York for capital punishment when it was clearly the will of the majority of New Yorkers? He answered lamely and to the groans of many in the audience that in one case the state was taking a life, in the other it was a woman's choice.[396]

Cuomo's quite sympathetic biographer Robert McElvaine summed up his own impressions: "The entire issue revolves around one question: is a fetus a living human being? If it is not, then there is no problem about abortion. If, however, it is once accepted that an unborn child is a human life, all the pragmatic arguments go out the window. Then abortion is murder and the obligation of the government to try to prevent that crime is clear. . . .

"Governor Cuomo tries to avoid the fundamental question of the humanity of a fetus. . . He answers: 'I have to conclude that the fetus is life or so close to life that it ought not to be disposed of casually.' That leaves him on thin ice."[397]

In Catholic moral theology, when the evil character of an action arising from its moral object — in this case the direct taking of an innocent human life — is so opposed to right reason, it cannot be altered or rescued by any external motive. Thus the excusing reasons alleged do not compensate for the malice of the act. McElvaine is correct: once one accepts that an unborn child is a human life, then excusing pragmatic causes "go out the window."

One year earlier Governor Cuomo had publicly congratulated the American bishops in these laudatory words: "As an American and a Catholic I am proud of you. It would have been easy to compromise your position so as to offend no one. You chose instead to tend to your duties as shepherds, to teach the moral law as best you can; you can do no more. Our Church has sometimes been accused of not having spoken out when it might have. Now you, our Bishops, show the courage and moral judgment to meet this issue of nuclear holocaust with a collective expression of where the Church in America stands."[398]

The governor, in 1990, praised the Catholic bishops for fostering the national debate on abortion but added something of a caveat: "We do not expect (the bishops) to be politicians . . . but (they are) not exempt from prudence in the political arena."[399]

When asked whether he would run for President in 1988, he wisely raised the question whether the United States was willing to elect an Italian American, a perspicacious perception to which might be added: a first generation New Yorker, one generation removed from Italy, and a Catholic. The judgment of the political pundits was that he would have trouble in the South. Yet he was justly described in the London *Tablet* as "the brainiest and most exciting personality on the American scene . . . a potential presidential candidate who could probably have the Democratic nomination for the asking."[400]

While he stoutly defended his position on abortion along the lines of his Notre Dame speech, under pressure from Sam Donaldson on TV, he not only asserted that his position was accepted by some Catholic theologians, but for the first time in public he cited a source, Father Richard McCormick, a Jesuit at Notre Dame University. Their agreement was, however, not necessarily on the question of abortion but rather on the criterion for laws on abortion, namely that a basic tenet of public policy is its feasibility. Both seemed to agree that a very prohibitive law would not be feasible, given the mentality and morals of the American public. Both, it would appear, would also agree that the wide-open abortion on demand is not feasible either. The public needs to be persuaded. Most Catholic theologians of whatever stripe judge abortion as a grave evil.

The governor in December 1991 took himself out of the race for President. Barring the distinct possibility of a popular draft at the Democratic nomination in New York City in the summer of 1992, he will remain something of an enigmatic character. His explanation that while he would very much like to run for President but had to remain in New York because of a budget crisis seemed rather lame.

His retreat to the fringe of presidential candidacies has fueled much speculation and second-guessing. Did he perceive an erosion in support over the years? In 1986, he scored a landslide victory over a rich and attractive Republican who was anti-abortion; in 1990 he lost considerable ground as he defeated a relatively unknown Republican candidate for governor. During the 1988 presidential campaign he openly queried whether the U.S. was ready for and willing to elect an Italian American. The question was severely exacerbated in January 1992 when presidential candidate Bill Clinton, governor of Arkansas, was heard to say on the excerpted tape furnished by Gennifer Flowers that Cuomo was "mean" and acts like a mafioso. Cuomo's response was that Clinton's remarks were "part of that ugly syndrome that strikes Italian Americans, Jewish people, blacks, women, all the different ethnic groups." Interestingly, he did not mention religion.

Did the shrinkage in support among the governor's own natural constituency (the Italian Americans, the Irish, Polish, Latino Americans) plus American Catholics in general have a major part in his decision? Public-opinion polls would answer in the negative; election results cast a shadow over the conclusions of the polls. The American Catholic is no longer an "automatic" Democrat, even at the congressional level.

According to pollster Patrick Caddell in 1982, sixty-three percent of the Catholic population voted for Democrats for Congress while in 1986 that number had fallen to fifty-five percent.[401] Coupled with the post-election diagnosis on the John F. Kennedy election that two million voted against him because he was Catholic, the governor could not help but wonder. He has been subjected to a single-issue litmus test of his "Americanism" because he is a Catholic and a double-issue litmus test on his Catholicism because he is pro-choice in abortion and anti-choice in education.

In any event, Governor Cuomo does deserve a great deal of credit for being willing at least to face up to the question of abortion and not hide and dodge like so many other politicians who are Catholic. As his biographer Robert McElvaine, pro-Cuomo and sympathetic to his dilemma, concluded: the governor tries to avoid the fundamental question of the humanity of the fetus. To be or not to be, that is the question, no matter whether the question is the right to life or the right to deny life. As one student of history wrote: "The bishops have a good case against Cuomo; he is politically speaking 'pro-choice' and seems to endorse uncritically the legal status quo."[402]

Consistency would seem clearly on the side of the bishops in their concern for human life.

Speaking from the same platform at Notre Dame just eleven days later and in an obvious reply to Mario Cuomo, Congressman Henry J. Hyde of Illinois, a Republican, delineated the parameters of the attacks on politicians who are Catholic. He saw not a simple anti-Catholicism but a Nativism as well.

"Our citizenship is on trial . . . for imposing our views and forcing our beliefs on the community . . . and our bishops accused of violating the constitutional separation of Church and State. . . . (We are told) literally to go sit in the back of the bus." The Catholic public official, he added, lives under a cloud of suspicion.

Recalling John Kennedy's famous speech in Houston, Hyde put forward the thesis that times have changed dramatically since that time. The chief question is no longer whether a commitment to Catholic teaching is compatible with public office in America but rather whether the American experiment can survive the sterilization in the public arena that takes place when religious-based values are systematically ruled out of order in public discourse.[403]

The bottom line for all who believe in the sacredness of the life of the unborn regardless of religion or politics was expressed by George Grant: "The fetus is a living member of our species. It is a fact accepted by all scientists, that the individual has his or her unique genetic code from the moment of conception. He or she is therefore not simply a part of the mother's body."[404]

On mixing religion and politics, Hyde seemed to agree with Cuomo that "Churches as institutions should not play a formal role in our political process both for the sake of their own integrity as the integrity of our politics," but their leaders should speak out on moral issues.[405] Why does the Reverend Jesse Jackson enjoy special immunity denied others? "All religious leaders should be held to the same standard . . . observe the same limits. . . . Consistency is one antidote to hypocrisy." Personal conscience and civic responsibility cannot be sundered, he concluded.

How then does a public official meet the challenge on abortion?

The congressman argued that the matter is not per se religious at all but clearly a moral and civil rights issue; there need be no appeal to the Bible, theology, or Church doctrine that the politician who is Catholic must make clear what is at issue, both the life of an unborn child and more the political health of America; that he reject the *absolute* separation doctrine in spite of the secularists and the feminists.

Do politicians change with the winds or rather with the public-opinion polls? Some undoubtedly do, Hyde inferred, as he quoted a private letter dated August 3, 1971: "While the deep concern of a woman bearing an unwanted child merits consideration and sympathy, it is my personal feeling that the legalization of abortion on demand is not in accordance with the value which must be recognized — the right to be born, the right to love, the right to grow old. . . .

"When history looks back to this era it should recognize this generation as one which cared about human beings enough to halt the practice of war, to provide a decent living for every family, and to fulfill its responsibility to its children from the very moment of conception.

This was "a beautiful statement in 1971," exclaimed Hyde, written by an unmarried "Senator, a prominent Catholic, perhaps the most famous of our Senators" who has repeatedly voted pro-abortion with tax money and, it might be added, opposed the Catholic schools in their quest for a modicum of equal treatment. Hyde described that senator as the most influential Catholic in the U.S. Senate without using his name.

Cuomo and Hyde stand very much in agreement in their general approach on the role of the bishops, in their objection to a single-issue litmus test, in the relationship of religion to public morality; but they part company radically on "parking one's religion at the door of the governor's office or of the legislature," or maintaining a personal position in private and a contradictory one in public in an area so fundamental and so basic as the right to life. Toleration extended to the killing of the unborn in the political order divides these two politicians fundamentally.[406]

If elected officials who were Catholic faced a special litmus test, nominees for the judiciary found themselves subjected to the same trial. The relationship between a moral standard on abortion and conduct as a judge became the diagnostic criterion, even for the highest tribunals.

One of the century's leading philosophers of law, the Supreme Court Justice Benjamin Cardozo (1932-38), put forward the picture of a judge with a conscience and a moral standard as he faced the law of the land: "What really matters is this, that the judge is under duty, within the limits of his power of innovation, to maintain a relation between law and morals, between the precepts of jurisprudence and those of reason and good conscience. . . . The constant insistence that morality and justice are not law has tended to breed distrust and contempt of law as something to which morality and justice are not merely alien, but hostile."[407]

Standing before an outdoor microphone at Kennebunkport, President Bush announced on July 1, 1991, his nomination of Judge Clarence Thomas for the Supreme Court. In his very brief reply to the President's words, Judge Thomas thanked not only his family members but with some emotion "the nuns" who were his teachers in elementary and secondary schools, sending ominous shudders and shimmers of panic and discomfort over the pro-abortionists of the nation and the public schools monopoly establishment.

Born into an impoverished black family in Georgia, the nominee was for a short time a student for the priesthood, a graduate of Holy Cross College, and the Yale Law School. When it was later revealed that he was attending the Episcopal Church with his second wife, he was still rendered suspect because he had attended Catholic schools. Father Robert Drinan, former congressman and professor of law at Georgetown University, predicted: "They will torture him."

No one did so more deftly than Alan M. Dershowitz, a Harvard law professor. In an article that had the veneer of objectivity, Dershowitz attacked in these words: "Few nominees to the Supreme Court has (sic) shown so many changes in fundamental attitudes in so short a time as has Thomas in the twenty odd years since he attended Holy Cross College." He added that Thomas had a good word for the "natural law" to the displeasure of the Harvard maven. The rapierlike thrust was both disingenuous and insidious, with an artful insinuating indirectness.

No other school was mentioned, just the Catholic one. Since the nomination concerned a judge already sitting at the appellate level, would it not have been more *ad rem* for the law professor to have referred to Thomas's law school and to have counted the years out of the Yale Law School, which would have made a shorter period to bolster his point? Did not the Yale Law School form the student in the law and the philosophy of law? Would not that fact be more germane?[408]

Holy Cross College, natural law, the nuns, the seminary training were just code words, seeming euphemisms — a fate so long suffered by the Afro-American, Asian American, Mexican American, and Jewish American segments of the population — that would mask the real objection: a Catholic, even a divorced man attending the Episcopal Church, could not be trusted on abortion because he attended Catholic schools. Was there a religious test for a Catholic seeking political office?

Feature writer Charles A. Coulombe hit the nail on the head when he wrote: "If Clarence Thomas is denied a seat on the Supreme Court, it will not be because he was born black, but because he was raised a Catholic."[409] Beneath it all, however, lay the question not of civil rights on which the

Church and its schools enjoyed a good record but of abortion and the right to life of the unborn.

Dershowitz named no other names of the "few"; his reference to natural law was a patent ploy, since most legal scholars in their study of the law must at times come across the natural law, whether in Aristotle, Aquinas, Grotius, John Locke, Kant, Jefferson, Madison, or John Marshall. Protestant theologian John C. Bennett put the matter this way: "We should also recognize that the natural law tradition in the various stages of its history has been a great treasure and that out of it has come much of the humanizing of western society and many gains for human freedom."[410]

As Dershowitz knew full well, the great body of American law has much of its origin in theories of natural law, variously conceived, vagrantly understood, and irresolutely interpreted. It was a slick maneuver to castigate Thomas, vague enough to avoid criticism of its perpetrator, and relatively immune to easy refutation. Actually the Harvard savant was employing a code word by interpreting natural law as propounded by the great scholastic philosopher St. Thomas Aquinas. In plain English, he was labeling the judge as "Catholic" and therefore suspect.

Virginia's Governor Douglas Wilder entered the fray, asserting that the abortion issue was fair game because of Thomas's Catholic education. Himself an Afro-American Baptist, Wilder put the key question: "How much allegiance is there to the Pope?" because "he (Thomas) has indicated that he was a devout Catholic," which, of course, Thomas had not.

Author Tom Clancy took aim at Wilder and others: "By what supreme arrogance does anyone demand that another person must step away from his religious beliefs in order to be a decent public servant?"

Editor Richard McMunn of *Columbia* magazine left no doubt that "in [Wilder's] view — shared by many others — Catholics are second class citizens, fit to hold public office only after passing a religious litmus test. Make no mistake about it, anti-Catholicism is not dead, though in recent years it has become more sophisticated and less overt. . . ."[411]

An aide to Wilder said the next day that the governor "apologized if he offended anyone." There was no question that he had deeply offended people and especially Catholics. Bishop Walter F. Sullivan of Richmond, Virginia, found the governor's remarks "inappropriate and unfortunate."[412]

The president of the Massachusetts State Senate, Billy Bulger, in support of Thomas, retorted, "How can a black governor lend support to a nascent doctrine of religious apartheid for the Supreme Court?"

Yet Senator Orrin Hatch of Utah supported Wilder: "I think it's fair to ask if his Catholic faith means he would blindly follow the Pope. You can ask the question in a sophisticated way that would be less offensive than what Wilder said. . . ." Within a few days Hatch's aides were backtracking, pointing out that the senator was in favor of the Thomas nomination and did not mean what the unfortunate quotations seemed to imply.

At any rate, the insidious deeper undertone of it all was the clear implication that Catholics do not and cannot think for themselves but must take orders from Rome, a throwback to the nineteenth-century climate in the twentieth century.

The Catholic League for Religious and Civil Rights questioned the Americanism of the questioners: "To implicitly call into question a nominee's fitness on the basis of his religious faith betrays a complete misunderstanding of the principles upon which this country was founded. The long discredited charge of dual loyalty against American Catholics, Wilder has revived. Such suggestions are unjust, intolerant and un-American."

Tom Clancy described what he plainly called bigotry: "We have come full circle. Here we have a black using against a black the same argument used by white bigots against a white."

Michael Devlin of Harmonton, N.J., wrote to the governor: "If similar litmus tests were required for Jewish or black Muslim candidates for Justice (Judge), the media outcry would be swift, vitriolic, compelling. So strong would be the response that politicians of your caliber (Wilder, i.e.) would know in advance that such comments could not be made."[413] He concluded: "What is particularly galling in your comments is that Catholics are a safe target for your obvious form of prejudice."

The attacks on Judge Thomas were both crude and subtle, but there was no mistaking that there was an explicit and an implicit religious test. The president of NOW, Patricia Ireland, vowed: "We will Bork him," referring to the successful campaign against Judge Robert Bork, largely because of his position on abortion. The *Washington Post* dug up a speech in which Thomas had said something favorable about "natural law," implying that it was an "alien philosophy," again a code word for Catholic and St. Thomas Aquinas, ignoring the fact that many of the Founding Fathers and legislators down the years used the same term in discussing legislation.

The nation's cartoonists had a field day with the nomination. Some, like the one in the *Chicago Tribune*, twitted the opposition by caricaturing three men asking seriatim for an Afro-American justice, a Hispanic, and a defender of civil rights, then showing profound shock by exclaiming: "Good God, a Catholic!" The *Philadelphia Daily News* showed a pompous bishop complete with miter and crosier proclaiming that he was pro-choice in education so that he could have the "State giving your tax money to parents to give to me so that I can teach their kids to be against choice in abortion." It was a two-edged sword, a cartoon that could easily be turned around to show that "pro-choice" to kill the unborn is scarcely the same as "pro-choice" to educate. The *Gazette Telegraph* of Colorado Springs showed likenesses of Senators Howard Metzenbaum, Edward Kennedy, Paul Simon, and two others of the Senate Judiciary Committee sharpening knives to carve up the nominee: "This could get tricky! We've got to figure out a way to carve him up without hitting his skin," a clear reference that extra-racial subjects must effect the defeat. Metzenbaum was the only senator who openly advocated putting Thomas on the spot on abortion; the others played it more cautiously, but, given their public positions on abortion, they could hardly keep up a disinterested façade. Years before, Senator Kennedy had said that it was "offensive to suggest that a potential justice of the Supreme Court must pass some presumed test of judicial philosophy."

Former Mayor of New York Ed Koch singled out Senator Metzenbaum, who had averred that if he disagreed on any specific issues, that fact would not affect his judgment. Koch cited the senators as not letting Thomas "get off the reservation because he didn't want a black on the court who doesn't want to take whites on a guilt trip." Acidly the mayor added: "Shall we impose the 'politically correct' views now sweeping our universities upon the courts as well?" The senator was evidently willing to make an exception and apply the litmus test on abortion.[414]

The "nun theme" was featured in the *Cincinnati Enquirer*, depicting a very fat and bloated Judge Thomas leading three equally grotesque nuns in black hoods like witches following him into the Court chambers singing Alleluia. Two justices, presumably Harry A. Blackmun and John P. Stevens, are depicted openly lamenting, "Well, there goes Roe v. Wade." The *Milwaukee Journal* choked on the word "nun," reporting only that the judge thanked his "mentors." *Time* magazine's depiction of the "nuns," who are not really nuns at all but simply religious Sisters in congregation, as "doting," drew a pert retort from the Sisters themselves, which *Time* published, assuring one and all that they were still working full time and were not at all in their dotage.

As might be expected from his long record of anti-Catholicism, Australian immigrant Patrick Oliphant published a cartoon showing an oversized nun with rosary in one hand and a ruler in the other, the Sister being white, towering over a small black youngster who had been just rapped on his knuckles, which were still hurting. The domineering teacher takes the role of prophet as she says: "Now once again, Clarence. . . . When we become a Supreme Court Justice, how do we rule on the abortion issue?" Two nuns stand in the background and the usual and characteristic jotting of this cartoonist adds the ominous warning: "Wait for the separation of Church and State — that's a real knuckle-buster."[415]

Oliphant was correct: he and many others were much more concerned about the "school question" than even abortion. But both issues were joined in Judge Thomas who magnanimously thanked the Irish-born American Sisters who were indeed his "mentors" in a segregated school where the nuns were the only whites.

As the date September 10, 1991, approached for the Senate hearing on the nomination, the attack became just slightly more subtle. The first waves of opposition were open and forthright; the subsequent not. The euphemism came into play: Where does Thomas stand on privacy rights? on Church-State problems? on affirmative action, covering up the litmus test on abortion already applied by the NAACP, the Urban League, and others previously? The NBC network flashed a picture of Thomas in cassock and surplice at the seminary that he attended for one year. The Senate hearings, not the public opposition, were touted to be decisive, that Judge Thomas was not *a priori* to be rejected.

The AFL-CIO opposed the nominee because of his stand on labor matters; the NAACP called him hostile to affirmative action and civil rights while not allowing its membership — then meeting in plenary session — to vote on the matter. Both of these giant organizations would have been more credible had they not just a few months earlier rammed through a pro-abortion resolution, much to the dismay of much of their membership. The AFL-CIO rescinded its original positions on abortion, "deferring to the individual judgments of its . . . members."[416] Both organizations could have come forward with cleaner hands.

Albert Shanker of the public school teachers' union, the American Federation of Teachers (AFT), publicly opposed Thomas, as did Planned Parenthood. The latter was particularly in bad faith because of its virulent opposition to "one-issue tests" in the past. Its president, Mrs. Faye Wattleton, continually positioned herself and Planned Parenthood as examples of "the American way."

The Senate hearings devolved almost entirely into a one-issue, a single-litmus, test that the senators had *ante factum* eschewed.

No impartial observer of the Senate hearings on the confirmation of Judge Clarence Thomas could possibly but conclude that there was only one test, the litmus test on where he stood on abortion. There were well over one hundred fifty instances that the matter was invoked. Senator Hatch complained that in the first two days Thomas had been asked the question over seventy times. Like football coaches trying to pierce a defense the senators tried straight-ahead bulldozing drives, fake reverses, end arounds, short passes, long passes, punts, counter reverses, play action plays, all the while telling the nation in effect that there is a litmus test, a one-issue demonstration and proof. The very ones who denounced the pro-lifers as "one-issue" fanatics became the one-issue inquisitors led by pro-abortion Senators Metzenbaum, Simon, Biden, and Kennedy. One end run was repeated over and over; it was introduced by Senator Joseph Biden under the title of "natural law." Was this not an indirect way to get at abortion and the Catholic judgment? It seemed so.

Judge Thomas cited in reply the Declaration of Independence as an endorsement of "natural law" with its God-given rights as evident and inalienable. It was pointed out that Judge Bork was repudiated at his confirmation hearings precisely because he did not believe in natural law; that Jefferson, Madison, Lincoln, John Locke, and many modern justices cited natural law in their opinions. The senators then disavowed having a "one-issue" mind, allowing a tolerance for natural law and an acceptance of the Declaration of Independence. But the merry-go-round on the question seemed utterly disingenuous: the senators could not afford to leave themselves vulnerable to a charge of religious bias. The press, however, saw the point.

Since Thomas attended only Catholic schools up to Yale Law, his idea of natural law would have to be that of one of its greatest expositors, St. Thomas Aquinas. Presumably Aquinas would be "pro-life" and hence a jurist could solve the Roe vs. Wade abortion case "from the sky."

Curiously, St. Thomas has often been cited as one who believed in a delayed hominization. "Relying on the state of biological knowledge of his day, Aquinas erroneously concluded that in human generation the male seed was the only active element. ... The earlier stages were succeeded by a human body informed by a human intellectual soul ... (with) a radical discontinuity ... among the bodies successively generated in the process of hominization." He even thought boys developed forty days ahead of girls.

Modern science does not mistake plant and nonhuman bodies for the human. Given his own principles, St. Thomas, with modern biological knowledge, would undoubtedly have concluded that "a human body must be animated by a human soul."[417]

On other grounds, Aquinas was anti-abortion and pro-life in his own times, precisely because he held to the natural law. Coyly, Senator Patrick Moynihan mentioned that an inscription on the Department of Justice Building in the U.S. capital reads: "Justice is founded on the rights bestowed by nature on man."

But all was fair in love and war and presumably in the Senate hearings.

Out of Washington, D.C., the Reuters News Service sent the following: "13th century theorist ideas to figure in Thomas hearings." The article described natural law: "The idea is strongly identified in the 13th century Catholic Theologian. ... (and) we hold these truths to be self-evident." Reuters continued: "Critics say Thomas' views based on religious beliefs put him (Judge Thomas) outside the mainstream of U.S. law."[418]

From his Birmingham jail years before, Martin Luther King, Jr., as he languished in his cell, wrote of just and unjust laws, citing both St. Augustine and St. Thomas Aquinas, adding that "a just law is a man-made code that squares with the moral law or the moral law of God. An unjust law is a code which is out of harmony with the moral order."[419] At any rate, the Senate Judiciary Committee finally found out the meaning of natural law and let the matter rest.

Syndicated New York columnist Anna Quindlen defined the natural law as "a tool of discrimination" in history or "just another name for personal religious beliefs and was apprehensive about what role such beliefs should properly play in the decision of the Supreme Court."[420] Similar comments were made by "experts" describing natural law: "It's God's law," "It's God's truth," "It's in the sky," and, in the words of Harvard's Dean Griswald, "a brooding on the presence in the sky" in sharp contrast to Judge Thomas's own definition, "the science of the rights of man," which was quite philosophical but not primarily theological or religious, much less denominational or Catholic.

When Judge David Souter was nominated for the Supreme Court in 1990 there was really a two-issue litmus test. Questions were raised not about his willingness to support public schools but about his willingness to aid the religious schools. In spite of the play-by-play TV exposure during several days of questioning, Souter refused to answer a specific question: a senator put the matter frankly: "The whole case has boiled down to one issue," namely abortion.

The media reporters badgered President Bush about Souter: "The first and almost only question asked of the President was 'Did you ask him about abortion?' " The President and Souter spent their time explaining that it was improper to select a justice on a single issue that would surely come before the Court. But if Justice Souter got off easy, Judge Thomas certainly did not; there followed the "one-issue inquisition," a new test for public office at the highest level. Is inquisition too harsh a word, too dipped in history and the past to be relevant?

Syndicated columnist Richard Cohen wrote that the "Salem witch trials of 1692 and the Clarence Thomas hearings have much in common." Two years earlier, the Senate Judiciary Committee had "trashed" William Lucas, a black conservative Republican candidate for governor in Michigan, graduate of Fordham University, and just incidentally a Catholic and anti-abortion, for a presidential appointment. Coincidence? Cohen didn't seem to think so. Afro-American columnist William Raspberry accused some of the senators of "going beyond the pale"; "Metzenbaum was close to McCarthyesque" and Kennedy seemed "either vicious or moronic." Thomas was, he wrote, being portrayed as someone foreign and alien to American jurisprudence.[421] One day later black Congressman John Conyers assured that "we have reached out to religious organizations; we have the churches mobilized" against Judge Thomas. Leaders in the black community were constantly saying that they would say the same things about a white candidate. Raspberry was direct: "I don't believe them."[422]

The Thomas hearings became even more heated and complicated with the sudden advent of Anita Hill, a university professor and former assistant to Judge Thomas. She accused Thomas of sexual harassment, pushing the daily soap operas off the air in favor of real-life drama. Without judging the merits of the show-trial, it may well be pointed out that the abortion question lay at the root of most of the encounter.

The virulently pro-abortion feminists promoted Miss Hill into a national martyr and a champion of women's rights, the first being the right to abort their unborn. While abortion had become the forbidden word, the euphemisms and code words had not. But at one point in the extensive questioning of Miss Hill, one Republican senator asked her if she disagreed with Thomas "philosophically." She answered in the affirmative. Did that mean that she supported abortion rights? She answered "yes" before Senator Biden shut off the conversation, ruling the matter out of order. But the cat was out of the bag: there was no question as to what the chief issue was. Miss Hill was the newly-discovered weapon of the pro-abortion feminist groups, their paramount issue being abortion and their chief target the Catholic Church.

The Judiciary Committee ended in a tie vote of 7 to 7, with six Republicans and Democrat Dennis DeConcini voting in favor of the nomination. On October 17, 1991, the Senate approved 52 to 48.

Faye Wattleton of Planned Parenthood vowed that abortion would be *the* issue in the 1992 elections. Polls showed, however, that blacks favored Thomas more than 2 to 1. The liberal state senator from Rhode Island, David Carlin, Jr., wrote on November 8, 1991: "If there were no abortion issue dividing the country, Thomas would have been confirmed by a lopsided majority. . . ."[423]

Just a few weeks later, William Barr sat before the same Judiciary Committee, which was battered and bent from the caustic and mordant criticisms of their erstwhile hearings on the Thomas nomination. Nominated by President Bush for the post of attorney general of the United States, Barr gave a very direct and forthright answer: yes, he was opposed to Roe vs. Wade. His response elicited an admiring rejoinder from Chairman Biden who said that in light of what had lately transpired, his answer was "refreshing" to say the least. But Biden went further: he told Barr that if he came before the Judiciary Committee as a nominee for the Supreme Court, he would oppose the presidential nomination. What was not said was that William Barr is a practicing Catholic.[424] Was it not another way to say: "No Catholics need apply"?

There had appeared then on the American scene a new litmus test for "Americanism." It was new because until the 1970s abortion was illegal in every state. The school question was not at all abandoned, but it had to take second billing to the issue of the right to life for the unborn. The U.S. courts had found a new liberty: the liberty to kill the unborn right up to and including birth.

Judge John Newsom of the First Circuit Court of the Federal Court of Appeals offered this judicial opinion: "Abortion and childbirth when stripped of sensitive moral argument are just two alternative methods of dealing with pregnancy." Judge John T. Noonan of the Ninth Circuit Court replied: "John Newsom's way of eliminating the moral issue lends itself to parody; stripped of the moral arguments surrounding them, embezzlement and the cashing of a cheque are simply two alternative ways of withdrawing money from a bank."[425]

In essence, what Judge Newsom and many more were saying was that in effect the churches should not mix morals and politics, that the churches, synagogues, and mosques should stay indoors and preach only to their own communities.[426] Morality, they insisted, had no place in the political and judicial contests over abortion.

Abortion had become *the* litmus test for all politicians, legislators, judges, and administrators who sought public service. But the argument was the same: it was un-American to be anti-abortion and pro-voluntary school, grades K through 12 only.

There was one difference, however, between the two issues. Abortion, at least in law, was not obligatory: Catholics or others, at least in theory, did not have to have abortions if they didn't want them. The school question was not the same: Catholics and others were subject to compulsory-education laws, and in the words of Supreme Court Justice Robert Jackson, "doubly burdened" to pay taxes for schools not used and tuition to sustain their choice. The same people who were so "pro-choice" on abortion were for the most part anti-choice on the school question; Catholics and others could be seen as pro-life and pro-choice respectively. But as Milton Himmelfarb said: Catholics (and others) have "a true grievance" on the school question.

Strange to relate, the guardian of the one-issue litmus test is the Internal Revenue Service, which is charged with seeing to it that tax laws forbidding certain political activities by tax-exempt organizations are observed, a perfectly understandable postulate. The IRS decided to take over policing chores as a sort of fair-campaigns committee, using its power to tax as its very potent weapon. Theirs has been a classic case of straining the gnat and swallowing the camel.

In 1978 and 1985, the IRS published its regulations directing that religious organizations may not participate in any political campaign on behalf of any candidate for public office, either directly or indirectly by participation or intervention, which "includes but is not limited to the publication or distribution of written or printed statements or the making of oral statements on behalf of or in opposition to a candidate." It further strictly limited the role of religious organizations in voter-education projects designed to inform the electorate of the views of candidates. Voter guides may state the position of a candidate on a wide range of issues but cannot evidence "bias on certain issues, even if not expressing support or opposition."[427]

This warning was sent to every Catholic bishop in the United States: don't allow participation in elections, directly or indirectly; muzzle your diocesan papers; cease pamphleteering; talk only of a wide range of issues, but don't say how a candidate stands for anything; and, of course, allow no single issue auto-da-fé for any politician. What was the IRS sanction? The tax exemption of the Church would be put in jeopardy.

This opéra bouffe was accented by a court case in New York challenging the tax-exempt status of the Catholic Church because of its stand on abortion, the action having been initiated by the Abortion Rights Mobilization (an arm of NOW), several abortion clinics, and Protestant and Jewish clerics, in 1980, and finally settled in 1991.

Ironically, the IRS found itself the sole defendant in this case, Judge Robert L. Carter dismissing the bishops' conference as codefendant. For nine years, however, the conference had to defend itself in the courts on this one case, spending about a half million dollars in defense and amicus curiae briefs.

The tax code prohibits tax-exempt entities from intervening in campaigns for public office. Another provision gives the churches the right to lobby, so long as it is not "a substantial part of its activities." On August 30, 1990, the IRS, after a five-year delay during which it harassed the bishops and the pro-life organizations, issued regulations about lobbying; there are recognized direct lobbying and grassroots lobbying. Churches, even if they qualify under section 501(h), still remain subject to 501(c)3, that is, under the old substantiality rule. Canons on how to transfer funds from 501(c)3 organizations to 501(c)4 lobbying organizations are spelled out, which would excuse the IRS from pursuing Planned Parenthood, NARAL, NOW, and others that make the distinction between funds tax exempt and not.

Add to these tergiversations the more fundamental question of the First Amendment in both its free-exercise and free-speech clauses and it is no wonder that Justice Scalia cried "chaos" on the Church-State legislation.

"Churches," according to an article in the University of Virginia Law School journal, "must act at their peril as they attempt to walk the obscure line between loss of exemption and faithfulness to the obligation to speak out on the moral dimension of important social issues."

It is not too harsh a judgment to label these efforts of the IRS bureaucracy as a cruel charade; worse, it showed its own bias and prejudices. Was the IRS seriously questioning the one-issue campaign for Israel, for Lithuania, for Palestine? Was it concerned about the Planned Parenthood's obsession with the abortion question? or NARAL? or NOW? The most blatant disregard and indeed flouting of its own regulations occurred during the presidential campaign of 1988. The IRS, which came down so hard on the Catholic Church and some of the right-wing Fundamentalist sects like Attila the Hun on Rome to see to it that elections were protected from the tax-exempt, itself soon became as silent and as active as the sphinx in Cairo.

Two Protestant ministers, American-born citizens of proper age, ran for the nomination of their parties: the Reverend Pat Robertson, Republican, and the Reverend Jesse Jackson, Democrat. Both won presidential primaries in several states. Their candidacies, although forbidden by Church law to Catholic priests, is not at issue here; the descent from fortissimo to pianissimo by the IRS certainly is.

With quite open abandon these two Protestant ministers made churches all over the land the anchors of their purely partisan campaigns. Without any scruples they registered communicants inside the churches; they delivered partisan political "sermons" from the sanctuaries; they organized Protestant clergy into active workers, advising them to do the same things in their own churches in partisan support; and quite unabashedly collected money for their campaigns within the church precincts themselves.[428]

While the silent acquiescence was not confined to the IRS, the media (press, radio, and television), the so-called "patriotic" organizations, and, of course, the ACLU were agreeably quiet; but these could not directly threaten a loss of tax exemption. None of them were silent when the Catholic Church taught that abortion is wrong because it extinguishes a human life; that true freedom in education meant a freedom to choose without penalty; and that family values in the U.S.A. were steadily being eroded — all clearly nonpartisan and applied to Republicans, Democrats, and other parties as well.

Virtually every Catholic in America would resent a politician speaking from his parish's pulpit on partisan politics, regardless of party affiliation. The Catholic bishops have made no endorsements of candidates, no collection of funds for them, and no partisan propaganda — all of which is very much anathema to most Church-going Catholics in the U.S. The rare exceptions would tend to prove the rule.

The *New York Times*, as has been mentioned, could blithely report that the presidents of the major Jewish synagogues formally endorsed Walter Mondale, the Democrat, for President, asking their people in and out of the synagogue to support him. The same paper that so reported, had no problem just a few weeks previously denouncing the American bishops: "It might as well be said bluntly. . . . The Catholic bishops' effort to impose a religious test on the performance of Catholic politicians threaten the hard-won understanding that finally brought Americans to elect a Catholic president a generation ago."[429]

In an attempt to get an answer to the seeming multiple and discriminatory standards employed by the IRS, a group of twenty graduate students sent four letters, properly and courteously addressed and registered, to the Honorable Fred Goldberg, commissioner of the IRS in Washington, D.C., asking for a clarification of 501-C, the regulation forbidding Church participation in single-issue politics and campaigns in general.[430]

The letter of March 12, 1990, respectfully called attention to the partisan political activities by tax-exempt organizations in favor of abortion and engaging so in an obvious "single-issue" campaign. It further mentioned the course of action by the Reverend Mr. Robertson and the Reverend Mr. Jackson. The letter specifically eschewed a "philosophical answer," only whether the promulgated regulations still applied. After sending four letters over a period of sixteen months, it became clear that the IRS was stonewalling, which called for a letter to a representative in Congress.[431] The letter from Congress got action but only to the House member. So a fifth letter, duly registered, was sent, which elicited a response three months later that the IRS "had no record" of the four letters, and that "generally" the IRS is prohibited from revealing confidential tax information and cannot tell of any action "we may take or have taken."[432] The letters to the IRS, nevertheless, did not ask for such information, only whether the regulations apply and are enforced.

There is no question in this opinion that the IRS has used a double standard, casting a blind eye toward the black politicians "for historical reasons"; it is less evident why the protective mantle around the pro-abortion forces was allowed. Yet the Catholic bishops were warned explicitly. The IRS was purblind and stonewalling but in a very selective manner: abortion was the real question. The single-issue complaint was bogus and Church activity selectively condoned.

Rabbi Arthur Gilbert asserted that "one answer does not reflect the candidate's loyalty to America and his freedom from church domination." Presbyterian theologian Robert McAfee Brown warned: "To isolate one issue, such as a candidate's religious affiliation, and make that the only issue on which to base one's vote seems to me to be political naïveté. A man's total voting record. . ." should be examined.

The IRS, however, showed great zeal about single-issue politics in the early 1980s, only to lose such zeal when the worm turned to pro-abortion. The Reverend Pat Robertson, who is pro-life, and his university were heavily fined in 1992.

The campaign for mayor in 1990 in Washington, D.C., right under the nose of the Internal Revenue Service, meanwhile, illustrated the point. Not only were Protestant ministers running for office, but all the candidates were using the churches and their staffs to collect money, mail literature, use telephones, and carry on a full-blown campaign.

In 1978 and 1985, the IRS could get away with its "single-issue" regulations. What happened to the separation of Church and State doctrine so dear to the secularists and secular humanists? Dozens of Protestant ministers, Jewish rabbis, and other clergy could ramble in the briar patch of partisan politics with abandon, but heaven help the grassroots protester of the killing of the unborn!

Why should not the religious citizen have equal rights to influence Congress, to lobby, and to help form public policy without being harassed by the media or government? Martin Luther King, Jr., was first of all a Protestant minister. Nor does anyone question (nor should they) an American Jew with dual citizenship in his lobbying for a country with its foreign policy based partly and deeply upon the Bible and the Talmud.

The point here does not intend or suggest even a scintilla of criticism of these activities by people clearly identified as using religion, churches, and religion-related organizations for their perceived just goals. As a prudential judgment, on the other hand, Governor Cuomo hit the nail on the head: "The American people will tolerate religious leaders taking positions for or against candidates, although I think the Catholic bishops are right in avoiding that position."

The IRS did take action that was upheld in the Supreme Court: Bob Jones University, the fountainhead of Fundamentalism and anti-Catholic action, was denied tax exemption but on the grounds, properly, of racial discrimination and not on the basis of partisan activity in politics or single-issue campaigning of which it has been equally guilty.

There has been preferential treatment in the government bureaucracy and in the media: Catholics are not treated equally. The IRS, for one, has its own selective morality in the application of regulation 501-C. Mr. Goldberg may well protest that the notice of 501-C was sent to all churches, synagogues, and temples. The question is: What has the IRS done about it? What of the ongoing apparent violations by the politicians, many operating in the nation's capital under the very eyes and ears of the IRS?

Why harass the Catholic bishops and ignore the Protestants and Jews?[433] Why refuse even to question the one-issue campaigns of the very vocal, vociferous, and semi-hysterical feminists of NOW and NARAL, one-issue partisans if ever there be such? Exemplars of one-issue politics par excellence? Was the IRS purblind or hiding in affected ignorance?

Over the years, however, Catholics have supported thousands of politicians who would not have passed a single litmus test on justice for voluntary schools or on the right to life. Up until the presidential campaign of George McGovern, with what most Catholics perceived to be a blatantly antifamily platform, most Catholics were Democrats and so voted.

They found no trouble in backing the presidents, many of whom were Freemasons, Truman being Thirty-third Degree; Generals Douglas MacArthur, Mark Clark, and others; governors galore, judges, senators, and congresspersons, even though they held out only slight if any hope for justice for schoolchildren. As stated already, they did not have to face abortion, homosexuality, euthanasia, modern techniques of contraception, and a host of other medical-moral questions. They accepted the premise that these men and women of good faith would be fair and just. At times their credulity was stretched to the limit.

Justice Hugo Black of the U.S. Supreme Court, formerly of the Ku Klux Klan, was bitterly hostile toward the Catholic Church, as already documented by his son.[434] His attitude toward the Church was so adverse and hostile that he was against lending secular textbooks to Catholic school-children for a special reason: "The same powerful sectarian religious propagandists who have succeeded in passing this bill to help religious schools carry on their religious purposes can and doubtless will continue their propaganda, looking toward complete domination and supremacy of their particular brand of religion. And it nearly always is by insidious approaches that the citadels of liberty are most successfully attacked." It was classic Nativism!

Not much different was the stance of Justice William Douglas who cited as his source Loraine Boettner's *Roman Catholicism*, a vintage Blanshard-type volume, whose thesis was, in her own words: "Our American freedoms are being threatened today by two totalitarian systems, Communism and Roman Catholicism. And of the two in our country Romanism is growing faster than is Communism and is the more dangerous since it covers its real nature with a cloak of religion." Douglas quoted Boettner further that "the whole education of the child is filled with propaganda. . . . Their purpose is not to educate but to indoctrinate and to train, not to teach Scripture truths and Americanism, but to make loyal Roman Catholics."[435] More classic Nativism!

Douglas's citation brought this acerbic comment from columnist George Will: "In an opinion against aid to parochial schools Justice William Douglas cited as a source of reliable evidence about Catholic attitudes, a vituperative anti-Catholic book comparable in spirit to the Protocols of the Elders of Zion."

Another assault was made on the pro-lifers in the form of the Racketeer Influence and Corruption (RICO) law, which was passed by Congress to catch within its net the racketeers of organized crime. The teeth in the law was the power of law enforcers to confiscate the assets of the drug dealers, the money launderers, and other assorted classes of criminals. This same law was then applied to the pro-life marchers and picketers who stood to lose their homes and assets by utilizing their constitutional right to protest. There was no question that some of the pickets went to excess and bombed some abortion clinics without loss of life, a tactic denounced, nevertheless, by the pro-life organizations as well as the bishops. Some pro-lifers were convicted under the RICO law; their cases have not as yet reached the higher courts. Interestingly, when the RICO law was applied to embezzlers, stock swindlers, savings and loan officers, and other white-collar criminals, many congressmen protested that such was not the intent of the law. But what of the pro-lifers? Are they RICO crooks?

Over half of congressmen in 1978, according to a Harvard study, would take no position on abortion, and were characterized as being cautious, avoiding meeting the question, and striving mightily to stay neutral. One congressman complained: "If you (as a Catholic) are against abortion and believe it to be a Catholic position and this priest [Congressman Father Drinan] is for it, what is a Catholic position?"[436] One fellow congressman described Congressman Rodino of New Jersey, one of the top leaders of the House and chairman of the House Judiciary Committee, as wearing a pin given him by the Pope and "even when he changes his suits"; moreover, "he hasn't lifted a finger." Another disclaimed that in no sense would this issue be a test of hostility toward Catholics by American institutions or society, assuring that "a revival of anti-Catholicism is impossible." One senator added that it was "not like the Al Smith days. I don't think abortion or parochial education can isolate Catholics today."[437]

Could the same be said in 1991? In 1884, the bishops of America saw a harmony between the Catholic Church and democracy particularly in its care of immigrants, of workers, of the poor, affirming that never has the Church been so free as in America. "Let us rejoice that in America by what special Providence the situation is highly favorable for real effective social Catholicism." The Church felt so free in America, said one observer, because it no longer carried the Bourbon (that is, royalty) heritage.[438]

At this very same time these very same bishops were carrying on a determined fight to defend the labor movement from both the threatened disapproval by Rome because of "socialist tendencies" and from the laissez-faire capitalists of the U.S. who wanted to enforce an economic royalist dictatorship of their own upon the working man and woman. Consequently, in light of this rich history and heritage down the arches of the years in defense of the rights of the worker, whether teamsters or farm workers or others, it comes as a sad denouement that many Catholics who are labor leaders fall into the same category as the politicians who hold to the Taney contradiction.

While there have been in American history many organizations that have opposed the Catholic schools down the years, the union labor movement has always stood for a modicum of justice and equity. The later alliance, however, of the AFT under Albert Shanker with the public school establishment and the anti-Catholic organizations has meant great hardship for families and teachers who believe in choice in education. With its 780,000 members the AFT packs considerable political clout; in conjunction with the NEA with another 800,000 members, it commands even more attention. The conversion of the entire AFL-CIO at the national policy level has been an example, according to a high national official of the Teamsters Union, of the tail wagging the dog. Conversion is the correct word.

In 1963, under President George Meany the AFL-CIO approved a report that kept the nonpublic schools in a sympathetic purview: "Proposals for federal aid to education have also become bogged down in the church-state controversy. No American whatever his religious beliefs can fail to recognize that non-public schools carry a large share of the burden of educating the young. These non-public schools face the same problems of mounting costs and increased enrollments as do the public schools. . . . They should receive as much assistance as is constitutionally possible."[439]

Two years later the convention accepted its report: "The AFL-CIO maintained that without any way of doing damage to the separation of church and state, it was possible and necessary to resolve this question of finding constitutional ways of giving aid to non-public schools."

The AFL-CIO strongly endorsed aid for private colleges that have "contributed substantially to the diversity of American education."

There must be, it continued, some sort of compromise on the question of aid to nonpublic schools.

> The Elementary and Secondary Education Act of 1965 more than justifies the AFL-CIO view.
> A few alarmists, undoubtedly well-intentioned, predicted that the limited aid available to pupils in non-public schools under the proposed legislation, would damage the principle of separation of church and state. Their fears have proved groundless. . . .
> Religious freedom and the separation of church and state rest upon solid foundations in America, and they show no sign of crumbling simply because a student in a parochial school is permitted to borrow a textbook paid for by federal funds.
> We believe that the principle of church-state separation is in fact strong enough to permit more extensive aid to non-public schools. . . .[440]

What a change twenty-six years later: the "few alarmists" took over the AFL-CIO, with Shanker listed on its letterhead in the first place after President Lane Kirkland and Secretary-Treasurer Thomas Donahue. His technique and arguments were the same: "Don't take money from the public schools and give to the rich private schools; don't take away from the poor and give to the rich; reject vouchers, tax credits and other means even for compensatory services; don't help the private and parochial schools because it will be a certain detriment and danger to public school education, and, of course, such things will weaken the role of public education as the foundation of our democratic system."[441] Union labor under the aegis of the AFL-CIO had made a hundred-and-eighty-degree turnabout.

The AFL-CIO's 1991 convention report begins with a glowingly patriotic sentence: "The fundamental promise of equal opportunity for all Americans can never be fulfilled until there is equal access for all to the means of acquiring a good and useful education." "All" did not really mean all, nor did "equal access" mean equal. The AFL-CIO's efforts have been singularly directed at depriving the nonpublic school children, parents, and teachers even of the meager scraps of assistance that government allots to them. A reading of the conversion from a liberal George Meany to a narrow Lane Kirkland leaves no doubt: one of the best ways to improve public school education is the hampering and eventual destruction of the nonpublic schools, especially the "parochial."

Such a judgment is made here with great sadness and genuine regret because union labor has usually been on the liberal side: "Let's give equal opportunity to all" and also, given the Catholic Church's history of support for union labor from its very inception and its educating scores of its leaders, even in 1992, Catholics could have expected better treatment. To bite the hand that fed it seems not to bother the AFL-CIO, neither at the national or state level. The attack has often been vicious, dishonest, and Nativist, abetted, of course, by the public school establishment, which funds its allies not only in the professedly anti-Catholic groups but sadly even in the labor movement. It was backing up the public school establishment, no matter what the charges.

On the Phil Donahue show on national TV where the discussion concerned the voucher system for all schools, the following exchange took place between Superintendent of Public Instruction for California (the largest system in the U.S.A.) Bill Honig and Congressman Patrick L. Swindall:

> Bill Honig: The public schools have to live by certain rules of what they teach. . . . You have tuition and no controls. You don't have to teach history. You don't have to teach science . . . (or) mathematics. There's really no common curriculum at all.
> Swindall: Bill, that's not true at all.
> Honig: It is in California.
> Swindall: Under the voucher system . . . that is not true. You would still have to meet accreditation.
> Honig: There are no accreditation standards for private schools in California.[442]

Sorry to relate, Honig has consistently raised these kinds of attacks, seemingly wishing to win a debating point no matter the means employed. He most certainly was being disingenuous, as the direct response of California Catholic school authorities made crystal clear:

> Half of the State's private school student population is enrolled in Catholic schools. Both Catholic and public high schools are accredited by the independent Western Association of Schools and Colleges (WASC). To also assure quality programming at the *elementary* level, in the 1970s a system of parochial school certification by the Western Catholic Educational Association (WCEA) was begun. To further assure school improve-

ment, in addition to WCEA certification, Catholic elementary schools in most dioceses hold WASC accreditation and regularly undergo outside independent review by WASC accrediting teams.

Over 400 California Catholic elementary schools hold WASC accreditation; only 65 public elementary schools hold accreditation. State law does not mandate accreditation for either public or private schools.

With respect to curriculum requirements, California Education Code Section 48222 requires that private schools "offer instruction in the several branches of study required to be taught in the public schools of the state." In the *California Private School Directory 1985-86*, published by Superintendent Honig's own Bureau of Publications, there is a section which addresses subjects "required by virtue of Education Code Section 48222 to be taught in all private schools attended by children between 6 and 16 years of age." Among subjects listed for study in grades 1 through 6 are mathematics, social sciences (including history) and science. The list of required courses of study in grades 7 through 12 also enumerates science, mathematics and social studies (including history).

But how many would read the reply, especially given the millions who watched the talk show? This line of "no regulation" of nonpublic schools is a favorite of Albert Shanker, but he goes way overboard.

The president of the teachers' union, the AFT of the AFL-CIO, regularly uses similar tactics on the same premise that to attack, denigrate, and savage "parochial" (his word) schools he somehow is helping the public schools. No type of argument seems beneath him and his cohorts.

The doomsday scenario is stock-in-trade: democracy is threatened, competition is unfair, private schools operate in secret, and the precedent will open the door "to cult, extremist, racist, ethnocentric or fly-by-night operations," all because of any kind of aid to nonpublic schools, whether tax credits or vouchers. Meeting himself coming and going, Shanker concluded his lobbying letter of November 18, 1991, to the U.S. senators with the assertion: "Finally other industrial countries do a far better job of educating their students than we do. None of them rely on a voucher mechanism for school excellence." He neglected to add that in most of the democratic industrialized nations the church schools are supported not by vouchers or tax credits, which are small contributions, but in the same way the state schools are and that they enjoy a measure of true parity with direct tax support for all bona fide schools without proliferation of cults, extremists, racists, ethnocentrics, or fly-by-nighters.

No one can read the propaganda from the public school establishment and not recognize the none-too-subtle Nativism that is at the foundation of the opposition to "private schools." Under Shanker's direction twenty-five national organizations are mobilized to save the U.S.A. from the religious schools in particular. Among them are the public school administrators, the

American Jewish Congress and American Jewish Committee, the Americans United for the Separation of Church and State, the Anti-Defamation League, the NEA, the PTA, the Unitarian Universalist Congregations, the Union of Hebrew Congregations, the United Church of Christ, and the General Conference of Seventh-Day Adventists.

Shanker has resurrected the term "parochiaid," which ordinarily is translated "Catholic"; he warns that assistance will favor "a few denominations" in this country and violate freedom of conscience, violate the First Amendment, "especially religious affiliated institutions" whose "primary mission . . . is to indoctrinate students in one religious philosophy. Worst of all these schools would divert funds from the public schools, amounting to taxation without representation." His attempt to identify in the public mind the Catholic schools with the nonexistent subversive schools is a variation on the same theme on abortion that identifies the Catholic Church with "the fundamentalists and wackos," a calumny on the Fundamentalists as well.[443]

Former Mayor Ed Koch, in his weekly column in *The New York Post* on November 30, 1991, wrote in support of the voucher program for schools. "Academics aside, I believe the Catholic schools have greater success because they have a value system not provided in the public schools." He denied that the schools are elitist: "In Manhattan 53% are Hispanic and 25% Black with 22% non-Catholic." He cited both the Rand study and the Howard University Press report in support of his thesis. He further pointed out that New York City spent $7,150 per pupil as against $1,768 per pupil in the archdiocesan schools of the city and $3,352 for each high-school youngster.

Such opinions like the May 21, 1991, issue of *Time* — which answered its title-story "Can Catholic Schools Do It Better?" quite bluntly: "Yes, with less money, more selectiveness and rigor, they produce better students. . ." — send Shanker and others into yet more paroxysms of jealousy and hatred. They have become absolutists: children, parents, and teachers not in public schools are to be treated as second-class citizens, a throwback to Harvard's President James Conant. The saddest part of it all is that this one union is swinging the entire AFL-CIO its way.

What was clearly enunciated by AFL-CIO Secretary-Treasurer Thomas Donahue and Dorothy Shields, director of the AFL-CIO department of education, was this: the primary and overriding "principle" is to preserve the jobs of the membership, that is, the administrators and teachers; "Can you blame him [Shanker]?" they added. To that end the AFL-CIO accepts the tendentious attacks on "private and parochial" schools as protection against them.

This position cannot be logically explained, however, simply as protection of the public schools because it has deep roots in anti-Catholicism and Nativism, even though the majority of labor leaders could not be found guilty of either.

A similar evolution from President Meany's hope that all bona fide schools could be accepted as cooperators in education to an adversary position has its parallel at the state level. California affords a case in point. For years, under the tutelage of the AFL top leader, Neil Haggerty, union labor favored some accommodation for nonpublic schools as part and parcel of American education.

In 1992, his successor, John Henning, has followed the Shanker line, bowing to the intense pressure of the AFT union, and the vote of the AFL-CIO executive council, to oppose assistance to the nonpublic schools, specifically a voucher program for choice in education. Labor leaders customarily admit privately that the question is not one of justice but simply of power and money.

More disappointing to Catholics has been the retreat of Catholic politicians and Catholic labor leaders on both the national and state levels, divorcing their expressed personal moral convictions from their public life. Many evils, as Governor Cuomo correctly argued, can be tolerated; but when the question gets down to something as basic as the very right to life itself and to justice, even of the most minute and meager kind, Catholics as well as others begin to wonder why. The list is lengthy: among those in the U.S. Senate are Daniel Moynihan, Edward Kennedy, Joseph Biden, George Mitchell, Patrick Leahy, Christopher Dodd, and John Seymour; there are also a number of congresspersons, governors, legislators, and local politicians.

So many of them in defense boast of their Catholic school education, yet subscribe to the Taney contradiction, "I'm personally opposed but...," and in some cases become actually hostile toward those who genuinely believe in the right to life and true choice in education. They are victims of the prevailing Nativism that in effect challenges their patriotism and devotion to the Constitution unless they support the so-called majority opinion as measured by the incessant polls. It is leadership by poll, "principles" subordinated to polls, policies dictated by polls, public conduct guided by polls. This technique was rightly described during the 1992 presidential campaign as "pandering."

One cannot blame them too much because they believe that their very jobs are at stake and that the very Catholics who criticize will not truly support them. Yet some "profiles in courage" might overcome the litmus tests.

One of the best exemplars of political profiles in courage has to be the governor of Pennsylvania, Robert P. Casey. Speaking at Notre Dame University on April 2, 1992, he charged that pro-abortion special interests have taken control of his own Democratic Party, thus deserting its natural constituency. Recalling that the party had fought over the years for human dignity, as well as for minorities, women, workers, children, families, the disabled, and the dispossessed, Casey challenged the party "to protect the most vulnerable, the most defenseless, the most powerless members of our human family . . . , to protect what should be a national constituency, our unborn children."

As a governor elected by the largest majority in the history of his state, Casey advised the Democrats to drop abortion as a litmus test for candidacy, and stop punishing pro-life candidates by shutting off major sources of campaign financing.

Perhaps Harvard law professor Mark DeWolfe Howe said it all at an open meeting on Church-State questions held at Harvard University: "What you think of all these questions depends on what you think of the Catholic Church."[444]

Chapter 16

The Land of the Free

Religious liberty in the U.S.A.? What has been the American Catholic experience since 1776?

The years have witnessed a phenomenal growth of the Catholic Church in America; an absorption of immigrants on an unprecedented scale; a rising economic prosperity in a minority and disadvantaged population; an increasing acceptance in social life; a qualified approbation in lower and higher academe; and a conditional affirmation in the political order. Throughout this history the ghosts of anti-Catholicism and Nativism were never fully exorcised, ghosts that have never died, even as ghosts perhaps are not supposed to die.

Like all history, that of Catholics is, to put it mildly, quite uneven. Both Protestants and Catholics brought to America a legacy from Europe, racial and religious, which was a fertile seedbed for controversy, animosity, persecution, outright violence, and overt injustice. Each body of immigrants, not to mention the native Indians, belonged to various interest groups, each with its own predilections and prejudices. Perhaps it is, in the hopeful aspirations of the Declaration of Independence, a mark of Divine Providence that America has not only arisen to the world's only superpower but in so many ways as the moral leader of mankind in pursuit of human rights based upon human dignity. Unfortunately "this nation under God" has had a hidden agenda, whole areas of unjust discrimination in the society that still call out for redress but not solely in the interest of each group, since the sum total of them does not add up to the common good. The specter of anti-Catholicism and of Nativism enjoyed a relatively secret agenda, its purveyors having been able to hide on the fringe of deniability. The origin and rise of Nativism had both positive and negative causes: Protestants as majority were the chief protagonists, Catholics as minority the chief antagonists. As in so many twentieth-century controversies around the world — Belfast, Beirut, Kabul, Jerusalem, Soweto, Khartoum, Dubrovnik, and a host of other places on earth — where religion is deemed the devil in the controversy, so too in early America. All of these factional struggles nonetheless had other and perhaps deeper causes, such as a preferred nationalism but always with a high correlation with religion. Nor was Nativism exclusively religious.

Over and above the irrational myths that fueled anti-Catholicism and Nativism, there stood status rivalries — in Higham's words, competition for prestige, for favorable positions in society, even for economic gain; in a word, for "inequality." Ethnic cleavage in America should not be attributed entirely to Nativism or even racism but also to a very human drive for status and power.

Nativism exists primarily as an antipathy to foreign groups, whether cultural, national, racial, or religious, picturing itself as safeguarding America from foreign threats. Over America's two hundred years it has included in its ranks sincere patriots, social reformers, bigots, and opportunists.[445] The fires of Nativism have been fueled over the years less by antagonism based on race and culture but more on one religion, leaving almost alone as its perennial target the Catholic Church and "popery."

That non-Catholics had good reason at least to question their Catholic fellow citizens about their allegiance in the early days of the Republic can scarcely be disputed. The Catholic Church had its own troubles during the two centuries. While it is dishonest to portray the past as better than it really was, that is, to whitewash the mistakes of the Church (whether of popes, councils, saints, clerical and lay, princely and proletariat, bright and dull, conservative and liberal), it is equally false to indulge in a revisionism that minimizes the extent and virulence of Nativism in its anti-Catholic species.

Conversely, the record of the anti-Catholics and Nativists should allow the chips to fall where they may: on Protestants, Jews, Muslims, and especially secularists, but only insofar as the record allows. There remains a certain reluctance on the part of most Americans to face up to that record, a ghost in the American closet, a queasiness not alien to many Catholics. The record is painful for all sides.

The two Vatican Councils furnish easy and valid pegs upon which to hang the data. The decrees and results of both could not be confined to merely internal workings of the Church, in-house matters that were of little concern to the world at large. Quite the contrary: there was scarcely any internal Church subject matter that did not excite curiosity on the part of non-Catholics and often gave rise to serious adverse judgment followed not infrequently with overt action. These reactions, especially in the United States, whether in the nineteenth or twentieth century, should have been seen in Rome as a lesson but unfortunately were not and were not promptly and adequately addressed.

The pivotal action in Vatican I was the declaration of papal infallibility. While as a doctrinal conclusion it was unexceptionable, clearly limited and confined to matters of faith and morals, yet it was perceived to be the final crowning of a temporal monarch of the Papal States with godlike character, subject to no one nor any moral law short of God Himself.

A sympathetic Protestant theologian, Robert McAfee Brown, pinpointed the issue: "This is really the nub of the matter. . . . The dogma . . . is precisely the area in which the greatest reservations be. No Protestant could ever accept such a claim. Why not? Because he felt that this is to make a claim for man which can be made only for God. It is to deny one's sole allegiance to God . . . contrary to Scripture."[446] He described his statement, and justly so, as given "not in bitterness and rancor, but out of genuine concern to get the problem located where it belongs — at the source of the greatest disagreement."[447]

Another unbiased Protestant theologian, Reinhold Niebuhr, wrote of "the assertion which we must regard as essentially heretical, it is the affirmation that the Church, a historical institution is divine."[448]

Leaving aside the much more complex theological intricacies in the dogmatic definition, the question might well be posed: If such reactions can happen in the green wood, what in the dry? The anti-Catholics and the Nativists were not concerned with theological distinctions and philosophical niceties; they had a convenient bludgeon made in Rome, an incendiary that would not lose its vim and vigor even a century later as the basis for other charges and accusations that could tend to compromise the patriotism of American Catholics. No cause, no election, no campaign involving Catholics but which could not be turned against them by those who believe, sincerely or otherwise, that the Pope is the anti-Christ or by those Nativists who more subtly seek power, whether personal or corporate, at the expense of Catholics. The doctrine opened a golden door of opportunity.

This doctrine, coupled with many questionable interferences by the Roman Curia in American affairs, kept the Catholic Church in the U.S.A. constantly on the defensive, partly undeservedly so, but partly not. Writing from Rome, Monsignor Denis O'Connell, rector of the North American College (1885-95), acidly remarked to Archbishop Ireland: "The nonsense of trying to govern the Universal Church from a purely European standpoint . . . will be glaringly evident." The doctrine of infallibility was not only widely misunderstood in the U.S. but seized upon as living proof that an American Catholic could not serve two masters; he was the Humpty-Dumpty that all the Pope's horses and all the Pope's bishops could not put together again. The Nativists had a ready pretext to campaign in the name of Americanism wrapped in the Stars and Stripes.

The pivotal action in what might be called the external affairs of Vatican II was indubitably the promulgation of the "Declaration on Religious Liberty." Here stood the American Church proud of its Catholicism and its Americanism, able to define in clear terms the relationship between Church and State born not of theory only but of almost two centuries of practice wherein the Church in the U.S.A. had become the largest and most powerful in the world.[449] Not only were the Americans bishops anxious to advance the cause of religious liberty in their own country but to influence the worldwide Church along similar lines. The result was a ringing declaration on religious liberty that could take its place proudly with the then recent cognate documents of the United Nations, the Helsinki Accords, and other splendid defenses of human dignity and human freedom.

While Catholics expected that the justified fears of men and women of good will would be laid to rest at last and the gratuitous suspicions and purblind religious prejudice of people of ill will would be substantially ameliorated, the results were mixed: the melody lingered on especially among not the average American citizen but what has been dubbed an elite, impugning the dedication of Catholics to the American experiment. Father John Courtney Murray's description before the opening of Vatican Council II seems a viable opinion a quarter of a century later: "A great many Americans still see their Catholic fellow citizens as vaguely alien and as narrow-minded servants of a theology ... (encumbered with clouds of suspicion)" and "taxed with everything from Spanish Catholic intolerance to Italian cynicism." Sardonically he averred that "the Pope crowned Charlemagne in 800 A.D.; today he could not crown a third-class postmaster in the U.S.A."450

Catholics in the United States experienced a double jeopardy throughout the two centuries. On the one hand, millions of Christians, sincere and God-fearing, many if not most with Evangelical or Fundamentalist leanings, gave assent to the proposition that Catholics — with their positions on the Bible, on Tradition, on faith, and the nature of the Church — were everything from second-class Christians to the fanatic followers of the anti-Christ. On the other hand, millions of Americans, many in mainstream America, gave assent to the proposition that Catholics could not be true Catholics and true Americans but were perforce obliged to live in a sort of schizophrenia in reconciling their position in the American commonweal.

Is the term American Catholic or Catholic American an oxymoron? Is America safe for Catholics? Are Catholics safe for America? Was it mere coincidence that the two streams of opposition holding that Catholics were not really true Christians and not really true Americans could join hands in opposition?

During the first century of the history of the United States, anti-Catholicism, already firmly planted in the Thirteen Colonies as a legacy from Europe, and its most virulent daughter, Nativism, sustained themselves with open violence, including arson of Catholic churches, convents, and schools. Legislators responded and crystallized into law anti-Catholic, anti-Semitic, and anti-Negro statutes, effectively establishing a second-class citizenship if not worse, the U.S. Constitution to the contrary notwithstanding.

During the second century unjust discriminatory legislation very gradually gave way to a more equal and more just participation of minority populations in the commonweal. The Dred Scott as well as Plessy vs. Ferguson decisions on slavery were slowly but only gradually overturned: slavery was not compatible with the Constitution nor were schools "separate but equal." The Alfred E. Smith campaign for President surrendered to the John F. Kennedy triumph, even if by a razor-thin margin.

271

Were the ghosts of Nativism thereby eradicated? Did the advent of the two famous Johns — John the XXIII and JFK — signal a substantive change of direction, at least among mainstream Americans? Many Catholic Americans held out the hope, negatively, that anti-Catholicism and *a fortiori* Nativism were at last truly dying if not already dead in U.S. society. Vatican II's "Declaration on Religious Liberty" fostered that hope.

The declaration itself was divided into two major sections: one philosophical, the other theological. Without any appeal to religion as such — for example, to the Bible or Christian Tradition or Church authority — the Council affirmed the dignity of every human being endowed with inalienable rights, including the right to religious liberty both as an individual and as part of a family, as a constituent of various private organizations, as a citizen of the state, and as a member of society. This right was both an immunity from unjust coercion and an entitlement to promote bona fide beliefs. Not only was the right a natural one but further protected as a civil right in law. The theological treatment elevated the question to the religious plane, espousing even higher motives of charity as well as justice, clearly mandated in Revelation and Church doctrine, nonetheless rejecting secularism as inimical to all freedom.

While many Catholics had hoped, somewhat quixotically, that the Council's declaration and the election of John Kennedy would constitute giant steps toward a true reconciliation in America on the matter of full citizenship and equal justice, the results were contradictory. Some even hoped that the American public informed by an alert and investigative media would learn of the official position of the Church on religious liberty. The tart rejoinder might well be that even the American Catholics are equally woefully ignorant in the area. A few Catholics even ventured to hope that perhaps a Supreme Court justice might make reference to and even quote the "Declaration on Religious Liberty" instead of the vicious and prejudice-laden anti-Catholic sources and profiles that disgrace some judicial opinions and poison their conclusions.

The American Catholic hoped for an American *modus vivendi* that would be entirely consistent with the theological and philosophical traditions come to fruition in the Council declaration and American constitutional theory and genius. American leaders, especially politicians, are, as a rule, quite ignorant of how the Catholic Church really works in the U.S.A., particularly the role of the local bishop who is among the most independent persons in office in the entire country. Perhaps the converse is also true that these bishops, as a rule, are ignorant of how the political — perhaps better, the legislative — branch of government operates.[451]

The turning point for many Catholics came in 1972 with the George McGovern campaign for President.

The judgment seems apt: ". . .feeling the anti-democratic contempt, many middle-class Americans, including a disproportionate number of ethnic Catholics, regretfully left the Democratic party . . . (and) became reluctant Republicans."

The old-time historical Nativist has been succeeded by a new modern breed; the time-honored French epigram that "the more things change, the more they are the same" seems to verify the opinion that the ghost had taken on a new life. Father Murray suggested a conclusion in words that he wrote on the eve of the Council: "The result has been Nativism in all its manifold forms, ugly and refined, popular and academic, fanatic and liberal. The neo-Nativist as well as the paleo-Nativist addresses to the Catholic community substantially the same charge: 'You are among us but you are not of us.' "452

The malevolence is quite arguably not as widespread as racism in America nor as virulent and venomous as anti-Semitism. The history of Afro-Americans and other racial minorities and of Jews has run along very parallel lines to that of Catholics. But Nativism has survived as chiefly anti-Catholic, although that matter can well be changing rapidly because of the great influx of immigrants from around the world. The 1991 gubernatorial election in Louisiana suggested a renewed xenophobia. The immigrant has once again joined the Catholic as target.

With the new and massive immigration from all continents into the United States and the resultant appearance, once again in its history, of the disease of xenophobia, all bona fide residents — whether the "originals" (among them Aleuts, Eskimos, Chamorros, and Hawaiians) or the newly-arrived refugees from the world's wars — wondered if the fact of the appearance of the nonwhite man and woman would compromise the right to purchase on the equality guaranteed by the Creator and recognized under law, especially into the twenty-first century. For Catholics it was more of the same.

Litmus tests have been resurrected for Catholics who aspire to public office. The ever-ancient and ever-new proof of "Americanism" rests on the response to the school question, whether favoring a monopoly of public schools but only at the elementary and secondary levels. The second is the position taken on the right to life and procured abortion. Both tests are directed almost exclusively at Catholics and have become the pretext if not the cause of "Catholic bashing," a phrase that irritates and annoys many, especially but not exclusively those American Catholics who describe themselves as "liberal."

Incongruously, these Catholics conveniently ignore the expressed judgment of their liberal star, Father John Courtney Murray, on the first and perennial litmus test, namely, on Catholic schools:

> The argument that has been made by Catholics in this country for more than a century . . . is not complex. Its principle is that the canons of distributive justice ought to control the action of government in allocating

funds that it coercively collects from all people in pursuance of its legitimate interest in universal compulsory schooling.

The fact is that these canons are not presently being observed. The solution reached in the nineteenth century reveals injustice, and the legal statutes that establish the injustice are an abuse of power. . . .

For my part, I have never heard a satisfactory answer to it.[453]

Liberal Adam Walinsky in the *New Republic* looked further for cause: "I think much opposition to Catholic schools is in fact anti-Catholic."[454] This judgment sent the representatives of the ACLU, NAACP, AFL-CIO, and others "through the roof."

The second test, with a life of its own because it had no significant American history beyond some thirty years in American law and custom, persists as the abortion question. Very often it is isolated as a "Catholic issue" involving yet another paroxysm of anti-Catholic and Nativist agitation against Catholics as not quite fully American. The themes are more muted in the 1990s, less overt, more sophisticated, and hence more subtle but nonetheless quite real.

There has been very little research on anti-Catholicism in the U.S.A. since 1930. The role of the public school establishment in its Americanization campaigns; the charge of intellectual inferiority; the practices of elite universities and in particular schools of education all in relation to Catholicism and Nativism — these cry out for historical, dispassionate investigation.[455]

How responsible are Catholics themselves as a cause or at least any occasion for anti-Catholicism in the United States? History provides a partial answer: the relationships with the Roman Curia and the reluctance of some to confront the question.

The long arm of the Roman Curia over America's past two centuries has most certainly not ameliorated matters. The Curia's clumsy interventions right into the 1990s; its ever-decreasing understanding of American Catholics; its lack of trust in the American bishops to guide the great Church within secure boundaries of doctrine, morals, and discipline; its rearguard action against the Vatican Council; its failure to learn its lessons from the schism and heresy of such "super-Catholics" under Archbishop Marcel Lefebvre (a European phenomenon in its origins) — all of these things have given the Nativists gratuitous ammunition. The Curia in many of its members has trouble, not unlike the Nativists, in believing that the American bishops can be at once truly American and truly Catholic.

American Catholics too must bear some of the burden without falling into a victimization complex. Should a Catholic object publicly that he is unjustly discriminated against because he is a Catholic? "The best people" leave such sleeping dogs lie.

Senator Moynihan, zeroing in on "the best people" who think that

Catholics have no rights on the school question and "who become embarrassed at asserting our own interests and claims," points out: "Now more and more I grow to believe that Nativism will prove to be the last and most persisting of American bigotries. Not simply because it touches something deep in our national experience, but primarily because Catholic institutions and Catholic intellectuals accept it."[456]

Even less irenic, Father Greeley puts part of the burden directly on Catholics themselves because of deference to "the best people."

"Catholic self-hatred is one of the principal reasons for the persistence of anti-Catholicism. Our own elite accept the judgments of 'the best people' about us. . . .

"As one who knows first hand, you get clobbered by your own kind for suggesting there are people in this country who hate Catholics and discriminate against them. . . . The 'best people' can go right on pushing us around."[457]

Nativism per se, however, is not the heart of the American problem: the nature of American democracy as lived in the U.S.A. is. If there were relative unity in religious belief as in some countries in the world — whether Catholic, Protestant, Jewish, Muslim, Buddhist, or Hindu — the answer would not be simple, but it would be easier. Yet pluralism in America is both a historical and existential fact that has bred doubt, distrust, and, above all, confusion. Four major groups have chiefly contributed to this confusion: Protestant, Catholic, Jewish, and secularist.

The secularist, as already detailed, would push all religion back into the sanctuary. His first and historical enemy has been and still is the Catholic Church, which stoutly and consistently denied the primacy of the state in society: one power, one law, one science, one art, and one civic faith; in actual fact, a denial of pluralism. Religion being a divisive force, he asserts, must be relegated to a purely private matter, with little or as little relevance as possible allowed in the public life of the state and society. The secularist calls for an aseptic society — that is, sanitized from religion, not unlike the state under totalitarian hegemony.

When religious-based moral and spiritual values are ruled out of the public arena as irrelevant, can the Republic long survive as an aseptic state? To use Abraham Lincoln's own word, can the American "proposition" survive bitter disagreement and basic dissension among its citizens?

There has been noticeable improvement in one area of Nativism: racism has been rendered un-American, obscene, and intolerable. Sad to say, the great migration of foreign-born to the U.S.A. has furnished yet the occasion for a revival of the dormant virus of Nativism. As for American Catholics, the ghost of Nativism never did go into hibernation but rather underwent a metamorphosis, adapting itself in sophisticated fashion to the changing times.

Can Americans fabricate a truly unified society while maintaining its religious pluralism? The ever-deepening antagonisms and divisions among the American people cannot be sustained if there is to be a just society. Murray calls for a new realism: "The free society . . . is a unique realization; it has inaugurated a new history. Therefore it might be possible within this new history to lay the ghosts of the past — to forget the ghettos and the autos-da-fé, the Star Chamber and the Committee on Public Safety; Topcliffe with his 'Bloody Question' and Torquemada with his rack; the dragonnades and the Black and Tans; Samuel F. B. Morse, the convents in Charleston and Philadelphia, the Know-Nothings and the Ku Klux Klan and what happened to Al Smith. . . ."[458]

There can, of course, be civic unity and at the same time religious integrity. The turmoil in American society demands a peaceful solution, which is a civic necessity; the history of the American proposition gives lessons on what succeeds and what does not, and the relationship between Church and State so crafted by the Vatican Council and by other worldwide documents makes equitable solutions not only desirable but feasible. The internecine discord that has degenerated into not only heated argument but even into physical violence threatens civic harmony.

Nativism, whether in its nineteenth- or twentieth-century form, is one such threat to the American proposition: "We the people of the United States, in order to form a more perfect Union, establish justice, insure domestic tranquility, provide for the common defense, promote the general welfare, and secure the blessings of liberty to ourselves and our posterity, do ordain and establish this Constitution for the United States of America."

The ghost of Nativism refuses to die but: "At first cock-crow the ghosts must go back to their quiet graves below" (T. Garrison).

May Nativism in all its forms rest in its grave in perpetuity!

Notes

1. Ray A. Billington, *The Protestant Crusade, 1800-1860: A Study of the Origins of American Nativism*, Macmillan, New York, 1938, p. 1.

2. John Gerard, *The Hunted Priest*, Fontana Books, London, 1951, p. 68. England had exiled its Jews almost two hundred years before the Spanish Inquisition.

3. *Rights of Colonists*, in Seldes, *The Great Quotations*, Citadel, Secaucus, N.J., p. 47.

4. D. L. Holmes, *The Episcopal Church and the American Revolution*, Forward Movement Publications, Cincinnati, 1976, p. 6ff.

5. John T. Noonan, *The Believers and the Powers That Are*, Macmillan, New York, 1987, p. 116.

6. Howard K. Beale, *A History of Freedom of Teaching in American Schools*, p. 96, quoted in James N. O'Neill, *Catholicism and American Freedom*, Harper, New York, 1952, p. 106.

7. E. Digby Baltzell, *The Protestant Establishment: Aristocracy and Caste in America*, Vintage, New York, 1964, p. 95.

8. William Lee Miller, *The First Liberty*, Knopf, New York, 1986, p. 282.

9. John Tracy Ellis, *American Catholicism*, University of Chicago, 1969, p. 36.

10. T. P. Draney, *The First Amendment and Religion in Education*, CSAA of New York State, Albany, 1975, p. 6.

11. Ellis, op. cit., p. 64.

12. Senator Daniel Patrick Moynihan, citation in his speech, Canisius College, Buffalo, N.Y., May 28, 1977.

13. Mark J. Hurley, *Church-State Relationship in Education in California*, The Catholic University of America, Washington, D.C., 1948, p. 2ff.

14. Ibid., p. 54ff.

15. Cf. Marie Lenore Fell, *The Foundations of Nativism in American Textbooks, 1783-1860*, The Catholic University of America, Washington, D.C., 1941.

16. Draney, op. cit., p. 8. One set of textbook readers depicted the popes in these words: "No other tyranny had ever been like theirs for they tyrannized over the souls of men."

17. Hurley, op. cit., p. 14.

18. For a detailed account cf. Billington, op. cit.

19. Dolores Lystak, *Immigrants and Their Church*, Macmillan, New York, 1989, p. 185.

20. Moynihan, op. cit.

21. Ibid.

22. John Higham, *Strangers in the Land: Patterns of American Nativism, 1860-1925*, Rutgers University, New Brunswick, N.J., 1955, pp. 28, 29.

23. Gustavacus Myers, *The History of Bigotry in the United States*, Random House, New York, p. 219ff.

24. Ibid., p. 231.

25. Donald E. Pelotte, *John Courtney Murray: Theologian in Conflict*, Paulist Press, New York, 1974, p. 143.

26. James V. Schall, *Christianity and Politics*, Daughters of St. Paul, Boston, 1981, p. 270.

27. In 1990, the Knights of Columbus with over a million and a quarter members had councils all over the U.S.A., as well as in Canada, Mexico, and the Philippines.

28. *Hartford Courant*, May 14, 1890, pamphlet.

29. Myers, op. cit., p. 312.

30. Ibid., p. 326.

31. Higham, op. cit., p. 190.

32. Ibid.

33. Ibid., p. 173.

34. Justice Felix Frankfurter, McCollum case, 1948.

35. *San Francisco Chronicle*, September 20, 1991.

36. Cf. Chapter 13.

37. Noonan, op. cit., pp. 374, 399. Cf. Chapter 14 on the school question.

38. Draney, op. cit., citing Otto F. Kraushaar in *American Nonpublic Schools*, Johns Hopkins University Press, Baltimore, 1972, p. 22.

39. Ibid., p. 12.

40. Lawrence P. Creedon, and William D. Falcon, *United for Separation*, Bruce, Milwaukee, 1959, p. 10ff.

41. Ibid., p. 88. Cf. also *Universe Bulletin*, Cleveland, August 12, 1949.

42. Paul Blanshard, *On Vatican II*, Beacon, Boston, 1966, p. 309.

43. Paul Blanshard, *Freedom and Catholic Power*, Secker, London, 1951, p. 245ff.

44. Ellis, op. cit., p. 193.

45. Ibid.

46. *Seminar on Religion in a Free Society*, no date or place of publication, 48 pages, Corrigan Library, St. Joseph's Seminary, Yonkers, N.Y.

47. B. Harrison, *Religious Liberty*, John XXIII Coop, Melbourne, 1988, p. 34.

48. O'Neill, op. cit., p. 88.

49. Marvin R. O'Connell, American Catholic Historical Society, December 30, 1978, address entitled "The Background of Vatican II's Declaration on Religious Liberty: The Daniel O'Connell Position."

50. Ibid.

51. James J. Hennessy, S.J., *The First Council of the Vatican: The American Experience*, Herder, New York, 1960, p. 132.

52. *Boston Pilot*, cited in Hennessy, p. 133.

53. Ibid., p. 131. The draft proposed on Church and State at Vatican I provided by the Roman Curia assumed the union of Church and State with the Church claiming powers over the state. The American bishops never had the chance to press their judgment on religious liberty. The prorogued Council, finding itself in the midst of the war in Italy, did not get to the question at all. Clearly they never would have accepted the European models as suitable for the U.S.A.

54. Ibid., p. 89.

55. Petrus Huizing, in *Concilium*, Vol. 18, Paulist Press, New York, 1966, p. 126.

56. In 1908, the Holy Office in Rome condemned the journal that had oriented it-

self toward implementing the thrust of Pope Leo XIII toward democracy. For a further treatment on "Americanism" cf. Chapter 3.

57. *The New Catholic Encyclopedia*, McGraw-Hill, New York, 1967, Vol. 7, p. 552.

58. Pelotte, op. cit., p. 4.

59. Marvin R. O'Connell, *John Ireland*, Minnesota Historical Society, St. Paul, 1988. The words are those of Archbishop Ireland of St. Paul in 1884, p. 265.

60. Ibid., p. 558.

61. Ibid., p. 269.

62. Ibid., p. 282.

63. Cf. Chapter 8 on John Stuart Mill.

64. President James H. Canfield of the NEA canceled the first invitation to talk; the furor caused in St. Paul prompted a second invitation, which the archbishop accepted. Again the episode illustrated the volatility of the Catholic school question. O'Connell, op. cit., p. 296.

65. Ibid., p. 297.

66. Ibid., p. 299.

67. Ireland to Cardinal Gibbons, December 22, 1890, cited in O'Connell, op. cit., p. 308. The archbishop of Milwaukee, German-born Michael Heiss, had strongly opposed a Bennett Bill in Wisconsin that mandated English in schools eliminating German; he viewed the bill as a threat to the existence of the parochial schools. Ireland took an opposite point of view.

68. Ibid., p. 314.

69. Neil G. McCloskey, *Catholic Education in America*, Columbia University, New York, 1964. The rector of the North American College in Rome, Monsignor Denis O'Connell, expressed similar sentiments: "There is no disposition here in any untainted priest to go to America except as a delegate or secretary" (O'Connell, op. cit., p. 558).

70. Ibid., p. 360, quoting letter of Satolli to Rampolla, New York, November 18, 1892.

71. Ibid., p. 365.

72. Illustrating the "Italian mentality" in the Curia and the maintenance of control, for the next hundred years all the apostolic delegates were Italian except one who was Belgian and all of the priest diplomatic staffs were also Italian except only one, an Irishman. Even English-speaking priests trained in the Roman Academia for diplomatic service, from Australia, England, India, etc., are rigidly denied appointment to the delegation (now nunciature) in Washington, D.C.

73. *Social Thought*, p. 50, Spring 1979.

74. Robert McAfee Brown, *Observer in Rome*, Doubleday, Garden City, N.Y. 1966, p. 82.

75. Pelotte, op. cit., p. 18.

76. Ibid., p. 1.

77. Ibid. Cf. also Robert McElroy, *John Courtney Murray and the Secular Crisis*, dissertation, Gregorian University, Rome, 1987, p. 108ff.

78. Ibid., p. 109.

79. Ibid., p. 119. This distinction between society and the state became the basis of the subsequent documents on religious liberty and education at Vatican II.

80. Ailred Graham, *Catholicism and the World Today*, Thames and Hudson, London, 1951, p. 9.

81. *Theological Studies*, June 1949, Theological Faculties of the Jesuits, Washington, D.C.

82. Ibid., p. 25. Only Jesuits are customarily allowed to publish articles in *La Civiltà Cattolica* of Rome.

83. Pelotte, op. cit., p. 21. Murray later wrote that Archbishop McNicholas's statement was not well-received in Rome, that is, "a certain part of Rome."

84. The Curia's Justice and Peace Commission published a brilliant document on racism in 1989 that was well received all over the world. However, it appeared to equate Capitalism and Communism, the U.S. and the U.S.S.R. as two equal villains on the world scene. Without publicity, American bishops took sharp issue with the equation.

85. The Vatican Council II discarded this anachronistic terminology. It was an unnecessary point of misunderstanding, especially in the English language.

86. J. W. Allen, *A History of Political Thought in the 16th Century*, Methuen, London, 1928, p. 67.

87. Ibid., p. 86. The sixteenth century was concerned chiefly with the relation of the State to Church, not vice versa; of the true religion; of the relation of ruler and subject; and whether rulers could be driven out of office.

88. Thomas More, *Dialogue Concerning Hereseyes [Heresies] and Matters of Religion*, p. 275.

89. A. Koestler, *The Invisible Writing*, Collins, Philadelphia, 1954, passim.

90. H. Belloc, *The French Revolution*, Holt, New York, 1911, p. 216ff. He insists that the French government was desperate for money and looked to the confiscation of property of the religious orders and monasteries as well as dioceses to ease taxation. "Even in our time [1911] the older men . . . cannot rid themselves of an imagined connecting between the Catholic Church and an international conspiracy against democracy." Napoleon's Concordat was believed to have settled Church-State problems. But it too was dissolved (p. 253).

91. *Reflections on the French Revolution*, Everyman, p. 122.

92. David O'Brien, *Public Catholicism*, Macmillan, New York, 1989, p. 226ff.

93. John F. Conley, in *America*, June 24, 1989.

94. Ibid.

95. Pelotte, op. cit., p. 119.

96. Miller, op. cit., p. 243.

97. Ibid., p. 18.

98. Ibid., p. 38.

99. Ibid., p. 49.

100. Ibid., Appendix One, p. 357.

101. Ibid., p. 73. John Courtney Murray remarked that "the French separation makes Jefferson's 'wall of separation' a split rail fence which regards the state as an end in itself," that is, a monism.

102. Moynihan, op. cit.

103. Ibid. Citing Cooley's "General Principles of Constitutional Law in the United States."

104. Ibid.

105. Ibid.

106. John C. Bennett, *Christians and the State*, in Jerome Kerwin, *Catholic Viewpoint on Church and State*, Hanover, New York, 1960, p. 107. Murray calls the Constitution "less a piece of 18th Century rationalist theory than a product of Christian history," *Time*, December 12, 1960.

107. Pelotte, op. cit., p. 130.

108. French law and custom still proscribe Catholic universities in France. Catholic "universities" are called "institutes" in an accommodation.

109. Joseph Leclar, in *Concilium*, op. cit., Vol. 18, p. 20. There was no official line on Spain. French Catholics were anti-de Rivera, anti-Gil Robles in 1933, and anti-Franco in 1936. Similarly a significant segment of American Catholics, led by the magazine *Commonweal*, was anti-Franco, contrary to American majority opinion, both civic and ecclesiastical.

110. Ibid., p. 105. General Franco in 1964 during the Vatican Council debate on religious liberty pledged that Spain would follow the Council; Spain did so in 1988 long after the general's death, implementing religious liberty in 1992.

111. Pelotte, op. cit., p. 47.

112. Theodore Hesburgh, *God, Country and Notre Dame*, Doubleday, New York, 1989, p. 224ff. Cf. O'Brien, op. cit., p. 226.

113. Vincent McCormick to Murray, August 5, 1958, cited in Pelotte, op. cit., p. 59.

114. John C. Bennett, *Christians and the State*, Scribner, New York, 1958, p. 254ff.

115. Ibid. It might be noted that Paul Blanshard and C. Stanley Lowell visited Rome during Vatican II and spent many hours with the American delegates, priests, bishops, and laity.

116. Brown, op. cit., p. 158.

117. *Catholicism in America*, Harcourt Brace, New York, 1954, "A Jew Looks at Catholics," Will Herberg, p. 41ff.

118. Will Herberg, in *Commentary*, March 1950.

119. There were ten original American priest-*periti* (experts) on the preliminary commissions: Joseph Fenton, Francis J. Brennan, William J. Doheny, John Steinmuller, Rudolph Bandas, George Higgins, John Quinn, Frederick McManus, Ulric Beste, and Edward Heston. Seven of these had close curial ties.

120. Miller, op. cit., p. 286.

121. Ibid., p. 287.

122. Ibid., p. 285. Ted Sorenson, one of Kennedy's closest advisers, was quoted as saying in 1960 that he now understood what was meant by the phrase that anti-Catholicism was indeed the anti-Semitism of the intellectual.

123. Pelotte, op. cit., p. 80.

124. Ibid.

125. *America*, September 2, 1967.

126. Huizing, op. cit., p. 124.

127. St. Cyril of Jerusalem *Catecheses on Faith and Creed, Week 31.*

128. John Henry Newman, *Development of Doctrine*, Longmans, London, 1909, p. 439.

129. Ibid., p. 39.

130. Ibid., p. 58.

131. John Courtney Murray, *Concilium*, op. cit., Vol. 15, p. 5.

132. Murray remarked that he drafted the speech which DeSmedt reworked to his own style. Pelotte, op. cit., p. 84.

133. Brown, op. cit., p. 160ff.

134. Pelotte, op. cit., p. 86.

135. Ibid., p. 87.

136. *New York Times*, December 2, 1963.

137. Lorenzo Dattrino, *Portare Cristo all'Uomo*, Estratto, Urbanianum, Roma, no date, p. 929. By seeming oversight, Tertullian was not mentioned in the footnotes on the final text.

138. *Concilium*, op. cit., Vol. 18, p. 100.

139. Ironically in 1989 Spain gave full recognition to Protestant churches and Jewish synagogues with equal treatment with Catholics, including freedom of education and parental choice, which are still denied to religious groups, teachers, and parents in the U.S.A. Implementation came in 1992.

140. Pelotte, op. cit., p. 89.

141. Ibid.

142. William K. Leahy, and Anthony T. Massimini, *Council Speeches*, Paulist, New York, 1966, p. 41.

143. Vincent A. Yzermans, *American Participation in the Second Vatican Council*, Sheed and Ward, New York, 1967, p. 626.

144. Ibid., p. 631ff. Major interventions were made by American clergy, including Cardinals Cushing of Boston, Meyer of Chicago, Ritter of St. Louis, Bishops Primeau of Manchester, Alter of Cleveland, Wright of Pittsburgh, and Father Joseph Buckley, superior general of the Marist religious order, in the debates of September 1964. One year later Cardinals Spellman, Cushing, Ritter, and Shehan as well as Bishops Charles Maloney of Louisville and Halliman of Atlanta presented an American perspective. Seventeen American bishops also submitted written interventions in support of the declaration.

Among the observers from the United States were Presbyterian Robert McAfee Brown, Methodist Albert Outler, Lutheran George Lindbeck, Anglican Massey Shepherd, Congregationalist Douglas Horton, Quaker Douglas Steere, Disciple of Christ Howard Short, and others. A total of twenty-eight different churches were represented by observer-delegates numbering eighty-two.

145. *Council Daybook, 1964*, NCWC (now USCC), Washington, D.C., 1965, p. 47.

146. Letter of Murray to Regan, January 31, 1967, in Pelotte, op. cit., p. 95.

147. Ibid.

148. Ibid.

149. Pietro Pavan, in *Concilium*, op. cit., Vol. 18, p. 37. Pavan became a cardinal in 1985.

150. John Courtney Murray, *We Hold These Truths*, Sheed and Ward, New York, 1960, p. 184.

151. *Issues in the Wake of Vatican II: Proceedings of the Eighth Convention of*

the Fellowship of Catholic Scholars, Paul L. Williams, ed., Northeast Books, Clarks Green, Pa., 1985, p. 43ff.

152. Cf. Chapter 15 for the discussion on natural law at the Senate hearings on the nomination of Judge Clarence Thomas.

153. Mark J. Hurley, *Commentary of Declaration on Christian Education of Vatican Council II*, Paulist Press, New York, 1966, p. 73.

154. Ibid.

155. Such a distinction was accepted in U.S. courts in 1991. In a very isolated case, cf. note 337.

156. Cf. Chapter 13.

157. Ibid.

158. Murray, op. cit., p. 149ff.

159. Ibid., p. 151. Cf. also Chapter 13.

160. Hurley, *Commentary of Declaration on Christian Education of Vatican Council II*, op. cit., p. 115.

161. Bennett, op. cit., p. 9. He makes a plea that those who became Communists in the 1930s and 1940s or fellow travelers should not be held accountable in the 1950s because they turned away from Communism. "What they did in the 1930's does not have the same moral meaning later." Yet curiously Bennett is holding American Catholics in effect culpable for what happened in Spain and in other states with Catholicism being the established Church. Op. cit., p. 142.

162. *The New Catholic Encyclopedia*, op. cit., Vol. 9, p. 334. In an interesting obiter dictum, Lawrence Uzzell in the *Christian Science Monitor*, February 6, 1990, commented: "Jews and Catholics have a lot to teach other Americans about how to push the U.S.S.R. toward freedom. After years of missed opportunities the Protestant-dominated National Council of Churches are finally ready to learn. Unlike mainstream U.S. Protestants, Jews and Catholics have demanded concrete Soviet progress on human rights. Jews demanded rights to emigration; Catholics freedom of religion for Ukrainians. More widespread, and therefore more damaging has been the 'liberal' Protestant practice of ignoring Soviet violations of religious freedom. . . . The NCC whitewashing of Soviet atrocities [makes it] impossible to calculate the harm such disinformation has caused Soviet Christians. . . . In the U.S.S.R. the Church separation is absolute in theory; in practice the government tightly controlled the Russian Orthodox Church to the point of all but crushing it."

163. A Berkeley (University of California) law professor complained: "Angela Davis, a Communist, was the speaker at my son's high school graduation. People have to listen to the most heavy handed dogmatism. Then suddenly the Constitution is violated if an agnostic hears the word God. This is absurd. If we have to put up with things we don't agree with, why is only God excluded?" *Time*, December 9, 1991.

164. Lorenzo Dattrino, op. cit., p. 929.

165. Walter M. Abbot, *The Documents of Vatican II*, American Press, New York, 1966, p. 685.

166. Ibid., p. 686.

167. Draney, op. cit., p. 24.

168. Ibid.

169. *Herder Correspondence*, Vol. I, No. O, Dublin, New York, and Berlin, p. 18.

170. A Minnesota Court of Appeals, in protecting the religious mission of a church school, judged that interference with religious freedom is permitted only insofar as necessary to protect the government's interest in "peace or safety" or "against acts of licentiousness."

171. *Concilium*, op. cit., Vol. 18, p. 133.

172. The author of this book signed the final document of the "Declaration on Religious Liberty" for the archbishop of San Francisco.

173. Ellis, op. cit., preface.

174. Bob Woodward and Scott Armstrong, *The Brethren*, Simon and Schuster, New York, 1979, p. 233.

175. Dinesh D'Souza, in *Crisis*, July-August 1991, p. 20.

176. Cf. Chapter 1, John Carroll in Canada.

177. Cf. Chapter 15, the role of the IRS.

178. Ibid.

179. Ibid.

180. Cf. Chapter 15, which presents an analysis of Cuomo's speech on the subject at Notre Dame.

181. Robert S. McElvaine, *Mario Cuomo: A Biography*, Scribner, New York, 1988, p. 91. The author maintains that liberal friends such as Janie Eisenberg argued with Cuomo for years before convincing him that abortion and homosexuality were private matters.

182. Ibid.

183. Ibid., p. 91ff.

184. Ibid.

185. On October 28, 1982, Cuomo vowed to fight for reproductive rights and to veto any restrictions on the use of funds. Yet in 1984 he kept repeating publicly, "I accept the bishops' position that abortion is to be avoided." Cf. *Catholic League Newsletter*, Vol. 14, No. 12.

186. Cf. Chapter 14.

187. Margaret E. Fitzgerald in American Irish *Newsletter*, December 1990. Cf. Chapter 1.

188. Cf. Chapter 14. In Europe, priests are still being elected to public office especially in Eastern Europe, for example, in Lithuania. The Roman Curia is silent on this matter.

189. Pierre Salinger, *With Kennedy*, Doubleday, New York, 1966, p. 35.

190. Fletcher Knebel, in *Look* magazine, May 23, 1961, p. 40ff.

191. The author questioned Archbishop Davis on the episode at St. Peter's Basilica during the Vatican Council. The Church tradition was expressed by Cardinal Suhard of Paris: "By giving the laity a free hand the Church is not making the best of a bad job and using them as substitutes until such time as she had reliable priests to take over the direction of the temporal order. On the contrary she fully intends without any ulterior motive to confide to the laity the full responsibility for human society" (Emmanuel Suhard, *Writings*, Fides, Chicago, 1953, p. 292).

192. Knebel, op. cit.

193. *America*, January 13, 1962, p. 462. It should be noted that when Robert Kennedy was a candidate for the Democratic presidential nomination, the religious issue was not generally raised against him. He won a smashing victory in California without having to face either the school question or the abortion dilemma. They would have undoubtedly come later.

194. Ibid.

195. Ibid., p. 461.

196. Fletcher Knebel, in our opinion, did not deserve to be mentioned in the same breath with the others. In a personal letter to the author, he wrote: "I merely quote what the *Kennedys* and their advisors say. . . . The piece was recounting what the *Kennedys* thought." Knebel told how he had tried to interview Cardinal Spellman, Cardinal Cushing, and Archbishop O'Boyle through Monsignors Broderick and Lally, and ended up with Monsignor Hochwalt, who was, however, an excellent spokesman. Letter of Knebel to Mark J. Hurley, National Press Building, Washington, D.C., no date.

197. The Republican nominee for president in 1940, Wendell Wilkie, told the nation: "I am not interested in being president of the United States to compromise my fundamental beliefs."

198. *Our Sunday Visitor*, Huntington, Ind., September 8, 1991. Cf. Chapter 14.

199. O'Brien, op. cit., p. 247.

200. *The Boston Globe*, September 17, 1984, David Farrell.

201. *America in Perspective*, Oxford Analytica editors, Houghton Mifflin, Boston, 1986, p. 116.

202. "Guido Sarducci" is a character on the TV program *Saturday Night Live* who parodies and pillories the Catholic Church. He masquerades as a priest. Many find him offensive, but there has been no outcry to get him censored or curtailed by the Catholic Church. He may be described as irreverent but not necessarily sacrilegious.

203. *Commonweal*, October 11, 1991. The list included William Bennett, Father Andrew Greeley, Cardinal Roger Mahony, Pat Buchanan, William Simon, Cokie Roberts, Hugh Carey, Robert Dornan, Bowie Kuhn, Father Richard Neuhaus (former Lutheran pastor), Cardinal John O'Connor, and Thomas Monaghan of Domino's Pizza.

204. Ibid.

205. Murray, op. cit., p. 20.

206. Moynihan, op. cit.

207. V. C. Blum, *Quest for Religious Freedom II*, Catholic League for Religious and Civil Rights, Milwaukee, 1986, p. 43.

208. Ibid., p. 24.

209. *America*, September 21, 1991.

210. *San Francisco Chronicle*, October 30, 1991.

211. TV program special, *Firing Line*, September 8, 1991.

212. *Our Sunday Visitor*, October 6, 1991.

213. *Law Briefs*, USCC, Washington, D.C., May 1991, p. 5.

214. Syndicated column by Andrew Greeley in *The Witness*, Dubuque, December 1978. Greeley insists that Nativism perdures "among the [American] cultural and intellectual elites." Cf. Greeley, *An Ugly Secret: Anti-Catholicism in North*

America, Sheed Andrews McMeel, Kansas City, 1977, p. 2. On the "sophisticated Nativism of the intelligentsia," cf. ibid., p. 78.

215. Harris poll, cited in *Catholic League Newsletter*, Vol. 7, No. 12.

216. Ibid.

217. John Higham, *Send These to Me*, Johns Hopkins University Press, Baltimore, 1984. Cf. *Catholic Historic Review*, XLIV. The president of Massachusetts Institute of Technology (MIT) in 1896 wrote in the *Atlantic Monthly* that "to continue to admit immigrants of these inferior races was only to degrade our own American race" (Greeley, op. cit., p. 18). Cf. Geoffrey S. Smith, in *The Encyclopedia of American Foreign Policy*, Scribner, New York, 1978: article on Nativism.

218. Ibid., *Send These to Me*, p. 154.

219. Ibid., p. 164. Frank was pardoned by the governor of Georgia and subsequently lynched by a mob.

220. Ibid., p. 169.

221. *Pastoral Letters of the U.S. Catholic Bishops*, Vol. II, NCCB, Washington, D.C., 1984, p. 41. A polling data analysis sponsored by the American Jewish Committee concluded that "anti-Jewish attitudes were at an historic low by most indicators." *San Francisco Chronicle*, January 9, 1992, from *New York Times*.

222. Arthur A. Cohen, in *American Catholics: A Protestant-Jewish View*, Philip Scharper, ed., Sheed and Ward, New York, 1959, pp. 130-131.

223. Greeley, *An Ugly Secret*, op. cit., pp. 20, 124.

224. Cohen, in *American Catholics*, op. cit., p. 183. For an in-depth treatment of the Jewish experience in light of Nativism, read: John Higham, *Send These to Me*, op. cit.; the Irish experience, Dale T. Knobel, *Paddy and the Republic*, Harper and Row, New York, 1986; the Mexican experience, Richard M. Peterson, *Manifest Destiny in the Mines: Nativism in California*, Rand E. Research, San Francisco, 1975; the New Jersey experience, Douglas Shaw, *The Making of an Immigrant City*, Arno, New York, 1976; the Pacific Northwest experience, Evangeline Thomas, *Nativism in the Old Northwest*, The Catholic University of America, Washington, D.C., 1936.

225. S. R. Lichter et al., *Media Coverage of the Catholic Church*, Center for Media Affairs, Washington, D.C., 1991, p. 9.

226. Higham, *Strangers in the Land*, op. cit., p. 79.

227. "Catholicism in America," in *The Critic*, 1976, article by Andrew Greeley, p. 18. Greeley noted also the "attempts of nativist dominated [state] legislatures to close down the Catholic school," p. 58.

228. Baltzell, op. cit., p. 21.

229. Ibid., p. 45.

230. Ibid., p. 96.

231. Ibid.

232. *Defamers of the Church: Their Character*, Nineteenth (Revised) Edition, Our Sunday Visitor, Huntington, Ind., booklet (no date, out of print), p. 5.

233. Greeley, *The Critic*, op. cit., p. 25.

234. Ibid. Greeley insists that Catholics are under-represented in senior faculty positions at the elite private colleges, Harvard, Yale, etc.

235. Francis T. Hurley, in *The New Catholic Encyclopedia*, op. cit., Vol. 10, p. 226.

236. Neil S. McCloskey, *Catholic Education Faces Its Future*, Doubleday, New York, 1969, p. 185ff.

237. This appropriation in the law was later deleted. Senator Inouye defended his position saying that the Hebrew school was a good one, serving French children and supporting their Jewish culture and religion. At the same time he was voting invariably to shut out Catholic-school Americans from even a scintilla of support as to other American children in nonpublic schools.

238. F. X. Curran, *The Churches and Schools: American Protestantism and Popular Elementary Education*, Loyola Press, Chicago, 1954, Chapter VIII.

239. Murray, op. cit., p. 144.

240. Ibid., p. 145.

241. These are precisely the two questions addressed by Vatican II in the "Declaration on Religious Liberty." Cf. Chapter 8.

242. Mark J. Hurley, speech to American Association of Public School Administrators, National Convention, San Francisco, February 28, 1961.

243. Murray, op. cit., p. 147.

244. Ibid., p. 148.

245. Greeley contends that public school administrators and deans of education were deeply involved in the religious and racial bigotry at the Americanization campaigns of the 1920s and 1930s. *An Ugly Secret*, op. cit., p. 75.

246. *Trestleboard*, November 29, 1920, p. 21. Cf. Hurley, *Church-State Relationship in Education in California*, op. cit. This book traces the school question in California from 1850 to 1943.

247. Ibid., November 1920, p. 35.

248. Ibid., December 1920, p. 34.

249. Hurley, op. cit., p. 94.

250. Letter of Charles L. Harney to Joseph T. McGucken, November 6, 1958.

251. A. P. Stokes, *Church and State in the U.S.*, p. 252, cited in W. J. Whalen, *Christianity and American Freemasonry*, Bruce, Milwaukee, 1958, p. 89.

252. Charles E. Chapel, assemblyman, speech, November 3, 1952, Radio KECA.

253. Ibid.

254. *The Christian Century*, August 8, 1951.

255. Press release, August 8, 1951.

256. Rev. Edward L. Whittemore to M. Lewis, October 17, 1952.

257. W. Earle Smith, Chairman, letter to brother ministers, July 23, 1952.

258. The official state record shows donations from the Shrines of New Orleans, Salt Lake City, San Mateo, San Francisco, Oakland, Minneapolis, and Alexandria, Va., as well as from Wyoming, the Virgin Islands, and Puerto Rico. Letter of Paul Morrison to Joseph J. Roseborough, January 19, 1953.

259. Culbert L. Olson, amicus curiae in Supreme Court, S.F. No. 19026.

260. Whalen, op. cit., p. 90ff.

261. Ibid., p. 95.

262. Florence F. Hoste, *The Catholic Church and Freemasonry*, St. Francis College, Ft. Wayne, 1953 Conspectus, p. 7.

263. *New Age*, February 1950, p. 67.

264. Ibid., August 1950, article by Glenn H. Rutley, Thirty-second Degree, p. 481.

265. Whalen, op. cit., p. 97.

266. Delmar D. Durrah, *The History and Evolution of Freemasonry*, p. 268, cited in Whalen, op. cit., p. 98.

267. L. Harold Anderson, Grand Master, annual breakfast, Los Angeles Board of Relief, Hollywood Palladium, Hollywood, March 31, 1957, mimeographed copy of the address.

268. Letter of Harold L. Billings to members of Fellowship Lodge No. 480 F and M, Oakland, Calif. (no date, received October 4, 1958).

269. Memorandum of Robert L. Osborne, October 1958. Osborne, an Oakland city councilman, contributed five dollars so that he would receive the literature of the campaign. He was a most active and strong supporter of the Catholic schools.

270. Reprint, *New Age*, Washington, D.C., March 1959.

271. Report of Committee on Education, to Supreme Council 33, A and A Scottish Rite, submitted and approved October 24, 1957, Henry C. Clausen, Chairman.

272. Letter of Grace M. Hoffman, Worthy Grand Matron, Order of Eastern Star, January 14, 1958.

273. Slip sheet given to a visitor at the Alexandria shrine, 1958. This line of argument and its very words were published in *New Age*.

274. Letter of W. F. McIntire to Justin McGrath, Washington, D.C., May 16, 1924.

275. Hearings, House of Representatives, May and June 1949, p. 775ff. It should be mentioned that the Scottish Rite for years testified against all federal aid to public schools but devoted most of its testimony against Catholic schools as such.

276. *Christianity Today*, Rev. Kenneth Cory, October 27, 1958. In the same issue, C. Stanley Lowell of the POAU had a long diatribe against Catholics under the title "If the U.S. becomes 51% Catholic!"

277. *Washington Daily News*, May 23, 1958.

278. Leaflet of invitation, First Baptist Church, San Francisco, June 1958.

279. The Knights of Columbus of California mobilized its members to fight the proposition and did so both by grassroots action and financial support.

280. *Commonweal*, July 25, 1958, letter of Mark J. Hurley.

281. Letter of Kenneth Freeman to NAACP, Berkeley, November 1, 1958. The *Oakland Tribune*, October 31, 1958, which had been very anti-Catholic in the 1920s and anti-Catholic school in later years, took positions on 17 of the 18 propositions on the ballot but not on No. 16 because it was "obscured by a religious controversy."

282. Bruce Felknor, speech, April 15, 1959, to National Conferences of Christians and Jews.

283. Letter of Ernest Besig, Executive Director, ACLU of Northern California, to Mark J. Hurley, November 10, 1958.

284. *Commonweal*, February 19, 1959.

285. James B. Conant, *Shaping Educational Policy*, McGraw-Hill, New York, 1964, p. 127.

286. *The Register*, Denver, April 27, 1952.

287. George Weigel, in *Catholic League Newsletter*, Vol. 12, No. 11.

288. Baltzell, op. cit., p. 276.

289. Wilbur Katz, *Religion in the American Constitutions*, Northwestern University, Evanston, Ill., 1963, p. 64.

290. Otto F. Kraushaar, *American Nonpublic Schools*, Johns Hopkins University Press, Baltimore, 1972.

291. Leo Pfeffer, *God, Caesar, and the Constitution*, Beacon, Boston, p. 257.

292. Higham, *Strangers in the Land*, op. cit., p. 68.

293. *Catholic League Newsletter*, Vol. 12, No. 10.

294. Bennett, op. cit., p. 235.

295. Loraine Boettner, *Roman Catholicism*, Presbyterian and Reformed Publishing Co., Philadelphia, 1974, p. 14ff, cited in Peter Stravinskas, *Constitutional Rights and Religious Prejudice: Catholic Education as the Battleground*, Buckmasters, New York, 1982, p. 145.

296. Stravinskas, op. cit., p. 144.

297. U.S. Supreme Court, Nos. 89, 569, and 570, June 28, 1971, Douglas and Black concurrence, p. 11.

298. Nyquist case, 72-694, concur and dissent, p. 8.

299. U.S. Supreme Court, No. 153, dissent, Tilton vs. Richardson, pp. 3, 6. Cf. *Catholics in America*, Robert Trisco, ed., NCCB, Washington D.C., 1976, p. 123ff.

300. Nyquist, op. cit., p. 8. For example, in Chicago archdiocese in one year (1990), twenty-three schools were closed.

301. Tilton, No. 153, dissent, p. 9.

302. Nyquist, op. cit., p. 8ff. Cf. Tilton, op. cit., p. 9.

303. *Law Briefs*, Mark Chopko, USCC, Washington, D.C., July 1985.

304. *Twin Circle*, September 14, 1991. New York spends $6,000 per pupil per year; the Catholic schools about half; New York has 6,000 administrators, the New York archdiocesan schools 30 administrators. Ibid. Freidman said that middle management, that is, administrators, have grown "like mad." Camden, N.J., public high schools were reported as costing $8,400 per student, the Catholic schools $2,370, to cite another example.

305. *Catholic Star Herald*, Camden, N.J., January 3, 1992.

306. Cf. Chapter 15.

307. James S. Coleman and Thomas Hoffer, *Public and Private High Schools*, Basic Books, New York, 1987. Cf. also *Private Schools, Public Schools, and the Public Interest*, National Opinion Research Center, University of Chicago. Cf. also *Reader's Digest*, November 1991, "Tale of Two Schools" by Trevor Armbrister, a comparison of Northwest High School and Cardinal Ritter Prep in St. Louis.

308. *Dubuque Witness*, July 15, 1990.

309. *Catholicism in America*, Commonweal Series, Harcourt Brace, New York, 1954, p. 40.

310. *Saturday Evening Post*, July 1983.

311. Ibid.

312. Ibid., p. 12.

313. James Yaffe, *The American Jews: Portrait of a Split Personality*, Random House, New York, 1968, p. 239ff.

314. Arthur A. Cohen, report, *Fund for the Republic*, p. 184.

315. Letter of George Reed, December 1, 1991, to author: Senate hearings on S. 1305 and S. 419; Max Lerner, in *PM*, May 18, 1947.

316. Greeley, *An Ugly Secret*, op. cit., p. 104.

317. Murray, op. cit., p. 19.

318. "First Things," in *Journal of Religion and Public Life*, January 1992, p. 7.

319. Yaffe, op. cit., p. 249.

320. Ibid.

321. *New York Times*, May 29, 1991.

322. Bennett, op. cit., p. 237.

323. Ibid., p. 236.

324. It should be noted that although the Supreme Court allowed textbooks under the federal Constitution, many states denied them under state constitutions as in California. Similarly, bus rides are denied by local public-school districts regardless of the law allowing them.

325. Lemon vs. Kurtzman, concur and dissent; Justice P. G. White: "The Court points to nothing in this record indicating that any participating teacher had inserted religion into his secular teaching or had any difficulty in avoiding doing so."

326. *The Freedom of Religion Clauses of the First Amendment*, Pennsylvania Catholic Conference, Philadelphia, 1990, p. 59.

327. H.R. 3 and H.R. 30, hearings, p. 389, 1989.

328. U.S. Court of Appeals, Pulido vs. Cavazos, May 21, 1991.

329. Douglas and Black in the Lemon case, June 28, 1971, p. 17.

330. Lemon case, op. cit., Douglas and Black, separate opinion.

331. Hunt-McNair, 71-1523, opinion, p. 9.

332. H.R. 3 and H.R. 30, p. 482f., 1989.

333. Lemon vs. Kurtzman, op. cit., p. 8, White.

334. Tilton vs. Richardson, opinion, 153, p. 9.

335. Nyquist, dissent (a) 72-694, White, p. 11.

336. Lemon case, op. cit., 4403 U.S. 614, "Total separation . . . is not possible in the absolute sense. Some relationship is inevitable."

337. *Law Briefs*, Chopko, op. cit., December 1989.

338. Nyquist, op. cit., p. 13.

339. Smith, 11 OS. Ct. 1595 (1990), cited in 9th Circuit Court of Appeals, p. 6265; Hanna Center case, August 7, 1991.

340. Lemon vs. Kurtzman, op. cit., 89-569 opinion: Burger, Black, Douglas, Harlan, Marshall, Stewart, Blackmun.

341. Stravinskas, op. cit., p. 79. Some leading scholars have called for reversal of the Lemon Test.

342. Joseph Costanzo, *This Nation Under God: Church, State and Schools in America*, Herder, New York, 1964, p. 170.

343. Ibid., p. 326.

344. Stravinskas, op. cit., p. 40.

345. Daniel Patrick Moynihan, "Why Private Schools Merit Public Aid," in *Independent School*, 37 (May 1978), p. 18. Cited in Stravinskas, op. cit., p. 15.

346. *Catholic League Newsletter*, Vol. 17, No. 10.

347. David M. Ackerman, Congressional Record Research Service, Library of Congress, January 17, 1992.

348. Lemon vs. Kurtzman, op. cit., 69 concur and dissent, p. 7.

349. Costanzo, op. cit., p. 170.

350. Nyquist, dissent A, White et al., op. cit., p. 9.

351. *Catholic League Newsletter*, Vol. 17, No. 10.

352. *Life Insight*, NCCB, Washington, D.C., December 1991.

353. In the city of San Francisco, for example, these points can easily be verified, not to mention New York. The State of California Superintendent of Public Education Wilson Riles tried to introduce under a veil of secrecy a thoroughly incompetent syllabus for sex education. It presented teaching units suitable at once for girls from eight to eighteen. The ridiculous program died aborning.

354. Meek-Pittinger, 73-1765 concur and dissent (b), p. 3.

355. Alvin Toffler, *Power Shift: Knowledge, Wealth, and Violence at the Edge of the 21st Century*, Bantam Books, New York, 1990, p. 346.

356. Ibid., p. 344.

357. Higham, *Strangers in the Land*, op. cit., p. 28.

358. *New York Times*, April 1982.

359. Nat Hentoff, "The Awful Privacy of Baby Doe," in *Atlantic Monthly*, January 1985, p. 56.

360. *Time*, December 9, 1991.

361. Cartoonist Patrick Oliphant has been particularly anti-Catholic, and anti-bishop. He depicted the American bishops as literally and physically stealing money from people, entitling his piece "America's Fighting Bishops Redistribute the Nation's Wealth" by strong-armed robbery. Cf. *San Francisco Chronicle*, November 24, 1984.

362. David H. Bennett, *The Party of Fear: From Nativist Movements to the New Right in American History*, University of North Carolina Press, Chapel Hill, 1988, p. 6.

363. David Feldman, *Birth Control in Jewish Law*, New York University, 1968, p. 261ff.

364. Nathanson stated that "the secular media are very biased toward pro-abortion" (*National Catholic Register*, May 17, 1981). He said: "I'm Jewish in the sense that I have a Jewish heritage and traditions, but I don't believe in God" (*This World*, October 6, 1985).

365. *National Catholic Register*, interview, May 17, 1981.

366. *This World*, October 6, 1985.

367. *Twin Circle*, February 2, 1992.

368. *Catholic Star Herald*, July 20, 1990. Bishop John F. Donoghue of Charlotte protested the cartoon by Mike Peters "for obvious insensitivity . . . and clearly known that [it] would be offensive to Catholics and others of good will."

369. *Newsweek*, April 1, 1991, p. 15.

370. *U.S. News and World Report*, April 1, 1991.

371. *Newsweek*, op. cit.

372. Woodward and Armstrong, op. cit., give a detailed account of the inside workings of the Supreme Court on abortion.

373. *USA Today*, January 23, 1992, p. 3.

374. *Media Monitor*, Vol. III, No. 8, October 1989.

375. Ibid. This fact does not necessarily mean that journalists are unfair. The question is what type of coverage was given.

376. Polls invariably show that abortion is very much down on the list below economic problems, housing and homeless, crime, drugs, etc. Cf. also *USA Today*, January 23, 1992, which makes the same point.

377. Shaw Report, *Los Angeles Times*, July 4, 1990.

378. *San Francisco Chronicle*, September 15, 1991.

379. Ibid.

380. Ibid., January 23, 1992.

381. Ibid.

382. Ibid.

383. Ibid., January 30, 1992.

384. Lawrence Lader, *Politics, Power and The Church*, MacMillan, New York, 1987, p. 11.

385. *Catholic New York*, March 21, 1991.

386. One of the Irish Sisters who taught Justice Clarence Thomas in St. Benedict's all-black school remarked: "He wondered as a child why he said the Pledge of Allegiance each morning because blacks weren't free and there wasn't justice for all."

387. Stringfellow Barr, in *American Catholics: A Protestant-Jewish View*, Sheed and Ward, New York, 1959, p. 18.

388. Ibid., p. 54.

389. Ibid., p. 73.

390. An interesting study would be a check on the contributions of drug companies, condom manufacturers, school-textbook publishers, food distributors, furniture factories to the respective organizations hiding behind charitable contributions, tax exempt.

391. A 1990 survey reported that thirty percent of the House of Representatives and twenty percent of the Senate listed themselves as Catholic, a figure quite consonant with the number of Catholics in the general population.

392. *U.S. News and Word Report*, April 1, 1991.

393. Cf. Chapter 9.

394. Mario Cuomo, speech, Notre Dame University, September 13, 1984.

395. Ibid. Cf. Mario Cuomo, *Diaries*, Random House, New York, 1984. "The laity have their own witness to bear, their specific problems to solve, and reforms to be undertaken, all on their own responsibility" (Suhard, op. cit., p. 291). The laity are irreplaceable; their vocation is not to be usurped by the clergy.

396. *The Harmonizer*, Ft. Wayne-South Bend, Ind., September 23, 1984.

397. McElvaine, op. cit., p. 95.

398. *Catholic New York*, July 7, 1983.

399. *New York Times*, March 14, 1990.

400. Senator David Carlin, "The Abortion Battle Ahead," in *The Tablet*, London, October 19, 1991.

401. Patrick Caddell in *Commonweal*, August 14, 1987. The vote of Catholics for Republican George Bush was significantly higher.

402. Peter A. Lawler, *Church Polity and American Politics*, Mary E. Sagers, Garland, New York, 1990, p. 176.

403. Ibid., p. 176.

404. Ibid., p. 192.

405. Ibid.

406. Cf. Chapter 9.

407. Benjamin Cardozo, *The Nature of the Judicial Process*, p. 134, cited in Bennett, *Christians and the State*, op. cit., p. 235.

408. *San Francisco Examiner*, July 24, 1991. Incidently, Professor Dershowitz showed a basic ignorance of the meaning of natural law as he compared it to positive law. Perhaps, however, his article was too short on this point to draw a final judgment. *Time* magazine, August 12, 1991, also published an article, "Judges, Democracy and Natural Law," which confused "natural law" with "laws of nature."

409. *Twin Circle*, July 28, 1991.

410. Bennett, *Christians and the State*, op. cit., p. 9.

411. *Columbia*, September 1991, Knights of Columbus.

412. Catholic News Service (CNS), July 3, 1991.

413. *Catholic Star Herald*, July 19, 1991.

414. *Wanderer*, July 25, 1991.

415. *Our Sunday Visitor*, under the title "Cartoon Bigotry," reproduced the cartoon August 11, 1991; cf. also *Catholic League Newsletter*, Vol. 18, No. 6. On March 17, 1992, the author was denied permission from the Universal Press Syndicate of Kansas City, Missouri, to reproduce the two Oliphant cartoons described in the text.

416. *Trade Union Courier*, New York, September 1990. Joann Cohen in the United Federation Teachers publication wrote that "the majority of rank and file trade unionists agree . . . that although 57% of the American people feel personally that abortion is wrong, 74% feel that women should decide [for themselves on an individual basis]. . . ."

417. *Ethics and Medics*, Vol. 17, No. 1, January 1992.

418. *San Francisco Chronicle*, September 11, 1991.

419. *The Wanderer*, October 17, 1991.

420. *San Francisco Chronicle*, September 12, 1991.

421. *Washington Post*, September 16, 1991.

422. Ibid., September 27, 1991.

423. David Carlini in *Commonweal*, November 8, 1991.

424. *San Francisco Chronicle*, November 16, 1991. The author of this book wrote to Senator Biden, a Catholic, about his statement published all over the U.S.A.; he did not send an acknowledgment, much less an answer.

425. John T. Noonan, *A Private Choice*, MacMillan, London, 1979, p. 98; Beal vs. Doe, 432 U.S. 438 (1977).

426. During the Senate hearings every Jewish synagogue in America was asked to mobilize its members to pressure Congress to grant an eleven-billion-dollar credit for Soviet Jews in Israel. Again, no word from the secularists, the ACLU, and the American Way on "mixing," regardless of the merits of the case.

427. Internal Revenue Service code, section 501, ruling 78-248, cited in John T. Noonan, *The Believer and the Powers That Are*, op. cit., p. 461.

428. Lawler, op. cit., remarks: "The pro-choice conversions of Jesse Jackson and Richard Gephardt seemed to have occurred out of expediency" (p. 179).

429. *New York Times*, October 18, 1984; September 15, 1984. Letter of graduate students, Yonkers, N.Y., March 12, 1990-June 1991.

430. Letter to Honorable Fred Goldberg, Institute for Advanced Education, from graduate students, Yonkers, N.Y., March 12, 1990.

431. Letter to Congresswoman Nancy Pelosi of San Francisco, October 21, 1991, from Donald R. Kehoe. A subsequent letter to Mr. Kehoe elicited a response from a lower level simply refusing to answer, claiming it could not "generally" divulge tax information, which was not the question. Letter of Mark J. Hurley, November 6, 1991, to D. R. Kehoe.

432. Letter of John Arbach, IRS, to author, December 3, 1991.

433. For nine years the ACLU and its allies sought through lawsuits to deny the Catholic Church tax exemption because of its position on pro-life. In 1985, the American Jewish Congress set aside "one million dollars to defend the separation of Church and State." The AJC appeared in court as plaintiff or amicus curiae against any aid to Catholic schools, even the most meager assistance.

434. Blum, op. cit., p. 129. The U.S. Postal Service has honored the memory of Justice Black with a five-cent stamp with his image on it (1991).

435. Cf. note 269.

436. Mary T. Hanna, *Catholic and American Politics*, Harvard, Cambridge, Mass., 1979, p. 150.

437. Ibid., p. 179.

438. Robert Pollock in *Commonweal*, June 30, 1939.

439. AFL-CIO convention proceedings, 1963, p. 179.

440. AFL-CIO report of Education Committee, December 13, 1965; also convention proceedings, p. 141.

441. American Federation of Teachers (AFT) pamphlet: "Labor the Champion of Public Education," 1985.

442. Phil Donahue show transcript No. 11105. Curiously, Honig's wife is a graduate of St. Mary's College, Moraga, Calif.

443. This material is taken from the printed materials, over one hundred pages, sent to each U.S. Senator by Shanker and the AFT in November 1991. Incidentally, there are no religious Fundamentalists on the U.S. Supreme Court.

444. Blum, op. cit., reported by Notre Dame law professor Robert Rodes, p. 128. Cf. Christopher Matthews, in the *San Francisco Examiner*, April 12, 1992.

445. Ira M. Leonard, *American Nativism*, Reinhold, New York, 1971, p. 6.

446. Robert McAfee Brown, in *American Catholics*, op. cit., p. 82. Cf. *Encyclopedia of American Foreign Policy*, op. cit., p. 566.

447. Ibid., p. 83.

448. Ibid., p. 94.

449. Brazil and Italy usually claim greater membership, but the figures are usually taken from a census that assumes the general population is *a priori* "Catholic."

450. *Time*, December 2, 1960. "While every form of clericalism, that is, every con-

fusion of jurisdiction, must be ruthlessly repudiated, the collective salvation and human perfection of the world is imposed on the priest as a duty" (Suhard, op. cit., p. 293).

451. Timothy A. Byrnes, *Catholic Bishops and American Politics*, Princeton University Press, Princeton, N.J., 1991, p. 4.

452. Murray, op. cit., p. 20. Cf. McElroy, op. cit., p. 108ff.

453. Ibid., p. 18.

454. *New Republic*, October 7, 1972, p. 18ff., cited in Greeley, *An Ugly Secret*, op. cit., p. 101.

455. Greeley, ibid., p. 20. Greeley asserts that there is a strong anti-Catholic feeling in the Jewish community and that "the empirical evidence shows it" (p. 104). It does not seem to be Nativist, however; John Courtney Murray, as pointed out in Chapter 13, makes a similar judgment: "There is the ancient resentment of the Jew, who has for centuries been dependent for his existence on the good will, often not forthcoming, of a Christian community. Now in America, where he has acquired social power, his distrust of the Christian community leads him to align himself with the secularizing forces whose dominance, he thinks, will afford him a security he has never known." Op. cit., p. 19.

456. Moynihan, speech, Canisius College, op. cit.

457. Andrew Greeley, Universal Press Syndicate column, June 1977.

458. Murray, op. cit., p. 24.

Index

93, 96, 99, 100, 102, 104, 105, 112,
113, 119, 129, 130, 134, 146, 161,
165, 177, 210, 216, 230, 232, 239,
242, 245, 246, 265
Constantinople, Council of — 79
Constitution — 10, 17, 19, 22, 24, 25,
26, 29, 40, 47, 61, 65, 66, 80, 94,
106, 112, 117, 126, 140, 141, 143,
146, 161, 165, 173, 190, 192, 193,
195, 198, 201, 203, 208, 237, 239,
266, 271, 276, 281, 283, 290
Constitution Advocates — 172, 179
Constitution of the Clergy — 62
constitutional state — 117
Continental Congress — 130
Conway, William — 121
Conyers, John — 253
Cooley, Thomas McIntyre — 66, 280
Cooper, Abraham — 137
Cornell, Robert J. — 140, 226
corporate freedom — 13, 66, 100
corporate liberty — 100
Corwin, Edward S. — 66, 205, 207
Coughlin, Charles E. — 141
Coulombe, Charles A. — 247
Council of Churches — 158, 172, 283
Cowles, John H. — 174, 177
Coxe, A. Cleveland — 46
Cranmer, Thomas — 18
crime — 18, 32, 115, 116, 128, 166,
178, 185, 198, 217, 219, 223, 243,
260, 292
CUA — *see* Catholic University of
America, The
Cuba — 50, 109
Cubberley, Ellwood P. — 34
Cuomo, Mario — 10, 126, 128, 129,
132-134, 136, 148, 150, 240-246,
259, 266, 284, 292
Curley, Michael J. — 50
Curran, Charles — 52

Cushing, Richard — 93, 94, 121, 282,
285
Cyril of Jerusalem, St. — 83, 281

D

Danielou, J. — 80
Dante — 58
Das Kapital — 38
Davis, Angela — 108, 155, 283
Davis, James P. — 144
Davis, Jefferson — 26
Declaration of Independence — 17-21,
65, 67, 80, 90, 111, 127, 130, 149,
203, 237, 238, 251, 252, 268
"Declaration of the Rights of Man" —
62
DeConcini, Dennis — 254
de facto discrimination — 9, 212,
213
deism — 66
deists — 63, 203
Delaney, James — 206
democracy — 12, 21, 25, 31, 33, 34,
36, 42, 51, 54, 61, 64, 66, 67, 72, 74,
135, 167, 169, 174, 181, 185, 186,
197, 261, 264, 275, 279, 280, 293
De Lubac, Henri — 80
Democratic Party's platform — 233
democratic school system — 182
Dershowitz, Alan M. — 157, 247, 248,
293
Descartes, René — 91
DeSmedt, Emil — 85, 86, 88, 90, 91,
96, 97, 282
despotism — 21, 28
despotism over the mind — 117
deterrence of atomic warfare — 150
Detroit (Michigan) — 30, 141
development of doctrine — 12, 41, 68,
70, 82-85, 87, 113, 281
Devlin, Michael — 249

excessive entanglement — 201, 202, 204, 207

experiment in justice — 101

F

faculty for judging — 113

Fagan, Maurice B. — 36

Fair Campaign Practices Committee — 179

Fairbault and Stillwater public schools — 47

farm workers — 120, 226, 261

Farrell, David — 147, 285

fascism — 72

Fauntroy, Walter — 130

feasibility — 244

Felici, Angelo — 97

Felknor, Bruce — 179, 288

Fenton, Joseph — 55, 57, 70, 71, 82, 88, 89, 281

Fernandez, Anecito — 96, 97

Ferraro, Geraldine — 135, 147, 148

fetus — 135, 217, 218, 243, 245

Fey, Harold E. — 172

First Amendment — 11, 12, 19, 31, 36, 55, 58-60, 65, 66, 94, 101, 105, 107, 115, 119, 128, 131, 133, 138, 141, 143, 149, 152, 155, 157, 184, 189, 200-206, 208, 210, 213-216, 236, 238, 239, 256, 277, 290

first Baptist president — 81

First Plenary Council of Baltimore — 44

First Vatican Council — *see* Vatican Council I

Florence, Council of — 79

Ford, Gerald — 147

Ford, Henry — 160

foreign potentate — 35, 44, 159, 206

foreign power — 17, 140

formulas of the past — 72

Founding Fathers — 9, 35, 59, 64, 66, 127, 176, 192, 203, 237, 249

fourteen propositions — 48

Fourteenth Amendment — 237

Fourth Estate — 211

Fourth Lateran Council — 112

Foxe, John — 59

France — 36, 38, 39, 41, 43, 59-63, 82, 92, 140, 163, 166, 281

Franco, Francisco — 92, 148

Frank, Barney — 135

Frank, Leo — 160

Franklin, Benjamin — 63, 130

free exercise of religion — 61, 68, 82, 93, 96, 107, 113, 115, 120, 152, 157, 203, 208, 210, 231

freedom from religion — 195

freedom of choice — 104, 127, 181, 186, 192, 208, 210

freedom of opinion of religion — 62

freedom of speech — 62, 66, 103, 138, 155-158, 205, 213, 219, 224, 231

freedom of the press — 62

Freemasonry — 35, 169-171, 175, 176, 287, 288

Freemasons — 23, 180, 259

French bishops — 91

French Revolution — 38, 54, 61, 62, 66, 68, 280

Freund, Paul — 205

Friedman, Joseph — 135

Friedman, Milton — 190

Friedman, Murray — 198

Fries, Amos A. — 178

Frings, Joseph — 97

Fry, Charles L. — 31

fundamental group unit of society — 103

Fundamentalists — 138, 161, 214-217, 265, 294

303

militarism — 53
Mill, John Stuart — 117, 279
Miller, William — 64, 81
Milwaukee Journal — 228, 250
Mitchell, George — 266
mixed commission — 96, 97
mobile classrooms — 198, 199
modern loyalty oath — 129
modern state — 84, 85, 107
modernism — 41, 42, 46, 63
Mohn, Reinhard — 211
monarch — 54, 117, 269
monarchy — 67
monasteries — 22, 280
Mondale, Walter — 132, 257
monism — 55, 63, 280
monopoly of education — 74
Moore, Paul — 224
moral code — 187
morality — 46, 60, 63, 64, 96, 114-116, 119, 120, 125, 128-130, 134, 157, 161, 165, 221, 227, 232, 240, 242, 246, 247, 255, 259
Morcillo, Casimir — 92
More, Thomas — *see* Thomas More, St.
Morrison, Paul — 172, 287
Morse, Samuel F. B. — 46, 276
Mosher, Steven — 156
Moynihan, Daniel Patrick — 134, 136, 154, 188, 193, 206, 213, 234, 252, 266, 274, 277, 280, 285, 290, 295
Muñoz Marín, Luis — 144
Murdoch, Rupert — 211
Murray, John Courtney — 10, 29, 37, 40, 52-57, 62, 68, 70, 71, 73, 80-85, 88, 89, 91, 93, 94, 96-98, 101, 106, 107, 114, 115, 118, 139, 144, 150, 153, 167, 168, 181, 187, 194, 196, 198, 271, 273, 276, 277, 279-283, 285, 287, 290, 295
Murrow, Lance — 216

Muslim(s) — 9, 18, 58, 69, 96, 108, 140, 185, 188, 217, 249, 269, 275
Mussolini, Benito — 177

N

NAACP — *see* National Association for the Advancement of Colored People
Napoleon — 60, 280
NARAL — *see* National Abortion Rights Action League
Nathanson, Bernard — 218, 228
National Abortion Rights Action League (NARAL) — 11, 146, 148, 149, 218, 224, 227, 233, 237, 239, 256, 259
National Association for the Advancement of Colored People (NAACP) — 158, 179, 239, 251, 274, 288
National Catholic Educational Association — 190
National Catholic Welfare Conference (NCWC — now USCC, or United States Catholic Conference) — 29, 282
National Conference of Catholic Bishops (NCCB) — 55, 135, 144, 226, 286, 289, 291
National Conference of Christians and Jews — 179
National Council of Jewish Women — 196
National Education Association (NEA) — 35, 47, 48, 133, 172, 186, 261, 265, 279
national employment service — 29
National Endowment for the Arts — 137, 219
National Institute for Education — 158
National Organization for Women

O

Puerto Rico — 144, 287
Purcell, John Baptist — 39
Puritan heritage — 18

Q

Quaker — 142, 282
Quanta Cura — 25, 38
Quebec Act — 20
Queer Nation — 232
Quest — 209
Quindlen, Anna — 253
Quinn, J. J. — 28
Quinn, John — 281
Quiroga, Fernando — 92

R

racial discrimination — 9, 10, 200, 212,
    226, 238, 259
racial equality — 30, 155
Racketeer Influence and Corruption
    laws — 223, 260
radical fringe — 137
Rahner, Karl — 80, 82
Rail-Splitter, The — 31, 32
Rampolla, Mariano — 48
Ramsey, Paul — 37
Randolph, Edmund J. — 237
Raspberry, William — 253
rationalism — 38, 61, 67
Reagan, Ronald — 147, 205
rednecks — 25
Reel, Bill — 128, 133, 223
Reform Judaism — 35, 196
Reformed Central Council — 132
Register — 182, 288, 291
Rehnquist, William H. — 184, 188,
    195, 197, 198, 207, 208
relation between law and morals — 246
religion — 9, 11, 19, 21, 23, 25, 28, 30,
    31, 34, 38-41, 43, 45, 47, 53, 54,
    58-69, 75, 82-84, 87, 88, 90-93, 95,

96, 99, 102-104, 107-121, 126, 127,
    133, 135, 139, 142, 143, 146,
    150-153, 155-159, 165, 167, 168,
    173-176, 179, 185, 188, 189,
    193-201, 203-210, 212, 215, 216,
    224-226, 228, 229, 231, 234,
    235-238, 242, 244-246, 259, 260,
    268, 269, 272, 275, 277, 278, 280,
    283, 287, 289, 290
religion of democracy — 197
religion of secularism — 208
religious apartheid — 248
religious bigotry — 18, 26, 31
religious crazies — 221
religious education — 104, 178, 207
religious nature of our people — 194
religious pluralism — 167, 276
religious test — 10, 132, 198, 247, 249,
    257
religious test for public office — 10,
    25, 65, 169, 173, 237
religious tolerance — 142
Republican candidates — 144
Republican platform — 233
Richard, Gabriel — 140, 225
Richardson, Friend William — 177
Richelieu, Jean du Plessis — 60, 140
RICO — *see* Racketeer Influence and
    Corruption laws
right to life — 102, 103, 115, 130, 149,
    227, 231, 234, 238, 242, 245, 246,
    248, 254, 259, 266, 273
right to organize into labor unions — 67
right to private property — 67, 101
right to property — 62
rights of man — 24, 62, 96, 253
Ritter, Joseph — 94, 97
Riyadh Daily — 190
Robertson, Pat — 130, 232, 257, 258
Robinson, Joe — 171
Roemer, Buddy — 127
Roman atmosphere — 71

Roman bureaucracy — 56

Roman Catholic(s); *also* Roman
  Catholicism — 18, 19, 36, 37, 46,
  47, 54, 72-74, 80, 128, 138, 142,
  143, 154, 169, 171, 174, 176-179,
  180, 187, 188, 198, 220, 260, 289

Roman Curia — 12, 39, 40, 42, 44-46,
  49-52, 56, 57, 59, 79, 85, 89, 90, 97,
  270, 274, 278, 284

Romanism — 23-25, 162, 169, 183,
  187, 260

Romish priesthood — 169

Roncalli, Angelo — 71

Roosevelt, Franklin D. — 30, 33, 34,
  141

Roosevelt, Theodore — 27

Rosenblatt, Roger — 241

Rossi, Cal — 223

Rotary Club — 172

Rogers, Elmer — 178

Ruffini, Ernesto — 79, 88, 91, 120

Rummel, Joseph — 135

Russia — 59, 163

Rutledge, Wiley B. — 189, 205

Ryan, James Hugh — 50

Ryan, John A. — 29, 50

S

Sacramento (California) — 230

Sacred Scripture(s) — 83, 86, 103, 110,
  111, 112, 116

saint by law — 237

Salem (Massachusetts) — 18

Salinger, Pierre — 142, 284

San Francisco (California) — 13, 22,
  50, 102, 108, 119, 147, 155, 156,
  170, 178, 180, 219-221

San Francisco Chronicle 23, 278, 285,
  286, 291-293

Saracens — 112

Sarducci, Guido — 152, 285

Satolli, Francis — 26, 46, 48-50, 279

Scalia, Antonin — 11, 184

Scandinavia — 96, 99

Schanberg, Sydney — 220

Schempp case — 208

Schlesinger, Arthur, Jr. — 80, 128, 132

Schlesinger, Arthur, Sr. — 30

school is a church — 106

school rights — 95

school-aid fight — 145

school-aid question — 10

Schumpater, Joseph A. — 108

scientific atheism — 95

scientific theory — 116

Scotch-Irish Presbyterians — 24

Scotland — 58, 99, 104

Scots — 24, 93

Scottish Rite Freemasonry — 35

Second Plenary Council of Baltimore
  — 45

Second Vatican Council — *see* Vatican
  Council II

second-class citizens — 166, 182, 198,
  265

secondary schools — 29, 181, 182, 191,
  195, 197, 199, 201, 204, 247

Secretariat for Ecumenism — 85, 97

secular humanism — 34, 55, 109, 114,
  130, 151, 153, 157, 194, 195,
  208-210

secular religion — 196, 197, 212

secular state — 54, 67, 68, 85, 107

secularism — 22, 27, 31, 47, 52, 53, 55,
  80, 87, 106, 112-114, 139, 150,
  194-196, 208, 236, 238, 272

secularization — 22, 23, 150, 182

segregation — 167, 168, 174, 185, 209

Senate Judiciary Committee — 33, 209,
  250, 252, 253

separate but equal — 9, 129, 203, 238,
  271

separation of Church and State — 10,

31-33, 35, 38, 62-64, 70, 74, 75, 80, 95, 99, 105, 107, 114, 125, 128, 130, 131, 132, 141-143, 148, 150, 173, 176, 184, 186, 187, 194-196, 202, 217, 229, 238, 245, 250, 258, 262, 265, 294

separation of the state from all religion — 63

Servetus — 59

Seward, William — 22

sex education in schools — 109

Seymour, John — 266

Shanker, Albert — 186, 193, 213, 251, 261, 262, 264-266, 294

Shaw, David — 223, 228

Shea, George — 88, 94

Sheen, Martin — 230

Shehan, Lawrence — 81, 82, 93, 282

Shields, Mark — 130, 223

Shriver, Eunice — 146

signs of the times — 67, 72, 90

Sikh — 9

Silber, John — 156

silencing of Murray — 71

Silent Scream, The — 218

Silva, Raul — 93

Simon, Paul — 166, 249

Simon Wiesenthal Center in Los Angeles — 137

sin and crime — 116

Siri, Giuseppe — 79, 120

Sixtus V — 58

Skills for Adolescents — 209

Smith, Alfred E. — 10, 30, 32, 37, 52, 125, 128, 132, 261, 271, 276

Smith, Chris — 232

Smith, Luther A. — 176

Smith, Matthew — 182

social justice — 198, 213, 233

social security — 185, 226

socialism — 67, 68, 72

society as civil — 67, 68

society as sacred — 67

Society of the Divine Word — 24

Sollicitudo Rei Socialis — 51

son of Noah — 218

Souter, David — 253

South African embassy — 230

Southern Methodist — 33

South Africa — 99

Soviet Union — 68, 92, 99, 109, 114

Soweto — 231, 268

Spain — 17, 18, 23, 36, 38-40, 52, 54, 59, 69, 72, 73, 81, 92, 93, 96, 99, 100, 112, 114, 120, 281-283

Spalding, John Lancaster — 49

Spalding, Martin J. — 45

Spanish — 23, 42, 50, 51, 53, 69, 70, 92, 93, 96, 97, 112, 271

Spanish Inquisition — 17, 26, 277

Speed, Joshua — 23

Spellman, Francis — 70, 82, 88, 107, 109, 121, 143, 144, 147, 282, 285

Spencer, John — 22

spiritual jurisdiction — 19

spiritual power — 41

Sports Illustrated — 235

Square and Compass, The — 164

St. Bartholomew's Day massacre — 163

St. Charles Seminary — 140

St. John Chrysostom's anti-Semitism — 112

St. Joseph's Seminary, Dunwoodie, New York — 43

St. Joseph's Seminary, Yonkers, New York — 278

St. Michael's Church — 140

St. Patrick's Cathedral — 219, 230

St. Paul's Outside the Walls — 79

St. Peter's — 39, 79, 84, 86, 87, 91, 92, 96, 102, 103, 284

Stalin, Joseph — 100, 160

Stalinism — 92

Stamp Act — 18